Cover Letter *Magic*

Wendy S. Enelow
Louise Kursmark

JIST Works

Cover Letter Magic

© 2001 by Wendy S. Enelow and Louise Kursmark

Published by JIST Works, an imprint of JIST Publishing, Inc.
8902 Otis Avenue
Indianapolis, IN 46216-1033
Phone: 1-800-648-JIST   Fax: 1-800-JIST-FAX   E-mail: editorial@jist.com

Visit our Web site at **http://www.jist.com** for information on JIST, free job search information and book chapters, and ordering information on our many products!

See the back of this book for additional JIST titles and ordering information. Quantity discounts are available for JIST books. Please call our Sales Department at 1-800-648-5478 for a free catalog and more information.

Acquisitions Editor: Michael Cunningham
Development Editor: Lori Cates
Cover and Interior Designer: designLab, Seattle
Proofreader: Gayle Johnson
Series Editor: Susan Britton Whitcomb

Printed in the United States of America
04 03 02 01 00   9 8 7 6 5 4 3 2 1

Library of Congress Cataloging-in-Publication data is on file with the Library of Congress

We have been careful to provide accurate information in this book, but it is possible that errors and omissions have been introduced. Please consider this in making any career plans or other important decisions. Trust your own judgment above all else and in all things.

Trademarks: All brand names and product names used in this book are trade names, service marks, trademarks, or registered trademarks of their respective owners.

ISBN 1-56370-732-2

Contents in Brief

Contents

Part III: The Total Job Search: Thank-You Letters, Recruiters, and Resumes

Introduction

WENDY S. ENELOW, CPRW, JCTC, CCM
President, Career Masters Institute
119 Old Stable Road, Lynchburg, VA 24503
Phone: 804-386-3100 Fax: 804-386-3200
wendyenelow@cminstitute.com

LOUISE KURSMARK, CPRW, JCTC, CCM
President, Best Impression Career Services, Inc.
9847 Catalpa Woods Court, Cincinnati, OH 45242
Phone: 513-792-0030 Fax: 513-792-0961
LK@yourbestimpression.com

January 5, 2000

Michael Cunningham
Editor-in-Chief
JIST Publishing
8902 Otis Avenue
Indianapolis, IN 46216-1033

Dear Mr. Cunningham:

Writing high-impact cover letters and job search communications is what we do best. That's why we have teamed together to write a new book, *Cover Letter Magic*. This publication is designed as a job seeker–friendly guide to developing powerful cover letters that get candidates noticed, not passed over. And, it's packed with more than 150 cover letter samples, all written by members of the Career Masters Institute, a prestigious professional association whose membership includes resume writers, career coaches, career counselors, recruiters, and others in the career and employment industry.

Let me briefly highlight the qualifications Louise and I bring to the table:

- We are published authors with a total of seven books between us, all published between 1995 and 1999.

- We have both been featured contributors to *National Business Employment Weekly* and countless other print and online job search publications.

- Both of us have had resumes and cover letters featured in numerous other JIST publications written by David Noble and Mike Farr.

- We have both earned our CPRW (Certified Professional Resume Writer), JCTC (Job and Career Transition Coach), and CCM (Credentialed Career Master) designations, clearly demonstrating that we are at the top of our industry.

- Combined, we have more than 25 years in the resume writing, cover letter writing, job search, coaching, and career marketing industries.

Enclosed is a detailed outline of our proposed publication, along with essential marketing information. I hope that you will give our proposal serious consideration; we think *Cover Letter Magic* will be a valuable addition to the JIST library of top-notch career publications. I'll follow up with you in two weeks.

Sincerely,

Wendy S. Enelow, CPRW, JCTC, CCM

Enclosure

The Cover Letter Is How It All Starts

Whether you're proposing a new book, product, service, advertising campaign, or anything else you are trying to sell, you begin with a cover letter. You write a letter in an attempt to generate interest, enthusiasm, and action from your reader. That is precisely what we did to interest JIST in publishing this book. And, see, it worked!

Your job search is no different. You have a commodity to sell—*yourself*—and you must approach your search campaign just as you would any other sales or marketing campaign. You begin by identifying the key features and benefits of that product (you!) and then work to develop a resume and cover letter that clearly communicate those specific points. It's that easy, yet that complex.

In this book, we focus almost exclusively on cover letter writing, although we do include a brief yet solid introduction to resume writing in chapter 15, "Winning Resume Strategies." Although you might think that writing job search materials is all the same, the difference between writing resumes and writing cover letters is dramatic. They are two entirely different documents, each with its own structure, strategy, and agenda.

> *Tip* If you have not yet written your resume, are having trouble with one section, are questioning the wording that you used, or are uncertain about its overall effectiveness, we recommend that you pick up *Résumé Magic,* the companion to this book, by Susan Britton Whitcomb, CPRW, NCRW, JCTC. Susan's book is one of the most comprehensive resources we've ever seen, covering virtually every topic imaginable related to resume development, strategy, writing, and production. No matter how obscure your questions are, you will find the answers in *Résumé Magic.*

Consider the following. When you're writing your resume, you're writing a document that you hope to use over and over, for almost every job search opportunity, advertisement, or referral. Of course, there may be times when you might have to modify your resume a bit, and there may even be situations when you have two or three different versions (depending on your objectives). The bottom line, however, is that you are writing a single document that gives a broad-based overview of your entire career.

The cover letter process is entirely different from resume writing. Almost every time you write a cover letter, you are writing a unique letter to a specific person for a particular reason and with a unique message. That process, in and of itself, requires that your letters be tailored to each individual situation.

Tip To optimize the impact of your cover letters and the response that they generate, you must be willing to invest the time and energy to create customized letters that sell you for a specific opportunity. Anything less will decrease your chances of capturing your reader's attention and being offered the opportunity for an interview.

How This Book Is Organized

Cover letter writing is an art that requires your ability to write a brief, hard-hitting document that catches the reader's attention. If you're not an experienced writer or you haven't used your writing skills in years, this can be a daunting task. But have no fear. We've made it easy for you with *Cover Letter Magic!* Here's how this book is structured.

The Introduction offers an exploration of the history of cover letters, how they have evolved, their purpose, and why cover letters are so important to your job search. The Introduction ends with "The Top Ten Strategies for Writing Winning Cover Letters."

Chapter 1 contains a comprehensive discussion of the "Ten Types of Cover Letters." You'll learn to identify the one that's right for each particular situation you encounter.

In chapter 2, you'll begin your preparation by developing your key selling points. This up-front work will make the actual writing of your cover letters much simpler and faster; you won't have to plan and write each letter from the ground up.

Then it's time to write. In chapter 3 we'll coach you in the process of writing a winning cover letter, from the strategy behind the words to the actual words themselves. We'll teach you how to write the three essential sections of every cover letter and give you a "Cover Letter Checklist" to guarantee that your letters are appropriate, on-target, and designed to produce results.

Chapter 4 follows with the unique characteristics of online cover letters, as well as similarities to and their differences from the more "traditional" cover letter.

Chapter 5 furnishes you with tools of the trade, so that you can improve the visual presentation and impact of your cover letters. Fonts, format, and paper are just a few of the topics we'll cover.

Then we'll move on to chapter 6 to discuss cover letter distribution and technology issues such as mail merge, e-mail broadcast campaigns, and other PC-based methods for cover letter reproduction and distribution. We round out our discussion with answers to frequently asked questions (FAQs). Should your letter *always* fit on one page? When should you discuss salary in a cover letter, and when is this topic best left for the interview?

Chapters 7 through 12 are what this book is all about: more than 100 "real-life" cover letters written by members of the Career Masters Institute—professional resume writers, career coaches, career counselors, recruiters, military and government transition specialists, and others in the career and employment industry. These letters were used in actual job search campaigns—successful campaigns with powerful resumes and cover letters as their foundation. Chapter 7 shows the "magic" of before-and-after cover letter transformations. Chapters 8 through 11 include letters for blue-collar/trades positions, new graduates/young professionals, mid-career professionals, and senior managers/executives. Chapter 12 finishes this section with letters devoted to technical and scientific professionals. You can quickly identify the chapter that is most pertinent to your situation and use the examples in that chapter as inspiration for your own cover letters.

Chapter 13 is dedicated to writing winning thank-you letters, the strategy behind them, and the style in which to present them. Also included are several outstanding samples that will help you make a thank-you letter work for you as a powerful marketing tool.

In chapter 14, we'll show you what recruiters are telling employers about you, and how you can write cover letters that get their attention.

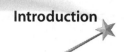

In chapter 15, we share information on writing winning resumes. Learn the best strategies, formats, and presentations for developing resumes that are powerful and well-positioned and produce the results you want—interviews and offers!

The appendixes provide hundreds of effective key words and action verbs to use in your letters. You'll also see a wealth of valuable Web sites, and get contact information for the professional writers whose work is featured in this book—find one in your area who can help you write your own winning cover letters.

Throughout this book, "Tips" and "Examples" are highlighted by special symbols. These sections provide quick insights to enhance the section you've just read, further explain specific strategies, and share insider strategies we've developed in our many years of writing cover letters. And perhaps most importantly, you'll find numerous "Action Item" lists that give you detailed and specific activities to complete as you go about the task of writing your own cover letters.

A Short History of Cover Letters and Their Evolution

Cover letters began to evolve several decades ago. In their original form, they were known as *transmittal letters*—brief letters indicating that the writer was transmitting a resume. Over the course of time, transmittal letters evolved into *cover letters*—letters that "covered" the resume and introduced the job seeker. Today, cover letters have again transformed themselves and can be much more accurately described as *career marketing letters*—letters that are designed to market the job seeker, highlight notable qualifications and career successes, and generate an invitation for a personal interview.

> *Tip* Throughout this book, we refer to these documents as *cover letters*, because that is still the most widely used terminology, but what we are really referring to are *career marketing letters*. The passive approach of "Here's my resume; give me a job" is out. The active approach of "Here's my resume; here's why you should hire me; now, give me a job" is what works!

Today, a job search is an intensely competitive process. For every position for which you apply, there are countless other unqualified, somewhat-qualified, and extremely well-qualified competitors. Compounding this is the fact that the employment market has changed dramatically over the past 10 to 15 years as companies have downsized, rightsized, reengineered, reorganized, streamlined, consolidated, merged, acquired, and reinvented themselves. What's more, businesses everywhere have globalized.

In fact, the world of employment has fundamentally changed. Job security exists only as long as you are providing value to the organization; the old model of joining a company for your entire career is essentially over. This radical shift means that smart workers are always prepared for new opportunities and that there is constant flux in employment. And, despite a historically low unemployment rate, thousands of dot-com startups, and a robust economy providing ample employment growth, companies are not content to fill open positions with just a warm body. They want the "best and the brightest" to capitalize on the enormous market opportunities that are present today. Thus, job search remains intensely competitive.

The successful job seeker understands how competitive the employment market is and knows that a job search must be approached as a marketing campaign. One of the most vital components of that marketing campaign is your cover letter. To ensure that you stay current with emerging trends and market conditions, you must remember that you are *not* writing a transmittal letter, and you are *not* writing a cover letter. Rather, you are writing a career marketing letter in which you must sell the product you are offering—yourself.

The Purpose and Objectives of a Cover Letter

Every time you sit down to write a cover letter, ask yourself the following question: "Why am I writing this letter?" Believe it or not, your answer will always be the same—"to ask for an interview." The bottom line is that there is no reason to forward your resume and cover letter other than to ask for an interview.

> *Tip* There are exceptions to this "rule." Consider the letter you write asking someone to pass along your resume to someone they know (to ultimately get an interview with them) or the letter you write when forwarding a copy of your resume to a friend for feedback (so that you can ultimately send it to someone else and get an interview with them). What about the letter you write to an old college professor who is now serving on the Board of Directors of a Fortune 100 company, asking for contact names and referrals (so that you can ultimately get an interview)? These are *not* what we traditionally refer to as cover letters; therefore, the "rule" of asking for the interview does not apply to these situations.

If only writing your cover letters were that easy—just a quick little note asking for an interview! Unfortunately, nothing worthwhile is ever that easy. Before you can ask for the interview, you must accomplish several objectives when writing your cover letters. These include the following:

- **Introducing** yourself and clearly defining "who" you are—a welder, teacher, sales manager, accountant, computer programmer, aerospace engineer, historian, chef, graphic designer, purchasing agent, security manager, or CEO.

- **Highlighting** your most notable qualifications, experiences, credentials, skills, and achievements.

- **Identifying** the value you can bring to the organization.

- **Capturing** your reader's interest in you, your resume, and your availability.

- **Motivating** the reader to call and offer you the opportunity for an interview.

What's more, whenever possible, you want to relate your qualifications, experiences, credentials, skills, and achievements to the specific needs of the company or recruiter to whom you are writing the letter. Sometimes this information is readily available (such as when the job advertisement lists the company's needs), other times you'll have to do some research (perhaps by talking to someone who already works at the organization), and on occasion you will not be able to find it. Whenever you are able to obtain company information, use that "market intelligence" to present your qualifications as they relate to that organization's needs. Position yourself as the best solution to the specific needs, challenges, or issues you have identified. Here are some examples:

- If you know that the company is looking for a production supervisor with extensive SAP experience, tell them about the SAP project team you managed.

- If you know that the criminal practice firm you're applying to is in desperate need of an experienced paralegal, be sure to highlight the fact that you have six years' experience as a paralegal for a criminal practice firm.

- If you know that the hospital you're applying to has had tremendous problems with retaining its JCAH certification, write about your years of experience managing relationships with JCAH accreditation personnel.

- If you know that an electronics firm wants a candidate with experience selling into both large and small accounts, relate your sales successes with both emerging companies and Fortune 100 accounts.

When writing your cover letters, picture this: You've taken each career experience, responsibility, and project you've ever had and laid them all out on a table. Every time you write a letter, you're going to look at everything on that table and then choose what to include based specifically on that company's needs.

What if you've been unable to learn much about the company and its specific needs? In that case, the best strategy is to make "educated guesses" about needs and concerns you can address for that company. A cover letter that presents you as a solution to business challenges is much more effective than one that simply presents your qualifications.

> *Tip* One-third of the individuals to whom you write a letter will never read it, one-third will always read it, and one-third may read it if the resume is interesting and catches their immediate attention. When writing your letters, remember that you are always writing to the latter two categories of readers— the ones who are most likely to read your letter and take action (such as extending you the opportunity for a personal interview). Because you do not know which readers fall into which categories, all of your cover letters must be powerful, well written, and well presented.

The Importance of Cover Letters in Your Winning Job Search Campaign

You may be wondering whether you need a cover letter. The answer to that question is simple and straightforward: *Every job seeker must have a cover letter.* There are virtually no exceptions to this rule, unless a particular company or recruiter has instructed you to forward just a resume, without a cover letter. (This rarely happens.)

There is no doubt that a great cover letter can make the difference in whether you get noticed or passed over. A great cover letter can be a powerful marketing tool that

- Positions you above the competition.
- Sells your qualifications and your successes.
- Demonstrates your knowledge, experience, and expertise.
- Creates excitement, enthusiasm, and action (an interview).

How can one letter do all of this? Is it the words you write? Is it the style or the tone of your cover letter? Is it the visual presentation? Is it the color of paper you choose and the typestyle you use? Is it the specific achievements you highlight? Is it the years of experience you have? Is it your educational credentials? Yes—to all of these!

As we will show you hundreds of times in this book, your cover letters can have a tremendous impact on the quality and success of your search campaign. To best demonstrate this concept, let's look at a typical job search situation in which you are contacting a company to express your interest in employment opportunities. You don't know of any specific job openings at the company. And you might not even know a specific person to address the letter to. This kind of letter is sometimes referred to as a "cold-call" letter.

Now, what are you going to send to that company? First, you will include your resume, full of factual information about your experience, educational credentials, and more. Your resume, in and of itself, is a powerful tool to sell your qualifications and highlight your achievements. However, the typical scenario is that you will prepare just one resume and use it for every employment contact you make—including cold calls, newspaper ad responses, online responses, networking communications, and more.

Your cover letter serves a different purpose. It is designed as a personal introduction to who you are, custom-made for that specific opportunity, and allowing you the chance to communicate a great deal of information about yourself—both the personal you and the professional you. In theory, you're taking excerpts from your resume—the most important excerpts as they relate to a specific position—and rewording them to communicate the same concepts, qualifications, experiences, and accomplishments, just in different words. It is not a good idea to type word-for-word the exact language that you've already used in your resume.

Tip Your cover letter should complement your resume, not repeat it verbatim!

The Rules: There Aren't Any!

Cover letters can be fun to write, although you may not think so. In fact, there may be little that you find fun at this point in your job search. But with the right perspective and a positive attitude, you will find that writing cover letters affords you great flexibility. There is no one set format in which they must be written. There is no one style in which they must be presented. There are virtually no rules for writing cover letters, other than a few basics, which we cover in "The Top Ten Strategies for Writing Winning Cover Letters," below. Because they are so flexible, cover letters allow you to positively present just those skills, qualifications, achievements, and credentials that you want to bring to a specific reader's immediate attention.

> *Tip* Cover letters allow you the opportunity to "paint the picture you want someone to see while remaining in the realm of reality"! You can pick and choose the skills and qualifications you want to highlight in each letter based on the requirements of a particular position. Cover letters provide you with the platform to create a vision of who you are that relates directly to the company's or recruiter's hiring criteria, while remaining 100 percent accurate and honest.

One of the other advantages of cover letters is that you can be creative in both content and presentation. There is no one standard format that you must follow. As we move into chapters 7 through 12 (the sample cover letter chapters), you will have the opportunity to review more than 100 actual cover letters that are unique in their wording and style, striking in their visual presentation, and successful in generating interest and interviews.

The Top Ten Strategies for Writing Winning Cover Letters

1. **Make it easy for someone to understand "who" you are.** Are you a sales representative, actuary, nurse, college professor, chemical engineer, restaurant manager, customer service agent, or architect? Be sure to clearly communicate that information at the beginning of your cover letter. Don't make someone read three paragraphs to find this critical information. No one is going to take the time and energy to figure it out!

2. **Use a unique and professional format when writing and typing your cover letters.** Don't fall into the trap of using cover letter formats that have been used for years and now appear worn out. Make your letters visually attractive and distinctive—not the overused "standard" formats. Take a look at all the samples in this book to see how creative yet professional you can be in writing the text and designing the presentation.

3. **Highlight your most relevant qualifications.** Use your cover letters to highlight your skills, experiences, qualifications, honors, awards, and credentials that are directly relevant to the company's needs and type of position and/or career path you are pursuing.

4. **Shine a spotlight on your most relevant achievements.** Be certain to highlight your career successes, results, and accomplishments that will be most meaningful to the intended audience of each specific letter.

5. **Include information that you know about the company or the position for which you are applying.** If you know any particulars about the company to which you are writing (for example, core issues, challenges, market opportunities, products, services, staffing changes, or management changes), be sure to address those items in your cover letter. What's more, relate specifically how your experience can meet the company's needs and provide solutions to its challenges.

6. **Explain why you want to work for this company in particular.** Do you want to work for the company because of its reputation, financial standing, products, services, personnel, location, or market potential? Why *this* company? Everyone likes a good "pat on the back" for a job well done. Companies are no different. Tell them what they're doing right that caught your attention.

7. **Be sure that your cover letters are neat, clean, and well presented.** Remember, cover letters are business documents, not advertising materials. They should be attractive and relatively conservative, not "over-designed."

8. **Double-check, triple-check, and then have someone else check your letter to be sure that it is error-free!** Remember, people don't meet you; they meet a piece of paper. And that piece of paper—your cover letter—reflects the quality and caliber of the work you will do on their behalf. Even the smallest of errors is unacceptable.

9. **Keep your cover letters short!** Cover letters are not essays. We recommend a one-page letter in nearly all circumstances.

10. **Always remind yourself why you are writing each cover letter, and be sure to ask for the interview!** Remember, securing an interview is your number-one objective for each cover letter you write.

In the cover letter on the next page, we show how each of these Top Ten tips is employed to create a letter that captures the reader's attention and "sells" the candidate for the Business Development position he is pursuing. The notated numbers (1–10) illustrate where each of the ten tips is used in the cover letter.

Timothy Lee

5723 Oak Manor Drive, Loveland, OH 45140

Home (513) 555-1234
Office (513) 555-1098

timlee@hotmail.com

September 5, 2000

Sandra Williams
Vice President / Sales and Marketing
Dot-Com Co., Inc.
2725 Lakeshore Drive
Chicago, IL 60623

Re: Business Development Position / Job #BDP-11, JOBS@DOT-COM.COM

Dear Ms. Williams:

You are looking for a passionate, results-oriented business development executive who can help lead Dot-Com to dynamic growth. My background gives me the experience, tools, and proven track record to build business through strategic partnerships and keenly focused marketing strategies, and I'm very interested in exploring how my qualifications may fit your needs.

With a successful 12-year career in sales, marketing, business development, and executive operations with technology and Internet access companies, I understand your markets and can capitalize on innovative opportunities for growth. One of my greatest strengths—consistently demonstrated throughout my career—is the ability to create partnership relationships and strategic alliances that build on the capabilities of each partner and pave the way for astronomical growth. My record shows that I can develop mutually beneficial relationships with key players—leading-edge companies in the telecommunications and computer industries. I'm confident I can deliver similar results for Dot-Com.

Most recently, having led the successful launch of Com-Tech, Inc., and firmly established the company as a leading supplier of Internet access and communications products, I am eager for new challenges. Your company is innovative and its future is bright; I'm excited about exploring opportunities where my talents can contribute to your mission.

I will follow up within a week to answer any questions you may have and schedule a time for a personal interview. Thank you.

Sincerely,

Timothy Lee

enclosure: resume

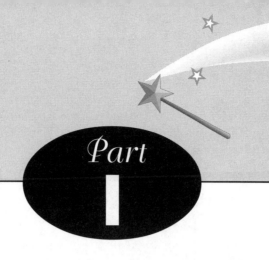

Part
I

Creating and Distributing Your Cover Letters

The Ten Types of Cover Letters

Writing cover letters can be one of the most difficult tasks in your job search. Although it may have taken you a while to prepare your resume, and it certainly required a great deal of effort, once it's done, it's done. Although there are exceptions, generally a job seeker will use just one resume throughout a job search. Cover letters, on the other hand, must be individually written to have the most impact and generate the most response. This means that you will have to create a new letter each time you send a resume. Why?

- **Cover letters are "situation-dependent."** Are you writing in response to an advertisement, writing to a network contact, following up on a past letter and resume you submitted, or just sending a general letter of inquiry? What if you're writing the letter in response to a specific referral from one of your colleagues? What if you're writing to recruiters who specialize in your industry or your profession? The situation dictates the strategy behind the cover letter and the specific information you will include.

- **You need to communicate different information to different people in your cover letter.** Suppose you're a customer service representative in the credit card industry interested in a similar position in the telecommunications industry. The focus in your letter is on (1) years of experience in customer service, and not your industry background. However, if you're seeking to transition into a human resources position in telecommunications, your letter would be focused on (1) years of experience in the industry and (2) the skills and qualifications you have that are transferable to human resources (for example, employee hiring, training, scheduling, and salary administration). *Remember, paint the picture you want the reader to see while remaining in the realm of reality!*

★ **You must be creative in presenting your qualifications in your cover letter.** Cover letters should complement your resume, not repeat it. Do not copy text, word for word, straight out of your resume. This means that you will have to decide how to communicate similar information in different words. Here's a quick example: If you're a sales representative and have highlighted specific sales achievements under each position in your resume, you do not want to repeat that same information in your letter. However, you still want to communicate that you've been successful. Instead of listing your individual sales achievements, you may want to summarize them to span your entire career or categorize them by type (for example, revenue growth, new account development, and new product introduction).

★ **Cover letters need to convey information that is meaningful in the particular situation.** For instance, if you're responding to an advertisement, your letter should address all (or most) of the hiring requirements as stated in the ad. Demonstrate that you are the number-one candidate. A great deal of information on this point follows later in this chapter.

★ **Some employers may require that you provide specific information in your cover letter.** If you are writing in response to an advertisement, the ad may tell you that you must submit requested information such as salary history (what you have earned in the past and in your current position), salary requirements (what your current salary expectations are), verification of U.S. nationality or residency, or other specific data.

To make cover letter writing easier, faster, and more efficient, we've classified cover letters into the ten most common and most preferred categories. Each letter you write will fit into one of the categories. Our list is an instant reference guide and map for you to use in developing your own cover letters.

Here's how to use the list. Simply determine why you are writing a specific letter and to whom. Then review "The Ten Types of Cover Letters" to determine which category your letter fits into. Read the section and follow the key points and recommendations. Then combine the recommendations with the writing suggestions in chapters 2 and 3, and you'll be well on your way to creating cover letters that are appropriate, on target, and powerful.

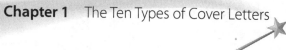

But before we get into the "Ten Types of Cover Letters," we need to look at the different formats that cover letters can take.

> *Tip* One of your most valuable assets for writing cover letters is the "Copy and Paste" function in your word-processing program. Although we will talk repeatedly throughout this book about how critical it is that letters be individually written to a specific company, individual, recruiter, venture capitalist, or other contact, you do not have to reinvent the wheel. If you've written a sentence, a paragraph, or a list of bullets that will work well in various letters, copy it in. Letters must be customized, but you can easily copy them and edit them for another use. Make it easy on yourself!

Cover Letter Formats

As we've stated, cover letters are business documents, and in most cases they should follow a fairly conservative, professional format. Only in rare circumstances is a wildly original cover letter appropriate. Unless you're in a creative or highly competitive field, we don't recommend unusual cover letter formats such as poetry, "wanted" posters, cover letters used as wrapping paper, advertisements, press releases, treasure hunts, or other innovative, nontraditional ideas. We do recommend a businesslike yet up-to-date and polished format.

Within this general guideline, there are three specific formatting styles you can use in the body of your letters:

1. Paragraph style

2. Comparison-list style (directly comparing your qualifications to the position requirements)

3. Bullet style (with introductory and closing paragraphs surrounding bullet-point statements)

Which style you should select depends on the following:

* Who you are writing to.

* Why you are writing to them.

* The type and amount of information you want to include.

- The tone of the letter.
- The writing style of the letter.

As you review the sample letters in this book, you'll see examples of all three of these formats, with the largest percentage falling into style #3—bullet style. This is often the preferred strategy. It allows you to "talk" to a prospective employer, using the paragraphs to introduce who you are and give some insight into your personality and your professional characteristics. You can then use easily skimmed bullet points to highlight credentials, experiences, special projects, honors, awards, and accomplishments that directly relate to the position for which you are applying.

> *Tip* No one style of cover letter is right for every situation. You must closely evaluate why you are writing a specific letter, determine what information is essential to include, and then determine which style works best with the information at hand.

Paragraph Style

Paragraph-style letters allow you to communicate information in the context of a "story" of what has happened, who you are, and what value you bring to an organization. Your paragraph-style cover letter should be well-written, position you as a qualified candidate, and energize your reader to action— an offer for a personal interview.

Comparison-List Style

Comparison-list style letters allow you to quickly and assertively respond to the specific requirements of a job as stated in an advertisement. If the advertisement is asking for five specific qualifications, directly compare your specific experiences and accomplishments to those qualifications, demonstrating how they match the company's stated needs. Your comparison-style cover letter should be brief, aggressive, and on target.

Sample Paragraph-Style Letter

Charles Tobin

| *Telephone in Japan:* 81-3-2749-8345 (+14 hours EST) | *U.S. Contact:* Mary Tobin, Boston, MA |
| *E-mail:* charlestobin@hotmail.com | Telephone (617) 555-8282 |

August 20, 2000

Mr. Frederick Staples
Crest Hills Country Club
75 Tanager Drive
Newton, MA 01579

Dear Mr. Staples:

At the suggestion of Sam Francis of Nicklaus Design, I am contacting you about the Golf Course Superintendent position at Crest Hills Country Club.

During my 15-year career, I have contributed to the successful construction and development of five courses, including world-class facilities in Thailand and Japan. Having worked closely with Nicklaus Design professionals the last eight years, I know first-hand the care and quality they bring to golf course design, and I am equally committed to maintaining design integrity and delivering the consistently excellent quality that will be expected by your members. The Nicklaus motto— " Get the job done right the first time" — is one that I live by as well, and one that I have successfully communicated to my staff, despite wide cultural differences.

You may not be familiar with the Asian courses I've built and managed. They are of superb quality and cater to very sophisticated clientele. The fact that these courses rank among the best in the world is borne out by the *Golf Digest* rankings they earned recently: Royal Thai was named #6 in Thailand, and Cherry Blossom (where I am currently Superintendent) was named the #2 course in Japan. I have enclosed several photographs of the courses in hopes of conveying their beauty and quality.

My eight years in the Far East have been professionally fulfilling, and it has been extremely satisfying to contribute to the successful development of these fine courses. However, having decided to return to the United States, I was extremely interested to learn about the Crest Hills opportunity. I am confident that your collaboration with Nicklaus Design will result in an immediately successful facility. I'd like to be a part of your organization and believe I have the professional skills and experience to contribute to your success.

May we explore this possibility at greater length? I am most easily reached via e-mail, and with notice I can easily arrange to travel to Boston to meet with you and other members of the management team. I look forward to learning more about your plans for the course and exploring how I can help you to make it successful.

Sincerely,

Charles Tobin

Enclosures: Resume; golf course photographs

Anna M. Ramirez

452 Broad Street, Englewood, NJ 07053 • 201/555-1208 • ramirez123@worldnet.att.net

October 15, 2000

Box J-7529
Englewood Times
75 Main Street
Englewood, NJ 07053

Re: Job No. SAL-475
            Medical Sales

With regard to your current need for a dynamic sales professional, I am confident you will be interested in my relevant accomplishments and experience detailed in the enclosed resume. You will note that my qualifications closely match your requirements:

You Require	I Offer
■ 3 years' sales experience	■ 5 years as a top-performing sales professional—recognized as "number one" in total sales in the region for 5 consecutive years
■ Medical sales background	■ 5 years in sales of medical products to physicians, hospitals, long-term-care facilities, and emergency centers
■ Territory management ability	■ In my first year with Medi-Quick, I quickly familiarized myself with a new territory and increased sales 200%. Over the past 5 years, I have dedicated myself to new account development and better coverage of my territory, and these efforts have paid off with significant increases in total territory sales.
■ Relationship-building with health care providers	■ The key to successful selling lies in customer relationships. I am skilled at developing positive long-term relationships with physicians, medical office staff, and hospital administrators. I provide the support, follow-up, and dependability they need to feel comfortable and confident buying from me, and I rely on strong interpersonal and organizational skills to establish rapport and maintain effective contact.

I would appreciate the opportunity to discuss your current needs and what I have to offer. With proven sales skills and a superior performance record, I am confident of my ability to help your company to achieve important sales goals.
Thank you.

Sincerely,

Anna M. Ramirez

enclosure

Less positively, however, this kind of letter, as its name implies, offers a *direct* comparison of your qualifications with the stated needs. Do not attempt to use this format unless you meet or exceed every qualification listed in the ad; otherwise, you will merely highlight where you are deficient. Further, this letter style does not allow you to "sell" any of your qualities other than through a direct point-by-point comparison. Although quite popular among some outplacement firms, particularly in the 1990s, this letter style is, in our opinion, the least effective of the three. We feel its use will continue to decline, primarily because of its limitations.

Bullet Style

Bullet-style letters allow you to take advantage of the best of the other two styles. You can begin with an introductory paragraph that communicates who you are and then follow up with a bulleted listing of the top achievements of your career as they relate to a particular company, position, or industry. Then go back to the paragraph style for your closing, communicating your interest in the position, detailing any specific information that you feel is appropriate, and asking for the interview. Bullet-style cover letters can often be the most powerful and most compelling, enticing your reader to closely review your resume and call to schedule an interview.

The Ten Types of Cover Letters

Now let's look at the ten types of cover letters. Remember, these categories are *situation-specific*—your reason for writing a specific letter will dictate the type of letter you choose. Simply skim through the following list for the situation that applies to your present circumstance and then use that type of letter. To illustrate each concept, we've included sample letters for each of the ten types, and we've recommended the most appropriate of the three styles (paragraph, comparison-list, or bullet) for each type of letter.

1. Ad-Response Letter to a Company

Recommended formats: Comparison-list style; bullet style

Writing letters in response to specific job advertisements will most likely be an ongoing part of your job search campaign. When you see an advertisement or job posting seeking a candidate with your qualifications, you'll want to respond quickly with a resume and cover letter. The only problem is that these letters are best written individually so that you can highlight how your experience and qualifications match the specific requirements for the job.

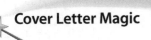

Example **Sample Bullet-Style Letter**

Chandra Parker
2357 Carpenters Lane
Cincinnati, Ohio 45242
(513) 555-0001

November 15, 2000

Mr. David Anderson
Vice President of Administration
Frontline Corporation
725 Walnut Street
Cincinnati, OH 45202

Dear Mr. Anderson:

Reading in today's *Post* about the innovative programs currently under way at Frontline, I was motivated to forward my resume to see whether my qualifications might be a good fit for current needs in your Sourcing Department. In particular, Frontline's focus on cost-improvement strategies mirrors my interests and contributions at AMC Packing, where I was instrumental in identifying and implementing significant cost-saving programs. These include

- Saving more than $1 million a year through distribution center reorganization.

- Reducing transportation expenses $330,000 annually through implementation of a highly effective outsourcing program.

- Negotiating contracts for services that delivered cost savings, reduced corporate obligations, and improved customer service.

My management experience includes identifying opportunities company-wide, developing implementation strategies, and executing plans to achieve results. I am an effective communicator across the organization and have a track record of developing positive relationships both within and outside the organization.

Frontline's potential for continued growth is exciting, and I feel confident that my strong bottom-line focus and leadership skills can benefit your company. May we meet to explore your needs and what I have to offer? Thank you for your consideration.

Sincerely,

Chandra Parker

enclosure: resume

So, instead of just printing a standard cover letter from your PC, you're faced with having to write a separate letter each time. Now, all of a sudden, getting out that quick resume and cover letter is not so quick.

Don't panic! There are ways to get around this and to make the process much easier. We recommend using a comparison or bullet style for ad-response letters. The items that you highlight in the bullets or columns—experience, positions, achievements, educational credentials, and so on—should directly match the needs of the hiring company. This type of cover letter is easier to write than a paragraph-style letter, because you're writing bulleted, stand-alone items and not a document in which each sentence must flow with the next. What's more, these letters are easily edited so that you can change an item or two and quickly create multiple versions of your letter within minutes.

> *Tip* Compile a comprehensive list of bullet-point statements about your career, employment history, positions, achievements, educational credentials, leadership performance, and so on, as ammunition for your cover letters. Then all you'll need to do is select the bullets from the list that match the requirements for each position for which you are applying. See "Step 1: Identify Your Key Selling Points" in chapter 2 for a detailed discussion on preparing these bullet points.

Be sure to reference the position title or number when writing an ad-response letter. You can do this best in one of three ways:

* Include a "position reference line" at the beginning of your resume. Type this between the inside address and the salutation. For example:

Example

```
Mr. Harry Jones
President
ABC Manufacturing Company
123 Main Street
Elm, WI 39393


RE: Purchasing Manager Position—Posting #34837-12


Dear Mr. Jones:
```

* Reference the position in the last paragraph of your cover letter with "I would welcome the opportunity to interview for the position of Purchasing Manager (#34837-12) and look forward to speaking with you." With

this approach, however, you run the risk of not capturing the reader's attention immediately by appealing to the advertised need.

* Reference the position in the first sentence of your cover letter with a sentence such as "I am writing in response to your advertisement for a Purchasing Manager (#34837-12)." This is our least-favorite way of referencing the position, because we prefer that cover letters start with a more dynamic and positive introduction.

Characteristics

Company ad-response letters are characterized by the following:

* **Targeted nature.** Because these letters are written directly in response to known hiring criteria and requirements, they closely target a specific position.

* **Bullet style.** Your objective when writing in response to an advertisement is to quickly and easily bring your qualifications to the forefront as they directly relate to the position requirements. Using bullet points is the easiest and "cleanest" way to accomplish this.

* **Comparison-list style.** You may choose to use the direct-comparison style in responding to ads; remember, this is effective only if you meet or exceed every single one of the stated requirements.

〈Example〉 Sample Ad-Response Letter to a Company

The company ad-response letter on the next page was written in response to an advertisement for a Vice President of Information Systems. Through a combination of paragraphs and bullet points, it addresses both the specific requirements (AS400 background, e-commerce initiatives) and the less-tangible skills (leadership, change management, strategy development) listed in the advertisement.

2. Ad-Response Letter to a Recruiter

Recommended formats: Comparison-list style; bullet style

Writing to recruiters in response to advertisements for specific positions requires exactly the same process as in section 1, developing company ad-response letters. You already know that

* These letters are best written individually so that you can highlight your experience in direct relation to the requirements of the position as outlined in the advertisement.

Terence Swift   2527 Garden Court, Tallahassee, FL 32301 — (850) 555-7506 — tswift@mediaone.net

June 20, 2000

Human Resources Department
Praxil Data Services, Inc.
2375 Capital Street
Tallahassee, FL 32301

Re: Vice President of Information Systems

Your recent advertisement describes interesting challenges that seem to be an excellent fit for the managerial, technical, and leadership strengths I offer. Effective leadership of Information Systems operations requires a strong technical background, and you'll note that I have extensive systems management experience that includes AS400 and multi-site/multi-platform networks.

Beyond technical skills, however, to accomplish corporate objectives it's essential to provide *vision, strategy,* and *execution* — to align IS activities with company-wide goals and to plan effectively for constantly changing technology and business needs. I have demonstrated strong leadership skills consistently throughout my career, and my record of contributions seems very relevant to your current needs:

- With Southeast Manufacturing, I was brought on board to implement a new IS Support Department for the rapidly growing and unwieldy technology area. After successfully launching this initiative, I was asked to step in as Interim Network Manager to "rescue" a floundering department. Through effective leadership and the establishment and enforcement of clear policies and requirements, a complete turnaround was achieved within 60 days.

- Since being promoted to Director of Information Systems, I have led our Y2K and Mainframe Migration projects to a success rate (projects completed on time and within budget) that is 49% above industry average.

- I understand the critical importance of an effective Internet strategy for forward-thinking companies, and since my experience includes e-commerce and EDI initiatives, I have both the leadership skills and the technical background to implement this strategy for your company.

- In all of my positions, I have focused on cost control and captured significant savings through a variety of initiatives, including process automation, improved/increased training, and effective vendor negotiations.

I am confident I can deliver similar strong results for Praxil. May we schedule a meeting to discuss the current opportunity and explore how my skills, strengths, and experience can benefit your organization?

Thank you.

Sincerely,

Terence Swift

enclosure

- Bullet-style letters are usually the most effective for this situation and are the easiest to edit for use from one position to the next.

- If you choose the comparison-list style, be absolutely certain that your qualifications are a perfect match for the position requirements.

- It is important to reference the position title and number in your letter.

There are two principal differences between letters you write to recruiters and those you write to companies. First, rather than refer to "you" or "your company," you will refer to "your client" or "your client's organization." This demonstrates that you understand that the recruiter acts as an agent for the hiring company. Second, it is common practice to include salary information, location preferences, and other inclinations that you would not mention in a letter directed to a company. In chapter 3 we elaborate on the additional information that should be included in recruiter letters and also give you suggested language for including this information in your letters.

Characteristics

Recruiter ad-response letters are characterized by the following:

- **Straightforwardness.** Don't mess around with recruiters! They know their craft and they know their business—to find a candidate who matches a company's hiring criteria to a "T" and nothing less.

- **Bullet style.** Generally speaking, you have even less time to catch a recruiter's attention than you do a company's. The bullet-style cover letter becomes even more important when you are writing to recruiters. Be honest, and be "quick."

Sample Ad-Response Letter to a Recruiter

The recruiter ad-response letter that follows was written in response to an advertisement for a Manufacturing Manager. The bullet points correspond to the specific requirements of the position; the paragraphs highlight additional "selling points" this candidate has to offer.

Gil Nanakara

gilnan@yahoo.com

2752 Florence Drive
Portland, Oregon 97219
(503) 555-0454

December 5, 2000

Alice J. Stanton
Management Recruiters, Inc.
235 Belvedere Drive, Suite 125
Portland, OR 97219

Re: **Manufacturing Manager** Position — 12/3/00 *Portland Tribune*

Dear Ms. Stanton:

My passion is to make manufacturing facilities work better: to accelerate workforce productivity, reduce costs, improve quality, maximize capital investments, and increase competitiveness.

Can I make these kinds of contributions to your client's organization? I offer:

- **Over 20 years of progressively responsible engineering and plant management experience** with Acme Products and Giant Manufacturing Company.

- Demonstrated ability to **deliver cost savings** and **operating efficiencies,** effectively **manage people and facilities,** and **introduce new product lines.**

- Effective **leadership skills** tested and proven in diverse environments; a record of successful solutions to a broad spectrum of engineering, staffing, and operating challenges.

- Keen ability to **motivate and develop people** to take on new challenges and advance within the organization.

- Strong **problem-solving skills** and an **innovative approach to technical and managerial issues.**

My expertise in consumer products manufacturing is well balanced and comprehensive, with accomplishments that display a record of sound, efficient, and profitable management of domestic and overseas manufacturing facilities.

If your client is interested in improving manufacturing productivity, profitability, and efficiency, please call me. I'd like to discuss how I can contribute my experience, drive, dedication, and leadership to the company's bottom line.

Currently, I am earning compensation in the low six figures and am available for relocation within the Pacific Northwest region.

Thank you for your consideration.

Sincerely,

Gil Nanakara

enclosure

3. Online Letter

Recommended formats: Comparison-list style; bullet style; paragraph style

When you write an online letter, you are generally writing in response to a specific advertisement on the Internet or in a print publication, in which you've been instructed to respond via e-mail. Just as with other ad-response letters, you should present your experience as it pertains to each and every one of the requirements outlined in the advertisement.

The strategy behind these letters is actually identical to that behind ad-response letters (aimed at either companies or recruiters). However, there are several things that differentiate these letters and make them unique, which is why we have put them in their own classification.

First of all, online letters are more brief than ad-response letters. No one wants to read a lengthy e-mail message, so keep your letters short and on target. Your challenge is to write a letter that meets all the criteria—defining who you are, highlighting your achievements and qualifications, clearly communicating your value, identifying the type of position you are seeking, and asking for an interview. The only issue is that you need to accomplish this in less space and with fewer words than the "traditional" ad-response letter.

In their visual presentation, online letters are "plain Jane." When you're preparing a letter that will be mailed on paper, you focus your attention on both the content and the look of the document. With online letters, there are no considerations regarding appearance. You simply type them as e-mail messages in the normal default font of your e-mail program. Although you can get fancy and include different types of highlighting, we recommend that you keep these letters as simple and straightforward as possible. Your reader is reviewing an e-mail message, not evaluating the quality and feel of a visually distinctive paper document. But do be certain to spell-check and proofread your online letter, just as you would a traditional cover letter. Typos and misspellings are no more acceptable online than they are on paper.

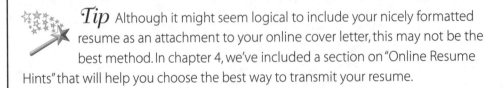

Tip Although it might seem logical to include your nicely formatted resume as an attachment to your online cover letter, this may not be the best method. In chapter 4, we've included a section on "Online Resume Hints" that will help you choose the best way to transmit your resume.

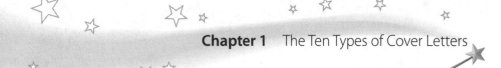

Characteristics

Online letters are characterized by the following:

- **Brevity.** Online cover letters are short and succinct, but long enough to include the top two or three most significant "selling" points of your career, experience, qualifications, and credentials. Although you want to keep these letters brief, you *do not* want to totally eliminate all substance.

- **Ease of readability.** Because most of these letters will be typed as e-mail messages (usually with your resume as an attachment or as part of that same message), their presentation is plain, easy to read, and quick to review.

Sample Online Letter

The online letter on the next page was written in response to an Internet job posting for a Product Manager. Note how the key requirements are highlighted in capital letters. All-caps is the only font enhancement available for use in an online letter. Even if your e-mail program lets you use bold and italic formatting, there is no guarantee that every recipient will be able to see the formatting.

4. Cold-Call Letter to a Company

Recommended formats: Paragraph style; bullet style

You may write cold-call letters to companies to express your interest in employment opportunities, without knowledge of specific advertisements or opportunities. Your challenge in writing this type of cover letter is to give your reader a broad introduction to your skills, qualifications, employment experience, achievements, credentials, and other notable traits that you anticipate will trigger their interest in you and make them offer you the opportunity for an interview.

When writing this type of letter, it is critical that you clearly identify who you are. Are you a sales professional, an accountant, a retail manager, a production operations manager, or a chemical engineer? A C++ programmer, a health-care administrator, a management executive, an advertising director, or a graphic designer? Who are you and how do you want to be perceived?

Re: Product Manager -- Job Posting PM-NE

Managing the development and marketing of technical products is what I do best. With a strong blend of pure marketing skills combined with in-depth expertise in the PC peripherals industry, I have been instrumental in the successful development, launch, and growth of innovative products in both broad and niche markets.

Your currently available Product Manager position calls for skills I have demonstrated during my 15-year career. Highlights include:

-- Successful experience in all phases of PRODUCT MANAGEMENT, from strategy development through product planning, positioning, launch, and ongoing line management.

-- Multi-product line experience with PERIPHERALS and POWER SUPPLIES.

-- Proven ability to work collaboratively with ENGINEERING, SALES, and EXECUTIVE MANAGEMENT and to promote a shared teamwork focus on common goals.

-- Experience with GLOBAL MARKETING CAMPAIGNS.

-- Consistently demonstrated strengths in PLANNING, ANALYSIS, COMMUNICATION, and team and project LEADERSHIP.

I am confident I can make strong contributions to your organization and look forward to exploring what I can bring to Mega Corp. as a Product Manager for your peripherals line.

Sincerely,

Megan Glass

Just as important, you must communicate what type of position you are seeking. No one is going to take the time to figure this out. Do you want to continue to work as a purchasing agent, or is your objective a purchasing management position? If you're a technology project leader, are you looking to make a lateral move, or are you interested in an IT management position, perhaps as CIO or CTO?

 Tip When writing a cold-call letter, it is critical to quickly identify *who* you are, what *value* you bring to the company, and what *type* of positions you are interested in. No one is going to take the time to read between the lines and make assumptions. Spell it out!

Characteristics

Cold-call letters to companies are characterized by the following:

- **Clarity.** Focus on creating a clear picture of yourself and your most notable attributes, skills, experiences, and qualifications. It is essential to quickly communicate this information, particularly when the company has not advertised for the type of position you are seeking.

- **Impact.** Again, because these letters are not in response to a specific opportunity, it is critical that they immediately and powerfully connect with the reader and move him to action to pick up the phone and call you. An effective way to motivate a response is to identify yourself as the solution to the company's problems or needs.

 ### Sample Cold-Call Letter to a Company

The company cold-call letter that follows was used by a technical writer to approach software companies. She identifies with the company needs, clearly states her expertise, and highlights her key selling points: her successful projects for other software producers.

Sharyn Walters

97 Liberty Street, Apt. 7-B • Philadelphia, PA 19103
(215) 555-6767 • sharynw@one.net

January 5, 2001

Patricia Randall
Director, Technical Communications
Quaker Technical Solutions
57 Broad Street
Philadelphia, Pa 19101

Dear Ms. Randall:

Good technical writing involves both science and art: understanding user needs, comprehending software functions, structuring content... then applying strong writing skills and creativity to develop documentation that is elegant, coherent, and, most importantly, useful.

As an experienced technical writer, I have consistently demonstrated strong skills in all of these essential areas. You may be interested in my track record:

- With XYZ, I created several versions of the manuals for the company's primary product line (manufacturing software). Nearly a decade ago, with computers on the factory floor just entering the mainstream, it was essential to carefully consider the learning abilities of users who were technology neophytes. This experience provided a strong foundation for the clear, well-organized, sensibly structured manuals that have become my trademark.

- Subsequently, I took on the challenge of writing manuals for software still in development. Close collaboration with the development team was necessary so that we could produce accurate documentation almost in concert with the software release.

I believe that strong software documentation is essential for customer satisfaction and directly contributes to business success. If you share this commitment and could benefit from my proven skills, then we should schedule a time to explore your needs and what I have to offer. When would it be convenient to meet for an interview?

Sincerely,

Sharyn Walters

Enclosure

5. Cold-Call Letter to a Recruiter

Recommended formats: Paragraph style; bullet style

Cold-call letters to recruiters are strategically identical to cold-call letters to companies. In essence, you are writing to the recruiting firm to introduce yourself (the *who* and the *value*) and explore your potential fit for current search assignments (the *type* of position).

There are two features that distinguish recruiter cold-call letters from company cold-call letters. First and foremost, it is important to disclose information about your job preferences—specifically, your preferences for type of position, type of company, and geographic location. If you are willing to consider only management opportunities, share that information with the recruiter. If you are interested in opportunities with only high-growth technology companies or medical device R&D firms, state that in your letter. If you know that you are not willing to relocate, say so. Or, if you are willing to relocate but only in the Southeastern U.S., communicate that. Be as specific as you can and don't waste anybody's time—yours or the recruiter's.

The other unique feature of a recruiter cold-call letter is the straightforwardness with which you present information about your salary and compensation objectives. We recommend that you provide some information to give the recruiter a concept of the level of salary or type of compensation you are seeking. You can do this in several different ways, generally in the last paragraph of your cover letter. The most common strategies for disclosing this information without giving away too much information include the following:

- **"Most recently, my salary has averaged $50,000 annually."** This is the best strategy if your salary has varied over the years.

- **"My current salary objectives are in the $100,000 to $150,000 range."** This clearly defines the range without stating a specific figure. If you state a specific number, it can potentially work to your disadvantage— either by taking you out of consideration because your expectations are too high, or shortchanging you with a salary that is lower than the company had expected to pay. And don't assume that a low figure will make you an attractive candidate. Both the recruiter and the company may assume that you lack the level of experience they're seeking.

> ★ **"My salary requirements are negotiable and can be discussed at the time of an interview."** This is our least-favorite alternative, because you have not disclosed any information. Use this type of response only when, for whatever reason, you do not want to provide any details.

> ★ **"My salary history can be discussed at the time of an interview."** Again, our least-favorite for the same reasons as above.

Note that you can use these same types of statements when writing in response to a company or recruiter advertisement that asks for your salary history or current salary requirements.

Mentioning salary in cover letters is a controversial topic. In fact, discussing compensation at this point in the job search process with any recruiter or company is an issue of constant debate. For a much more comprehensive discussion on this topic, please refer to "Step 5: Write the Closing," in chapter 3.

Characteristics

Cold-call letters to recruiters are uniquely characterized by the following:

> ★ **Disclosure of job, company, and geographic preferences.** Lay your cards on the table and be specific about your job preferences.

> ★ **Disclosure of salary and compensation information.** Unlike cold-call letters to companies, where you should never discuss compensation, it is a good policy to at least "define the ballpark" when writing to a recruiter.

Example **Sample Cold-Call Letter to a Recruiter**

The recruiter cold-call letter that follows was written for a senior executive looking for a new top-level opportunity. Pay close attention to both section #1 (which highlights his general management competencies) and section #2 (which highlights his most significant career achievements). By demonstrating strong experience across a broad range of functions and combining that with tangible achievements, this letter positions Joseph for a variety of senior-level opportunities.

Also note that his e-mail address is prominently displayed, clearly communicating that he's in sync with the technology wave; he's modern, not a stuffy "old" executive.

JOSEPH R. GRANNSON

jrg@inmind.com

13876 Wilson Park South #1403
Memphis, Tennessee 38134

Phone: (901) 555-3726
Fax: (901) 555-3683

August 15, 2001

Don Pardo
Managing Partner
SES Search, Inc.
8888 N. 154th Street, Suite 1212
New York, NY 10024

Dear Mr. Pardo:

Building corporate value is my expertise. Whether challenged to launch a start-up venture, orchestrate a turnaround, or accelerate growth within an established corporation, I have consistently delivered strong financial results. Now I'm looking for a new executive opportunity with a company poised for solid growth and performance.

The value I bring to an organization can best be summarized as follows:

- More than 10 years of direct P&L responsibility across diverse industries and market sectors.
- Strong, decisive, and profitable leadership of global sales and marketing organizations.
- Keen financial, negotiating, and strategic planning performance.
- Consistent and measurable gains in operations, quality, and efficiency productivity.

To each organization, my teams and I have delivered strong and sustainable operating, market, and financial advantages critical to long-term growth, profitability, and competitive performance. Most notably, I:

- Increased sales 19.6%, reduced staff 32%, shortened lead times 50%, and improved quality performance 300%.
- Orchestrated successful turnaround and return to profitability of $54 million corporation. Cost reductions surpassed $2 million, account base increased 15%, and annualized cash flow improved $1.2 million.
- Accelerated market growth of well-established market leader in a highly competitive and volatile market, increasing revenues 45% and delivering equally significant reductions in operating costs and corporate debt.
- Advanced rapidly during tenure with the Raffert Corporation, becoming the youngest corporate executive in the 52-year history of the company.

My goal is a top-level management position with an organization seeking to achieve market dominance as well as aggressive revenue and profit projections. I am open to relocate nationwide and would anticipate an annual compensation package of $200,000+.

I look forward to the opportunity to speak with you regarding any current search assignments appropriate for a candidate with my qualifications, and thank you in advance for your consideration.

Sincerely,

Joseph R. Grannson

Enclosure

6. Referral Letter

Recommended formats: Paragraph style; bullet style

When you are writing a referral letter, you are writing to a particular individual at a company or recruiting firm at the recommendation of someone else. These letters may be very similar in style and strategy to cold-call letters. You're not sure whether the company has a specific need for someone with your talents. You don't necessarily know the company's situation. Is it on a growth track? Are they downsizing? Do they have new products to introduce? Are they making money? Are they losing money? So, just as with the cold-call letter discussed earlier, these letters are often more "general" in their presentation and not necessarily focused on a particular position. As mentioned above, you want to give your reader a broad-based introduction to who you are, what expertise and qualifications you have, and why you would be valuable to their organization.

Although referral letters may be very similar in style to cold-call letters, the one major exception is the introduction, in which you immediately reference the individual who referred you to that person, company, or recruiter. It is critical that you mention that person's name and, if appropriate, his or her company or professional affiliation, as the very first item in your cover letter, to ensure that the recipient will read on.

> *Tip* For a referral letter to be effective, the person who referred you must be immediately recognizable to the reader because of name, company affiliation, or status within the business community or industry. There are no exceptions! If the name is not recognizable, the impact of your letter is negated, and its value is nonexistent.

Referral letters can work for individuals at all levels. For the senior executive, a referral letter can highlight contributions to revenue and profit growth, strategic leadership, organizational development, turnaround, and other senior-level functions. For the college graduate, a referral letter can focus on academic performance, internships, leadership, enthusiasm, and interest in the organization. The message may change; the strategy remains the same: "Sell" who you are in a broad-brush fashion in the hope that something within the breadth of your experience will capture your reader's attention.

Characteristics

Referral letters are characterized by the following:

- **Introduction.** All referral letters begin with an immediate reference to the person who referred you to that organization. This is the single distinguishing qualification of referral letters.

- **General in composition.** Because you do not know whether the company is hiring, or for what types of positions, it is best to sell as much about yourself, your experience, and your career as possible in an attempt to find "common ground" with the company.

Example   ### Sample Referral Letter

The referral letter on the next page was written by a CFO looking for a similar type of position. He referenced the name of the president of his current company to capture the reader's immediate attention, and then followed with a brief yet hard-hitting summary of his expertise. This letter positioned him as an incredibly qualified candidate.

7. Networking Letter

Recommended format: Paragraph style

Networking letters are written to your personal and professional network of contacts and are one of the single most vital components of your search campaign. No matter who you are, what you do for a living, or where you do it, you have developed a network of contacts over time, whether deliberately or not. Networking is a natural process that you almost can't avoid. Now, you can use those network contacts to your advantage in identifying employment opportunities, getting interviews, and shortening your job search cycle.

Who are your networking contacts? They can be divided into several categories:

- **Professional network.** This network includes coworkers, colleagues, supervisors, and managers from both past and current employers. If you are a senior executive, this network may also include bankers, investors, business partners, vendors, and others within your professional community.

- **Community network.** Business professionals from your local community—bankers, lawyers, real estate brokers, and others you have some personal relationship with—can be an important part of your network.

ARNOLD L. LEBERSTEIN

P.O. Box 38283
Worcester, Massachusetts 01605

Home (508) 555-3372   Fax (508) 555-3777

March 21, 2001

Michael R. Mannley
President & CEO
LRL Products Manufacturing, Inc.
89 Leicester Road
York, PA 18763

Dear Mr. Mannley:

John Johnson recommended I contact you directly. I know that you and John see each other often at the regional CEO meeting each month. I've worked for John for the past six years but will be leaving the company as they shift their operations to Mexico later this year. John knew that you were looking for a new CFO and thought our timing might be perfect.

For the past 20 years, I have served as Chief Financial Officer for two billion-dollar-plus corporations (John's company and Rubbermaid). The scope of my responsibility has been extensive, including the entire finance, tax, internal audit, transactions, information systems, and administrative functions for both corporations. As such, I'm recognized as one of a small number of executives credited with leading both of these corporations through dramatic growth and financial success.

Equally notable is my significant experience in corporate transactions – IPOs, LBOs, acquisitions, divestitures, public financings, investment financings, and more. I have earned a reputation for my ability to identify opportunities, then structure and negotiate complex transactions to achieve growth, expanded market presence, and strong bottom-line results. This experience includes transactions in the U.S. as well as major international markets in Europe and Asia.

Now that the time has come to look for new executive opportunities, I would welcome the chance to meet with you. John believes that we are definitely a good match, and I look forward to exploring that potential. I'll phone next week to schedule a convenient time for an interview. Thank you.

Sincerely,

Arnold L. Leberstein

Enclosure

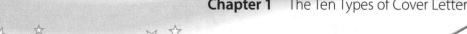

- **College/university network.** College alumni, professors, and administrators can be a priceless source of leads and contacts for your campaign.

- **Association network.** Professional and community associations to which you belong are an extremely valuable networking source.

- **Personal network.** This network includes friends, neighbors, and relatives.

Networking letters can often be the most creative missives you write. Because you are writing to individuals whom you know—either personally or professionally—you can "let your hair down" and develop a letter that is a bit more informal than you would write to a stranger. In turn, you can be more creative in your presentation, tone, language, and style.

The message you want to communicate in your networking letter is "I need your help." You're writing to these individuals for their assistance, guidance, referrals, and recommendations—not for a job. (If they happen to have a job opening themselves, however, they'll probably mention it as a natural response to reading your letter.) If you approach your contacts in this manner, you're very likely to receive a positive response. The key to successful networking is to ask only for what your contact can give you. Everyone can give advice, and most people enjoy helping friends and associates. But if you ask for a job, and it's not in your contact's power to give you one, you'll create a "dead end" with that networking contact.

> *Tip* You want at least one of three things from each of your network contacts: (1) a recommendation or referral for a specific employment opportunity; (2) information about specific companies; or (3) additional contacts you can add to your network. The whole trick to networking is to expand your contact base by getting new names from your existing network. Leverage their contacts to your advantage.

Just as with cold-call letters, your referral letter should give a strong summary of your skills, experiences, achievements, and credentials. You have no idea what opportunities a particular contact may know of, so you want to be sure to highlight a broad range of qualifications.

This letter is easier than most in that you can often use the same letter for all of your network contacts. There may be instances in which you want to change it a bit, particularly at the beginning, where you may want to start with something a bit more personal: "It's been a while since you and I have seen each other. In fact, I think the last time was at the AMA meeting several months ago in Chicago. I've been meaning to catch up with you since then, but we've been immersed in a new company acquisition, plus Jenny just had our second child. I can hardly keep up with it all!"

Characteristics
Networking letters are characterized by the following:

- **Familiar tone.** Because you are writing to individuals whom you know, your letters should be hard-hitting, powerful, and results-oriented, yet written in a less formal manner than you would write to a stranger.

- **Request for help and contact information.** Remember, the two most valuable results of your networking efforts are (1) specific leads that you will receive from the network and (2) contact information for people and companies you can then add to your network.

Sample Networking Letter
The networking letter on the next page was written for a CFO looking to make a transition from the restaurant industry. It uses a conversational yet not-too-informal tone. Note the request for an in-person meeting.

8. Follow-Up Letter
Recommended formats: Paragraph style; bullet style

Follow-up letters are just that—letters that you write to follow up on previous correspondence (your resume and cover letter) that you sent but from which you have had no response. When writing follow-up letters, you have three primary objectives:

- To reiterate your interest in the advertised position.

- To highlight your most relevant experience, skills, and qualifications.

- To ask for an interview.

Robin Madison

4723 Plantation Place, San Diego, CA 92138 ▪ 619-555-0008 ▪ robinmadison@aol.com

April 27, 2001

Stanley Prince
Principal
Tyson Consulting
129 Brookline Avenue
Boston, MA 02142

Dear Stan:

May I ask your advice and assistance?

Having completed a turnaround of the financial operation at Le Jardin (a 5-restaurant chain with $14 million in anticipated revenue this year), I have assessed my career options and decided to launch a search for a new position. Whether in a new industry or with a larger organization, I'm ready for new challenges and feel that my track record will be meaningful to any company interested in business growth and tight financial controls.

In the past 15 years, I've had the good fortune to be associated with rapidly growing organizations, and to be in on the "ground floor" of the accounting/finance operation. Many times, I learned "on my feet" — to implement accounting systems, to negotiate financing, to prepare reports and analysis for venture capitalists, and to meet a wide array of both accounting/finance and general operating challenges. The results have been satisfying — as you'll note from the accomplishments highlighted in my resume.

Now, I'm eager to transfer my skills and experience to an organization where I can continue to make a difference — and where I'll also continue to learn and expand my professional skills.

My expertise and interest are in service industries, and my financial experience has encompassed businesses from start-up to $20 million.

Since I value your experience and perspective, I would greatly appreciate a few minutes of your time to discuss my career options and glean any suggestions you can offer. I'll phone you in the next few days to see if we can get together for a brief meeting.

Thanks very much.

Best regards,

Robin Madison

enclosure: resume

When you write these letters, you will select a letter category identical to the first letter that you sent. If your first letter was a letter in response to a company advertisement, you are going to send that same type of letter again. The only difference is that you are going to change the text and not send the exact same letter. Just as you want your letters to be complementary to your resume, you want your follow-up letters to be complementary to, not repetitive of, the first letter that you sent. Communicate similar achievements of your career using different language, examples, and highlights.

Follow-up letters generally begin with a reference to your previous correspondence and the reason for your contact: "Several weeks ago I forwarded a letter and resume in response to your advertisement for an Insurance Agent, and I would like to reiterate my interest in the position. My six years of experience in insurance sales and brokerage services have provided me with precisely the skills and qualifications highlighted in your advertisement."

With that introductory paragraph, you've immediately communicated

- Why you're writing to that company.
- The fact that you've previously contacted them.
- That your experience is identical to their requirements.

Always be certain to include another copy of your resume with your follow-up letter, even though you sent one previously. If you are fortunate enough to capture your reader's attention with the letter, you want him or her to be able to quickly review your resume, not spend an hour searching through a pile of resumes collected over the past month.

Here's a typical scenario of when you would send a follow-up letter. You see an advertisement in your local newspaper for a Production Scheduler with a large manufacturing company and immediately forward your resume and cover letter. Three weeks pass with no response from the company. You may even see the position advertised again in the Sunday paper. Because your qualifications are so perfectly suited to what the company asked for in its advertisement, you send a follow-up letter with another resume.

When Is It Appropriate to Send a Follow-Up Letter?

* When you have recently (two to four weeks ago) forwarded your resume and cover letter in response to a specific advertisement and you meet the hiring criteria almost to a "T."

* When you have not heard back from an individual who said he would contact you within a specific period of time. Often, based on the situation and your relationship with that individual, a phone call is a more appropriate and certainly more proactive method of follow-up contact. After your conversation, you can determine whether another letter would be of value—a letter highlighting and responding to specific points from your phone discussion.

* When an individual said that she would provide you with some information or contact names, forward your resume to a contact, or initiate some other action on your behalf. Again, make the determination whether a letter or phone call would be more appropriate, based on the specific situation.

* When you sent a cold-call cover letter to a company and now see an advertisement for a position with that company that closely matches your qualifications. This is one instance when the style of letter you send will change based on the circumstances; now you'll send an ad-response letter (being certain to communicate how your qualifications match their specific requirements) rather than a general-interest letter.

When Is It Not Appropriate to Send a Follow-Up Letter?

* To a targeted direct mail or e-mail campaign that you've sent out within the last month. Whether your mailing was to the 100 fastest-growing technology companies or to 1,000 recruiters specializing in your profession, you must remember the strategy behind targeted mailings. It is not wise or thrifty to send a follow-up letter to all of these contacts after just a few weeks. However, if several months have passed and you're still in the market, you might think about targeting the same list of contacts again. In this instance, however, your letter will be more like a cold-call letter and less like a follow-up letter, although you might briefly mention that you have contacted them previously.

⋆ If you have received a "rejection" letter from the company or a letter stating that they will keep your information on file. Unfortunately, that's just a nice way of saying, "Thanks, but no thanks. We're not interested."

⋆ To a recruiter with whom you have spoken about a particular position for which you believe you are precisely qualified, but for which the recruiter does not think you are an appropriate candidate. We have seen so many job seekers invest time and effort in trying to convince recruiters that they are the right candidate when, for whatever reason, the recruiter has determined that they are not. You are never going to change the recruiter's mind, so don't waste your energy. Once a recruiter has made up his mind about a candidate, there is no way to change that perception. By sending follow-up letters or making follow-up calls, you are accomplishing nothing. The only appropriate correspondence at this time would be a quick letter of thanks that requests you be kept in mind for other opportunities.

⋆ To the recipients of a broadcast letter mailing. (A broadcast letter is a detailed career-summary letter that you send without an accompanying resume to senior executives at your target companies. It is described more fully in letter type #9, below.) If you could not capture the reader's attention the first time, chances are that the company does not have a need for someone with your qualifications. Save your time and energy for more productive activities.

Characteristics

Follow-up letters are characterized by the following:

⋆ **Introductory paragraph.** Follow-up letters begin with three essential elements: why you're writing, that you've contacted them before, and that your experience closely matches their requirements.

⋆ **Creativity.** When writing follow-up letters, you must think of new words and phrases to describe your experience, highlight your accomplishments, and capture your reader's attention. These letters must not repeat word-for-word what you've already said in your resume and your first cover letter.

Sample Follow-Up Letter

The sample follow-up letter that follows is a prime example of how to reference your initial contact, reiterate your interest in the position, and highlight your qualifications.

GARY RANDOLPH JONES

24 East 56th Street
Hartford, CT 06106
Home: (860) 555-8763   Work: (860) 555-5777
E-mail: grj@new-world.com

December 10, 2001

Allen Archer, Jr.
Executive Vice President
Grantview Media Ltd.
3838 N. Wards Road
Allentown, PA 18766

Dear Mr. Archer:

Three weeks ago I forwarded my resume in response to your advertisement for a General Manager. I assume you've received quite a bit of response, but in an effort to bring special attention to my qualifications, I would again like to submit my resume. My career can be best summarized as follows:

Recruited to RAPER Technology in 1984, I am one of the five senior executives responsible for the dramatic growth of the company, from a $7 million privately held venture into a $100+ million NYSE high-tech organization with operating subsidiaries worldwide. My contributions have been diverse, with dual emphasis in my roles as *General Manager* and *General Counsel.* Most notably, I offer:

- Sixteen years of increased responsibility as General Counsel, building and expanding the corporation's in-house legal and risk-management organization as the company has grown, diversified, and expanded. In this capacity my role has been vast, ranging from M&A and IPO transactions to VAR and OEM contracts to commercial litigation, employment law, and pension plan administration.

- Three years' experience as President of the $220 million Text Systems Division. With full P&L and operating management responsibility, I launched two next-generation technology products, created a global distribution network, and delivered a better than 40% contribution to bottom-line profits.

- Extensive qualifications in negotiating complex, multimillion–dollar technology sales, partnership, and intellectual property agreements with major corporations worldwide (e.g., Microsoft, IBM, Hughes, Unisys, Computer Sciences, McDonald's, Ernst & Young, and Transamerica).

- Conceived, created, and orchestrated a global investor relations and corporate communications program that consistently strengthened the company's market presence, investor ratings, and corporate image.

Perhaps most significant have been my contributions as an internal business consultant, advisor, and team leader, working with management to devise strategic business plans, implement tactical action, and drive forward favorable financial results across all core operating units. My leadership style is direct and decisive, yet I am flexible in responding to constantly changing business, market, financial, and organizational demands.

I believe my qualifications are an exact match for your requirements and would welcome the opportunity for a personal interview. I will follow up in 10 days if I haven't heard from you. Thank you for both your time and consideration.

Sincerely,

Enclosure   Gary Randolph Jones

9. Broadcast Letter

Recommended format: Paragraph style

Broadcast letters are an unusual hybrid job search strategy and can best be summarized as merging the resume and cover letter into one document. The one distinct advantage that broadcast letters offer is that these letters avoid the knee-jerk reactions employers have to many resume and cover letter packages. These "preprogrammed" actions might include: (1) forwarding it to the human resources department; (2) setting it aside to review later; or (3) depositing it in the "circular file." With a broadcast letter, you are delivering a personal piece of correspondence with no visual cues as to its purpose. Therefore, an individual must read (or at least peruse) your letter in order to determine its content. This allows you the opportunity to communicate your message without being immediately "dismissed" as you may have been by using the more traditional approach of a cover letter with a resume.

Broadcast letters are extremely controversial. Some people praise their effectiveness, believing that they generate more interest because they eliminate the visual cues. Others deplore them, believing that they attempt to manipulate the truth, changing the reader's perception of who you are. This, indeed, may be true. The greatest value of a broadcast letter is its ability to create a "different" picture of who you are.

Another point of controversy relating to broadcast letters is that they clearly try to circumvent the traditional human resources resume-screening process. After all, a broadcast letter is a personal letter sent directly to a senior executive. If that executive is interested in you, she will pick up the phone and call you, or perhaps route your letter to a lower-level manager who is the hiring authority for your functional area. While it's true that one important function of the HR department is to recruit, screen, and recommend candidates, our job-seeking clients have told us time and time again that they have benefited tremendously from conducting a "guerrilla" campaign, working around HR.

Our belief is that, in very select circumstances, broadcast letters written to companies can result in a decisive competitive advantage over the traditional cover letter and resume package. Some of the situations in which you might want to consider using a broadcast letter are the following:

* **When you are transitioning from one industry to another.** The sample letter at the end of this section is a prime example of this situation. The individual portrayed was attempting to transition into the corporate market after more than 20 years in the nonprofit sector. Undeniably, the broadcast letter was by far his most effective marketing tool, allowing him to demonstrate his senior management performance without immediately eliminating him from consideration for lack of corporate experience.

* **When you are not quite right for a particular position but are well-qualified.** Here's the situation. You see an advertisement for a Health Care Administrator. The ad states that you must have experience in six core management functions. Well, you've got five of the six and, in fact, a tremendous amount of experience in the first three. Use your broadcast letter to aggressively "sell" your qualifications with particular emphasis on the skill sets in which you are most qualified. By focusing on your assets and never mentioning your liabilities, you are positioning yourself as a well-qualified candidate who has "the right stuff."

* **When your relevant experience was acquired years ago.** Consider the following scenario. For 12 years, you worked in training and development for a large corporation. You then took a promotion to the operations management team, where you have worked for 11 years. Your goal is to return to training and development. If you prepared a traditional chronological resume, your relevant experience would be near the end of your resume. With a broadcast letter, however, you can bring all your training and development experience to the forefront to capture your reader's immediate attention.

* **When your age is a liability.** Unfortunately, for all too many job seekers, age is a discriminating factor, particularly when you're more than 50 years old. With the traditional resume, a prospective employer can glance at your resume, see that you were working in the 1960s or 1970s, and ascertain instantly that you are over 50 years of age. To avoid being immediately eliminated from consideration, develop a broadcast letter that sells your experience, qualifications, skills, and most notable career achievements but does not include specific dates for employment and education as your resume does. This gives a prospective employer the opportunity to be impressed with your career track first, before finding out that you are over 50.

★ **When you have not worked for years.** This situation may be most typical for women who left their careers to raise their families and are now returning to the workforce. If you sent a resume, as soon as someone glanced at the dates of your employment experience, it would be obvious that you had not worked for quite a while. However, with a broadcast letter, you can highlight your experience, qualifications, and achievements without ever mentioning dates. This type of letter may end with a paragraph briefly explaining why you have not been working recently, how your situation has changed so that you are now able to return to the workforce, and, of course, the type of position you are seeking.

★ **When you want to bring to the forefront something that has been only a sideline in your career.** Suppose you have worked in field service management for 15 years, in which your primary responsibilities include directing a regional PC field service operation. On the side, as time permitted, you also worked with the product R&D team to create new technology products and applications. Now your objective is a position in technology development. The broadcast letter gives you the opportunity to bring those aspects of your career to the forefront while simply acknowledging your responsibilities for field service.

★ **When you are at an extremely senior level in your career track.** A broadcast letter is an exclusive, high-end marketing tool for introducing yourself as the first step in an executive job search process. Further, it is a more confidential process than traditional resume distribution. You're writing a personal letter to another top executive, rather than sending along a resume, which (1) immediately communicates that you're looking for a job and (2) allows word to get out that you're in the market. You never know how many people may see your resume and mention it to others. For example, if you are the CEO of a Fortune 100 company, secure in your position yet interested in other executive opportunities, consider a broadcast letter as a high-level and confidential communication that you can use to "test the waters" and see what type of initial response you receive.

Unfortunately, we cannot list each situation for which broadcast letters would be appropriate. It's a judgment call each time. Ask yourself this question: "Am I trying to draw significant attention away from what I have done principally throughout my career and focus on a smaller aspect?" Or:

"Am I trying to draw significant attention away from the industry or type of organization in which I have worked and position my skills for a different industry?" If your answer is yes, you might consider the value a broadcast letter would bring to your campaign.

One final point about broadcast letters: Although there are select circumstances when you might write a broadcast letter to a company, we do not recommend sending them to recruiters. Recruiters want chronological facts and figures, which the broadcast letter does not provide. Recruiters want to be able to quickly peruse your resume and see where you have worked, what positions you have had, and how long you held them. They want to glance under "Education" to see your credentials. They'll spend only five to ten seconds. That's it. Broadcast letters are not designed to provide such a quick review of factual information. Rather, broadcast letters "tell a story" that one has to read to understand. Recruiters, as a whole, are not willing to invest the time to interpret these letters and extrapolate relevant facts. It's not their job!

Characteristics

Broadcast letters are characterized by the following:

- **Depth and quantity of information,** which is greater than a traditional cover letter as outlined in any of the other categories in this list.

- **Number of pages.** It is more than acceptable for a broadcast letter to run two or even three pages, as appropriate to a particular situation.

Example   Sample Broadcast Letter

The broadcast letter that follows is an excellent example of transitioning your skills from one industry to another. This individual worked as an executive in association management for more than 20 years and really did have a distinguished career. However, his goal now was to transition that experience from the nonprofit sector into "corporate America." What he wanted his readers to focus on was his experience, not the environment in which it was acquired. Had he sent a traditional cover letter and resume, the very first thing someone would see would be a list of his employment experience, all in association management. Most likely, the person would have gone no further. With his broadcast letter, he was immediately called for an interview.

RONALD R. JOHNSON
12 St. Paul Street
Baltimore, Maryland 21098

Phone: (410) 555-0876   Fax: (410) 555-6549   E-mail: rjj2@mindspring.com

April 11, 2001

Gary Meyerson, President
Marteenson Partners, Inc.
55 Greenbelt Parkway
Washington, DC 20056

Dear Mr. Meyerson:

As one of the top three executives in a national organization, I am recognized for my expertise in building strong, efficient, cost-effective, and productive operations responsive to our customers' needs. My efforts were the foundation for our tremendous financial and operational success.

When we started years ago, the organization was an unknown entity. Through our efforts in building a strong business culture, developing sound financial policies, introducing advanced technology, and driving business development, we now boast of a national reputation and strong bottom line. My contributions to that organization and the value I bring to Marteenson Partners are best summarized as follows:

Financial Leadership

I built the entire financial, accounting, internal auditing, and budgeting infrastructure from the ground floor. This included developing a progressive cash-management program, managing payroll and related tax affairs, negotiating lines of credit, and managing investments valued in excess of $3 million. Further, I launched a series of aggressive cost-reduction initiatives that reduced overhead costs within specific categories by as much as 40%. Through my efforts, we ended 2000 with a solid 22% net profit and cash reserves equivalent to one full year's operating expenses.

Revenue & Profit Performance

During my tenure, annual revenues grew from $18 million to more than $50 million, with annual profits averaging 18% for 10+ consecutive years. My specific contributions focused on creating new sources of revenue through both product and service development. In addition, I personally negotiated several key contracts that have been instrumental to our sustained growth.

Human Resources Leadership

When I joined NBEO there was no HR function. Under my leadership, we developed a complete HR function, recruitment and benefit programs, retirement plans, training programs, job descriptions, employee manuals, and more. Today, we have a fully integrated HR organization able to support the organization as it continues to grow, expand, and strengthen its operations.

Information Technology

In an attempt to keep pace with the rapid emergence of new technologies, I spearheaded the acquisition and implementation of a host of computer systems. Further, I led the acquisition of several generations of telephone/telecommunication systems. I bring to Marteenson a good working knowledge of the technology and telecommunication tools available to meet the needs of our industry and enhance our productivity.

Please also note that I have an MBA in Finance and Administration and a B.S. in Business, both from New York University. I have been characterized as a strong and decisive leader, able to make difficult decisions. Just as vital, is my ability to be flexible and respond to constantly changing organizational, financial, and market demands.

Currently, I am confidentially pursuing new senior management opportunities. My goal is to transition my experience into a new, faster-paced, and higher-growth organization where I can contribute to the organization while advancing my professional skills. I would welcome a personal interview to discuss your current executive staffing requirements and would be pleased to provide any additional information you require.

Sincerely,

Ronald R. Johnson

10. Sponsor Letter

Recommended format: Paragraph style

Sponsor letters are a relatively new phenomenon that has emerged in recent years. They can be best described as letters written by other individuals to their network of contacts on your behalf. In theory, it's John Smith writing to his colleague, Jane Doe, to tell her about Sam Wilson (the job seeker) and what a valuable employee he would be. Sponsor letters leverage some-one else's network on your behalf. These letters are appropriate for only a small percentage of job seekers, because the sponsor letter has one essential requirement: someone who is willing to be your sponsor.

For sponsor letters to be effective, you must have the "right" sponsor. It must be an individual who has a strong network of personal contacts, has an excellent reputation, has impeccable credentials, and is willing to "go the extra mile" for you. The impact of the sponsor letter rests almost entirely on the credibility of your sponsor. If you select a sponsor who does not possess these qualifications, the letters will ultimately be of little or no value to you.

When deciding who you might approach to be your sponsor, consider the following three critical criteria:

- **Your sponsor must be "appropriate."** Your sponsor must be at a high-enough career level to have contacts at the level you are seeking—individuals who can get you in the door for an interview and make hiring decisions. Most likely, your sponsor is more senior-level than yourself, with a higher level of management responsibility.

- **Your sponsor must have contacts other than those you already have.** Although the level of your sponsor may immediately indicate that she has contacts outside your own personal network, also be sure that your sponsor has contacts in different circles than you do. If you already have a contact at AT&T, you don't need your sponsor there. Where you need her is in getting you in the door with companies and recruiters with whom you do not have a relationship.

- **Your sponsor must be willing to leverage his network of contacts on your behalf.** When you ask someone to be your sponsor, you're asking a great deal of him. You want him to dedicate time and effort to this project and "put his neck on the line" for you. That's right. When John Smith contacts Jane Doe about you, it's his reputation and credibility that he risks. If you ask someone to be your sponsor, you'd better be sure that you can live up to his expectations and your promises.

A good strategy for managing a sponsor letter campaign is to ask your sponsor to write to ten of his most senior-level contacts. The letter should serve to introduce you, praise your performance, highlight your accomplishments, and communicate the value you bring to that organization. Your sponsor can write the letter, or you can offer to write a draft, making the process easier for your sponsor and faster for you.

Characteristics

Sponsor letters are characterized by the following:

- **Authorship.** Sponsor letters are written about you by a third person. They are not written by you, the job seeker.

- **Impact.** These letters generally have tremendous impact because of the reputation and credibility of the individual writing the letter.

 ### Sample Sponsor Letter

The sponsor letter that follows is a prime example of how someone else's contact can work to your benefit. This individual is currently working as a general manager in the telecommunications industry. His company has just been sold, and he is now interested in applying for several national sales management positions with other industry leaders. One of this individual's closest friends is a college friend from 20 years ago, now the mayor of a small Northeastern town. Because of his high-profile political career, he knows everyone, including several presidents of some of the area's most prominent telecommunications companies.

JOHN S. JOHNSTON, MAYOR
Leicester Town Square
1 Main Street
Leicester, New York 14890
(716) 555-3766

July 29, 2001

Mr. John E. Taylor, Jr., President
Dreamport, Inc.
5355 Town Center Road
Boca Raton, FL 33486

Dear Mr. Taylor:

Can I tell you about Bart Brogan's professional career? No. Can I tell you how many millions of dollars in profits he has helped to generate? No. Can I tell you how tremendously effective he is in reengineering, streamlining, and optimizing business and finance operations? No.

What I can tell you is about Bart Brogan, the man – an individual with strong character, impeccable ethics, and keen business insight. He is a man who has earned the respect of other business, civic, and political leaders.

I first met Bart back in college at Brown University, where we both participated in competitive athletics. It was then that I first realized that Bart really was someone unique and talented. I watched him at the competitions and saw his intensity and drive to succeed. What I also witnessed was his innate leadership skill and the camaraderie he elicited. I was impressed.

After graduation, Bart and I went our separate ways, but we have always stayed in touch with one another. He's had a tremendously strong corporate career; mine has focused in the political arena. Nonetheless, we have maintained a personal connection for years, supporting one another in whatever ways possible and challenging each other to achieve our personal best.

What I do know about Bart's professional career is that he is an astute businessman with excellent credentials in strategic planning, finance, general management, and information systems/technology. I am also aware that he has negotiated and structured several significant mergers, acquisitions, and other corporate initiatives.

If you are considering adding to your executive management team, I guarantee you can't go wrong with Bart. Not only would you be hiring an individual who is well respected within the professional community, you would also be hiring an individual whose liaison, networking, and relationship-management skills will be of certain value to Dreamport.

If there is any additional information I can provide, please contact me directly at (716) 555-3766.

Sincerely,

John S. Johnston, Mayor

Chapter

2

Preparing to Write

We are making a few assumptions about you, our reader. We're assuming that you've already invested a great deal of time, effort, and energy in writing and designing your resume. If you've hired a professional resume writer, you also have a financial investment. Now that your resume is complete, we want you to use it!

We're also assuming that since you've purchased this book, you have hit a stumbling block in writing your cover letters that, in turn, is preventing you from sending out your resumes. Maybe you've already drafted a letter and are a bit uncertain about the language that you've used. Perhaps you've written cover letter notes to yourself but just can't seem to tie them all together into a cohesive structure. Possibly you were pleased with the letter you wrote, but it isn't getting any response. Or maybe you can't get any further than a blank piece of paper or computer screen.

To improve the ease and confidence with which you write cover letters, we've created a step-by-step process and structure that will allow you to quickly and easily write your cover letters and get your resumes out—*now!* Although you may admire the prowess with which you typed and formatted your resume, love the color of paper you selected, or are thrilled about the quality of your resume, if it is just sitting on your desk, it is not working for you. Your resumes are of no value to you or anyone else if they are not in circulation.

To get your resumes out, all you need to do is follow this five-step action plan to produce a cover letter from start to finish:

Step 1: Identify Your Key Selling Points

Step 2: Pre-Plan

Step 3: Write the Opening Paragraph

Step 4: Write the "Meat"

Step 5: Write the Closing

Step 6: Polish, Proofread, and Finalize

The most time-consuming of these is step 1, identify your key selling points. To make that process easier, we've devoted this entire chapter to helping you collect an arsenal of information about yourself and your career that will be available for you to consider for *every* letter that you write. By investing time and effort now, you'll make the process of producing each unique cover letter practically painless! Once you begin the actual writing process with step 2 (in chapter 3), you'll see how your advance work really pays off.

Step 1: Identify Your Key Selling Points

What qualifications, experiences, achievements, and skills do you bring to a company? It's time to evaluate and quantify what it is that makes you unique, valuable, and interesting to potential employers.

The best place to start is by clearly identifying *who* you are. Are you an accountant, realtor, or construction project manager? A sales professional, customer service representative, teacher, or nurse? An advertising specialist, social worker, architect, or librarian? A CFO, CIO, COO, or CEO? It is critical that you be able to clearly and accurately define who you are in an instant. Remember, an instant is all that you have to capture your reader's attention, encouraging him not only to read your cover letter in full, but to read your resume and contact you for a personal interview.

Just as important, you must be able to clearly identify why a company or recruiter would be interested in you. Is it because of the companies you've worked for? The industries in which you've been employed? The positions you've held? The promotions you've earned? The financial impact you've had? What you accomplished? Your specific skills and qualifications? Your licenses and educational credentials? Your patents? Your technical expertise? Your leadership skills? Your foreign language skills and international experience? Why would someone be interested in you?

These are critical questions to ask yourself. What's more, the answers to these questions will directly impact what you write in your cover letter and how you present that information. You must determine what you have to offer that relates to that company's needs, what will be of interest to that company, and what will entice them to read your resume and offer you the opportunity for an interview.

Action Items

We designed this book to give you both theory and practical exercises to guide you in creating your own winning cover letters. The "Action Items" you see below and in later chapters will lead you step by step through the process. You may prefer to hand-write your responses or type them on your PC. In either event, take the time to complete each action item carefully and thoroughly, and you'll create valuable resources and tools that you can use for every cover letter you write.

1. Know Your Career Goal

Fill in the following blank with your job title or profession. I am a _____. The more brief and concise your answer, the better. Clarity is the key to effectively communicating who you are to a prospective employer.

What if you are pursuing more than one career goal and can identify yourself with more than one "WHO" statement? If your options are quite different (for instance, programmer and project manager), it's best if you repeat these exercises for each of your professions. Why? It's quite likely that what is highly significant for one profession will be less important for the other—and remember, you are focusing on why employers would be interested in you, so it's important to convey your experience, skills, and accomplishments that are most directly related to that particular position. On the other hand, if your professions are closely related (marketing manager and product manager), you can create a hybrid job title ("Marketing / Product Manager") and encompass the key points of both.

2. Write Responsibility Summaries

Write strong summary sentences that detail all of your job responsibilities from each of your current and past positions. Be as detailed as possible, and try to remember

continues

continued

everything you did in each position. Obviously, if you've been working for 15, 20, or more years, you can eliminate some detail in your earlier positions, but only if they are not relevant to your current objectives. We recommend using a separate page for each position so that you can easily add other items as they come to mind.

Remember that your cover letter is not designed to be a listing of job responsibilities and functions. Rather, it is designed to point out the most notable responsibilities and highlights of your career as they relate to the needs and interests of the prospective employer. Once you've invested the effort in preparing a complete list, you can use it over and over, hundreds of times, as the foundation for virtually every cover letter you write. In theory, it will be your "cheat sheet," a single reference source containing all the different items, qualifications, highlights, responsibilities, and other bits of information you might include in a cover letter.

Your resume is a good place to start in preparing this list. In fact, your "prep work" for creating your resume can also be the foundation for the material you'll develop for your cover letters. You'll save time and effort in this exercise if you can use your notes, old resumes, and other career summary materials you used to develop your resume.

To best demonstrate what a summary sentence is and its value to you in writing your cover letters, here's a quick example: "Managed daily and monthly accounting operations for a $200 million company with 11 operating locations throughout the Midwestern U.S."

With that summary sentence, you've immediately communicated to your reader that not only did you manage accounting, but you managed accounting for a large and diverse operation. This probably included accounts payable and receivable, general ledger, payroll, financial reporting, bank reconciliations, month-end account reconciliations, staffing and training, and all related computer operations.

So, with just one little sentence, you were able to tell your reader what you were responsible for and the level of that responsibility. Remember, your cover letter should be relatively brief and not repeat all the information that is in your resume. Your only objective with the letter is to pique someone's interest to read your resume and invite you for an interview.

 ## Sample Summary Sentences

To help you create your list of responsibilities, we've compiled a sample portfolio of 45 summary sentences for various professions. This list is by no means comprehensive; it was created to give you ideas and help get your own juices flowing.

Check off all that apply to you and your career, and then read the sample summary sentences under each. These sentences will give you an idea of the type of information you may want to highlight, depending on your particular career experience. It would be nice to think that you could just take a summary sentence we've provided and drop it right into your cover letter. Unfortunately, chances are slim that the following samples will be precisely accurate for your career track. These are simply provided as a tool to help you come up with your own summary sentences.

☐ **Accounting and Auditing**

> Supervise a six-employee accounts payable, accounts receivable, and internal audit operation for one of the area's largest commercial heating and air-conditioning companies.

☐ **Administration**

> Administrative Manager for a large health-care practice with responsibility for staffing, budgeting, equipment acquisition, financial reporting, regulatory reporting, and all departmental staffing and training functions.

☐ **Advertising**

> Designed and produced a portfolio of multimedia advertising, marketing, and promotional materials to increase Amazon.com's market image and consumer awareness.

☐ **Association and Not-for-Profit Management**

> Member of six-person management team directing fund-raising, community outreach, member development, member services, and all administrative affairs for the American Medical Association's Specialty Practices Division.

☐ **Banking**

> Participated in the start-up, staffing, and sales of First National's first Private Banking Program, one of their nationwide initiatives designed to increase market reach and build long-term customer relationships.

☐ Clerical/Administrative Support

> As assistant to one partner and six managers in a Big Five consulting firm, prepared presentations, proposals, project documentation, and final reports to present a consistently professional image to clients.

☐ Communications

> Worked with a team of 22 in-house professionals responsible for the conceptualization, design, development, and production of a portfolio of print, video, and multimedia communications to support IBM's new-product roll-out programs.

☐ Computer Programming

> Designed new computer programs for Finance, Accounting, Administration, Purchasing, and Vendor Management departments of Ford Motor Company's $200 million parts division.

☐ Construction

> Construction Manager for the $40 million renovation of Park City Plaza Hotel, including full responsibility for architectural design, contractor selection, competitive bidding, field supervision, and regulatory affairs.

☐ Consulting

> Launched entrepreneurial consulting venture specializing in strategic planning, market planning, new product development, and joint venture negotiations for electronics companies expanding into the Asian marketplace.

☐ Corporate Finance

> Senior Finance Executive for Merck's $2 billion international sales division, including full decision-making responsibility for banking, tax, treasury, financial analysis, financial reporting, contract negotiations, mergers, acquisitions, and capital funding programs.

☐ Customer Service

> Responded to customer calls, faxes, and e-mails, independently addressing a wide range of product, quality, billing, and general customer satisfaction issues for $1 million industrial supplies company.

☐ Education and Educational Administration

> Advanced rapidly from Classroom Teacher to Grade Chairperson to Assistant Principal to Principal with full leadership responsibility for a 1,000-student high school.

☐ **Energy and Environmental**

Member of the Environmental Engineering Task Force traveling to Mobil locations nationwide to evaluate site conditions, assess potential hazards, negotiate with local regulators, and manage field remediation teams.

☐ **Engineering**

Joined four-person Engineering Task Force leading the redesign and optimization of all product engineering systems for Quaker's entire U.S. operation (six manufacturing plants, 2000+ employees, and close to $2 billion in annual revenues).

☐ **Food and Beverage/Food Service Operations**

Fast-paced customer service position in one of the area's largest restaurants, serving up to 500 customers per day.

☐ **Government**

Acted as Chief Operating Officer of a federal government agency responsible for the administration of all educational grant and foundation funds to nonprofit teaching institutions throughout the U.S.

☐ **Health Care**

One of six nurses in a 350-bed teaching hospital selected to participate on a new coordinated health-care team providing care to neonatal and pediatric ICU clients.

☐ **Hospitality**

Held a series of progressively responsible positions in Reservations, Front Office Operations, Guest Services, and Special Events for a 1000-room Hilton hotel.

☐ **Human Resources**

Senior HR Director with full responsibility for staffing, training, leadership development, benefits, compensation, employee relations, labor relations, and HRIS for a $45 million retail sales company.

☐ **Human Services**

Provided comprehensive counseling support, interagency referrals, and program development for a caseload of 32 juvenile offenders on probation through a joint court/community outreach program.

☐ **Insurance**

Top-producing insurance sales agent with the highest revenue and lowest loss ratio out of 200+ agents in a five-state territory.

☐ **International Business Development**

Independently planned and directed all marketing, new business development, new product launch, and joint-venture programs for Ericsson throughout Central and South America.

☐ **Investment Finance**

Sold/marketed a portfolio of mutual funds, stocks, bonds, and low-interest, mortgage-backed securities to private investors and small-business investors throughout the New York metro area.

☐ **Law Enforcement**

Distinguished career with the Los Angeles Police Department, earning 12 promotions over 20 years, six honorable decorations, and regional media coverage for personal success in resolving a potential life-threatening hostage situation on the campus of UCLA.

☐ **Legal Affairs**

General-practice attorney specializing in civil matters, personal injury, real estate law, personal tax law, and family law.

☐ **Logistics**

Led business development teams in analyzing, proposing, and implementing logistics programs that focus on value-added service and cost savings for clients around the country.

☐ **Manufacturing**

Independently directed the production of over 2000 SKUs each year, from the initial stages of production planning and materials acquisition through floor production, quality testing, and final customer distribution.

☐ **Marketing**

Conceived campaign and directed production team responsible for introducing Kellogg's newest breakfast product into the national market, building it into a $2 million well-known consumer brand.

☐ **Operations Management**

> Held P&L responsibility and oversaw all branch activities in support of contracted accounts for national delivery service; supervised clerical, administrative, and customer-service staff.

☐ **Product Development**

> Full leadership responsibility for all new product development and commercialization projects for the $28 million Internet Systems Division of ABC.

☐ **Project Management**

> Brought on board as first project manager for a rapidly growing technology consulting company to oversee its largest-ever contract, a $4+ million software installation for a major national retailer.

☐ **Public Relations**

> Launched high-profile nationwide public relations campaigns to support Jesse Ventura's 2000 presidential campaign.

☐ **Purchasing**

> Directed the purchase of over $50,000 annually in office supplies and materials to support the operations of a prestigious civil engineering firm.

☐ **Real Estate**

> Managed advertising, leasing, maintenance, and tenant relations for a 332-unit garden apartment complex catering specifically to senior citizens.

☐ **Research and Development**

> Team Leader directing all technology R&D programs funded by a $2 million grant awarded from the Department of Energy for the design of alternative residential heating systems.

☐ **Retail**

> Train and supervise a staff of six retail associates responsible for product merchandising and display, sales, customer service, and loss prevention.

☐ **Sales**

> Maintain consistently high sales volume in retail sales of jewelry to both established and walk-in clientele of a six-store jewelry chain's flagship downtown location.

☐ **Scientific Research**

> Pioneer in the theoretical research of genetic anomalies associated with the aging process and physical deterioration.

☐ **Security**

> Member of a six-person industrial security team working to introduce new security standards, technologies, and systems to guard against further corporate espionage activities.

☐ **Senior Management**

> Senior Management Executive with full strategic planning, operating, marketing, and P&L responsibility for a $20 million emerging telecommunications company anticipating an IPO within the next 16 months.

☐ **Technology**

> Acquired, customized, and implemented emerging database, client/server, Internet, and e-mail technologies to transition a small fabric design company into the 21st century.

☐ **Training**

> Selected for newly created 100% training position, serving as primary operations and applications trainer for all new hires of $7 million hardware/software reseller firm.

☐ **Transportation**

> Recruited to Ryder Integrated Logistics to redesign its business model, restaff key positions, and revitalize field marketing in an effort to regain #1 market position in the industry.

☐ **Travel and Tourism**

> Planned, scheduled, and managed all corporate travel programs for the executive management team of Macy's and its 22 operating subsidiaries.

One final note regarding your key selling points relates to the types of organizations with which you have been employed. Do you have experience with any of the following types of companies?

- ☐ Start-up venture or new enterprise
- ☐ Turnaround company
- ☐ High-growth company
- ☐ Fortune 10, 50, 100, 500, or 1000 company

You can use this information to further strengthen your qualifications and sharpen the impact of your cover letters. For example, if you have experience in turning around poor-performing companies and you're writing to an organization in need of an aggressive turnaround, sell your experience in reorganizing, revitalizing, and redesigning businesses to improve operations and financial performance. By doing so, you clearly communicate that you've met the same types of challenges that the company is currently facing. Be sure to "talk the right talk" to each audience.

Action Item

3. Write Your Achievements

Write your achievements for all of your positions. Just as with item #2 above (responsibilities), you're going to create a single resource—your cheat sheet— that lists all of your career achievements, accomplishments, and contributions. Again, the more comprehensive your list, the more usable a resource it will be in developing your cover letters. Remember, achievements sell, and cover letter writing is selling—selling you!

Let Your Achievements Sell for You

Your achievements are what set you apart from others with a similar background. They answer the reader's all-important question—"What can you do for me?"—because they tell precisely what you have done for someone else. Cover letters and resumes without achievements are simply dry compilations of position titles and responsibilities. They don't sell your unique attributes, and they don't compel readers to pick up the phone and invite you in for an interview.

In thinking about your achievements, ask yourself how you've benefited the organizations where you've worked. In general terms, you can help an organization by:

- **Making money** (revenues, profits, earnings, ROI/ROA/ROE increases, new customers)

- **Saving money** (cost reductions, streamlining, automating)

- **Creating new things** (systems, processes, products, technologies, operations, companies)

- **Improving existing things** (reengineering, redesigning, developing new processes, consolidating)

- **Improving performance** (productivity, efficiency, quality, delivery, customer service)

- **Winning honors, awards, and commendations**

In writing your achievements, think about the two key pieces of information you want to convey: what you did and how it benefited the company. Without either of these components, an achievement is incomplete. Let's compare two achievement statements:

- Spearheaded project team that designed, developed, and launched ATP's next-generation software systems.

That's fine, but it's incomplete. When writing about your achievements, make sure you include bottom-line results—with numbers, whenever possible—to make those results tangible.

- Spearheaded project team that designed, developed, and launched ATP's next-generation software systems, which **generated $8.5 million in first-year sales.**

This one sentence—this one achievement—communicates not only success and financial contribution, but a great deal of information about the individual's specific skills. We would surmise from reading it that her qualifications include software engineering, cross-functional team leadership, quality assurance, product testing, product documentation, manufacturing, and product commercialization. We might also assume that she has experience in project budgeting, costing, purchasing, scheduling, and project reporting. We got all that information from just one sentence—one achievement.

The specific achievements you include in your cover letters will depend entirely on your professional career, skills, experiences, qualifications, and competencies. Achievements can vary widely—from installing new word processing software in your office to launching a new business venture that generated $100 million in revenues—and everything in between.

Identify Your Achievements

The following list will help you identify your achievements. Just as you did in the previous section, check off every item on this list that applies to you, and then write specific achievement statements for every example you can think of from your career. You'll need to do this for each of your positions in order to create a consistent record of accomplishment.

To get you started, here's a quick example: If you checked off the first item ("Increasing sales revenues"), you might then reword it as "Increased district sales by 22% in just one year for Myers-Baker-Anderson." For another position, you might write, "Grew territory by 27%, nearly twice the regional average of 14%." And if your revenue accomplishments weren't quite so stellar, you can still find a positive way to state your contribution: "Met all performance goals for revenue growth, new business, and customer retention."

Here's the list. Ask yourself if you have managed, participated in, helped with, or contributed to any of the following:

- ☐ Increasing sales revenues
- ☐ Improving profitability
- ☐ Improving customer service
- ☐ Improving customer satisfaction ratings
- ☐ Improving market share ratings
- ☐ Capturing new customer accounts
- ☐ Penetrating new business markets
- ☐ Increasing sales within existing accounts
- ☐ Penetrating new geographic markets
- ☐ Identifying new market opportunities
- ☐ Reducing operating costs

- ☐ Reducing overhead costs
- ☐ Developing new technology
- ☐ Implementing new hardware, software, or other systems
- ☐ Coordinating team-building and team-leadership efforts
- ☐ Designing new training programs or educational curricula
- ☐ Developing new products or expanding product lines
- ☐ Building new facilities or expanding existing facilities
- ☐ Sourcing new vendors
- ☐ Reducing annual purchasing costs
- ☐ Negotiating contracts
- ☐ Improving productivity
- ☐ Improving the quality of operations or products
- ☐ Improving efficiency
- ☐ Introducing new performance standards
- ☐ Streamlining operations, functions, or support activities
- ☐ Exceeding specific performance expectations
- ☐ Simplifying business processes
- ☐ Eliminating redundant work activities
- ☐ Realigning staffing to meet business demand
- ☐ Structuring or negotiating strategic alliances, joint ventures, or partnerships
- ☐ Structuring or negotiating mergers or acquisitions
- ☐ Directing IPOs, private placements, or other corporate financings
- ☐ Appearing on local, regional, national, or international media
- ☐ Coordinating special-event programs
- ☐ Improving the company's image
- ☐ Managing fund-raising programs
- ☐ Solving persistent problems that affect any area of business operations

Other achievements that you can highlight, as appropriate to the type of position you are seeking or company to which you are writing, may include the following. Check those that apply to you, transfer them to your list of achievements, and write a powerful statement of achievement.

- ☐ International experience
- ☐ Public speaking experience
- ☐ Print and online publishing experience (books, articles, newsletters)
- ☐ Industry honors, awards, or credentials
- ☐ Academic honors, awards, or credentials
- ☐ Industry licenses and registrations

> *Tip* If your list of achievements is particularly long, divide it into "functional" sections such as Sales & Profit Achievements, Technology Achievements, Human Resource & Leadership Achievements, Major Projects, New Products, Marketing Campaigns, Organizational & Productivity Improvements, New Clients, Cost Savings, Start-Ups, Turnarounds, and so on. Each time you sit down to write a cover letter, refer to your list and select the achievements that are most appropriate to the position for which you are applying. You'll be amazed how much faster you'll be able to write your letters.

Sample Achievement Statements

To help you get started, we've compiled a list of thought-provoking ideas for achievement statements related to 45 different professions and industries. Find your profession, review the list of achievement ideas for it, determine which are appropriate to your specific experience, and incorporate those concepts into your own unique achievement list.

Accounting and Auditing

- Identifying misappropriated or uncollected monies
- Implementing integrated computerized systems to link different business units
- Contributing to revenue growth, cost reduction, and profit improvement

Advertising

- Capturing or managing major clients, contracts, and campaigns
- Demonstrating a combination of creative talent and business skills
- Earning honors, awards, media coverage, and other "reputation-building" recognition

Association and Not-for-Profit Management

- Increasing membership, geographic expanse, and prominence
- Increasing membership fees, revenues, and funding
- Influencing favorable legislative policies

Banking

- Growing lending volume, deposits, and customer base
- Expanding into new markets, new products, and new services
- Reducing A/R, write-offs, and risk and asset exposure

Clerical/Administrative Support

- Streamlining work processes and improving work flow
- Eliminating redundant or repetitive tasks
- Automating previously manual office functions

Communications

- Writing marketing, advertising, and customer communications
- Designing multimedia systems for conventions and trade shows
- Crafting speeches and investor presentations

Computer Programming

- Writing new programs for new applications
- Improving user-friendly software capabilities and support
- Enhancing system productivity and performance

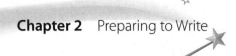

Construction

- Securing or managing major projects, clients, and contracts
- Delivering projects on time
- Achieving cost savings and avoidance

Consulting

- Capturing prominent clients and accounts
- Delivering quantifiable revenue and profit contributions and cost reductions
- Participating in new product/technology development, new market development, and other innovations

Corporate Finance

- Contributing to revenue and profit growth, cost reduction, and/or ROI, ROA, or ROE gains
- Negotiating major corporate deals—mergers, acquisitions, financings, private placements, IPOs, and so on
- Managing collateral operating, strategic planning, HR, information technology, and administrative functions

Customer Service

- Improving customer-service performance and customer-satisfaction ratings
- Introducing new customer-service and support programs
- Retaining customer accounts in highly competitive markets and industries

Education or Educational Administration

- Increasing student test scores and academic rankings
- Expanding educational programs and improving course curricula
- Influencing favorable public policy and legislation

Energy and Environmental

- Completing major remediation, haz-mat, or regulatory projects
- Discovering or implementing product and technology innovations
- Making financial contributions

Engineering

- Developing and commercializing new products
- Delivering process, design, and performance improvements
- Contributing to new revenues or cost reduction

Food and Beverage/Food-Service Operations

- Improving front-of-the-house and back-of-the-house operations
- Increasing revenues and reducing operating and labor costs
- Earning industry recognition and ratings

Government

- Implementing new programs, policies, and initiatives
- Delivering budget, deficit, and cost reductions
- Negotiating or managing public/private partnerships

Graduating Student

- Achieving academic or athletic honors
- Demonstrating leadership skills
- Acquiring professional skills through "nonprofessional" employment, internships, and so on

Health Care

- Improving quality of care, utilization, and health-care policy
- Participating in emerging health-care markets—managed care, PPOs, and so on
- Contributing to improved financial performance and regulatory ratings

Hospitality

- Improving guest services and guest satisfaction ratings
- Increasing revenues and bookings
- Upgrading facilities and amenities

Human Resources

- Leading organizational, cultural, and productivity improvements
- Capturing cost savings
- Developing and implementing new HR programs, services, and technologies

Human Services

- Delivering new programs and services
- Amassing a record of client, program, and project successes
- Contributing to funding, budgeting, regulations, and legislative affairs

Insurance

- Growing premium volume and number of insureds
- Reducing risk and volume of claims
- Introducing new products and expanding into new markets

International Business Development

- Achieving revenue and profit growth
- Developing and expanding new markets
- Negotiating international deals, joint ventures, acquisitions, and alliances

Investment Finance

- Delivering growth in investment yields and portfolio performance
- Expanding range of investment product expertise
- Demonstrating successes in new-product development and client-relationship management

Law Enforcement

- Apprehending more criminals than any other officer
- Achieving the highest arrest-to-conviction percentage
- Promoting public education and community outreach programs

Legal Affairs

- Handling high-profile cases
- Demonstrating diversity of corporate and industry expertise
- Demonstrating diversity of legal practice expertise

Logistics

- Improving purchasing, warehousing, inventory, distribution, and transportation operations
- Reducing overhead and operating costs
- Negotiating innovative vendor partnerships and strategic alliances

Manufacturing

- Delivering measurable improvements in productivity, efficiency, workflow, process, and product yield
- Reducing labor, material, equipment, and overhead operating costs
- Introducing innovative technologies and systems

Marketing

- Managing notable new-product-launch campaigns and quantifying financial performance
- Contributing to revenue, market share, earnings, and company growth
- Demonstrating a combination of strategic and tactical marketing expertise

Operations Management

- Streamlining, consolidating, and improving operations
- Reducing costs and improving net profit margins
- Introducing advanced systems, technologies, and processes

Product Development

- Developing and commercializing new products, with subsequent revenue performance
- Coordinating cross-functional design, engineering, manufacturing, and sales teams
- Developing notable co-development alliances, partnerships, and joint ventures

Project Management

- Completing projects ahead of schedule or under budget
- Managing cross-functional project teams and personnel
- Negotiating with third-party vendors, contractors, and business partners

Public Relations

- Increasing visibility and market recognition
- Managing PR, special events, and other media-targeted programs
- Coordinating executive liaison affairs

Purchasing

- Managing significant purchasing volume and commodities
- Developing U.S. and international vendor sourcing and contracts
- Achieving quantifiable cost reductions and inventory improvements

Real Estate

- Developing new projects and properties
- Selling large numbers of properties or generating large dollars
- Managing high-profile properties, resorts, complexes, and buildings

Research and Development

- Developing and commercializing new products
- Creating new techniques, processes, and procedures
- Generating new revenue and profit streams

Retail

- Increasing sales revenues
- Improving customer service and repeat clientele
- Managing loss prevention and merchandise control

Sales

- Increasing sales and growing market share
- Developing new accounts and new markets
- Introducing new products

Scientific Research

- Pioneering new research methods and techniques
- Making new scientific discoveries
- Increasing funding and appropriation

Security

- Managing sensitive corporate or institutional security programs
- Thwarting potentially hazardous events and emergencies
- Managing relationships with law-enforcement agencies

Senior Management

- Increasing revenues, reducing costs, and improving bottom-line profits
- Outperforming the competition and dominating the marketplace
- Leading performance, process, organizational, and technological improvements

Technology

- Developing new technologies
- Commercializing existing technologies
- Implementing major projects

Training

- Developing and delivering new training programs
- Creating training manuals, curricula, trainer guides, and other instructional materials
- Training other trainers

Transportation

- Capturing cost savings
- Achieving productivity and efficiency improvements
- Reducing operating costs

Travel and Tourism

- Booking large events, excursions, and corporate programs
- Increasing agency revenues
- Upgrading computer technology

There! You've completed the most time-intensive preparation for writing your cover letters. With these comprehensive lists of *responsibilities* and *accomplishments* in your toolkit, you're ready to move quickly through the remaining steps to get your cover letters off the drawing board and into circulation.

Chapter 3

Writing Your Cover Letters

Remember the six steps to creating your cover letters start-to-finish that you read about in chapter 2?

Step 1: Identify Your Key Selling Points

Step 2: Pre-Plan

Step 3: Write the Opening Paragraph

Step 4: Write the "Meat"

Step 5: Write the Closing

Step 6: Polish, Proofread, and Finalize

If you're working your way through this book step-by-step, you devoted a great deal of time to identifying your key selling points in chapter 2 and creating two lists—one highlighting overall skills and responsibilities of each of your positions (summary sentences) and the other highlighting all of your successes, contributions, accomplishments, and special projects (achievements). Now that you've done all your preparation work, let's write a cover letter!

The process of writing your cover letters starts with a brief pre-planning session to identify the specific purpose of that particular letter. Then you move into the actual writing of each of the three distinct parts of the cover letter: the opening, the "meat," and the closing.

The easiest way to master this approach is to work on an actual letter. Rather than having you complete exercises and write samples that, although educational, leave you with no final product, let's work on the real thing—you and your career.

To begin, find an advertisement you want to respond to, a network contact you want to reach, a recruiter you'd like to introduce yourself to, or any other situation in which you'd like to write a cover letter. Use that letter as we go through each step of the process. When you complete step 5, you'll be done, and you'll have a letter that's ready to go! We call this a "practical" learning exercise because it has practical application—a finished product.

Just as in the previous chapter, there are Action Items for you to complete at the end of each step. You can do this either manually (on paper) or electronically (on your PC). Whichever way you choose, be sure to complete the Action Items in their entirety. The notes you take will become the foundation for, and in some instances the actual wording of, your cover letter.

Step 2: Pre-Plan

Before you begin writing a single word of your cover letter, you must determine the appropriate strategy for that particular letter. You're not ready to write until you can clearly answer the following questions:

- ★ **Why am I writing this letter?** Am I writing in response to a print or online advertisement, sending a cold-call letter to recruiters or companies, contacting someone in my network, writing to a company at the recommendation of someone else, or writing a follow-up letter to a company to which I already sent a resume? The answer to this question will significantly impact the content of your cover letter—the introduction in particular. After you've answered this question, review the "The Ten Types of Cover Letters" (in chapter 1) and select the type that fits your particular situation.

- ★ **Have I researched the company and the position?** There will be instances where you know, or can find, information about a company you are writing to, the products it sells, the services it offers, the positions that are open, the types of candidates it hires, its key hiring

requirements, and much more. Do your research! The more you know about the company and the position, the more on-target you can write your letters, relating your experience to their identified needs. If you know the company sells electronic components and you've worked in that industry, sell your related experience! If you know the company is on a growth track and you've worked for two other growth companies, highlight it! If you are an expert in multimedia communications and the cable company you are writing to has just bought a broadcast company, tell them you know the industry! Your goal is to find common ground between you and the company, and then leverage that to your advantage.

> *Tip* By researching a company and finding out all that you can, you will be able to write a cover letter that directly relates your experience to that company's needs. The company will see your immediate value to them, and you will have a remarkably solid advantage over your competition.

Do I have a contact name? Have I double-checked the correct spelling of the name and the person's job title? Do I have the full mailing address or e-mail address? The fact is that if you write to the Human Resources department of a company, you'll never quite know where your letter and resume have landed. However, if you write to a particular individual, you not only know who has your resume, you also know who to follow up with. This is critical!

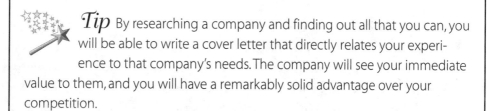

Action Items

1. Choose a Type

Write down the type of cover letter you are writing from the list of "The Ten Types of Cover Letters" (in chapter 1) that best fits your reason for writing this letter. Then, carefully review the section that describes that type of letter in detail.

2. Compile Information About the Company

Write down everything that you know or have learned about the company—industry, products, services, number of employees, annual sales revenues, and more.

continues

continued

3. Compile Information About the Position

Write down everything that you know or have learned about the position—the specific job duties, minimum requirements, supervisor's name and title, "inside" information from a source within the company, and anything else that is pertinent.

4. Write Contact Information

Write down the name, title, and full mailing address of the individual you will be contacting. If you are sending an online letter, also note that individual's e-mail address.

An Example: Chris Matthews

To make the process of cover letter writing easier and faster for you, we've created a fictitious job seeker, Chris Matthews. Chris is an experienced technical project manager who, for the past four years, has worked extensively on Y2K-compliance projects. With the need for these specific skills eliminated, he pursued additional training and recently earned his certification as a Web programmer. Now he's ready for a programming or management position that will use his new skills while also benefiting from his strong project management and team leadership abilities.

Chris knows that a Web site and electronic commerce capability are fast becoming a business necessity for virtually all companies. Since he can help them build and launch their Web sites, he plans to approach companies in his local area that do not currently have fully functioning e-commerce capabilities.

Work along with Chris as you both progress through steps 2 through 6, creating a cover letter from start to finish.

Here are Chris's completed "Action Items" for "Step 2: Pre-Plan."

1. **Choose a type.** To begin his job search, Chris will use letter type 4: Cold-Call Letter to a Company. Using the local Chamber of Commerce directory, he has compiled a list of midsized companies that do not currently have e-commerce capabilities. He has prioritized these into

those he feels could benefit the most from developing a site. His first letter will be to Funky Fashions, a small chain of eclectic clothing stores.

2. **Compile information about the company.** Through his research, Chris has learned that Funky Fashions has a region-wide following, offers unique and trendy items, and sells clothing with an average retail price of $50. Further, the company's customer list includes many fashion-conscious and computer-savvy young adults. Funky Fashions advertises on TV, on the radio, and in the newspaper. It also sponsors radio promotions and event tie-ins to promote a "hip" image to its core customer base. The management team is headed by the company's founder, a 48-year-old woman who is known for her creativity and business savvy, but not for being a technology pioneer.

3. **Compile information about the position.** Since Chris is writing a "cold-call" letter, he does not know whether a position is available. However, he is envisioning his ideal role with the company as a leader of e-commerce development. He would like to combine his programming skills and project management experience with the company's creativity, fashion sense, and business expertise to create a Web site that helps the company connect with and sell to existing and new customers.

4. **Write contact information.** Since the company is not technologically advanced, Chris will use a traditional mailed letter. He plans to write to the president of the company. He located her name in the local business journal feature on "The Top 200 Companies in Chicago."

```
Cynthia Mars, President
Funky Fashions, Inc.
1230 Lakeshore Boulevard
Chicago, IL 60616
```

Step 3: Write the Opening Paragraph

The opening paragraph of your cover letter is your hook—your "sales pitch" of who you are and why you are of value to that specific organization. It should be written to entice the recipient to read your letter in its entirety and then take the time to closely review your resume. And, because it is so critical, the opening paragraph is often the section that will take you the longest to write.

> *Tip* If you're having trouble writing the opening paragraph of your cover letter, leave it for the time being and move on to the body of the letter. Once you've written the rest, the opening paragraph will usually flow much more smoothly and quickly.

There are three specific questions you must address in the opening paragraph of your cover letter:

1. Who are you?

2. Why are you writing?

3. What message are you communicating?

There are literally hundreds of opening paragraphs you can use that differ in style, wording, impact, tone, and presentation. The type of opening that you choose will depend on two key criteria:

1. **What is appropriate for the specific situation?** Are you writing in response to an advertisement or following up with a network referral? Are you writing to Fortune 100 companies to explore potential opportunities, or are you responding to a posting from an Internet job site? The specific situation almost always dictates the type of opening you select.

2. **What feels right?** When you read the samples below, you'll really like a few of them, feel lukewarm about others, and definitely not like some of them at all. That's okay. People differ; cover letter styles differ. Select one that not only fits the situation, but one that you feel good about, like its tone, and believe will work for you.

Example **Sample Opening Paragraphs**

We've chosen our favorite 41 opening paragraphs to share with you. Some are aggressive; some are mild-mannered and conservative. Some are typical in style; others are vastly different from anything you've probably ever seen before. Read them all and select the ones that you are most comfortable with.

Sample 1: Ad-Response Letter to a Company or Recruiter

```
I am writing in response to your advertisement for a (NAME OF
POSITION) and have enclosed my resume for your review.
```

Advantages:

- Direct, clear, and concise.

- Immediately identifies the position for which the candidate is applying.

Disadvantages:

- Passive and a bit passé.

- Reads the same as hundreds of other cover letters the company or recruiter has read before.

Sample 2: Ad-Response Letter to a Company or Recruiter

```
You will want to interview me for the Administrative Director
position with Pfizer because I
```

- Managed all administrative and business support functions for Merck's four-person senior executive management team for 12 years.

- Implemented the full suite of Microsoft Office programs and coordinated on-site training for 200+ administrative personnel.

- Saved $10,000 in annual purchasing costs.

Advantages:

- Immediately asks for the interview.

- Highlights experience in the same industry (both companies are large pharmaceutical manufacturers).

- Quick and easy-to-read style.

Disadvantages:

- Can be interpreted as too aggressive (but we don't think so).

Sample 3: Ad-Response Letter to a Company or Recruiter

> Born and educated in Australia, I have lived and worked around the globe—from Asia to Latin America, from the U.S. to the Philippines. The strength of my cross-cultural experience, combined with 15+ years of senior management experience, places me in a uniquely qualified position for your search for a **Director of International Business Development**.

Advantages:

- ✶ Interesting, informative, and fun introduction.
- ✶ Communicates the candidate's overall expertise.
- ✶ Clearly highlights the position for which the candidate is applying.

Disadvantages:

- ✶ Candidate could be perceived as "older" due to 15+ years and such extensive global experience.
- ✶ Conversational rather than hard-hitting—requires reading the full paragraph to determine the specific reason for writing, though the bold type certainly helps to make this information more noticeable.

Sample 4: Ad-Response Letter to a Company or Recruiter

> Your recent advertisement for an Operations Manager calls for skills and experience I have demonstrated throughout my career—most recently as Director of Operations for Office Depot's Corporate Accounts Warehouse.

Advantages:

- ✶ Clearly identifies why the candidate is writing.
- ✶ Appeals to the company's interests by referring to its advertised needs.
- ✶ Immediately communicates a highly relevant position with a well-known organization.
- ✶ Links the candidate's experience to the specific position.

Disadvantages:

- ✶ Appropriate only if the candidate's experience is directly relevant to the advertised position.
- ✶ Rather bland.

Sample 5: Ad-Response Letter to a Company or Recruiter

```
There is nothing that I have found that offers more challenge
than "closing the deal." The strategy, the partners, and the
money involved can be complex. But when the deal closes, the
personal satisfaction is tremendous. It is this expertise
that I bring to the position of Venture Funding Manager.
```

Advantages:

- ⚹ Unique, interesting introduction.

- ⚹ Immediately identifies the candidate's number-one qualification.

- ⚹ Links the candidate's experience to the specific position.

Disadvantages:

- ⚹ Appropriate only if the candidate's number-one qualification is what the hiring company is focused on.

Sample 6: Ad-Response Letter to a Company or Recruiter

```
When I was 7, like many others, I seriously planned to be-
come a professional baseball player. Unlike so many others,
however, I found a way to stay involved in sports despite
not making it to the major leagues. Playing baseball through
high school and college, then becoming involved as Clubhouse
Manager for a AAA baseball club, were natural outlets for my
interest and ambition. I then "fell" into a sales position,
where I've excelled for three years. Now I see an ideal
opportunity to combine my deep interest with my proven
professional skills and would be delighted to interview
for your Sports Sales Associate position.
```

Advantages:

- ⚹ Unique and interesting introduction that, in the right circumstances, can really captivate the reader.

- ⚹ Gives a quick but comprehensive "life" summary.

- ⚹ Clearly states the position for which the candidate is applying.

Disadvantages:

- ⚹ Applicable only for a candidate seeking to transition from one industry to another.

- ⚹ Could be interpreted as too "homey."

Sample 7: Ad-Response Letter to a Company or Recruiter

I would like to submit my name for consideration for your
advertised Warehouse Manager position. My qualifications
follow.

Advantages:

- Clear and concise.

- Immediately communicates the position the candidate is applying for.

Disadvantages:

- Boring, with no "hook" to grab the reader's attention.

Sample 8: Ad-Response Letter to a Company or Recruiter

Success. I believe that it lies in one's ability to merge
the strategic with the tactical, to understand the market
and the competition, to effectively control the finances of
a company, and to build a strong and committed workforce.
No one function is accountable for performance. It is the
integration of it all and the combined strength of the
management team. This knowledge and hands-on approach to
executive management is what will distinguish me from
your other candidates for the position of CEO.

Advantages:

- Communicates that this candidate understands business and executive management.

- Uses a unique style and executive-level presentation.

Disadvantages:

- Style is appropriate only for a mid- to senior-level position.

- Can be interpreted as too vague, theoretical, or obscure.

Sample 9: Ad-Response Letter to a Company or Recruiter

Please accept this letter and enclosed resume as application
for the position of City Manager. You will find that not only
do I have the specific qualifications you are seeking, I am a
strong business leader, a graduate of McAllen Leadership
Conference, and a current resident of the city with a wide
network of personal, professional, and political contacts.

Advantages:

- Immediately identifies the position for which the candidate is applying.

- Highlights what the candidate considers to be her three most significant selling points.

- Combines a traditional introduction ("Please accept…") with proactive style ("…strong business leader…").

Disadvantages:

- May not be addressing the "hot buttons" of the hiring committee.

- Language may be viewed as stodgy or old-fashioned.

Sample 10: Ad-Response Letter to a Company

A start-up company is only as good as the people behind it, and when you're in the Internet arena, you need people who are experienced and knowledgeable in this rapidly growing and ever-changing medium. I believe your search for the newest addition to your team is over if you seek an entrepreneurial-minded sales professional with expertise in formulating, managing, and marketing emerging Internet services.

Advantages:

- Distinctive introduction that will stand out from the crowd of competitors.

- Makes an immediate industry connection between the candidate and the hiring company.

- Alludes to the specific position for which the candidate is applying.

Disadvantages:

- May be telling people what they already know ("A start-up company is only as good…") and, therefore, may be considered somewhat condescending.

- Recipient must read the whole paragraph to "get it" and to identify the position for which the candidate is applying.

Sample 11: Ad-Response Letter to a Company

```
Your search for a Retail Sales Manager is over if you are
interested in someone who can ignite sales, reduce losses,
and build a top-performing sales and customer-service team.
I have done it in the past and will continue to do it in the
future—ideally with Lazarus Retail Management. I present to
you my resume for your consideration for a position on your
management team.
```

Advantages:

- ★ Powerful and confident introduction that is most appropriate for candidates in sales, marketing, and business development (demonstrates that you really can sell).

- ★ Highlights overall areas of expertise and achievement.

Disadvantages:

- ★ Could be interpreted as a bit too boisterous for some organizations.

Sample 12: Ad-Response Letter to a Recruiter

```
I meet all the hiring criteria for your search for an Admin-
istrative Director. Briefly summarized, my qualifications
include the following:
```

Advantages:

- ★ Clean, clear, and concise.
- ★ Briefly addresses hiring criteria as stated in the advertisement.

Disadvantages:

- ★ Passive approach that is similar to hundreds, maybe thousands, of letters the recruiter has previously seen.

Sample 13: Online Letter to a Company or Recruiter

```
I submit my qualifications in response to your job posting
for a Nurse Manager and have attached my resume at the bottom
of this letter.
```

Advantages:

- Clear and concise opening suitable for abbreviated online letter format.

- Immediately identifies the position for which the candidate is applying.

Disadvantages:

- Boring, but appropriate for "quick-read" e-mail letters.

Sample 14: Online Letter to a Company or Recruiter

```
With 12 years of experience as a high school teacher, I more
than meet your hiring requirements for the Teacher Training
Specialist position. My resume is available at http://
www.cminstitute/1rosen.html for your review.
```

Advantages:

- Concise and straightforward introduction is ideal for an online cover letter.

- Connects the candidate's experience with the advertised position and its specific requirements.

- Demonstrates technological proficiency (by including the Web site address).

Disadvantages:

- Does not entice the recipient to want to read on or provide any captivating information.

Sample 15: Cold-Call Letter to a Company or Recruiter

> Are you in need of a top-producing sales professional? An individual who has built new sales territories, delivered double-digit revenue growth, and consistently outperformed the competition? An individual who excels in transitioning customer relationships into profitable partnerships?

Advantages:

- Can be a powerful introduction if the reader answers "yes."

- Can entice readers if the candidate has used the right key words to grab their attention.

- Demonstrates that the candidate knows how to sell (the letter is a sales pitch).

Disadvantages:

- Is virtually worthless if the reader answers "no."

Sample 16: Cold-Call Letter to a Company or Recruiter

> Recruited to RAP Technology in 1989, I am one of five executives responsible for the dramatic growth of the company, from a $7 million privately held government contractor into a $200+ million NYSE high-tech systems provider with operating subsidiaries worldwide. My contributions have been diverse, with dual roles as Senior Vice President of Operations and Chief Technology Officer.

Advantages:

- Immediately communicates that the candidate has value. RAP recruited him, so others must want him as well.

- Demonstrates significant achievement and outstanding financial performance.

Disadvantages:

- Is appropriate only if the candidate was recruited for his last position.

- Is appropriate only if the candidate has one very significant achievement to highlight.

- Does not immediately communicate the type or level of position the candidate is interested in.

Sample 17: Cold-Call Letter to a Company or Recruiter

As one of the top three executives in a national nonprofit
organization, I have been recognized for my expertise in
building strong, efficient, cost-effective, and productive
operations that are responsive to our members' needs. When we
started three years ago, the organization was an unknown
entity. Today, we have increased our membership 400%, increased our funding 200%, and are recognized as one of the
top 500 nonprofits in the country.

Advantages:

- ✶ Immediately identifies who the candidate is and his level of experience.

- ✶ Highlights quantifiable achievements that are quite significant.

Disadvantages:

- ✶ Appropriate only if the candidate is writing to an individual in the same industry (in this instance, nonprofit).

Sample 18: Cold-Call Letter to a Company or Recruiter

Beginning my professional career as one of the first female
engineers ever hired into MCI, I progressed rapidly through
a series of increasingly responsible technical, product
development, marketing, and sales management positions
with MCI, Sprint, and AT&T. And to each, I delivered
financial results.

Advantages:

- ✶ Demonstrates innovation and fast-track promotion.

- ✶ Communicates significant industry expertise.

- ✶ Vaguely highlights success and achievement.

Disadvantages:

- ✶ Unclear as to what this candidate's current objective is.

- ✶ Niches this candidate into one specific industry—telecommunications (fine if that's where her search is strictly focused).

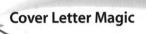

Sample 19: Cold-Call Letter to a Company

> Building corporate value is my expertise. Whether challenged to launch a start-up venture, orchestrate an aggressive turn-around, or lead an organization through accelerated growth and expansion, I have consistently delivered strong financial results.

Advantages:

- Aggressive, powerful, and high-performance.

- Most appropriate for a senior management or executive-level position.

Disadvantages:

- Can be interpreted as too aggressive (though we don't think so).

- Not focused on any particular type of company (start-up, turnaround, or growth) that the candidate is interested in—is "all over the place."

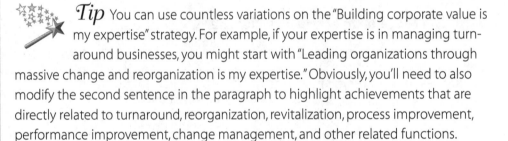

Tip You can use countless variations on the "Building corporate value is my expertise" strategy. For example, if your expertise is in managing turn-around businesses, you might start with "Leading organizations through massive change and reorganization is my expertise." Obviously, you'll need to also modify the second sentence in the paragraph to highlight achievements that are directly related to turnaround, reorganization, revitalization, process improvement, performance improvement, change management, and other related functions.

Or, if your success has been in developing new products, you could begin your cover letter with "Developing new products that have generated millions of dollars in new sales revenues is what I do best." Then continue with your next sentence that high-lights relevant achievements, functions, and key words.

These types of letters do not have to be restricted for use at just the senior manage-ment or executive level. Suppose you're an office manager whose expertise is creat-ing order from chaos. You might consider writing "Creating efficient, productive, and well-organized business support operations is the value I bring to your company."

If you like this strategy, first identify your number-one qualification or area of expertise, and then work on developing a strong and powerful two- to three-sentence intro-ductory paragraph.

You will find numerous variations of this opening in the sample letters in chapters 7 through 12.

Sample 20: Cold-Call Letter to a Company

I am writing and forwarding my resume in anticipation that
you may be "in the market" for a well-qualified President and
CEO. Highlights of my professional career that may be of
particular interest to you include the following:

Advantages:

* A "toned-down" version of sample 19.
* Immediately identifies who the candidate is, level of experience, and type of position being sought.

Disadvantages:

* If the reader is *not* "in the market," the letter is of little value.

Sample 21: Cold-Call Letter to a Company

Never in the history of the U.S. industrial revolution has
the pace been faster, the competition stiffer, or the economic factors more complex. With the rapid emergence of the
information technology marketplace, each and every company is
faced with tremendous challenges and unlimited opportunities.

Are you prepared to compete and win?

I can make a positive impact. With 20+ years of experience in
the information technology industry, most recently in data
warehousing, digital communications, and e-commerce, I bring
a wealth of technical and managerial expertise to Blue Ridge
New Media Partners.

Advantages:

* Quickly communicates that this is a senior-level candidate.
* Demonstrates industry knowledge and expertise.
* Is unique in style and presentation.
* Does not communicate an immediate message of "I want a job."

Disadvantages:

* Takes quite a while before the reader understands "who" this candi-date is, and, therefore, may lose the reader's interest.
* Does not quickly communicate why the candidate is writing, and, therefore, may lose the reader's attention.

Sample 22: Cold-Call Letter to a Company

> During my ten-year career with Westinghouse I earned seven
> merit promotions, advancing from Management Trainee through a
> series of increasingly responsible production assignments to
> my current position as Manager of Production Scheduling. Now
> my goal is to transition my experience into a smaller,
> higher-growth organization such as Excelsior Technology.

Advantages:

- Communicates promotion, achievement, and success.

- Quickly and effortlessly explains the reason for leaving her current position.

Disadvantages:

- Does not state a particular position in which the candidate is interested.

- Highlights experience with a large corporation when the candidate is currently looking for opportunities with small companies.

- Communicates a focus on the candidate's career and goals rather than the company's needs; an employer's knee-jerk reaction could be, "So what?"

Sample 23: Cold-Call Letter to a Company

> Twenty years ago, consumer electronics virtually sold them-
> selves. With just a bit of advertising, a company was set to
> launch a new product. Today, things have changed dramatically,
> and marketing has become one of the most vital components for
> any successful company. With both global competition and new
> product roll-outs at an all-time high, it is no longer enough
> just to develop a great product. You need an astute marketer,
> and that is precisely what I am.

Advantages:

- Immediately communicates who the candidate is.

- Demonstrates substantial industry experience.

- Captures interest and should command immediate agreement with the philosophy expressed.

Disadvantages:

* Can be interpreted as condescending (doesn't everyone already know this information?).

Sample 24: Cold-Call Letter to a Company

I am currently employed as the Hotel Manager with The Emerald Suites in San Diego. After eight years, I have decided to confidentially explore new opportunities and am contacting a select group of hotels that would be most interested in a candidate with my qualifications.

Advantages:

* Immediately communicates who the candidate is.

* Highlights years of experience in the hotel industry.

* Drops the "right" name (assuming that The Emerald Suites is a prestigious property).

Disadvantages:

* Not particularly exciting or captivating.

* Unclear as to what type of position the candidate is seeking (although we can guess).

* May convey an impression of self-importance—and there's definitely more focus on the candidate's interests than the employer's needs.

Sample 25: Cold-Call Letter to a Company

If you are looking for an experienced Pharmaceutical Sales Representative who can increase market share, build strong physician relationships, deliver effective presentations, and capture competitive business, then you will be interested in the experience and accomplishments highlighted in the enclosed resume.

Advantages:

* Immediately communicates who the candidate is.

* Identifies with the company's needs and promises the ability to deliver results.

* Immediately communicates why the candidate is writing.

Disadvantages:

- If the company is not looking for someone with these qualifications, the first paragraph will not capture interest.

Sample 26: Cold-Call Letter to a Company

> If you ask any one of my colleagues, employers, or clients, they will all tell you the same thing about me: I am a unique combination of **Technical Expert** and **Customer Service Specialist**. It's what I have done for years, it's what I enjoy, and it's the value I bring to TXT Systems, Inc.

Advantages:

- Unique letter style and tone.
- Who the candidate is stands out boldly.

Disadvantages:

- Does not state the specific type of position the candidate is seeking.
- May be considered somewhat pompous (although we do not think so).

Sample 27: Cold-Call Letter to a Company

> I am a well-qualified Bank Manager seeking a new and more challenging career opportunity with a financial institution in need of strong strategic, operating, and management leadership.

Advantages:

- Clearly and immediately communicates who the candidate is.

Disadvantages:

- Vague in terms of what type of position the candidate is currently seeking.
- Not particularly exciting, interesting, or captivating.

Sample 28: Cold-Call Letter to a Company

When I joined the investment management team at USF&G, I knew I was in for an exciting opportunity. Little did I know that during my five-year career, the company would be acquired twice and experience better than 200% market growth. In response to the dramatic changes within the organization, not only was I retained during each of these transitions, I was promoted three times to my current position as Director of Retail Investor Services, the exact type of position I am now seeking with your financial institution.

Advantages:

* Interesting and informative introduction.

* Communicates the candidate's fast-track career, promotion, and value to his current employer.

* Communicates the type of position the candidate currently holds and relates it directly to the position being sought.

Disadvantages:

* Leaves the reader wondering why this individual is seeking new employment opportunities if his career with USF&G has been so phenomenal.

Sample 29: Cold-Call Letter to a Company

I am a well-qualified marketing professional with 15+ years of experience. Most notable have been my achievements in new market development, new business development, market research, service/product line expansion, and customer management. Now, after a long and successful career with ABC, I am seeking to relocate to Atlanta and am quite interested in opportunities with your local network affiliate.

Advantages:

* Clearly communicates this candidate's expertise and core skill sets.

* Communicates the candidate's generalized achievements.

* Highlights that the candidate is (or will be) available in the local market, and therefore no relocation is required.

Disadvantages:

- 15+ years' experience can be interpreted as maybe 20, 30, or more years and, therefore, makes this look like an older candidate.

- Candidate appears to be moving downward in the career cycle.

Sample 30: Cold-Call Letter to a Company

> Do you seek the missing link to connect your U.S. operations with your expansion into Latin America? If so, we should meet. You will be particularly interested in the past five years of my career, during which I have provided the knowledge and experience to build Allied Signal's presence throughout the entire Latin American region. Starting with virtually nothing, I built a multimillion-dollar market that continues to grow at better than 25% annually.

Advantages:

- Captures immediate attention if the reader is interested in expanding into Latin America.

- Clearly communicates the candidate's experience and success.

- Highlights a very tangible achievement.

Disadvantages:

- Potential exists that the recipient could answer "no" to the introductory sentence, making the letter virtually powerless and a waste of time.

Sample 31: Cold Call Letter to a Company

> As I begin to launch my new career, I am looking for a company with a reputation for continual growth and achievement. From its beginning in 1899 as Brown Telephone Company, Sprint has grown tremendously and positioned itself as one of the industry's leaders. Sprint has precisely the spirit and drive that I that I seek as I near graduation and begin my career in human resources.

Advantages:

- Demonstrates that the candidate has devoted time to researching the company and its history.

- Communicates the specific type of position the candidate is seeking.

Disadvantages:

- Immediately identifies that this candidate (a graduating student) has no relevant experience.

- May be interpreted as manipulative and pandering to the company.

- Gives no reason why the company should be interested in this candidate.

Sample 32: Cold-Call Letter to a Company

FOR IMMEDIATE RELEASE

Lew Johnson, the current Sports Information Director at Maine State University, recently announced his desire to contribute his three years' experience in sports and public relations to a Division I school. Johnson's contract with MSU expires in May, and he sees this as an opportunity to meet bigger challenges. Johnson's performance at MSU has brought a great deal of attention to the athletic department, from athletes, students, parents, and the general public. He knows he can do the same for a larger athletic department at a larger school.

Advantages:

- Unique format that is particularly enticing for a public relations or marketing communications position.

- Demonstrates creativity, innovation, and the ability to capture the reader's interest.

- Clearly identifies who the candidate is, his experience, and his current employment objectives.

Disadvantages:

- Could be interpreted as a traditional press release and either forwarded to the PR department or discarded.

- May be too creative for a traditional or conservative university.

- Written in the third person, which is generally not advisable.

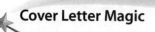

Sample 33: Cold-Call Letter to a Recruiter

I am writing in anticipation that you may be working with a client company seeking a well-qualified candidate for a position in Technology R&D. Highlights of my career that may be of particular interest to you include the following:

Advantages:

- One of the preferred methods when writing to a recruiter.

- Clear and concise as to the type of position the candidate is seeking.

- Immediately identifies the candidate's industry preference.

Disadvantages:

- Passive and passé.

- Similar in tone and presentation to thousands of letters the recruiter has previously received.

- Nothing distinguishing to immediately capture the reader's attention.

Sample 34: Referral Letter

Walter Clark recently described your broker-training program to me, and it certainly caught my attention as I seek to start a new career in the financial services industry. Mr. Clark is familiar with my extensive professional experience and recommended I submit my resume directly to you for consideration for one of your vacant investment professional positions.

Advantages:

- Highlights the name of the referring individual, who is someone the recipient knows.

- Communicates that it was Mr. Clark's recommendation that this candidate contact the company, because Mr. Clark believes there might be a match between the company and the candidate.

- Identifies the type of position the candidate is most suited for.

Disadvantages:

- The letter could potentially be passed on to someone not familiar with Mr. Clark, thereby negating the impact of the letter.

- Does not highlight any particulars about the candidate's experience.

Sample 35: Referral Letter

John Greene of CIO Enterprises suggested I contact you regarding your search for a Corporate Counsel. I've worked closely with John and his executive team for the past 18 months to facilitate their private placement and subsequent IPO. With the successful conclusion of that assignment, I'm now interested in other corporate funding and development projects, so John thought we might be a good fit for one another.

Advantages:

- Highlights the name of the referring individual, who is someone the recipient knows.

- Clearly communicates the value the candidate can bring to the company through the example of what she has done for CIO Enterprises.

- Is clear about the type of position the candidate is seeking.

Disadvantages:

- If the company has no corporate funding and development projects on the horizon, the candidate's experience will not capture the reader's interest.

- The letter could potentially be passed on to someone not familiar with Mr. Greene, thereby negating the impact of the letter.

Sample 36: Networking Letter

> As a fellow CEO, I've most likely dealt with many of the same issues that you have—issues related to reducing costs, optimizing operations, improving staff competencies, and, ultimately, strengthening bottom-line financial performance. My particular achievements have been in the transportation industry, but the skill sets I demonstrated are easily transferable to another industry.

Advantages:

- Immediately communicates the level of this candidate's expertise.

- Best used when approaching network contacts for their assistance and recommendations.

- Builds camaraderie with the reader.

Disadvantages:

- Clearly communicates that the candidate does not have experience related to the recipient's industry and, therefore, may immediately exclude him from consideration.

- Not focused on any particular opportunity.

Sample 37: Networking Letter

> Your name came to my attention recently as I began researching the pharmaceutical and medical research industries. I am interested in a career in sales and am looking to gain further insight into these industries and major players like yourself. I hope that you will help me in this pursuit of information by meeting with me to answer a few questions. Please understand that I am not asking for a job, but rather for some of your time to increase my knowledge.

Advantages:

- Excellent introduction for a letter requesting an informational interview (as opposed to a job interview).

- Alerts the recipient to that fact that her name is well-known and well-respected in the industry.

- Not asking for a job, just for information and time.

Disadvantages:

- Appears as a novice in the industry with no relevant experience.

- May be interpreted by the reader as a waste of her time.

- May be construed by the reader as an indirect attempt to secure employment.

- There is no personal reference; the writer is essentially "cold-calling" the recipient.

Sample 38: Follow-Up Letter to a Company or Recruiter

Three weeks ago I forwarded my resume for consideration for the position of Advertising Specialist with WRKR Broadcasting. I'm sure you received quite a response and have had to devote time to reviewing the qualifications of each of the candidates. At this time, I would like to reiterate my interest in the position and assure you that my qualifications not only meet, but exceed, your hiring requirements.

Advantages:

- Connects the candidate's experience to the company's specific hiring requirements.

- Demonstrates that the candidate follows up on a task that he has initiated.

- Reconfirms the candidate's interest in the position.

Disadvantages:

- May be a waste of time if the hiring manager did not respond to the first inquiry.

- May be interpreted as "pushing" the hiring manager too hard to follow up (we don't think so).

Sample 39: Follow-Up Letter to a Company or Recruiter

After we met last month at the AMA meeting, you asked that I forward my resume to you. Assuming that you've received it by now, I wanted to follow up to schedule an interview with you. During our conversation, you mentioned that you were interested in a candidate with an extensive background in the insurance and risk-management industries. That is precisely my background and the value I bring to AAA.

Advantages:

- Brings to the reader's immediate attention that she has already met the candidate and, at that point, asked the candidate to forward his resume.

- Clearly communicates who the candidate is.

- Clearly communicates the experience the candidate brings to the company.

Disadvantages:

- May be a waste of time if the hiring manager or recruiter did not respond to the first inquiry.

- May be interpreted as "pushing" too hard to follow up (we don't think so).

Sample 40: Sponsor Letter

After our leadership conference last week and our discussion about your search for a new Director of Procurement, I think I've found just the right candidate for you. Jonas Viens has been an employee with our organization for eight years and currently serves as Assistant Director of Purchasing and Vendor Relations. His level of expertise in vendor sourcing, price negotiations, and contract administration is outstanding and a valuable asset to our organization. However, Jonas has decided to relocate to Miami, a real loss for us but a potentially outstanding opportunity for you.

Advantages:

- Excellent example of a sponsor letter introduction.

- Clearly communicates who the candidate is and his value to the hiring organization.

- Immediately connects the candidate with the hiring company's needs.

Disadvantages:

- Can be used only if written by a third party—a candidate's sponsor.

- Appropriate only if this senior executive is writing to a colleague— another senior executive.

Sample 41: Sponsor Letter

Mary Morton is a winner. I know from experience. Mary worked for me for 14 years, first as Sales Manager and then as VP of Sales and Marketing during my tenure as CEO of Ryder Dedicated Logistics. Her performance was top-of-the-line, consistently exceeding revenue and profit objectives and winning major accounts. What's more, she knows our industry, how the marketplace works, and what it takes to win. If you're looking for a VP of Sales to replace Roger, you can't go wrong with Mary.

Advantages:

- Powerful introduction and testimonial from a third party.

- Clearly communicates who the candidate is.

- Clearly communicates the need the candidate fills.

Disadvantages:

- Can be used only if written by a third party—a candidate's sponsor.

- Appropriate only if this senior executive is writing to a colleague— another senior executive.

Action Item

1. Write the Opening Paragraph

Write the opening paragraph for the cover letter you have selected to write for this exercise. You can select one of the samples above and edit it to your experience, qualifications, achievements, and the specific situation at hand. Or, if you prefer, you can write an entirely different introduction that is both appropriate and "feels good" to you.

 ## Chris Starts His Letter

Remember Chris Matthews? He's about to start his letter to Funky Fashions to see if he can "sell" his qualifications to develop the company's e-commerce site.

Chris wants to appeal to the owner's business sense and show how technology can help the company.

Here's how he starts his letter:

> Today's most exciting technology is electronic commerce. It can deliver enormous business gains and competitive advantages for companies that dedicate the resources necessary for a high-quality, easily navigated, flawlessly performing e-commerce site.
>
> **That's where I can help your company.** I can communicate what is unique about Funky Fashions—your products, image, and unique fashion focus—on a Web site that will increase your sales, expand your market reach, and solidify your connection with your technology-savvy customer base.

Step 4: Write the "Meat"

After reading and progressing through step 3, "Write the Opening," you're now ready to tackle the real task at hand. You're ready to write the "meat" of your cover letter—the substance, key qualifications, accomplishments, successes, and whatever other information you can highlight that will entice the reader to closely review your resume and offer you the opportunity for a personal interview.

> *Tip* Before you begin writing, again consider why you're writing the letter you have chosen for this exercise. Regardless of your profession, the type of position you are interested in, your industry experience, your professional skill set, your technical proficiency, or any other variable, you have just one purpose in writing the letter:
>
> **To sell the product—and the product is you!**

In order to sell any product, you must highlight the attractive *features* and *benefits* of that product. Put yourself in the buyer's shoes, and ask yourself:

- What will catch my attention?
- What's interesting about this candidate?
- What's innovative or unique about this candidate?
- Why is this candidate different from (or better than) other competitive candidates?
- Do I understand the value I'll get from this candidate?
- Do I need this candidate?
- Do I want this candidate?

Whether you're conscious of it or not, every time you buy something, you ask yourself these questions and others. It's the typical process that everyone goes through when they're deciding whether to make a purchase. It is imperative that you remember this as you begin to write your cover letters. Understand that you must clearly communicate the answers to these questions in order to get people to want to "buy" you.

> *Tip* Your cover letter *should not* be written as "Here I am; give me a job." Instead, it should be written as "Here I am; this is why I am so valuable; *now* give me a job." Focusing on the value and benefits you have to offer is a good way to capture the reader's attention. Remember, the employer's most compelling question is "What can you do for me?," not "What do you want?"
>
> Your challenge is to convey that value in a short and concise document—your cover letter.

Refer to the lists of responsibilities and achievements you developed in "Step 1: Identify Your Key Selling Points." Your lists include information from both your current position (if you are currently employed) and all of your past positions. The sole reason that you completed this task was to prepare for what you are going to do now: write the "meat" of your cover letter.

Unfortunately, there are no rules to guide you in selecting what to include from your lists and what to omit. It is entirely a judgment call based on the specific situation at hand. Consider the following scenario:

You're currently employed as a customer service manager with a large telemarketing company. If you're applying for a similar position in the credit card industry, the responsibilities and accomplishments you will highlight in your cover letter are those related to customer service, problem resolution, team building, and business unit management. You will *not* highlight your years of experience in the telemarketing industry.

If, on the other hand, you're applying for a position in sales in the same industry, the responsibilities and achievements you will highlight are those related to customer relationship management, account management, and product/service support, as well as your extensive experience in the telemarketing industry.

So, as you can see, what you highlight in your cover letter is determined exclusively by the specific situation at hand—the position, the company, the industry, and the required qualifications and experience. It is not necessarily based on what you consider to be your most significant responsibilities and achievements from throughout your career, but rather what is *most relevant to the hiring company and its needs.*

Achievements, accomplishments, contributions, and successes are the cornerstone of any effective cover letter. It goes without saying that you want to demonstrate that you have the right skills, qualifications, and experience for a particular job. However, you do not want your letter to be a "job description"—a listing of job responsibilities. First of all, you've addressed a great deal of that information in the resume that you'll be sending along with your cover letter. Remember, you do not want your letter to simply reiterate what's in your resume. The challenge is to write a cover letter that complements the resume and brings the most notable information to the forefront, as related to the particular position or situation.

Secondly, when you write in your cover letter that you have "Seven years' experience managing electronics purchasing for GE," you've immediately communicated a whole set of implied skills (such as vendor sourcing, contract negotiations, inventory planning, competitive bidding, product review, and knowledge of electronic products). To keep your cover letter short and succinct, do not waste space simply listing all of your skills and competencies as they are noted on your resume. Instead, highlight the notable achievements that will set you apart from the crowd and give readers a good idea of what you can do for them.

Depending on the format of your letter, you can convey this information in paragraph format style, comparison-list style, or in bullet points. If you're writing full paragraphs, make sure they are fairly short to promote readability. Edit and tighten your copy so that every word and phrase conveys information that relates to the employer's needs and your most relevant qualifications.

Your lists of responsibilities and achievements are your tools. First review what you know about the company and the position (your action items from "Step 2: Pre-Plan"). Then carefully review your lists to determine which responsibilities and achievements are most appropriate to this particular situation and incorporate them into your letter. Sometimes you'll use them exactly as you have written them, sometimes you'll edit them to integrate them into the flow of your cover letter, and other times you may consolidate several of them into one statement or achievement. However you elect to use these lists, use them wisely. You have gone to the effort of preparing them. Now let them work for you as the foundation for every letter you write.

Action Items

1. Write the "Meat"

Write the "meat" of the cover letter you have selected to write for this exercise. You can use a paragraph style, comparison-list style, or bullet style, depending on the particular reason you are writing this letter. Be sure to focus on your achievements so that you can quickly and accurately communicate your value and strength in performance. Use the samples in chapters 8 through 12 to give you ideas on how to write powerful text that communicates a positive message of performance.

 Chris Writes the "Meat" of His Letter

Chris Matthews continues his letter to Funky Fashions with a few short paragraphs that convey his key qualifications—remember, he offers a mix of both Web programming skills and technical project management. He is careful to appeal to the company's business interests and convey that he knows what is special about Funky Fashions.

> With recent training in Web programming combined with an extensive background in technology project management, I have both the technical skills and the business focus to help your company achieve its goals for electronic commerce. I offer:
>
> - **Advanced web programming skills**—to translate your company's products, services, and image to a highly functional, unique, "funky" Web site. I have honed these skills through a recent in-depth Web programming course, where I was #1 in my class.
>
> - **Strong project-management abilities**—Managing mission-critical projects for Saks Fifth Avenue, Northern Electric, and Ralston Purina, I delivered all projects on schedule and under budget and was recognized for inspiring a strong team environment across multiple departments of each company.
>
> In short, I have the technology skills and project management experience to take your e-commerce site from the drawing board to the World Wide Web.

Step 5: Write the Closing

Now that you've written your introductory paragraph and the balance of your cover letter, all you have left to write is the closing paragraph. Simple enough—in fact, this is generally the easiest section of your letter to write. To get started, ask yourself these two simple questions:

1. What style of closing paragraph do I want to use?

2. Is there any specific personal or salary information I want to include that was requested in the advertisement to which I am responding?

When it comes to choosing style, closing paragraphs are easy. There are only two styles—*passive* and *assertive*. There are, obviously, various options within each of these styles, and we explore these below. The distinction between the two styles is evident.

- **Passive style:** A passive letter ends with a statement such as "I look forward to hearing from you." With this sentence, you are taking a passive approach, waiting for the hiring company or recruiter to contact you. This is not the strategy we recommend.

- **Assertive style:** An assertive letter ends with a statement such as "I look forward to interviewing with you and will follow up next week to schedule a convenient appointment." In this sentence, you are asserting yourself, telling the recipient that you will follow up and asking for the interview!

We strongly recommend that you always end your cover letters with an assertive closing paragraph. If you think back to the Introduction, you'll recall that the number-one objective of your cover letter is to get an interview. Ask for it!

Furthermore, we also advise that you outline an agenda that communicates that you will be expecting their call and, if you don't hear from them, you will follow up. This puts you in the driver's seat and in control of your job search. It also demonstrates to a prospective employer that once you've initiated something, you follow it through to completion. This is a valuable trait for any professional.

Inevitably, there will be instances in your job search when you will not be able to follow up:

- If you are responding to a blind advertisement with a P.O. box, you won't know who to call.

- If you are responding to an advertisement that states "No phone calls," don't call.

- If you are sending out 1,000 letters to recruiters across the nation, don't waste your time trying to follow up on each of them. If a recruiter is interested or has an opportunity for which you are suited, they'll call you.

- If you know that you'll never get the individual you want to speak with on the phone, don't waste your time or money trying.

>
> *Tip* Follow up with a phone call after forwarding a resume and cover letter only when the situation is appropriate. You do not need to follow up every single contact with a phone call.

The closing paragraph of your cover letter is also the preferred placement for any personal or salary information you will include. There are generally only two times you will want to include this type of information:

* **When it has been asked for in an advertisement.** Common requests include such things as salary history (what you have made in the past and are currently earning if you are employed), salary requirements (what your current salary objectives are), citizenship status, or geographic preference.

Example

> I look forward to interviewing for the Sales Manager position and can assure you that the strength of my sales production, sales training, and account management experience will bring measurable value to Centric's sales organization. In response to your specific requests, my salary requirements are in the $50,000 to $70,000 range, I am a U.S. citizen and am open to relocation anywhere in the Southwestern U.S. Thank you.

> *Tip* You will have already addressed the skill and qualification requirements of the position earlier in your letter—in your opening paragraph and in the body of the text. Save the closing paragraph for the "extras" that you may need to include.

* **When you are writing "cold-call" letters to recruiters.** When contacting recruiters, we recommend that you at least minimally address your salary requirements (a range is fine) and any geographic preferences in the closing paragraph of your cover letter.

Example

> If you currently have an open search for a Logistics and Distribution Manager, I would welcome the opportunity to interview for the position. Be advised that my current salary is $45,000 annually and I would anticipate a 10% to 15% increase in my next position. Thank you for your consideration. I look forward to speaking with you.

The Salary Question

Before we present the various sample closing paragraphs we've developed for your use, let's take a few minutes to discuss salary and how you can best deal with divulging salary information when it is requested.

First, keep in mind that it is never to your advantage to volunteer salary information. If you do so, you give employers a reason for screening you in or out of consideration, and you place yourself at a disadvantage in later salary negotiations. On some occasions, however, such information may be specifically requested. What do you do in those cases?

If an employer or recruiter asks you to provide a salary history (what you have made in your past and current positions), you have four basic options:

1. You can provide brief information in your cover letter, such as "My salary history has averaged $100,000 to $125,000 over the past five years." This defines the "ballpark" of your salary range and is usually quite adequate for the first contact you'll have with a recruiter or hiring company. If you choose to disclose salary information, we recommend this type of response.

2. You can provide more detailed information in your cover letter, such as

   ```
   My salary history is as follows: Retail Sales Man-
   ager—JC Penney ($75,000/year); Retail Sales Manager—
   Kmart ($62,000/year); Sales Department Manager—Kmart
   ($45,000/year); Sales Associate—Kmart (progression
   from $18,000 to $35,000/year).
   ```

   In this example, you've still been brief but managed to include a great deal of information while demonstrating consistent growth in your compensation.

3. You can prepare a separate page—titled "Salary History"—that lists your employers, job titles, and both beginning and ending salaries. The following is a sample format:

   ```
   Customer Service Representative    Beginning Salary—
                                      $22,000/year
   Sir Speedy Printing Company        Ending Salary—
                                      $35,000/year
   ```

Here's another format that may be appropriate if you've held several positions with the same company:

Example

```
IBM—NEW VENTURES DIVISION

General Manager                      $137,000/year
National Sales Manager               $102,000/year
Regional Sales Manager               $ 85,000/year
Key Account Manager                  $ 55,000/year
Sales Associate                      $ 38,000/year
```

4. You can choose not to provide this information, either ignoring the request entirely or addressing it without disclosing salary information: "I will be glad to discuss salary once we have determined that I am a good fit for the position, responsibilities, and environment." There is the risk, of course, that the reader will be annoyed that you did not supply the requested information. In our experience, however, the most common response of hiring managers and HR people is, consistently, to *look at the resume anyway*. By not disclosing salary history, you are probably not hurting your chances of being asked for an interview, and you are maintaining a decided advantage in any ultimate salary negotiation. Of course, if the advertisement states "Responses without salary history will not be considered," you must comply. (See the next section, on salary requirements, for a detailed discussion of the pros and cons of supplying and not supplying this kind of information.)

If an employer or recruiter asks you to provide your salary requirements (what your current salary objectives are), you again have four basic options:

1. You can provide a range, such as "My salary requirements are in the $55,000 to $65,000 range." This "ballpark figure" is generally enough information for this initial stage of contact with a potential employer or recruiter. In fact, this is our preferred method of response.

2. You can provide a specific number in your cover letter, such as "My salary requirements are $90,000 per year." This is not a particularly good strategy, because it limits you. The position for which you are applying may be slated for a $100,000 salary. However, you've already agreed to work for $10,000 less a year. What a bargain for the company! Or, a specific number can hurt you in the other direction. Suppose the company is prepared to pay only $75,000, but it's a great opportunity. You might just consider it, but potentially you've excluded yourself from consideration with an overinflated salary expectation. And finally, any salary requirement that is too high *or* too low

can effectively "screen you out," particularly in the first stages of re-sume review. When a recruiter or HR person is flooded with hundreds of resumes, his or her first response is to weed out anyone who doesn't fit each and every aspect of the job profile.

3. You can "take the fifth" and reply with, "My salary requirements are negotiable and can be discussed at the time of an interview" or "My salary requirements are flexible and will be discussed when I know more about the position and your company." Either way is really avoiding the question, but at least you are acknowledging that you saw the question. The only time we recommend this strategy is when you have absolutely no idea what a position will pay and don't want to oversell or undersell yourself.

4. You can ignore the request and not divulge your salary require-ments. There are definite benefits to this strategy. First, you will not be screened out based on salary. Second, you won't "paint yourself into a corner" with a salary figure that may be much lower than the company is willing to pay. Third, you are able to keep the focus on what's really important: whether you're the right person for the job. As every shop-per knows, once you've found an item that you love, you're nearly always willing to pay just a bit more than you budgeted. By avoiding salary discussion until the company is convinced it wants to "buy" you, you give yourself a definite negotiating advantage. And both formal and informal research supports the finding that resume reviewers look at the resume anyway, even when salary requirements are not included.

This approach can definitely work in your favor—but if you choose not to divulge salary requirements in your letter, you must prepare yourself to answer salary questions when they arise. The best strategy is to continually steer the conversation back to the matter at hand: whether you're the right person for the job, whether you have skills and experience that can help the company, and so forth. Spend the time to learn salary negotiating techniques (through a book or a coaching session with a career professional) so that you can handle these questions professionally and consistently throughout your search. And finally, this strategy will *not* work with recruiters. As we've stated several times, it's important to be up front with salary and personal requirements when dealing with recruiters. They won't take your candidacy any further unless they know you're in tune with their client's needs.

Depending on your level within the management ranks, there may be other information you will share in your cover letters relative to your salary and overall compensation package. This might include such items as signing bonuses, performance bonuses, equity interest, stock options, profit-sharing plans, deferred contribution plans, deferred compensation plans, and other management and executive incentives. Regardless of your career level, we recommend that you read *Job Offer! A How-To Negotiation Guide* by Maryanne L. Wegerbauer (JIST Publishing, 2000) for an in-depth exploration of the strategies, tips, and techniques for effective salary and compensation negotiations.

 ## Sample Closing Paragraphs

The following are 35 sample closing paragraphs. These are quick and easy to review. Note that some closing paragraphs are indeed one paragraph, while others may be two paragraphs, largely to improve readability. Simply select the samples that you are most comfortable with and adapt them for your use.

Sample 1: Ideal if responding to a recruiter advertisement

> If you are working with a client company seeking a candidate with my qualifications, I would welcome the opportunity to speak with you. Be advised that I am open to relocation and that my current compensation exceeds $85,000 annually. Thank you.

Sample 2: Solid closing for company ad-response letter

> I think you'll agree I meet and exceed your needs for a Firm Administrator. I would appreciate the opportunity to meet with you and can be reached at (555) 333-2838 to schedule an appointment or for more information. Thank you for your time and consideration. I look forward to meeting you in the near future.

Sample 3: Aggressive closing for company ad-response letter

> After you review the enclosed resume and visit with me, I think you'll agree I'm the missing piece to your team. My experience in the industry is solid, my knowledge of the technology vast, and my client contacts of tremendous value to IBM. I will follow up next week to schedule an interview, and I look forward to meeting you. Thank you.

Sample 4: Strong closing for response to company ad

Aware that you are currently recruiting for a Quality Engineer, I would welcome the opportunity to interview for the position. I guarantee that the depth and quality of my experience and technical skills are ideally suited and would bring measurable value to your organization. Thank you. I appreciate your confidentiality.

Sample 5: Ideal closing for ad-response letter (to recruiters or companies)

My goal is a top-level management position with an organization seeking to achieve market dominance as well as aggressive revenue and profit projections. I am most interested in interviewing for the position of General Manager—Aeronautics Division, where I will provide the strategic and tactical leadership critical to succeed in today's fast-moving environment.

I look forward to interviewing with you and the other principals involved in the hiring process. Thank you.

Sample 6: Clearly positions the candidate as an asset and highlights qualifications for a specific position

I am confident that I can make a meaningful contribution to Archer Associates as the link between your growing offices. I am willing to travel in the U.S., Canada, Latin America, and Europe, and would be pleased to relocate to Orlando.

I would appreciate the opportunity to meet with you to discuss your growth objectives and how I can help you in achieving them. Please feel free to contact me for further information to support my candidacy for this position. Thank you.

Sample 7: Closing for cold-call letter to a recruiter

Currently, I am exploring finance and accounting management opportunities within the medical technology market. As such, I would welcome the opportunity to speak with you regarding any current search assignments. Please note that I prefer to remain in the Miami metro market and that my salary requirements are negotiable. Thank you.

Sample 8: Concise and versatile closing for ad-response and cold-call letters

I am confident I can deliver similar results for your company. May we meet to explore your needs and how I can contribute to your growth and success?

Sample 9: Cold-call letter closing

I would appreciate the opportunity to speak with you about how I can help your company live its mission by improving customer service, productivity, and efficiency through information technology. I will call in a few days to arrange a meeting that is convenient for you. In the meantime, if you need more information, please feel free to call me at (555) 555-1234. Thank you.

Sample 10: Concise and direct closing for a cold-call letter to a company

Currently, I am exploring new engineering and project-management positions within the chemical industry. If you are seeking a decisive, action-driven, and technically astute leader for your engineering organization, I would welcome a personal interview. I'll follow up on Tuesday to arrange a mutually convenient time for our meeting. Thank you.

Sample 11: Focuses on how to contact the candidate

I am confident I can make a quick and valuable contribution to Robbins & Robbins and am sure you'll agree once we've had the opportunity to meet. Because of my travel schedule, it is easiest to reach me via e-mail at sallysmith@inmind.com. I look forward to meeting with you and the rest of the sales and customer-service team.

Sample 12: Focuses on relocation requirement

I am willing to relocate for the right opportunity—one that provides a challenge, a way for me to make an ongoing, positive impact, and the potential to grow with the dealership. I would appreciate a personal interview at your earliest convenience and will call to schedule a convenient time. Thank you for your consideration.

Sample 13: Ideal if the candidate is seeking a position that requires relocation or travel

I would welcome the chance to meet with you to explore international sales opportunities and do appreciate your time and interest. On a personal note, I am single and currently renting my home. Therefore, relocation or travel can be immediate. Thank you.

Sample 14: Ideal if the candidate wants to remain in the same geographic area

Currently in the process of leaving Brenview Associates, I am anxious to remain in the area and am contacting a select number of companies I believe would be interested in a candidate with my broad general management and operations experience. Can we meet to explore such opportunities? I can be available at your convenience and will follow up in the next ten days to schedule a time.

Sample 15: Focuses on personal attributes and the reason for wanting to work for a specific company

Characterized by others as creative, intuitive, flexible, and decisive, I believe my strongest value is my broad operational and business perspective. The opportunity that you are offering with Bayer has tremendous potential and unlimited opportunities—thus my interest in meeting with you to further discuss the position, your needs, and my capabilities. Thank you.

Sample 16: Focuses on personal attributes

The enclosed resume describes my qualifications in some detail. But it is difficult to convey on paper the personal qualities I bring to every challenge: drive, focus, commitment, a high energy level, and a strong work ethic. I am eager to take on new challenges and confident that I can deliver strong results for Megacorp's Medical Products Division. May we meet to explore your needs and what I have to offer?

Sample 17: Focuses on professional competencies

My experience lies principally in the product, service, and distribution industries, and my track record clearly demonstrates my ability to deliver strong financial results. I thrive in challenging, fast-paced, and results-driven organizations where teams work cooperatively to achieve aggressive business goals.

May we meet to explore your current and anticipated executive staffing needs? I can guarantee that the quality of my leadership performance will have a significantly positive impact on your operations. Thank you. I'll follow up next week.

Sample 18: Explains past employment experience

Since leaving EDS in 1998 after a long and successful career, I have been engaged in a number of consulting assignments while I've evaluated new opportunities, trying to find just the "right fit" for someone with my combination of leadership, customer management, and technical expertise. Your advertisement appears to require precisely the qualifications I bring to an organization. As such, I would welcome the opportunity to further explore the position, and I thank you in advance for your time and consideration. I'll follow up next week if I haven't yet heard back from you.

Sample 19: Explains the candidate's reason for leaving the company

After two years of success at Miller, the company is now poised for dramatic growth. However, the investor group has decided to pull the funding, and without a strong cash infusion, our growth and development opportunities have been significantly hindered. This has prompted my decision to leave the organization.

Through this experience I've found that I have enjoyed the constant interaction with the investor group and the accountability it demands. Therefore, I am contacting a select group of firms where I believe the opportunities are the strongest and my experience would be of most value. May we meet to explore such an affiliation? I'll call to speak with you, and we can go forward from there. Thank you.

Sample 20: Explains why the candidate is seeking to return to an industry where he had previous experience

My goal is to return to the financial services industry in a mid-level management capacity. I am open to a number of opportunities that would allow me to use the diversity of my management skills across various disciplines—operations, sales/marketing, finance, and IT. I would also anticipate that the position would have a strong international focus to capitalize on the wealth of my experience abroad and my foreign-language skills.

I would welcome the chance to meet with you and look forward to your immediate response. Thank you for both your time and your consideration.

Sample 21: Explains why the candidate is interested in changing careers and industry focus

Now, at this juncture in my career, I am seeking the opportunity to transition my experience into either an investment or large commercial lending institution where I can continue to plan, strategize, negotiate, and execute favorable transactions—thus my interest in meeting with you to explore such opportunities. Thank you. I'll follow up next week.

Sample 22: Explains why the candidate wants to work for that particular company

Currently, I am exploring new senior-level sales, marketing, and business development opportunities where I can provide both strategic and tactical leadership. Aware of the quality of your products, your commitment to global expansion, and your focus on customer service, I would be delighted to meet with you to discuss potential employment. I thank you in advance for your consideration and look forward to speaking with you.

Sample 23: Explains why the candidate is transitioning from consulting back to corporate

Most recently, I have provided operating, strategic, and marketing expertise on a consulting basis to an organization in need of strong hands-on leadership. This assignment has been quite rewarding, but I miss the dynamics of working "on the inside." As such, I would welcome the opportunity to interview for the position of General Manager with Zion Corporation and will phone next week to schedule an interview.

Sample 24: Explains why the candidate is remaining in the profession, just changing industry focus

My goal is to continue in association management; however, my direction has changed. Throughout my career, I have been quite interested in the building, construction, and housing industry, and in fact worked for a $200 million REIT early in my career. Through this experience, I developed a strong foundation and understanding of the industry, its partners, its financial demands, and its operating requirements. Years later, I earned my real estate license, just to keep my "fingers in the pot." Now, I am ready to make a full transition to an association whose mission is to service that industry—thus my interest in your announcement for an Executive Director of BOMI and my request for a personal interview.

Sample 25: Excellent strategy to explain why the candidate is in the job market

Now that HHXT has been acquired, I am working to facilitate a seamless transition to the new ownership team. Concurrently, I am exploring new executive opportunities and would welcome a personal interview for the CEO position at your earliest convenience. Thank you.

Sample 26: Explains why the candidate is choosing to leave a company after years of employment

Please note that I am currently employed with Metropolitan and that they are not aware of my decision to leave the corporation. However, after eight years of intense legal, financial, and regulatory issues that have dramatically impacted the company's operations, I am ready to move on to new opportunities and new challenges. As such, I would welcome a personal interview for the advertised position and guarantee that there are few Senior Auditors with the breadth of experience and technical qualifications that I bring to your organization.

Sample 27: Clearly communicates why the candidate wants to remain in a particular industry

I have found the energy industry to be demanding and competitive, yet exciting with unlimited opportunity. Even though I have been offered positions outside of the industry, my objective is to continue to advance my career in energy distribution and operations management. I look forward to interviewing for the position of VP—Energy Distribution and thank you for your consideration. I'll follow up next week.

Sample 28: Demonstrates strong leadership and communicates a positive message of performance

These achievements are indicative of the quality and caliber of my entire professional career. Whether challenged to accelerate growth, orchestrate a top-to-bottom turnaround, or position an organization for long-term growth, I have provided strong leadership and even stronger financial results. Now I am seeking a similar professional challenge and would welcome an interview for the position of CEO with KTZ Partners.

Sample 29: Communicates stability with current employer

I am slated to return to the U.S. this spring to manage a large domestic production operation for my current employer. It is a tremendous opportunity. However, before accepting, I have decided to confidentially explore other senior management positions within the industry—thus my interest in speaking with you as soon as possible to determine my fit for your Manufacturing VP position. Thank you.

Sample 30: Communicates performance and accomplishment

Never satisfied with the status quo, I strive to build profitable businesses by clearly understanding the market, the competition, and what needs to be done to retain a competitive lead. This is the strength and track record I bring to QSR.

May we meet to discuss your search for an Operations Manager? I'll call to arrange a mutually convenient time. Thank you.

Sample 31: Follow-up letter to a recruiter, announcing that the candidate has accepted a new position

More than excited about my new position, I feel honored to be part of Centric's new management team. However, as any astute business professional today will tell you, it's never wise to close yourself off from other potential opportunities. As such, if you ever receive an exciting search assignment for which I fit the bill, I'd appreciate a quick call. Thank you.

Sample 32: Informal network contact

I would appreciate any ideas, recommendations, or referrals you could offer and will, in the future, be delighted to do the same for you if the situation ever arises. I've enclosed a copy of my resume and will follow up with you shortly to get your feedback. Thanks so much.

Sample 33: Formal network contact

Now that the time has come to move on, I am anxious to identify new executive opportunities where I can combine my legal and general management skills to provide strong, decisive, and actionable leadership to another technology venture. In anticipation that you may be aware of an organization seeking an individual with my skill set and track record of performance, I have taken the liberty of enclosing my resume.

Any assistance you can offer would be most appreciated. I thank you for this effort and those in the past. If there is ever anything I can do for you, please do not hesitate to contact me.

Sample 34: Ideal for a network contact with someone the candidate knows quite well

```
I'll follow up with you in two to three weeks to get your
feedback and recommendations, and I can't thank you enough
for your help. If I can ever return the favor, please do not
hesitate to get in touch. My best to you and your family.
```

Sample 35: Effective, professional closing for use when writing to a venture capital firm

```
Currently, I am confidentially exploring new professional
challenges and opportunities and would be delighted to speak
with you about such positions with one of your portfolio
companies. I guarantee that the wealth of my financial exper-
tise, combined with strong strategic, operational, and lead-
ership skills, will add measurable value to your investment.
Thank you. I look forward to your call.
```

Action Item

1. **Write the Closing Paragraph**

   Write the closing paragraph of the cover letter you have selected for this exercise. You can select one of the samples above and edit it as appropriate, or you can write an entirely different closing that is appropriate and that you "feel good" about.

 ## Chris Writes His Closing Paragraph

Chris Matthews has written a letter that is fairly lengthy. To counterbalance that, he wrote a closing paragraph that is short, succinct, and concise.

```
Can we meet to explore your need for an e-commerce leader
within Funky Fashions? I'm confident I can deliver strong
business results by positioning the company as a leader in
cutting-edge technology as well as cutting-edge fashion.

Thank you for your consideration. I will call next week to
follow up.
```

You're Done with the Writing Part!

Congratulations! By completing all the Action Items in this chapter, you've written a cover letter for a specific job search situation. Now that you've done it once, simply repeat the steps for each cover letter you write. You'll find that the process becomes easier and faster each time you do it, and you'll create a variety of cover letters that will be applicable for many differ-ent situations during your search.

Chris' Cover Letter

Chris has also finished his cover letter. Here's the final product:

CHRIS MATTHEWS

123 Park Avenue   Phone: 555.444.3627
Chicago, Illinois 60606   E-mail: cmatthews42@aol.com

April 2, 2001

Cynthia Mars, President
Funky Fashions, Inc.
1230 Lakeshore Boulevard
Chicago, IL 60616

Dear Ms. Mars:

Today's most exciting technology is electronic commerce. It can deliver enormous business gains and competitive advantages for companies that dedicate the resources necessary for a high-quality, easily navigated, flawlessly performing e-commerce site.

That's where I can help your company. I can communicate what is unique about Funky Fashions—your products, image, and unique fashion focus—on a Web site that will increase your sales, expand your market reach, and solidify your connection with your technology-savvy customer base.

With recent training in Web programming combined with an extensive background in technology project management, I have both the technical skills and the business focus to help your company achieve its goals for electronic commerce. I offer:

- **Advanced web programming skills**—to translate your company's products, services, and image to a highly functional, unique, "funky" Web site. I have honed these skills through a recent in-depth Web programming course, where I was #1 in my class.

- **Strong project-management abilities**—Managing mission-critical projects for Saks Fifth Avenue, Northern Electric, and Ralston Purina, I delivered all projects on schedule and under budget and was recognized for inspiring a strong team environment across multiple departments of each company.

In short, I have the technology skills and project-management experience to take your e-commerce site from the drawing board to the World Wide Web.

Can we meet to explore your need for an e-commerce leader within Funky Fashions? I'm confident I can deliver strong business results by positioning the company as a leader in cutting-edge technology as well as cutting-edge fashion.

Thank you for your consideration. I will call next week to follow up.

Sincerely,

Chris Matthews
Enclosure

Step 6: Polish, Proofread, and Finalize

The process we've recommended for writing your cover letters suggests that you first craft the opening, then the middle, then the closing of each letter. Although this step-by-step process makes the task fairly quick and easy, you will probably find that your letters need final polishing, wordsmithing, and tweaking to ensure that each section "flows" into the next and that you have a cohesive-sounding whole.

Take the time to proofread your letter thoroughly and carefully. Read it for sense and flow; then read it again to check for spelling errors, punctuation mistakes, and grammatical inconsistencies. As we've suggested before, have your spouse or a friend proof your letter—and then read it one more time to be absolutely certain there are no errors. We cannot emphasize this point enough. The people who receive your cover letter and resume *do* judge your professionalism based on the quality and accuracy of these documents. In fact, in a survey of hiring authorities conducted for a prior book, *90 percent of respondents* mentioned quality and appearance factors (typos, misspellings, smudged print, low-quality paper) as reasons for *immediately discarding a resume package.* Don't take a chance that your carefully written letter and resume will end up in the "circular file" before your qualifications are even considered.

Here are a few things to look out for during the polishing phase:

- **Spelling:** Use your computer's spell-checker, but don't rely on it totally. The spell-checker won't flag an "it's" that should be "its" or a "there" that should be "their." Make triple-certain you've correctly spelled all names: people, organizations, software programs, and so forth.

- **Grammar and punctuation:** If you're not confident about your grammar and punctuation skills, purchase an all-purpose reference guide and use it as often as you need to. Don't let your cover letter be discarded because of basic grammar and punctuation errors.

- **Interesting language:** As much as possible, avoid cliches and outdated language (for example, "Enclosed please find my resume."). It's difficult to find new ways to express familiar sentiments (such as "I would appreciate the opportunity for an interview"), and it's certainly not necessary to come up with unique language for every phrase. But make sure that your cover letter doesn't sound like a cookie-cutter, one-size-fits-all letter that could have been written by any job seeker.

Before sending your cover letter, be sure to review chapter 5, "Cover Letter Presentation," for tips on making your letter look its best.

Tips and Tricks from the Top

Don't Reinvent the Wheel

Much of our discussion has focused on the fact that your cover letters should be written individually based on the specific situation. And that is quite true. The more focused your letters, the greater the impact and the more likely you are to get a response and an opportunity to interview. However, you *do not* have to reinvent the wheel with each and every cover letter you write. If you're a sales representative writing in response to advertisements for other sales positions, you can very often use the same letter with just a few minor editorial changes to match each opportunity.

Remember your "copy and paste." It's a great tool!

Specialist Versus Generalist Letters

This is a difficult concept to grasp, so pay very close attention. In today's competitive job search market, companies hire specialists to solve specific problems, manage specific operations, or perform specific functions. The "general management" layer that existed for so many decades has been virtually obliterated as the entire world becomes more specialized. This has permeated virtually every industry, including technology. Just think about it. We don't have just programmers now. We have C++ programmers, Java scripters, and Web designers!

Now, consider this concept as you begin to write your cover letters and market yourself. It is to your advantage to be a specialist—regardless of your profession or your industry. People can immediately understand the value you bring to their organization when you specialize in one or a group of related functions. Of course, the general manager will always exist, but the opportunities are much tighter and the positions much harder to find. It is our opinion that if you position yourself as a specialist, you will find that your job search moves along much faster and more positively.

Of course, you may position yourself as a specialist in several different (though usually related) careers. Let's say your career has been in sales. You started as a field sales representative, moved up to a sales-management role, and most recently have been the director of sales training for your organization. As you contemplate a career move, you're considering a wide range of positions under the general "sales" umbrella. If you try to sell yourself as a "jack of all trades," you may not find many takers. But you can position yourself as a specialist in sales, sales training, or sales management—and promote your related strengths as added value you bring to the organization.

Sell It to Me; Don't Tell It to Me

Cover letter writing is sales—pure and simple. You have a commodity to sell—yourself—and your challenge is to write a marketing communication that is powerful and pushes the reader to action. (You want him to call you for an interview!) Therefore, it is essential that you "sell" your achievements and don't just "tell" your responsibilities. Here's a quick example. If you are an engineer (and we all know how much they like to write!), you could "tell" your reader that you've worked on developing new products. Sounds pretty exciting (not)! Or, you could "sell" the fact that you've participated in the design, development, testing, and market launch of 12 new products that now generate over $2 million in sales each year. Which letter would capture your interest?

Getting Over Writer's Block

Very often, the most difficult part of writing a cover letter is getting started. You can sit and look at that blank piece of paper or computer screen for hours, frustrated and wondering whether the whole world has such a hard time writing cover letters. If you are in a profession that requires you to write—such as advertising, marketing, communications, or public relations—the process can be much easier. (However, both of us have had plenty of clients from these "writing" professions who have told us they found writing their own career marketing materials the most difficult writing tasks they've ever attempted.) And if you are in finance, engineering, purchasing, quality, production, or another "non-writing" career track, cover letters can be an especially formidable task. That's why it's so important to follow the step-by-step process we have created. It is guaranteed to make cover letter writing faster, easier, and much less painful!

If you're still having trouble, consider this simple thought: *You do not have to start at the beginning!* Even after writing thousands and thousands of cover letters, we sometimes sit stumped, unable to come up with just the right opening paragraph. Rather than wasting time and brain power, and getting frustrated, we just leave it alone and move on to another section in the letter that we feel more confident writing. You'll find that once you get going, new ideas will pop into your head and the more difficult sections will come much more easily and confidently.

Answer the Employer's Most Important Question: "What Can You Do for Me?"

A powerful cover letter can help you get what you want: a new, perhaps more advanced, more convenient, more satisfying, position. And it is certainly important that you understand what you want to do, the kind of company you'd like to work for, and the environment in which you'll be most productive. Yet you must remember that employers aren't really interested in you. They're interested in *what you can do for them.* If you do not keep this thought in the forefront of your mind when writing your cover letters, you're likely to produce a self-centered "here I am" letter that probably won't do much to advance your job search.

When writing your cover letters, consider the employer's needs, and make sure that you communicate that you can add value, solve problems, and deliver benefits for that employer. You can do this through a strong focus on accomplishments ("Ah, she did that for Acme Widgets; she can do the same for me.") and through careful attention to the wording and tone of your letter so that you appear to be more interested in contributing to the company than satisfying your own personal needs.

Cover Letter Checklist

Before mailing, faxing, or e-mailing each cover letter you prepare, complete the following checklist to be sure that you have met all the rules for cover letter writing. If you cannot answer "yes" to *all* of the questions, go back and edit your letter as necessary before mailing it.

The only questions for which a "no" answer is acceptable are questions #5 and #6, which relate specifically to the company to which you are writing. As we have stated previously, there will be instances when you can find this information, but there will also be instances (such as when writing to a P.O. box) in which you cannot.

	Yes	No
1. Do I convey an immediate understanding of who I am within the first two sentences of my cover letter?	☐	☐
2. Is my cover letter format unique, and does my letter stand out?	☐	☐
3. Have I highlighted my most relevant qualifications?	☐	☐
4. Have I highlighted my most relevant achievements?	☐	☐
5. Have I included information I know about the company or the specific position for which I am applying?	☐	☐
6. Have I highlighted why I want to work for *this* company?	☐	☐
7. Is my letter neat, clean, and well-presented without being over-designed?	☐	☐
8. Is my letter error-free?	☐	☐
9. Did I have someone else proof my letter?	☐	☐
10. Is my cover letter short and succinct, preferably no longer than one page?	☐	☐
11. Do I ask for an interview in the letter?	☐	☐

Anatomy of a Winning Online Cover Letter

This chapter is short, succinct, and to the point.

Why?

Because online cover letters are short, succinct, and to the point.

Why do online cover letters get a chapter all their own?

Because the way we communicate has been forever altered by the rapid emergence of e-mail as a primary channel of communication in today's fast-paced business world. Consider how our letter writing has changed over the past century:

- In 1900, when a gentleman wrote a letter to his associates, it was elegantly composed and beautifully handwritten. Magnificent imagery and symbolism virtually jumped off the page.

- In 1942, when Winston Churchill wrote to his advisors, his letters were a bit less grandiose, but still detailed, informative, and well-executed.

- In 1987, when Frank Barnes (MBA and CFO) wrote to Xerox for a position on its executive management team, he prepared a comprehensive, one-page letter on his PC summarizing his career track and highlighting his most notable achievements.

Today, in 2000, when Julie Jones, Esq., wrote to Microsoft for a position on its corporate legal team, she e-mailed her materials—a six-sentence cover letter with her resume. The letter was extremely brief, highlighted her two most notable career successes, and asked for the interview. No fluff, no flowery language, no imagery, and no real detail. There was just enough to whet her reader's appetite and get him to read her resume and offer her the opportunity for a personal interview.

Julie's letter is typical of most online cover letters. They are characterized by their brevity and their impact. There are no wasted words. There is no grand introduction or career overview. They are hard-hitting, concise, and on target for the particular position.

What characterizes an online cover letter?

- Brevity
- To-the-point style and tone
- Written in brief paragraphs or a bullet-style format
- Generally written in response to a specific advertisement or online posting
- Most similar in style to "company ad-response" and "recruiter ad-response" letters as outlined in chapter 1

Just like other ad-response letters, online cover letters *must* highlight the specific qualifications, experiences, skills, and accomplishments you offer as they relate to the requirements of the position. However, your challenge with online letters is to do this as quickly as you can. You have even less time than with the traditional "paper" resume and cover letter to catch someone's attention and interest. Therefore, your online letters must immediately present your unique qualifications, highlight your most significant achievements, and ask for the interview.

Online Cover Letter Hints

To make your online cover letter most effective, follow these simple suggestions related to the unique needs of this format:

- Always reference the position for which you are applying in the subject line of your e-mail message. By doing so, you alert recipients to your reason for contacting them before they open your message.

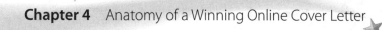

* *Do not* include the recipient's full mailing address as you would in a typical "paper" cover letter. Use only the salutation line (Dear Ms. Brown:).

* As with other ad-response letters, be sure to address any additional requests for information that were stated in the advertisement (such as salary history, salary requirements, ability to relocate, citizenship or residency status, foreign-language skills, and technology proficiency).

Online Resume Hints

In addition, you will always want to send your resume along with your online cover letter. You have four distinct options available for transmitting your resume electronically:

* **Paste your resume into the e-mail message itself.** This is by far the most efficient method of transmitting your resume electronically. Computer viruses have permeated the Internet, making individuals quite apprehensive about opening file attachments from strangers. Unfortunately, although this is the easiest method, it's also the least attractive. When you paste your resume into an e-mail message, all the effort you invested in making it look good is virtually gone. Your resume is now just words on a page with a minor bit of formatting that you can add back in.

* **Send your resume as an attached word-processing file.** Point 1: *Very* few people will open attachments from strangers. When you send your resume as a word-processing file, you will never know whether the recipient ever saw your resume. Point 2: If, for whatever reason, you are sending your resume as an attached word-processing file and do not know what word-processing software the recipient has, send it in Microsoft Word—by far the most common word processing program used by businesses today. If you send it in WordPerfect, ClarisWorks, Microsoft Works, or any other format, you run the risk that the recipient will not be able to open the file. There are certain industries in which this is not the case; for instance, in the legal industry, WordPerfect is still the preferred word-processing program. But unless you know otherwise, it's safest to assume that Word is the preferred format.

* **Send your resume as an attached text file.** Point 1: Again, you run the risk of the employer not opening and reading your resume. Point 2: If you choose to send your resume as an attachment, consider sending it in a text file. That way, anyone can read it in any software program. However, just as in the e-mail version, all formatting will be lost.

* **Post your resume on a Web site.** This is perhaps the best solution of all, combining the ease of e-mail transmission without cumbersome attachments with the impact of a sharp visual presentation. Be sure to include in the text of your e-mail message the URL of the Web site where your resume is posted so that someone can just click on it and go right to the Web site. If you choose this option, we recommend that you also include the text version of your resume in the e-mail message (option 1, above), thereby giving readers immediate access to your resume and then the option of obtaining a fully formatted version to view and download if they wish.

If you choose to post your resume on a Web site, it's best to get a stand-alone site just for your resume rather than including it on a personal or family site. Don't distract the employer or embarrass yourself by including your resume on a site with family updates, children's cute sayings, or a scanned-in picture of your spouse doing the limbo on your Caribbean vacation. In a job search, it's to your best advantage to keep your communication professional at all times.

 ## Sample Online Cover Letters

The following are two examples of our preferred style for online cover letters.

Preferred Online Cover Letter Style for Companies

```
From: "Seth Sefert" <ssefsdf@yahoo.com>
To: "Shanna Miller" <s.miller@co.com>
Subject: Plant Manager -- Newcastle Management
Date: Mon, 28 Feb 2000 15:42:43

Dear Ms. Miller:

My strong qualifications for your Plant Manager
position have prompted me to contact you. They include:

-- 10 years' experience in Plant Management and
Operations Management.

-- Management of 220-person manufacturing operation and
$145 million annual operating budget.

-- Annual productivity gains averaging 18% and cost
reductions totaling over $2.8 million.

-- Implementation of SPC, MRP, SAP, and other automated
technologies.

I am currently employed as the Plant Manager for STS
Machinery in Yorktown, Pennsylvania. As you may be
aware, the facility has recently been acquired by Dow
Chemical and production will be moved out of state this
June.

My resume follows at the end of this message, and I
have attached a Word-formatted copy if you prefer to
download it.

I appreciate your consideration and look forward to
meeting with you. Thank you.

Seth Sefert
```

Now, let's take that same letter and modify it for sending to a recruiter. We have highlighted the areas that differ from the original letter above so that you can quickly see what additional information we have added and what information we have changed.

Preferred Online Cover Letter Style for Recruiters

From: "Seth Sefert" <ssefsdf@yahoo.com>
To: "Richard Hanson" <r.hanson @recruiter.com>
Subject: Plant Manager -- Newcastle Management
Date: Mon, 28 Feb 2000 15:42:43

Dear Mr. Hanson:

My strong qualifications for the available Plant
Manager position have prompted me to contact you. They
include:

-- 10 years' experience in Plant Management and
Operations Management.

-- Management of 220-person manufacturing operation and
$145 million annual operating budget.

-- Annual productivity gains averaging 18% and cost
reductions totaling over $2.8 million.

-- Implementation of SPC, MRP, SAP, and other automated
technologies.

I am currently employed as the Plant Manager for STS
Machinery in Yorktown, Pennsylvania. Our facility has
recently been acquired by Dow Chemical, and production
will be moved out of state this June.

I am available for immediate relocation to the Toledo
area and would anticipate a salary of $125,000 to
$150,000 per year.

My resume follows at the end of this message, and I
have attached a Word-formatted copy if you prefer to
download it.

I appreciate your consideration and look forward to
meeting with you. Thank you.

Seth Sefert

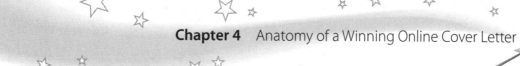

Final Thoughts About Online Cover Letters

When writing online cover letters, be sure to pay close attention to spelling, grammar, and tone, just as you would with a traditional cover letter. Perfection and accuracy are vital, as always.

The greatest advantage of online communications is immediacy. If you send cover letters and resumes to 500 recruiters, you'll receive e-mail and telephone responses within a day or two, compared to a week or more delay for responses to your mailed letters. In our experience of helping job seekers at all levels, we find that e-mailed resumes are very effective when used in broad campaigns to recruiters, as responses to online postings, and as a method of immediate communication with people you've already spoken to. They also are very effective—even essential—for people in highly technical fields.

But do be wary of the impersonal nature of e-mails and the ease with which they can be ignored! When sending a follow-up to an online letter, you can again communicate via e-mail, but it may be preferable to make a phone call and attempt to establish "live" communication. It's very easy for the recipient to overlook your letter in a sea of e-mails received daily. By telephoning, you can set yourself apart and build a more personal relationship.

A Word About Scannable Resumes

Electronic scanning of resumes—and sometimes cover letters—has become common practice at large companies. Resumes that are scanned or downloaded become "searchable" documents that are stored in a central database and can be accessed quickly through an electronic key-word search.

While many modern scanning systems can accommodate type enhancements such as bold, italics, and underlining, to be certain all of your text is entered correctly it's best to prepare a plain-vanilla version of your resume that can be scanned by any type of scanning system. Remove all type enhancements, vertical and horizontal lines, and fancy bullets. Choose a clean sans serif font such as Arial for maximum readability, and make certain that you haven't condensed the font or reduced the letter spacing such that letters touch each other—this is likely to cause scanning errors.

When applying to large companies, consider sending your resume and cover letter in both traditional and scannable format; or avoid the scanning controversy altogether by sending your resume via e-mail or the company's online application form.

Chapter
5

Cover Letter Presentation

We've worked with you for hours, maybe longer, to help you develop high-impact, attention-grabbing cover letters. You probably thought that you were done and your letter is ready to go. Wrong! Writing is only the first step in preparing your letter. Now that you've written the words, we'll focus our attention on the visual presentation of a winning cover letter.

Developing Winning Visual Presentations

What makes a winning cover letter different in presentation from other cover letters? Isn't one letter just the same as another? Quite clearly, the answer is "no."

Winning cover letters are distinguished by the following:

Professionalism. Take just a quick glance at any cover letter in this book, and you'll quickly see that these letters look extremely professional. They were not typed on an old electric typewriter. They were not typed on onion-skin paper (remember that?). They were not photocopied or scanned. They were each originally produced and offer a sharp, high-impact presentation. Remember, the quality of your cover letter is a direct indication of the quality of work you will produce for an employer!

* **Clean, neat, and easy-to-read presentation.** Take another look at some of the sample letters in this book. They are neat, with even margins and equal spacing throughout. The size of type is easy to read without being too large or looking too "elementary." They are quick to read because they are so well presented.

* **Perfection.** Every winning cover letter is perfect and totally error-free. We recommend that you proofread each cover letter a minimum of three times and then have a friend, relative, or coworker proofread it again. Your objective—your only objective—is 100 percent accuracy. Nothing short of that is ever acceptable.

Design Considerations

Many of the issues in this section—cover letter format, font, type of paper, and color of paper—may be decisions you already made when you prepared your resume. It is our recommendation that you use those same specifications when preparing your cover letters. Through consistent presentation, you will create a top-notch professional presentation. A consistent image demonstrates thought and planning in preparation—another great message to communicate to a prospective employer!

Many of these design considerations are really just personal preferences. The format that you chose for your resume, for example, is most likely one that you liked (as well as one that "worked" to present your qualifications as you would like them to be perceived). The same thing is true of cover letters. Pick a style that you like, that is appropriate, and that is consistent with your resume.

If you really like ivory-colored paper, for instance, use it for everything—your resume, cover letters, thank-you letters, and any other job search correspondence. If you really like purple paper, use it for the invitations for your next party, and select something that is more professional, more conservative, and more appropriate for your career correspondence.

What do we mean by appropriate? Consider this. You're the manager of an accounting department interviewing candidates for a bookkeeping position. The first resume and cover letter you receive are neat and conservative, typed in a sans serif typestyle (without the little curlycues) such as Arial, and on bright white paper. The presentation is precise, neat, and clean, visually demonstrating exactly the qualifications you are seeking in a bookkeeper. Then you pick up the next resume. It's also neat and clean, but it's "loud." Both the resume and cover letter are typed in italics, they're difficult to read, and the gold paper is, well, interesting. Now, remember, you're hiring a bookkeeper. Which candidate would you be more interested in? The answer is obvious! Let your visual presentation match what you do for a living and how you want to be perceived by a prospective employer.

Although the resume in italics on gold paper is not appropriate for a book-keeper, it can be appropriate in other situations. What about a young graphic artist? Or a theatrical stage designer? Those professions require creativity, flair, and the ability to visually capture an audience's attention. Now italics on gold doesn't seem quite so unusual. Again, it's a question of matching your visual presentation with the image you are working to create. Let's explore some specific design considerations. Consider the following questions:

What Format Should You Use?

There are two basic cover letter formats—block style and modified block style. Which style you select depends entirely on your personal preference. There is no right way; there is no wrong way. Our only recommendation is that once you have selected the style you prefer, stick with that style for *all* of your correspondence so that the presentation of all your materials is consistent.

Here are examples of both:

Block-Style Letter: Everything Is Flush Left

```
November 21, 2000

John Doe
President
ABC Manufacturing Company
123 Main Street
Greensburg, PA 15601

Dear Mr. Doe:

Building top-performing sales territories is what I do best.
Whether challenged to build a new sales region, accelerate
growth within an established market, or launch the introduc-
tion of a new portfolio of products, I have consistently
delivered strong revenue results.

…

Sincerely,


Greg LaMontica

Enclosure
```

Modified Block-Style Letter: Indented Date, First Lines of Paragraphs, and Closings

```
                        November 21, 2000

John Doe
President
ABC Manufacturing Company
123 Main Street
Greensburg, PA 15601

Dear Mr. Doe:

   Building top-performing sales territories is what I do
best. Whether challenged to build a new sales region, accel-
erate growth within an established market, or launch the
introduction of a new portfolio of products, I have consis-
tently delivered strong revenue results.

   …

                Sincerely,


                Greg LaMontica

                Enclosure
```

What Font Should You Use?

Twenty-five years ago there were two fonts for resumes and cover letters—Courier and Elite. These two typestyles came in two sizes (10-point and 12-point). That was it. Your choice of font and size depended on what kind of typewriter you were using. Today, your choices run in the hundreds. If you're like most of us, your PC came with more fonts than you can count, most of which you've never even looked at. You've chosen a few that you like and use them for just about everything.

The list below includes fonts that are commonly used for cover letters and resumes. You'll note that the list is divided into "Serif" and "Sans Serif" categories. A quick glance at each font will tell you that serif fonts contain tiny header and footer strokes on each letter; sans serif fonts are cleaner-looking, without extraneous strokes. Which is better? It's simply a matter of personal preference. Traditional wisdom says that serif fonts are easier to read; we don't necessarily agree or disagree—it really depends on the individual font. Some fonts look better than others in larger sizes; others lose readability at small sizes.

One area where sans serif fonts may have an advantage is in documents meant for computer scanning. Letters without extraneous strokes are easier for the scanner to read and leave less room for misinterpretation. For that reason, we recommend sans serif fonts for scannable resumes and cover letters.

Serif	Sans Serif
Times New Roman	Helvetica
Bookman	Arial
Souvenir	Tahoma
Soutane	Century Gothic
Fritz	CG Omega
Palatino	Krone
Garamond	Gill Sans
Century Schoolbook	Lucida Sans

The Times New Roman typestyle requires its own discussion. It is by far the most widely used of any font, and, in some ways, that's great. It's clean, conservative, highly readable even in smaller sizes, and appropriate for almost every profession and industry. What's more, virtually anyone can download a resume and cover letter file that you send to them, and you're pretty much guaranteed that when they print your materials, they'll get exactly the same presentation that you get. Everyone has Times New Roman.

The negative side of this is that the font lacks visual distinction. For every 100 resumes and cover letters we see, 80 to 90 of them are typed in Times New Roman. After awhile, even though they may use different formats, they all begin to look the same. Your goal is to create a document that is neat, conservative, industry-appropriate, position-appropriate, and visually distinctive—a document that stands out from the crowd and gets you noticed. So perhaps you should consider a different font.

Exercise: Experiment with Type Styles

If you're uncertain about what typestyle to use for your materials, take a few minutes and do the following exercise.

Type the following resume excerpt exactly as it is typed below using bold, italics, and underlining just as we have. Note that we've used a resume in this instance (as opposed to a cover letter) because of the many different type enhancements resumes contain. Then copy and paste the paragraph 10 or 20 times, changing the typestyle each time. Print your test pages, and you'll see what each typestyle looks like and whether it's appropriate for your job search materials.

Sales Manager—*Veterinary Products Division*   1998 to Present

SMART PETS, INC. (*Division of AAA Veterinary*), Portland, Oregon

Independently plan and manage all sales, marketing, customer service, and business-development programs through a four-state region in the Western U.S. Challenged to increase sales revenues, expand market penetration, and improve competitive industry ratings.

- Built regional sales from <u>$2.8 million to $6.4 million</u> in 12 months.

- Launched the introduction of <u>18 new products generating $1.2 million</u> in new sales revenues.

What Type Enhancements Should You Use?

If you're unfamiliar with the terminology of type enhancements, these simply refer to **bold,** *italics,* SMALL CAPS, ALL CAPS, and underlining—things you can do to a typestyle to make its presentation more noticeable. In the exercise above, you can easily see what type enhancements can do to make things stand out in a document.

Just as in the excerpt above, we're sure that you have many type enhancements in your resume. And you should. But cover letters are not resumes. They are letters—fairly formal and conservative business documents. As such, you should severely limit your use of these type enhancements. In fact, you might not use any of them at all in your letter. If you do, you should use them quite sparingly, and only to highlight really important things that you want your reader to see quickly.

What types of things might you choose to highlight visually in your cover letters?

- Notable achievements (particularly numbers and percentages)
- Notable educational or professional credentials
- Notable company names (employers, partners, vendors, customers)
- Notable honors and awards (academic and professional)
- The position for which you are applying

Do not type an entire letter in italics or in bold print. You may think it looks different. You're right. You may think it looks distinctive. You're right. You may think it looks sharp and professional. Not necessarily! Unless you are looking for a position in a creative industry such as graphic design, theater, art, film production, media, or something related, keep your cover letters clean and conservative—and, most importantly, *readable.*

What Paper Color Should You Use?

Ah, the infamous paper color question! We've responded to questions about this for decades now. Is plain white paper the best? Sometimes. Is ivory paper an acceptable standard? Yes. Is light gray paper recommended? Sometimes. What about papers with borders? Sometimes. Paper with logos and graphic designs? Occasionally. Parchment paper? Perhaps. What about really distinctive colors such as blue, pink, brown, or gold? These are appropriate only in certain instances.

As you can see, there are no rules for color selection. Just as with all of your other design considerations, the paper color you select is based largely on your own personal preferences and the appropriateness to your career. To make your selection process a bit easier, here are a few of our standards for paper selection:

- White and ivory paper are always appropriate for virtually any job seeker in virtually any situation.

- Light gray paper offers a conservative presentation with a degree of sophistication and visual distinction. This color is particularly recommended for the following professions: accounting, finance, insurance, general management, and executive management.

- Papers with borders can also offer a conservative yet distinctive presentation, as long as the papers are nicely designed and not flamboyant.

- Papers with logos and graphic designs are a relatively new addition over the past ten years. Have you ever seen a teacher's resume with an apple logo in the corner? What about a sports marketing director's resume with basketballs, soccer balls, and baseballs on the bottom? These papers can be unique. Yet there is controversy. In fact, our opinions differ. One of us believes that papers like this are distinctive and eye-catching. The other thinks that they are generally "too cute." You be the judge, but wisdom should dictate that if you have any reservations, do not select this type of paper. And if you do choose to include graphics, make certain they are appropriate to your profession and not chosen simply because you "like cats."

- If you are not familiar with parchment paper, it's two-toned with a look that's often described as marbleized. Ten or 15 years ago, parchment paper was a common selection for job search materials. Over the years, it has become much less frequently used, for no particular reason that we could identify. Our only reason for not using it is our personal preference. We don't like it, but you might, and that's fine as long as the presentation is conservative.

- Our final category is colored paper—blue, pink, brown, tan, gold, green, yellow, or any of a number of other distinctive colors. For the average job seeker, these papers are not recommended. Remember, your objective is to create neat, clean, conservative, and visually distinctive resumes and cover letters, not advertisements!

There are exceptions to this rule, however. Consider the female graphic artist with her resume on a blush-colored paper. It can be sharp! What about the geologist preparing his resume on rusty-brown paper? Or the nurse who uses a light blue paper? Certain colors "match" certain professions and, when appropriate, can be a unique presentation that will quickly grab your reader's attention.

Suppose you're a manager hiring a landscape designer. You're looking through a pile of 50 or more resumes that you've received, most of them on white and ivory, with an occasional gray one thrown in. Then, all of a sudden, you come across a resume on a great green paper. It immediately communicates landscaping, doesn't it? Colored paper can work in certain circumstances, but *only* in certain circumstances.

What Type of Paper Should You Use—Bond, Linen, Cotton, or Parchment?

This decision is strictly personal preference, because all types of paper are acceptable and widely used. One of us definitely prefers linen papers because they feel so nice, while the other uses only cotton papers because they feel heavier than linen. Be advised that virtually all papers are now available for laser printers. If you're using this type of printer, the extra few pennies spent on high-quality laser-compatible paper are well worth the investment. These specialty papers have been manufactured so that they do not smear as easily when you run them through your laser printer, significantly improving the quality of your finished product.

> *Tip* Consistency in design and presentation will distinguish you from others competing for the same position *and* communicate that you are a professional concerned about the quality and image of your work product—a great message to send to a prospective employer!

Meet the Challenges and Beat the Odds

If looking for a job were an exact science, life would be so much easier!

When you add 82 + 11, it always equals 93. When you add 2 parts hydrogen to 1 part oxygen, you always get water. When you watch the earth revolve around the sun, you know that on June 20th or 21st, the summer solstice will always occur.

These are not questions. They are facts. There is no discussion; there are no surprises. Each is measurable, predictable, and consistent. Each is an exact science with an exact answer to an exact question. There is no room for personal interpretation.

Unfortunately, there is nothing that is measurable, predictable, or consistent about any aspect of a job search, including cover letter writing. Looking for a job is not an exact science, and there are no exact answers. In fact, the answer to almost every question is *"It depends"*—on the situation, the job seeker, the position, the industry, the economy, the location, and any one of a number of other factors. Thus the challenge of your entire job search campaign: It all depends!

Frequently Asked Questions

Ask yourself this question: "Should a resume always be just one page?" Keep your answer a secret, and ask that same question of five other people. How many different answers did you get? Several, we would assume. No one ever agrees on job search issues. There is constant conversation and disagreement about virtually everything—from the number of pages to the color of paper; from providing salary information to selecting envelope size; from how to address the letter to when to follow up. The list goes on and on.

With more than 25 years' combined experience in resume and cover letter writing, career coaching, and job search marketing, we've heard just about every question imaginable, and then some. Following are what we have found to be the most frequently asked questions—along with our professional opinions and recommendations. But bear in mind that these are not *facts*. Your own circumstances could dictate a different action than we recommend.

How Long Should Your Cover Letter Be?

Should your cover letter always be one page? It depends.

Generally, cover letters should be one page in length. This is true for approximately 90 percent of all cover letters. Remember that your cover letter has three main purposes:

1. To tell your readers why you are writing.

2. To highlight your most relevant experiences, skills, qualifications, and achievements.

3. To ask for the interview.

Your goal is to whet the reader's appetite, intrigue him, and get him to closely read the information you have submitted. In the vast majority of circumstances, you can accomplish this on one page.

There may be instances, however, when one page is just not enough. If you believe that the information you are including in your letter is essential information that is not communicated in your resume, go ahead and prepare a two-page letter. But be sure that everything you've included is vital to favorably presenting yourself to a company or recruiter.

Two-page letters are most frequently used by the following types of job seekers:

* **Career changers.** When you're faced with positioning yourself for a new career path, it may take more than one page to communicate relevant experiences, skills, and accomplishments that may not have been highlighted on your resume. It is critical that these cover letters clearly emphasize your transferable skills and qualifications to demonstrate your eligibility.

* **Industry changers.** If you are attempting to change industries, you may also find that your cover letter is longer than the traditional one page. In this situation, you must focus your letter on your skills and qualifications that are transferable from one industry to the next.

* **Senior executives.** These individuals may want to communicate a wide range of expertise and accomplishments across a broad spectrum of disciplines (such as management, leadership, products, industries, technologies, countries, customer markets, operations, finance, human resources, administration, sales, marketing, advertising, public relations, and investor relations). Because the information is so extensive, it may require a second page. And with senior-level candidates, hiring authorities are usually looking at more than *what* you've done. They want to know *how* and *why* you've done it so that they can assess your style and strengths with regard to their existing management team and organizational needs.

* **Scientists and technologists.** Often, due to the complexity of your technical qualifications and associated management and business skills, a two-page letter is necessary to communicate all of the relevant information.

* **People seeking government jobs.** What do we all know about government? Paper counts! Even though we often hear about a government's shift to a paperless environment, trust us: There are still volumes of paper in virtually every government office. When writing for a position with a state, local, or national government agency, if you have a great deal of valuable information that you believe is essential to communicate, you do not have to be as concerned about keeping it all on one page.

People seeking university and academic appointments. Academia is much like the government in its unique relationship with paper and documents. Again, if you believe the information is important and will favorably position you, be sure to include it even if it takes two pages.

> *Tip* We recommend that, if possible, you keep your cover letter to one page. If appropriate and warranted, two pages are acceptable. But your cover letter should *never* be longer than two pages.

There is one specific type of cover letter that is almost always two to three pages in length—the *broadcast letter.* You'll remember from chapter 1 that broadcast letters are used in place of the more traditional resume and cover letter package and can best be described as a combination of both documents.

When you send a broadcast letter, you do not include a resume. Therefore, it is critical that you communicate more information about your career history, qualifications, accomplishments, educational credentials, and other related skills and experiences than you would in a "regular" cover letter. For broadcast letters to be effective, exciting, and enticing, you must include specifics to capture your reader's attention. These specifics may include employment experience, college degrees, technology skills, professional affiliations, publications, and other information that clearly demonstrates your knowledge and expertise. As such, these letters are longer than traditional cover letters.

Should You Include Salary Information in Your Cover Letter?

It depends. We are of two minds. We offer dual recommendations in two situations but agree with one another on the other two situations. See which rationale feels most comfortable to you.

If you are responding to an advertisement that has requested your salary history or salary requirements:

Supply the information. If you do not provide this information when requested, certain companies and recruiters will not look at your materials.

Don't supply the information. Repeated surveys show that nearly 100 percent of readers admitted that they will look at your resume and call you for an interview even if your salary information is not included. Why give them ammunition to screen you out?

If a personal contact or source you've uncovered during your search has requested your resume and salary information:

Supply the information. To do otherwise would seem unresponsive and impolite.

Consider addressing the issue without providing numbers that can be detrimental in a future salary negotiation. Say something such as "I'd be glad to discuss salary when we meet, once I learn more about the position and you have the chance to assess my fit for your needs."

When contacting companies either as a cold call or in response to an ad where salary information has not been requested.

Do not supply the information. It is much better to have this conversation in person and not on paper. Always try to defer any discussion of salary until you have been offered the position.

When writing "cold" to recruiters.

Always offer salary information. It helps them to determine your "proper fit" within a hiring organization. A recruiter will not work with you without knowing whether you match the requirements (including salary) for the specific position she is attempting to fill.

How Can You Best Communicate Salary History or Salary Requirements?

Review the suggestions presented in Chapter 3—"Step 5: Writing the Closing." Multiple examples are given; choose the one that feels most comfortable to you.

Should You Send Your Resume to Human Resources?

If you are writing "cold" to a company (not in response to a specific advertisement), should you address your resume to the Human Resources department? The answer to this question is a resounding "NO!" HR departments "process" and evaluate resumes. They generally do not make hiring decisions (except for HR positions). Instead, send your resume to the President, CEO, COO, CFO, Vice President of Sales, Director of Customer Service,

Accounting Manager—whoever is the decision-maker for the department or function in which you are interested. These individuals have the authority to schedule an interview and make a hiring decision. It is much more efficient to work "down from the top" than to get out of the HR department.

Should You Follow Up a Faxed Resume?

If you've faxed or e-mailed your resume and cover letter to a company or recruiter, should you follow up with a paper copy in the mail? No! Times have changed. If you had faxed your resume and cover letter five years ago, the answer would have been "yes." If you had e-mailed your resume and cover letter two years ago, the answer again would have been "yes."

Today, however, we recommend that you do not mail a hard copy if you have already transmitted your information electronically. Electronic communication is now a totally acceptable method of communication in virtually any business, industry, and market sector. The only time you should follow up with hard copy is when it has been requested. Try to control the paper flow!

What Size Paper Should You Use?

Should you use Letter size or Monarch size paper for your cover letters? It depends. Which do you like best? That's what we recommend that you use. We have never found that the size of paper made any difference in whether an individual job seeker was offered the opportunity for a personal interview.

Here are the pros and cons of both:

- Monarch-size paper (7 x 9 inches) does stand out from the more traditional letter-size paper and visually presents itself more like a piece of personal correspondence. However, it can easily be misplaced and lost in the daily shuffle.

- Letter-size paper (8½ x 11 inches) is the standard, is an acceptable presentation in any circumstance, is easy to file, and is less likely to be misplaced.

Should You Use the Same Paper for Everything?

Should your cover letter be on the same paper as your resume? It depends. Generally we do recommend that you be consistent. If you've chosen ivory paper, you should use it for everything—your resume, cover letters, thank-you letters, and any other job search correspondence. The presentation is quite professional.

However, there are instances when you may choose to use a paper that is different but complementary. Consider the following circumstances:

- You're a business professional or executive and have printed your resume on a light gray paper with surrounding white border. It's really sharp! You may elect to print your letters on a high-quality white paper as a unique enhancement to your presentation.

- You're a talented graphic artist competing for a position in metropolitan New York. You want someone to immediately notice you and your artistic talent. In this instance, you might select a blue and white pinstripe paper with your personal logo design in the background for your resume, and matching plain blue paper with logo for your cover letters. In fact, graphic artists and other creative professionals should use their resumes and cover letters to demonstrate their visual creativity. For those individuals, the resume is not just communicating words. It should also communicate a powerful visual image.

- If you have printed personal stationery that complements your resume, feel free to use it. It presents a professional, high-quality image.

Do Your Communications Need a Consistent Look?

Should your resume, cover letter, and other job search communications "look" the same? Yes!

Pick a standard presentation (font style, font size, heading, format, and paper) for your documents and stick with it. Consistency breeds familiarity and familiarity can breed confidence in your ability. Furthermore, it creates a more professional, elegant, and high-quality presentation.

What Size Envelope Should You Use?

Should you mail your resumes and cover letters in large envelopes (9" x 12") or regular #10 business envelopes? It depends and, just like the size of paper, is really based on your personal preferences. The vast majority of recipients really don't care—and even if they do have a preference, they will not discriminate against you because your presentation is different. Here are our recommendations:

* Use regular #10 business envelopes for most of your mailings and communications. The savings in postage will add up quickly.

* Use larger envelopes if you're trying to make a really top-flight impression. Large envelopes are most appropriate for high-level network contacts, direct mail to executives, and responses to senior-level advertisements.

* Use larger envelopes if you are sending more than three sheets of paper or if your paper is extremely heavy. Thick stacks of heavy paper do not fold well. And if, for instance, you are a graphic designer sending design samples, then by all means send them flat in a larger envelope for the best possible appearance.

* Consider using larger envelopes to mail resumes and cover letters that are intended to be scanned. Creasing and folding laser-printed pages sometimes causes laser toner to smudge, flake, or create "ghost" impressions that could reduce the scannability of your resume.

 Tip No one has ever made a hiring decision based on the size of an envelope. And there's always the chance that the hiring manager may never actually see the envelope itself—just the contents. Use what you like and don't fret!

What If You Don't Know the Addressee's Name?

How do you address a letter when you don't have a specific name? Here it doesn't depend. It's personal choice. Take a look at a few possible salutations:

* **Dear Sir/Madam**—All-purpose and inoffensive, although it may be perceived as stodgy and old-fashioned.

* **To Whom It May Concern**—Another standard. Has the downside of being impersonal and old-fashioned.

- **Dear Hiring Executive (or Hiring Committee)**—Formal, but appropriate.

- **Dear Human Resources (or Human Resources Representative)**—Acceptable only if you're writing to a P.O. box and you cannot call to get a specific individual's name.

- **Dear Hiring Authority**—Acceptable only if, despite your best efforts, you have been unable to uncover the name of the non-HR person to whom you're sending your resume.

- **Good Morning (or Good Day)**—A bit more up-to-date, but it reminds us of junk-mail greetings that try (unsuccessfully) to be personal.

- **Re: Job Title You're Applying For** (leaving off a specific salutation)—A useful method for replying to want ads, when you truly don't know to whom your resume is being sent. We think it's preferable to the "Dear Human Resources" greeting.

- **No Salutation** (begin your letter immediately after the inside address)—Again, perfectly acceptable for want-ad replies. May be an improvement over old-fashioned, non-specific greetings.

Here are a few that we *do not* recommend:

- **Gentlemen**—This is no longer politically correct. You cannot presume that you're writing to men.

- **Dear Sir**—Again, no longer politically correct or necessarily accurate.

- **Dear Gentleperson**—Great for a 19th-century romance novel, but not particularly appropriate for today's job search market.

What If You Are Unsure of the Addressee's Gender?

How do you address a letter when you have a name but don't know whether it's a man or a woman? It doesn't depend here, either. Simple answer—Dear M. Smith. But do make an effort to find out the person's gender so that you can address your letter as "Dear Mr." or "Dear Ms."

Should You Follow Up with a Phone Call After Each Resume and Cover Letter You Send?

It depends. Telephone follow-up can be quite costly and time-consuming, and it is often difficult to get the person you want to speak with on the phone. You can try calling at off-hours (such as 7 to 9 a.m. or 5 to 8 p.m.) when an individual is most likely to answer the phone himself. If you call during the day, be sure to make an effort to establish some rapport with the gatekeeper (for example, the administrator, secretary, assistant, or receptionist). That individual can have tremendous power, making the difference in whether you get through or you're blocked out.

We do not recommend that you call after each and every resume and cover letter you've sent. It would be a poor investment of your time to spend your entire day leaving phone messages, not to mention the frustration.

The situations in which we do recommend that you call are the following:

- When you have a top-level contact at a company.
- When you consider yourself an ideal candidate for a position (and we mean *ideal*).
- When you have been referred by someone to a specific person.

Another strategy is to follow up with a quick e-mail message. This will encourage the recipient to respond to you as she goes through all of her e-mail messages. Plus, you've given her the chance to respond quickly, at her own convenience, and with minimal effort.

Do You Need to Mention Why You're in the Job Market?

It depends. There's certainly no requirement that you do so, but if your reason is particularly legitimate (such as a plant closing or a management change due to the successful IPO you were instrumental in negotiating), then mentioning this information may send a positive message. In any event, be prepared for the question "Why are you leaving your current job?" or "Why are you looking?" to come up early in your search, and practice a concise, positive, and believable response. Never bad mouth your company, boss, or coworkers.

Do You Need to Make Your Cover Letter "Scannable"?

What does "scannable" mean, anyway? Scannable simply means machine-readable. Many companies now scan resumes into a database and then search by key words for candidates who match specific requirements. To be scannable, your resume should not contain italics, underlines, or graphics, and the font should be clear, readable, and at least 11 points.

Some companies scan cover letters along with resumes; others do not. It certainly could not hurt to check your cover letter format for scannability. It should not be difficult to change any nonconforming elements to make sure that every valuable word is correctly entered into the database.

Tip For a great deal more information on computer scanning and keyword inclusion in your career marketing documents, see the section on "Scannable Resumes" in our companion book, *Résumé Magic*, by Susan Britton Whitcomb, CPRW, NCRW, JCTC.

Using Your PC in Your Job Search

As we turn the corner into the 21st century, it is estimated that more than half of all job seekers manage their job search campaigns using a PC. Over the past decade, job seekers have become more savvy in managing their campaigns, and PC technology has become commonplace. Assuming that you fall into this category, you may be using your PC for a variety of applications, including the uses detailed in the following sections.

Word Processing and Desktop Publishing

You can use word processing and desktop publishing programs to prepare resumes, cover letters, thank-you letters, and other job search correspondence.

To take full advantage of your computer's capability, learn to use features such as envelope and label printing and mail merge (see the following section). Word processors offer advanced formatting features such as variable line spacing, font width and spacing adjustments, bullet-shape variations, and paragraph boxes and rules (lines) that can enhance your visual presentation quite nicely. The samples in this book use many of these features—particularly in the headings. Skim through the samples, select a few you like, and see if you can replicate them on your PC.

To give your documents a truly polished appearance, follow these two typesetting rules:

- Use only one space after a period (instead of the two you were taught when you learned to type).

- Avoid underlining; use paragraph rules (borders) instead.

Mail Merge

Mail merge is an advanced word-processing feature that allows you to type a cover letter in one file, a list of names and addresses in another file, and then merge them to print individualized letters. Mail merge is a tremendously powerful application that will allow you to produce hundreds and hundreds of individualized cover letters and envelopes with just a few simple commands.

The most frequent use of mail merge is for bulk mailings (for example, sending your resume and cover letter to 200 sales recruiters in the Northeastern U.S.). Although we have focused, and will continue to focus, on the fact that your cover letter should be written individually to address a specific opportunity, company, or situation at hand, there are times when individual letters are not necessary. Direct mail is one of those times. When you are writing "cold" to a group of recruiters or companies, all in the same profession or industry, you can often use the same letter word for word. Mail merge now allows you to produce those letters quickly and easily with minimal cost. You can merge your letters into new documents and then print and mail each letter. Or, for an e-mail campaign, you can merge your letters into e-mail messages that automatically appear in the "out" box of your e-mail program.

Database Management

Many job seekers use their database and contact-management programs (such as Access, ACT!, and FileMaker Pro) to manage their contact lists and information. As your job search proceeds, you will begin to accumulate more and more contact information—advertisements, referrals, network follow-ups, and so on. Keeping track of this information can be a daunting task. Some job seekers prefer the index card method, others prefer the notebook method,

and others now turn to their PCs and take advantage of the database method of contact management. Choose whichever method works best for you, but choose one. If you think that you can manage all this information "in your head" or on scraps of paper, you're wrong. We guarantee you'll get lost in the process, misplace some vital contact information, or lose the name of the hiring manager at the company you really want to work for!

> *Tip* Managing your contacts is one of the most critical aspects of your job search. The more contacts you develop, the more new contacts you'll get and the more opportunities will be open to you. Keeping track of all that information—whether on paper or with your PC—is vital to a quick and successful job search.

PC-Based Calendars and Appointment Books

You may also find that your PC offers an easy-to-use calendar and appointment book for scheduling interviews, follow-up phone calls, follow-up correspondence, and all of the other commitments that will arise as part of your job search. Almost every PC that you purchase today has a built-in appointment calendar. Use it to your advantage. Or, if you prefer, use a paper calendar. But just as with your contact information, write it all down and do not rely on your memory. A missed appointment is a lost opportunity.

Internet Access

The Internet offers vast, powerful, and readily accessible information sources. It's also an inexpensive and immediate method of communication. Use it wisely and you can accelerate your job search, gain access to wonderful opportunities, and gather the information you need to make good decisions about jobs, pay, relocation, and other career issues.

With the proliferation of job sites, resume-posting sites, and career information available online, the Internet has become an important element in many job searches. The following activities will allow you to take full advantage of this enormous resource.

Create a Text (ASCII) Version of Your Resume

You can do this easily by using your word processing program's "Save As" feature. Save the file in a Text Only or ASCII file format with a new file name, and then close and reopen the newly saved file. You'll see that your resume has been transformed to plain-Jane formatting in Courier type. Relax! You still have the fully formatted version of your resume under its original file name, and your new version is perfect for transmitting via the Internet, with full readability guaranteed for any recipient. You can go through this version and add extra blank spaces and typewriter symbols to improve readability. Here's an example, using the resume excerpt we worked with in chapter 5:

```
= = = = = = = = = = = = = = = = = = = = = = = = =

1998 to Present

Sales Manager—Veterinary Products Division

_____

SMART PETS, INC. (Division of AAA Veterinary), Portland, Oregon

Independently plan and manage all sales, marketing, customer-
service, and business-development programs through a four-
state region in the Western U.S. Challenged to increase sales
revenues, expand market penetration, and improve competitive
industry ratings.

===  Built regional sales from $2.8 million to $6.4 million in
     12 months.

===  Launched the introduction of 18 new products generating
     $1.2 million in new sales revenues.
```

With this version of your resume, you're ready to post your resume on the Internet, reply to online job postings and advertisements, and apply for jobs directly at company Web sites.

Post Your Resume on Resume Web Sites

Resume sites, or resume banks, are enormous repositories of resumes that are "searchable" by employers and recruiters—sometimes for free and sometimes for a fee. If your resume has the right key words for a particular search, you will be contacted by the hiring company or recruiter. Disadvantages to posting your resume include a lack of confidentiality (your current employer just might come across your resume while searching for new additions to the staff) and the inability, in most cases, to remove your resume once it's been posted. You also leave yourself open to contact from candidate-hungry recruiting and placement firms that may not screen your resume thoroughly and call you for totally irrelevant jobs; and you can be sure you'll start receiving "junk" e-mails and perhaps even phone calls from companies that want to sell you some fantastic product or service to help you in your job search.

Visit Job-Posting Sites

By entering your own key words on the hundreds of job sites available, you can look for positions that are a good match for your current career goals. You can find both general and specialized sites. Some of these sites are free, and some require you to become a subscriber.

Visit Professional Association Sites in Your Field

Check the professional associations of which you're a member to see whether they have a Web site with a career section; quite often, you'll find highly relevant job postings for which you can apply.

Explore the Sites of Companies That Interest You

Many companies post their available jobs on their Web sites, either instead of or in addition to their traditional (and much more expensive) methods of advertising for help or engaging the services of a recruiting firm. In addition to job postings, you'll find a wealth of information about the company's culture, mission, and operations that you can incorporate into your cover letters and use to your advantage during interviews.

Research Companies, Industries, Business Trends, and Salaries

As a research tool, the Internet is immensely valuable. You can find great quantities of detailed information about almost any topic—including specific companies, industry trends, business activity, and so forth.

Knowledge is power—and never more so than when you're negotiating your salary. On the Internet, you can research salary information to find out industry averages and other information. And you can compare the cost of living in various cities to see how much a move will affect your financial situation.

Distributing Your Resumes and Cover Letters

Picture this. It's 1980 and you've just prepared your resume and 25 individual cover letters to launch your job search campaign. How did you distribute your resumes back then? Then answer is simple because there was only one answer—via the U.S. Mail. ·

Ten years later, in 1990, you're ready to launch another search. Now you have a decision to make. Should you send your resumes and cover letters via mail, or should you use the latest and greatest technology—the fax machine?

Today, the process for resume and cover letter distribution has become even more complex. Not only can you mail or fax, you now have e-mail at your disposal. Undeniably, e-mail is the quickest, easiest, and lowest-cost method for distribution. But which method is right for you? Do you have to select just one method, or can you use a combination of all three? How do you know what works, for whom, and when?

As of the writing of this book in the spring of 2000, the jury was still out. In an informal survey of some of the nation's top resume writers and career coaches, the decision was split 50/50 between mail and e-mail, with few advocating the use of fax campaigns (although they are increasing in their acceptance and their frequency). Mail campaigns were preferred because of their strong visual presentation. E-mail campaigns were chosen because of their ease, efficiency, and immediacy.

To best determine which distribution method is right for you and your campaign, let's evaluate the pros and cons of all three:

	Pros	Cons
Paper Campaigns	Paper resumes and cover letters retain their formatting and sharp visual presentation of you and your qualifications.	It is the most expensive method of distribution.
	People can "touch" and "feel" your paper resume, making a stronger and more immediate impression.	It is the slowest method of distribution.
	It is the preferred method of written communication for senior executives.	Resumes and cover letters can be entered into a database (for retention) only if the recipient is willing and able to scan them.

	Pros	**Cons**
E-Mail Campaigns	E-mail campaigns are immediate. E-mail campaigns are the lowest-cost method of distribution. E-mail messages can be saved in a database for future use and retrieval.	E-mail messages can be easily ignored and deleted. The sharp visual presentation of a paper resume is lost. It is extremely difficult to get all the e-mail addresses you need, particularly if your search campaign is targeted to companies (versus recruiters). Not everyone has an e-mail address; therefore, some of your potential contacts will be eliminated.
Fax Campaigns	Faxed resumes and cover letters retain their formatting and sharp visual presentation. Faxing is immediate. Faxed documents are much harder to ignore than e-mailed documents. They are slightly less costly than paper campaigns.	Fax campaigns are more costly than e-mail campaigns. It is extremely difficult to get all the fax numbers you need, particularly if your search campaign is targeted to companies (versus recruiters). Not everyone has a fax; therefore, many of your potential contacts will be eliminated. There is a higher rate of transmission failures as compared with the U.S. Mail. Some visual appeal is lost, and clarity of transmission may be affected by both the sending and the receiving fax machine.

To further help you determine which of the three methods of distribution—paper, e-mail or fax—is right for you and your campaign, consider the following facts:

- Senior-level people and senior-level decision-makers tend to prefer paper. That's it! Therefore, senior-level campaigns should always be on paper unless: (1) you are looking for a position in a technology industry, in which case you would send your resume and cover letter via e-mail; or (2) you have been specifically instructed to send your resume and cover letter via either e-mail or fax.

- Anyone looking for a position in a technology industry should use e-mail as the primary method of distribution. E-mail has definitely become the preferred method of communication for technology companies and their leadership teams.

- Do not conduct an e-mail campaign that is targeted directly to companies unless you have called each and every company to obtain the correct e-mail address of the specific individual (by name or by job title) that you want to contact. Unless that company has posted a position advertisement and listed an e-mail address, you have no assurance that your letter will get to the right person. You can't simply e-mail your resume to ibm@ibm.com and expect it to miraculously get on the right desk.

- Traditional print campaigns are always appropriate unless an electronic (e-mail or fax) response has been requested. The power of paper can be extraordinary and can leave a lasting impression on your reader.

- If you're conducting an e-mail campaign, do not send your resume as an attachment. Most people will not open an attachment from a stranger for fear of viruses. If you have chosen to distribute your resumes and cover letters via e-mail, always paste your resume into the e-mail message, include a Web site address where your resume is posted, or offer to submit a formatted copy on request.

Whether you choose to do your campaigns yourself, or hire a professional who specializes in the preparation of job search campaigns, is entirely up to you. If you have the technical expertise and the data you need, producing your own job search campaign may be your best and lowest-cost strategy. However, if you do not have access to the right data, you are technologically

challenged, or your time is at a premium, you may want to consider contracting with a company that can provide these services to you. Remember, do what you do best and let other experts do what they do best!

Managing the Paperwork and the Process

One of the greatest challenges you will face in your job search is managing the paperwork process. If you're not careful, it will overtake you, and you'll find yourself buried in a pile of paper, faxes, e-mails, notes, and scraps of paper. You must devise—and *stick to*—a structured process to manage it all. If you don't, your job search will be disorganized, you'll misplace important contact information, you'll forget interviews and scheduled follow-ups, and you'll be forever lost in the process.

You have basically two choices as to how you will manage your search campaign. You can do it either on paper or on your PC. The choice is yours. Whatever is the easiest for you to manage and control is the method you should select.

Managing Your Campaign on Paper

If you choose to manage your search campaign on paper, you'll need a good supply of index cards and a notebook. We recommend that you write on an index card the full name and information (company name, address, phone number, fax number, e-mail address, URL) of every job search contact you have. Include the date that you forwarded a resume and cover letter, the specific advertisement you responded to (if applicable), and the date you received a response. If the response is not positive, simply note it on the index card, and you've finished (at least for the time being) with that contact.

If the response is favorable, create a notebook page for the company and transfer all relevant information from the index card onto the page. Use the notebook to continue documenting all of your communications, meetings, interviews, and contact names with that company or recruiter. Be sure to write down each and every thing that transpires between you and that company or recruiter. If, after the interview process and other communications, you are not offered the position, simply move that piece of paper to an inactive section in the back of your notebook.

One of the greatest advantages of managing your search on paper is that the information is always at your fingertips. No matter who calls or when, you can quickly pull an index card or open your notebook to have immediate access to information about the position, the company, the requirements, the salary, the location, and much more.

You'll obviously also need a calendar to keep track of appointments, follow-up calls, interviews, and your other commitments. Spend the extra few dollars and buy a calendar that is 8½ x 11 or 5 x 8 so that you have plenty of room to write down everything.

Even if you elect to manage your search campaign on paper, you will still need your PC for word processing and e-mail applications.

Managing Your Campaign with Your PC

If you choose to manage your search campaign on a PC, you'll need a database or contact-management program and a calendar. You will do precisely the same as we outlined above. The only difference is that all of your documents will be maintained electronically.

On one hand, this appears to make your job search much more efficient, and in many instances this is true. However, the one downside is that you are entirely dependent on your PC for all of your information. If you're standing in the kitchen one evening at 8 p.m. and a prospective employer calls, you don't have the information immediately at your fingertips. Was this a sales position or a marketing position? Is it the company calling or a recruiter? What were the specific requirements of the job? What were they looking for in an ideal candidate?

With a paper system, you have all of this information at your immediate disposal. When you're dependent on technology, you have to

1. Wing it.

2. Ask them to hold for a minute while you run to your office and turn on your PC.

3. Ask them if you can call them back in five minutes.

We do not recommend any of these strategies, but if you are faced with this situation, we recommend either #1 or #2. Don't ever put a prospective

employer off by using #3. Their response can quite easily be, "Well, if you're not interested, I'll call someone else." The opportunity can evaporate in an instant.

Perhaps the best approach is to start with #1 (wing it) and, while continuing the conversation on a cordless phone, walk to your office, turn on your computer, and hope that you can access any necessary information before the end of the conversation.

Helpful Hints

Here are a few other helpful hints for effectively managing your job search process and the flow of information, paper, faxes, and e-mail messages.

Keep Everything

We like paper. We like to be able to touch it, feel it, and put it somewhere for retention. You never know when that scrap of paper, old business card, or notes on a new company moving into the area will be of value in your job search. To keep track of it all, we suggest a file cabinet or file drawer devoted exclusively to your job search and your career. File cabinets are great inventions and are remarkably more efficient than the old "pile it on the floor" system that we all know so well.

Touch Everything Only Once

Part of what consumes such a great deal of our time is shuffling paper around. Paper now enters our lives at such a breakneck pace that we can hardly keep up with it! The key to improving your organizational skills is to try to touch everything only once. When you receive a fax, an e-mail message, or a piece of mail, look at it, do what needs to be done, and then put it away finished. This simple task alone will dramatically improve your efficiency and is much more effective than the traditional "throw it in the pile and look at it later" method.

Write Down Everything

As basic as it may sound, write down everything—appointments, networking luncheons, interviews, follow-up calls—everything! Don't rely on your memory. This is particularly true for those of us who have "senior moments" when we know that we know something, but just can't remember it! And don't think for a minute that you have to be a senior citizen to have a senior moment. It happens to all of us.

Checklists Are Great Things

Checklists are some of our favorite things! Why? It's not because it makes us more organized. It's not because it makes us more efficient. It's because we get to cross things off! That, in and of itself, is really motivating and rewarding.

If you live by the "Post-it Note management strategy," give checklists a try. It's not a huge leap from piles of little pink notes to a single sheet of paper, so the transition is relatively easy. You'll be amazed by (1) how much neater your desk is when there are not 100 Post-it Notes on it, and (2) the thrill and exhilaration of crossing things off your list.

Develop a Schedule and Stick to It

Flexibility is one of the keys to success for any job seeker. You can "go with the punches" and quickly respond to changes and opportunities. That's great. But just as critical is your ability to manage and control your time.

The only vehicle that will provide you with such control is a definite schedule—a schedule that you stick to 100 percent of the time (barring situations that you consider emergencies). No matter how many times you may be tempted to make an exception, don't, unless it's an opportunity for an interview or networking contact. When you developed your schedule, we assume you devoted the time to create a job search management tool that fit your life. Stick to it!

Use this schedule as a model for developing your own.

8:00 a.m.–10:00 a.m.	Follow-up phone calls and networking contacts.
10:00 a.m.–noon	Preparing resumes and cover letters for distribution.
Noon–12:30 p.m.	Lunch.
12:30–4:00 p.m.	Interviews.
4:00 p.m.–6:00 p.m.	Follow-up phone calls and networking contacts.

 Tip If you're sharper in the morning, you may want to schedule your interviews for the morning and your writing time for the afternoon.

Now, does all that sound great? The problem is, it won't work nearly that efficiently. On Monday, you'll have an interview scheduled for 9 a.m., and on Wednesday, you'll have interviews the entire day. Therefore, you must juggle your schedule to accommodate someone else's interviewing schedule. In a job search, this is essential.

And if you're employed, obviously you can't spend 8 or 9 hours daily on your job search. So it's even more critically important that you structure times in your already overcrowded day for your job search. Unless you make the search a priority, it will not be successful. Here's a sample schedule you can adapt for your use if you're currently working:

7 a.m.–8 a.m.	Follow-up phone calls and networking contacts.
Noon–1 p.m.	Working lunch: Get out of the office to a secure, private location. You can schedule initial (brief) interviews for this time, as well as continue your networking activities.
5 p.m. – 7 p.m.	Interviews, follow-up phone calls, and networking contacts.

For more lengthy interviews, you will need to arrange for time off from work.

Part II

Sample Cover Letters

Chapter 7

Before-and-After Cover Letter Transformations

This chapter—and the five that follow it—contains examples of excellent and successful cover letters written by career professionals for their clients. You can use these examples to help compose your own winning cover letters.

A tremendous amount of thought and effort went into selecting the letters that would be included in this book. It was our objective to assemble a "user-friendly" collection of the very best cover letters written by top professionals in the careers and employment industry. To find such a source of qualified talent, we turned to the Career Masters Institute and its membership—professional resume writers, career coaches, career counselors, recruiters, outplacement consultants, military and government transition specialists, and others.

All cover letter submissions were carefully reviewed against stringent standards for quality, writing style, tone, visual presentation, impact, creativity, and diversity. Only those letters that met our requirements have been reprinted for your use. Each includes the name of the author. We list contact information for each author at the end of the book, in case you'd like to get in touch with him or her personally.

A note about credentials: Nearly all of the contributing writers have earned one or more professional credentials. These credentials are highly regarded in the careers and employment industry and are indicative of the writer's

expertise and commitment to professional development. Here is an explanation of each of these credentials:

Credential	Awarded By	Recognizes
CCM: Credentialed Career Master	Career Masters Institute	Specific professional expertise, knowledge of current career trends, commitment to continuing education, and dedication through *pro bono* work
CPRW: Certified Professional Résumé Writer	Professional Association of Résumé Writers	Knowledge of resume strategy development and writing
JCTC: Job and Career Transition Coach	Career Planning and Adult Development Network	Training and expertise in job and career coaching strategies
MA: Master of Arts MS: Master of Science MBA: Master of Business Administration M.Ed.: Master of Education MFA: Master of Fine Arts	Accredited university	Graduate-level education
NCC: National Certified Counselor NCCC: National Certified Career Counselor	National Board for Certified Counselors (affiliated with the American Counseling Association and the American Psychological Association)	Qualification to provide career counseling
NCRW: Nationally Certified Résumé Writer	National Résumé Writers' Association	Knowledge of resume strategy development and writing

Any additional certifications earned by our contributors are spelled out in full (for example, Certificate in Career Planning & Development).

To contact any of our cover letter writers for help with your own job search, see Appendix D, "Geographic Index of Cover Letter Authors."

Note that there is a special section at the end of each of the next five chapters that includes "A Magic Example"—a cover letter written by Susan Britton Whitcomb, CPRW, NCRW, JCTC, author of our companion book, *Résumé Magic*. These letters are some of the best we've ever seen. Be sure to pay close attention to their style, tone, and presentation.

How to Use the Samples

Among these samples you may find a cover letter that is almost identical to your needs and written for someone with a background similar to yours. Great! Take that letter, edit it as necessary, and you're ready to go. More likely, however, you'll find bits and pieces from a letter here and a letter there that are in line with your particular situation.

Even if you have to start writing from scratch, reviewing these letters will get the wheels rolling in your head and give you ideas for strategies, formats, opening paragraphs, presentation of accomplishments, closing paragraphs, and more—in fact, every element of your cover letter.

1—Before

101 Queen Street
Centreville, Ontario
A2A 3B3
(905) 555-6000

January 27, 2001

Mr. Amol Sandhu
Manager
Human Resources
OmniTech Services Inc.
555 Valley Drive
Centreville, Ontario
B3C 4D5

Dear Mr. Sandhu,

I would like to apply for the position of Electronics Technician
(Job # 555) you have advertised.

I have been repairing and servicing electronics equipment for the
past 22 years. I have experience with the C460 series printers,
colour printers, inkjet and laser printers, and audio/visual
equipment. In addition, I have excellent customer service and
troubleshooting skills.

I am available for interviews. Please contact me at the above
phone number and I look forward to hearing from you.

Sincerely,

James Muirfield

This "before" sample is a straightforward response to an advertised position. It lacks visual appeal and only briefly mentions qualifications.

Writer: Ross Macpherson, MA, JCTC; Pickering, Ontario

1—After

James Muirfield

101 Queen Street ❖ Centreville, Ontario A2A 3B3 ❖ (905) 555-6000

January 27, 2001

Mr. Amol Sandhu
Manager, Human Resources
OmniTech Services Inc.
555 Valley Drive
Centreville, Ontario
B3C 4D5

Re: Job # 555 "Electronics Technician"

Dear Mr. Sandhu,

It is with great interest that I respond to your advertisement for an Electronics Technician. I believe that both my experience and skills are a perfect match for the position, and I would appreciate your careful consideration of my credentials as presented below and in my attached resume.

As my resume indicates, I have **22 years of solid experience** as a service and repair technician. Over the course of my career, I have consistently proven my ability to provide outstanding customer service and solve the most difficult of technical issues.

I have been recognized by past employers for the following personal strengths, and it is these same qualities and results that I would bring as a technician with OmniTech Services:

    ❖ **Outstanding technical proficiency and expertise**

    ❖ **Proven ability and perseverance to solve the toughest technical issues**

    ❖ **Highest level of customer service and client relations**

    ❖ **Friendly, punctual, and willing to take the extra step to ensure customer satisfaction**

I am very excited about this position and would appreciate the opportunity to meet and discuss my qualifications. Thank you for your consideration, and I look forward to hearing from you soon.

Sincerely,

James Muirfield

Resume attached

In this version of James Muirfield's cover letter, his strong qualifications are well highlighted—both technical skills and personal attributes such as customer service skills and punctuality. This letter also effectively communicates his enthusiasm for the position.

2—Before

To Whom It May Concern:

I have worked for Galt Grocery Outlet from October of 1989 until the present time. I am looking for stable job that will better my experience in the construction or fencing business.

While working for Galt Grocery Outlet, I was a manager assisting in running the store and managing the employees. Experience learned: Driving a forklift at Galt Grocery Outlet and the Pear Shed during the summer and I also learned communication skills from working with customers and employees.

I have received my diploma from Galt High School graduating with a 3.0 GPA and also had a year and a half of college studying the Administration of Justice.

My hobbies include weight lifting, hiking and fishing in my spare time.

Throughout my years working with Galt Grocery Outlet I have received Employee of the Year, and employee of the month three times.

Richard Carpenter

92743 Rich Road
Galt, California 95632
(209) 555-4092

This candidate tried unsuccessfully to combine a resume and cover letter. With formatting errors, both first- and third-person writing, inclusion of high school G.P.A., a hard-to-find address, and hobbies not directly related to the career objective, it's easy to see why this document was relegated to the "circular file."

Nancy Karvonen, CPRW, JCTC, CCM; Galt, CA

2—After

RICHARD CARPENTER

92743 Rich Road
Galt, California 95632
(209) 555-4092

January 28, 2001

Mark Morgan
Director
California Warehouse Distributors
7388 Murieta Drive
Rancho Murieta, CA 95683

Dear Mr. Morgan:

Are you looking for an experienced warehouse manager or heavy equipment operator? I'm certain that you occasionally come across a safety-oriented candidate with excellent people skills who stands out from the crowd, and I fit that description. You will find my resume enclosed.

✓ Throughout my career, I have consistently delivered solid quantifiable results for my employer through productive and cost-effective methods.

✓ In reviewing my background, you will find that I have succeeded in providing effective leadership, direction, and management; and skillfully operated a variety of forklifts in fruit packing and warehouse environments.

✓ I have been instrumental in generating long-term benefits for the firms that I have served—benefits that can best be summarized as:
   1. increased financial support
   2. increased public support
   3. increased organizational efficiency and safety

At this point in my career, I am seeking new challenges and opportunities to continue to provide strong and decisive leadership and improve financial results. If you could benefit from a dedicated and goal-directed employee with proven skills and abilities, I would welcome a personal interview where we might establish a mutual interest. Thank you for your time and consideration.

Sincerely,

Richard Carpenter

Enclosure: Resume

This revised cover letter, which emphasizes relevant experience and results, helped him land a job within one week.

3—Before

ELEANOR SANDOVAL
75 Netherland Court, Apt. 6-C
New York, NY 10021
(212) 555-8765

October 22, 2001

Peter Rockhouse, Esq.
Evans, Rockhouse & Stanford, LLP
725 Avenue of the Americas
New York, NY 10027

Dear Mr. Rockhouse:

Given your mission to curb the tide of attrition among the ranks of your Associates and provide a more harmonious environmetn, I feel confidnet that I could make a substantial contribution as Director of Associate Relations. For the past twenty-one years, I have been a successful legal recruiter from all sides of the recruitment spectrum – business, school and law firm. Four of those years were spent as Director of Legal Recruiting for Abrams, Howe & Castor. It was my charge to upgrade the level of legal talent and to aid and abet in providing a more congenial atmosphere at the firm. To every task set by the Partners, I achieved well beyond their expectations.

What I have disdovered after an eighteen month return to headhunting is that while monetarily successful, I miss the day to day operation of a law firm and quite frankly, I miss the atmosphere. My experience, creative approach and personality combined to create a job I not only excelled in but loved. It has always been a tenet of my professional faith that if a person loves the job, it is done superbly.

After reading yesterday's New York Law Journal, I felt strongly that this positon literally had my name on it. Therefore, I have takent he liberty of submitting myr esume to you as Managing Partner of Evans, Rockhouse & Stanford. I eager await word from you.

Sincerely,

Eleanor Sandoval

This version of the cover letter is obviously a rough draft, with no attempt made to polish the formatting or even spell-check for typographical errors. Much of the information included is relevant and interesting, however.

ELEANOR SANDOVAL

75 NETHERLANDS COURT, APT. 6-C
NEW YORK, NY 10021
(212) 555-8765

October 22, 2001

Peter Rockhouse, Esq.
Managing Partner
Evans, Rockhouse & Stanford, LLP
725 Avenue of the Americas
New York, NY 10010

Dear Mr. Rockhouse:

After reading yesterday's *New York Law Journal,* I felt strongly that the position of Director of Associate Relations literally had my name on it.

For the past 21 years, I have been a successful legal recruiter from all sides of the recruitment spectrum – business, school and law firm. Four of those years were spent as Director of Legal Recruiting for Abrams, Howe & Castor, where it was my charge to upgrade the level of legal talent and provide a more congenial atmosphere among Partners and Associates at the firm. To every task set by the Partners, I achieved well beyond their expectations.

What I have discovered after an 18-month return to headhunting is that while financially successful, I miss the day-to-day interaction and operation of a law firm, and, quite frankly, I miss the atmosphere. My business experience, creative approach, and service-oriented personality combined to create a job I not only excelled in, but loved. It has always been a tenet of my professional faith that if a person loves the job, it is done superbly.

Given your mission to curb the tide of attrition among the ranks of your Associates and provide a more harmonious and productive environment, I feel confident that I could make a significant contribution to Evans, Rockhouse & Stanford and have enclosed my resume for your consideration.

I would appreciate the opportunity to meet and speak with you directly regarding some of my ideas for attorney recruitment and retention that would complement your firm's goals. I will call your office next week to see if we can arrange a mutually convenient time to meet.

Sincerely,

Eleanor Sandoval

enclosure

This letter opens with a strong statement that was buried in the previous version. The writer did an excellent job of reorganizing the information and improving the professional tone. Note the appeal to the reader's interests in the last paragraph.

4—Before

134 Merrick Road, Apt. 5D
St. Albans, NY 11135
Telephone (718) 555-9001

March 3, 2002

Philip Barnes
Parkway Elementary School
320 E. 241 Street
New York, NY 10000

Dear Mr. Barnes:

Thank you for taking a moment to review my attached resume. I am submitting it to you for employment consideration for your recent opening for a teacher.

For the past four years, I have dedicated myself in helping children grow academically as well as socially. Working with children has been and is a wonderful adventure to me.

I trust you find my academic and employment experience suitable in qualifying for employment with your organization. Please feel free to contact me should you need more information.

I look forward to speaking with you.

Sincerely,

Cameron Anderson

This "before" sample is a classic example of a "transmittal letter"—a letter that merely announces a resume and does little to sell the candidate.

Writer: Christine Magnus, CPRW; Bronx, NY

4—After

Cameron Anderson

134 Merrick Road, Apt. 5D, St. Albans, New York 11135
(718) 555-9001

March 3, 2002

Philip Barnes
Parkway Elementary School
320 E. 241 Street
New York, NY 10000

Dear Mr. Barnes:

A rewarding and successful teaching experience motivates me to bring my commitment to the Parkway School. I offer four years of experience, dedication, and a talent for motivating students to achieve academic excellence.

As a substitute teacher at Holy Trinity, I developed a homework assistance program that significantly improved students' academic performance. My determination in bringing the program to reality was fueled by my desire to help students succeed.

My determination and commitment have also allowed me to do the following:

- Help students overcome problems affecting their academic performance.
- Deliver lessons in a creative and meaningful manner to facilitate comprehension of subjects.
- Empower students and increase their levels of academic performance.

Is it possible to meet with you to discuss how my skills can help your students? If you have any questions or require additional information, please contact me at (718) 555-9001.

Sincerely,

Cameron Anderson

"I highly recommend Cameron. She is a self-motivated person who takes the initiative and follows through."

Tina Foxworth
Principal
Holy Trinity School

This dynamic and effective "after" version of the letter is enhanced by a quote from a very credible source: the principal of a school where this candidate worked.

5—Before

Todd R. Clementson
265 Charlotte Street
Asheville, NC 28801
(828) 555-1212

February 14, 2001

Roland Pharmaceuticals
Att: ABA-Ash
2346 Oswalk Blvd.
Asheville, NC 28801

Dear Personnel Director,

Having a BSBA in Marketing, one year of outside sales in advertising, as well as excellent communication and analytical skills, I would like to express my interest in the position of Pharmaceutical Sales Representative with your organization. Having recently been interviewed by the Jason Pharmaceuticals organization, I found myself completely enthralled in the interviewing process. Through that experience I have become apprised that Pharmaceutical Sales is the career I want to persue. Although I was not rewarded this job due to the competitive nature of this field, I was contacted by the District Manager and informed that I ranked extremely high among the other candidates, and that I have great potential in the pharmaceutical sales field. If you have any reservations concerning a possible interview due to the lack of sales experience, I'd like to urge you to contact Jon Novella, District Manager for Jason. He conducted my first three interviews and would be more than happy to inform you of my potential in the pharmaceutical field. He can be contacted at 828-555-1313.

I greatly appreciate your time and consideration and look forward to the opportunity of interviewing with you to further discuss this endeavor.

Sincerely,

Todd R. Clementson

Salary Requirements:
39,900 + Bonuses

This "before" sample contains a gold mine of valuable information, but the effect is lost because of dense paragraphs, grandiose language (complete with a few incorrect word choices), and bland formatting.

Writer: Dayna Feist, CPRW, JCTC; Asheville, NC

5—After

Todd R. Clementson
265 Charlotte Street • Asheville, NC 28801 • (828) 555-1212 • Clementson@aol.com

February 14, 2001

Mr. C.W. Morgan
Roland Pharmaceuticals
2346 Oswalk Blvd.
Asheville, NC 28801

Dear Mr. Morgan:

Please consider this: I have a BSBA in Marketing, one year of outside sales experience, outstanding communication and analytical skills, and I would like to be your Pharmaceutical Sales Representative.

In a sense, I have been selling—building effective relationships—all my life. Through my performance, management style, and product/process knowledge, I have garnered respect and credibility from upper management at my current position, and my opinions are important to them when we interact professionally and socially. As a housing manager, I used a professional style of communication regardless of the socioeconomic status of the tenant (even during evictions!), and income revenues reflected that. As advertising sales consultant for a community newspaper, I functioned as the company troubleshooter for problem accounts.

If you have any reservations about interviewing me because I lack "official" sales experience, I would urge you to contact Jon Novella, district manager for Jason Pharmaceuticals. It was during the interview process with Jason that I realized how very serious I am about pursuing a pharmaceutical sales career. Jon conducted my first three (out of 5) interviews. He thought enough of my potential to offer to act as a reference. He can be reached at (828) 555-1313.

I would like to bring my energy, enthusiasm, organization, and persuasive ability to your team. Will you grant me the opportunity of an interview? I guarantee you will not be sorry you did.

In closing, I want to thank you very much for your time and attention. I look forward to your reply.

Sincerely,

Todd R. Clementson

enc.

Even though the candidate didn't get the job mentioned in the letter, this experience is turned into a strong reference that counterbalances his lack of sales experience. The second paragraph communicates that the candidate knows what's important for success in sales and has demonstrated those key skills.

6—Before

September 23, 2001

Mr. Jerome Skinner
Manager, Human Resources
Canada Pharmaceuticals
1000 Central Street North
Augusta, Ontario
A5B 5C5

Dear Mr. Skinner,

I am graduating from the Augusta Institute of Pharmaceutical Technology and am interested in a position in your Research & Development department.

I am a very hard working student and have received excellent grades on my lab projects.

For example, I successfully created a formulation matrix for IR tablets and determined its strength by copying penicillin V potassium tablets. In another project, my group examined confounding, standard order, experimental error, significance testing via ANOVA, polynomial equations, and optimization in pharmaceutical application of 2^{4-1} fractional factorial design.

I am very interested in a position at Canada Pharmaceuticals in the Research and Development department. You are welcome to review my attached resume. Thank you for your consideration.

Sincerely,

Catherine Westbrook
31 Masters Road
Augusta, Ontario
A2B 2C2
(905) 555-4455

The formatting and language of this letter convey a less-than-professional message, and the information highlighted is only a small part of what this candidate has to offer.

Writer: Ross Macpherson, MA, JCTC; Pickering, Ontario

6—After

CATHERINE WESTBROOK

31 Masters Road
Augusta, Ontario A2B 2C2

Phone: (905) 555-4455
E-mail: cwestbrook@mail.com

September 23, 2001

Mr. Jerome Skinner
Manager, Human Resources
Canada Pharmaceuticals
1000 Central Street North
Augusta, Ontario
A5B 5C5

Dear Mr. Skinner:

As a graduating student from the **Augusta Institute of Pharmaceutical Technology**, I am particularly attracted to Canada Pharmaceuticals as a progressive leader in pharmaceutical research and development, and as an employer that can provide both the challenge and opportunity I am seeking.

Pharmaceutical research and development offers the opportunity to work on the cutting edge of medicinal innovation and discovery, and it is for this reason that I pursued it as a field of study. My academic experience has exposed me to the challenges and excitement of working in a team toward a common goal, and it is within this dynamic environment of teamwork, innovation, and a collective desire to succeed that I particularly thrive. It is exactly Canada Pharmaceuticals' dedication to these very principles that makes me confident that I would be a valuable contributor and that excites me about opportunities within your company.

In addition to my academic qualifications, I would bring the following personal strengths to a position in Canada Pharmaceuticals:

> **An enthusiasm for challenges, especially those that require new ways of thinking and collaborative input across scientific specialties.**
> **Outstanding teamwork and leadership skills, where I have demonstrated my ability to both contribute and motivate.**
> **A dedicated work ethic and desire to make a difference, which is reflected in my academic, work, and volunteer experience.**

I would appreciate the opportunity to meet and further share with you my qualifications and enthusiasm for joining the Research and Development team at Canada Pharmaceuticals. Thank you for your consideration, and I look forward to hearing from you soon.

Sincerely,

Catherine Westbrook

Enclosure

Although it contains a great deal more information, this letter retains its readability through effective formatting. The first two paragraphs compliment the company and give strong reasons for wanting to work there.

7—Before

October 25, 2000

Box W0XX1
24 Heber Plaza,
Miami, FL 33132

Dear Sir or Madam:

I am responding to the position of International Regional Sales Manager advertised in The Miami Newspaper, October 24, 1999.

My academic credentials include a Masters in Business Administration, which has provided the foundation for my extensive international professional experience. This international work includes experience in various markets including Latin America and the United States.

I have been a Marketing Manager and Deputy General Manager at Swiss Watch Corporation in Panama, where I successfully met the challenge of introducing Swiss Brands to the Central American market and South American market. In addition, in my capacity as an International Account Executive for Video Services, I have been marketing 3D model home simulation services to foreign construction companies. Furthermore, I have worked in the area of Customer Relations with non-linear editing systems manufactured by Avis Technology. All of my international experience has been enhanced by the fact that I speak various languages proficiently, including Spanish, French, English, Hebrew and have a working knowledge of Portuguese.

I would like the opportunity to further discuss my experience and qualifications with you. Please feel free to call me at (305) 999-0624. Thank you for your consideration.

Sincerely,

Gabriel Hamda

This letter is full of "I" statements and shows very little knowledge of or relevance to the employer's needs. Further, it is not written in a style and format that are commensurate with the midlevel management position being pursued.

7—After

Writer: Lisa LeVerrier, MA, MS, CPRW, JCTC; Boca Raton, FL

GABRIEL HAMDA

142 E. Ocean Club Drive
Aventura, FL 33180

(305) 999-0624
gabrielhamda@mindspring.com

October 25, 2000

Box W0XX1
24 Heber Plaza,
Miami, FL 33132

<u>RE:</u> International Regional Sales Manager

Dear Hiring Professional:

Building corporate value and delivering sustained revenue growth is my expertise. For the past eight years, I have proven my ability to lead aggressive market expansion into international markets. Highlights of my professional career include:

- Introduced innovative simulation technology into international territories including Brazil, Mexico, Venezuela, Costa Rica, and Colombia.
- Increased *Swiss Watch* sales by 35 percent, resulting in $2 million in additional annual revenue.
- Negotiated successful corporate partnership with Kodak in El Salvador—result was 56 new distribution channels with over $200,000 in annual sales.
- Spearheaded successful launch of *Swiss Watch* products in Panama, Colombia, and Bolivia, resulting in huge mass-media campaigns.

My strengths lie in my ability to conceive and implement strategic action plans to identify new market opportunities, introduce state-of-the-art technologies/products, and negotiate strategic partnerships to drive Latin American market expansion and revenue/profit growth. Equally notable are my strong qualifications in public relations and promotion, recruiting and training, customer relations, and cross-cultural communication (fluent in English, Spanish, and French).

Currently, I am seeking a mid-level management position where I can continue to provide strong and decisive sales and marketing leadership. If my experience and abilities are a match for your goals, I would welcome the opportunity for a personal interview. I can assure you that my international sales and marketing expertise will be of value to your organization.

Sincerely,

Gabriel Hamda

Enclosure: resume

Opening with a strong statement that conveys value to the organization, the "after" version of this letter goes on to emphasize specific accomplishments that are relevant to the hiring company's needs. The closing is assertive and professional.

8—Before

Tammy Eaton
555 Wonder Valley Road
Vicksburg, OR 95555
(555) 555-5555
tmeaton@or.aha.org

May 19, 2002

Search Committee
American Heart Association, Middletown Chapter
555 East Main Street
St. City, OR 55555

Attn: Search Committee

Please accept this letter in application for the Middletown Chapter Manager position. Enclosed please find my resume and letters of recommendation. I am available for relocation.

My resume outlines my 19 years of experience with American Heart Association. I am a "people person" and enjoy working with staff, contributors, volunteers, healthcare professionals, and the community at-large. I also have strong management experience as an Acting Chapter Manager with the Downtown Chapter and as a National Projects Coordinator with the national level. As an Acting Chapter Manager, I maintain excellent communications between the chapter and it's constituencies, oversee budgets and control expenditures, update the Vice President of Community Services on activities of the chapter, make management recommendations as appropriate, and provide supervisory oversight and support to my staff.

I am confident this experience would enable me to build internal and external relationships, maximizing limiting operating resources, with enhancement of the delivery of services to ensure that the mission and goals of the American Heart Association continue.

Thank you. I look forward to hearing from you.

Very truly yours,

Tammy M. Eaton

Enclosure

This letter fails the first rule of referral letter writing: Immediately name your referral source in the first sentence of your letter. The letter is also vague, short on measurable results, and contains a serious grammatical error ("it's" should be "its") that might torpedo his chance for an interview.

Writer: *Susan Britton Whitcomb, NCRW, CPRW; Fresno, CA*

Tammy M. Eaton

555 Wonder Valley Road
Vicksburg, OR 95555
(555) 555-5555
tmeaton@or.aha.org

May 19, 2002

Jennifer Marks
Search Committee Chair
American Heart Association, Middletown Chapter
555 East Main Street
St. City, OR 55555

Dear Ms. Marks:

Jack Hennesey, Terry Carver, and Joe Piceda have urged me to apply for the American Heart Association's Middletown Chapter Manager position. As an ardent and longtime supporter of Heart, I am pleased to submit my resume for the position.

Qualifications I can deliver to the chapter stem from my 19 years with Heart. Included in this tenure is significant management experience at the national and chapter levels. Specific contributions in the disciplines of operations, corporate relations, fund development, finance and accounting, human resources, and technology are outlined on the enclosed resume.

Most recently, under my direction as Acting Chapter Manager, the Downtown Chapter enjoyed a 21 percent increase in fund development, operated in the black for the first time in four years, partnered with Saint Joseph's Medical Center to implement "Healthy Hearts" in K–12 schools, and resurrected an advisory panel made up of committed and talented business and community leaders.

In an era when societal and economic influences have yielded a decline in volunteer services and financial resources, your committee no doubt wants an individual with proven leadership experience in the not-for-profit sector. I believe my track record is indicative of the ability to build internal and external relationships, maximize limited operating resources, and enhance the delivery of services to ensure that this chapter of the American Heart Association continues to thrive.

I look forward to learning more about how I can assist in meeting the chapter's immediate needs and long-term goals.

Sincerely,

Tammy M. Eaton

Enclosure

Starting strongly with multiple referrals, the "after" version of the letter goes on to state verifiable accomplishments along with general qualifications. And, very importantly, it identifies with the mission of the nonprofit organization.

Winning Cover Letters for Blue-Collar and Trades Positions

The Top Five Cover Letter–Writing Tips for Blue-Collar and Trades Positions

1. Be certain to highlight your technical qualifications as they relate to the position. Often these specific technical requirements—such as a cosmetologist's license, heavy-equipment operator's certificate, or welding certification—are bona fide job requirements, and without them you cannot be considered for the job.

2. Nowadays many blue-collar positions are hard to fill, and turnover is high. If you can stress traits such as work ethic and a strong performance record, you will be a prime candidate.

3. Use language that is comfortable for your educational level and vocabulary, but be certain that your letter sounds professional and is absolutely correct in grammar, spelling, and punctuation.

4. Mention any recent education, training, or other evidence of continuing professional development; this shows you are serious about your profession and dedicated to improving your skills.

5. Just as with any other type of profession, consider the needs of the employer and sell yourself as the solution to those needs.

9

Writer: Susan Guarneri, NCCC, CPRW, CCM, JCTC; Lawrenceville, NJ

Timothy O'Neill
37 Paramount Drive, Lawrenceville, NJ 08648
(609) 555-5555

January 18, 2002

Mr. John Hogan
Main Street Manufacturing
17 Main Street
Lawrenceville, NJ 08648

Re: **Machinist or Maintenance Machinist** position

Dear Mr. Hogan:

If you believe that properly maintained equipment, and machinery are vital to manufacturing production deadlines, we think alike.

If you need customized parts, equipment and machinery to meet rush orders, we should talk.

If you are looking for a dependable and conscientious machinist, maintenance machinist or industrial machinery repairer, please consider my qualifications:

- **18 years of experience as a Machinist** producing or repairing parts and equipment for major industrial manufacturers, pharmaceutical companies, and research organizations

- Completed rush order projects on time and with **quality results**

- Experienced with a wide variety of equipment, tools, fixtures, and materials— which means I can bring **immediate value** to your operation

- Loyal, dedicated, and **dependable** hard worker

- Quick learner with a knack for **solving problems**

To help you learn more about my qualifications, I have enclosed my resume. Throughout my work history I have been successful as a machinist because I have acquired excellent skills, planned carefully for projects and kept on good terms with people at all levels.

It would be a pleasure to meet with you at your convenience to discuss the contributions I would make to your team. I am ready to put my energy and experience to work for you. May I hear from you soon?

Sincerely,

Timothy O'Neill

Enc.

Opening with interest-generating statements and continuing with bullet points that highlight key qualifications, this cover letter grabs and keeps the reader's attention from beginning to end.

Writer: Rhoda Kopy, CPRW; Toms River, NJ

10

JOHN A. KEARNEY
1812 Diamond Drive • Toms River, NJ 08753
732-555-3132

May 15, 2001

David Carlisle
Piedmont Properties
1866 Bradley Boulevard
Eatontown, NJ 07724

Dear Mr. Carlisle:

I am interested in securing a position as a Maintenance Technician / Supervisor, with full responsibility for overseeing the maintenance of a large apartment complex or housing development. My resume is enclosed for your review.

With over 10 years of experience in all aspects of building maintenance, I can be a valuable addition to your staff. My expertise in the areas of carpentry, plumbing, electrical work, painting, landscaping, and pool maintenance has led to the present occupancy rate of 98 percent in the apartment complex I presently oversee.

I was specifically selected to rectify serious safety and health hazards and initiate extensive repairs and renovations at two apartment complexes. The ability to accurately assess needs and promptly implement solutions has contributed to my success. Through effective planning and scheduling, I have consistently demonstrated the ability to keep complexes in tip-top shape with minimal manpower. While other complexes of comparable size require a work force of four, I get the job done with a work force of two.

If you are searching for a maintenance professional who is committed to high standards of workmanship, relates well with residents, and is used to being on call around-the-clock, please contact me to arrange an interview.

Thank you for your consideration.

Sincerely,

John A. Kearney

Enclosure

By addressing such key issues as occupancy rate, safety, economy, and tenant relationship-building, this letter strongly appeals to the interests of its primary audience: property owners.

11

Writer: Meg Montford, CCM; Kansas City, MO

John W. Bridges

525 W. Harrison
Olathe, KS 66061
913-555-9999

2860 Fast Street
Santa Ana, CA 92703
714-555-8888

November 30, 2000

Human Resources Manager
City Hall
105 Central Street, Room 120
Santa Ana, California 92701

Position: **STREET SUPERINTENDENT**

My 20 years of experience in all facets of Public Works make me an ideal candidate for
your next Street Superintendent. Having the longevity with one city employer speaks to
my dedication and strong work ethic. Supervisors have applauded my dependability,
punctuality, and ability to meet established project deadlines. My current manager has
commented, "Last winter John never missed a call out for snow. This is the type of
leadership this shop needs if we are to be successful."

The city of Olathe is the fastest-growing city in Kansas. Classified the third-largest city
in the state by area, Olathe has 1500 lane miles and continues to add 10–12 lane miles
per year. It is a suburb of Greater Kansas City. I have worked for this city during its rapid
growth and have conquered the challenges this growth process has provided its city
workers.

Training and technical development are very important to me, and I take advantage of
every opportunity to acquire the knowledge that will advance my skills. As a crew leader,
I have directed many workers on the job sites and am confident of my ability to oversee
your staff of 27. Work zone safety is a critical issue in our field, and I take pride in my
proactive approach to using safety equipment, meeting safety requirements, and
following procedures.

In January 2001, I will be relocating to your city for family reasons, but can be available
for an interview before then. Please contact me at my Olathe telephone number to
schedule a meeting. Thank you for considering my application.

Sincerely,

John W. Bridges

This letter packs a lot of information. The candidate reinforces his qualifications with a very effective
quote, gives enough information about his current employer to show relevance with the city to which
he's applying, and informs the reader that he will be relocating to that city in just a few months.

12

Writer: Carole S. Barns; Woodinville, WA

HAROLD S. MILLER
1341 Pinehurst Avenue NE ▪ Boston, MA 02266 ▪ (617) 555-1144

February 6, 2000

Douglas Turkell, District Secretary
Fire Protection District 101
145 NW Lester Lane
Boston, MA 02266

Dear Mr. Turkell:

Enclosed is a resume in application for testing for promotion to Career Lieutenant in Fire Protection District 101. As a current Firefighter in the District who has served as an Acting Lieutenant for the past 5 years, I have the skill, the knowledge, and – most importantly – the dedication and commitment to ensure the citizens and businesses are provided with safe, efficient, and quality fire prevention, education, and management. Let me highlight a few of the areas where I believe I am exceptionally qualified to fulfill the requirements of the position:

YOUR REQUIREMENTS	MY QUALIFICATIONS
▪ First Class Firefighter for one year. Training in up to 276 hours of specialized firefighting programs. Possess valid EMT certification.	▪ I have been a Firefighter since 1991 and achieved my First Class Firefighter status in April 1992. A graduate of the University of Massachusetts, I also have a degree in Fire Command and Administration from Bunker Hill Community College. All of the required courses — from Supervision to Time Systems — have been taken. I completed my formal studies with a GPA of 3.8. I am a certified EMT.
▪ Supervise strategic and tactical emergency operations and/or Command System (ICS).	▪ I have completed 28 hours of instruction on ICS and have an excellent working knowledge of the system. Tactics are among my strongest skills. I achieved the District's highest score on the most recent tactical exercise.
▪ Be able to effectively use personnel and resources in both emergency and non-emergency situations.	▪ As Acting Lieutenant for the District for the past five years for up to 75 percent of my shifts, I am frequently responsible for the day-to-day operations of the crew. My leadership skills generate trust because I believe in fair and equal treatment of others and that all leaders are more effective if they lead with a team mentality.
▪ Excellent communications and public relations skills.	▪ With strong written and verbal communications abilities, I am particularly effective in dealing with the public. I am an enthusiastic provider of public education programs and enjoy going the extra step to promote a positive, helpful image of the Fire Protection District among our "customers."

I look forward to the examination and evaluation process and the opportunity to demonstrate before the Review Committee my abilities to handle tactical, personnel, and citizen issues.

Sincerely,

Harold S. Miller

Enclosure: Resume

This letter expands on a simple comparison-list style with some strong selling points for each qualification. Applying for a promotion within the fire department where he works, the job seeker still "sells himself" just as if he were an outside candidate.

13

Writer: Janet Beckstrom; Flint, MI

Samantha T. Coles

258 DeMarl Avenue
Mt. Morris, MI 48458
810-555-2391

June 4, 2002

Mount Hope Community College
Attention: Employment Office
3300 Selmer Avenue
Mt. Hope, MI   48654

Dear Employment Director:

I understand that Mount Hope Community College has an opening for a professional cosmetologist to teach in your Cosmetology program. As a graduate of the Mr. David's School of Cosmetology and a soon-to-be graduate of the Cosmetology Management program at Mount Hope, I hope you will consider me for this position. My resume is enclosed.

As you can see from my resume, I am a licensed cosmetology instructor in addition to being a licensed cosmetologist. I currently run an 11-chair salon I opened in 1990. In addition, I maintain my own clientele as a hairdresser.

My skills as a cosmetologist have been recognized by Mount Hope's *On the Town Magazine,* which named me the "Most Creative Stylist." Also, Her Products (a beauty supply wholesaler) asked me to work as a platform artist at several beauty shows across the country. I even demonstrated the use of their products in an instructional video they produced.

I'm sure I have the right combination of education and experience to make an excellent cosmetology instructor. I hope you will call me to arrange a personal interview. I can be reached at the above number or in my salon at 810-555-1815. Thank you for your consideration.

Sincerely,

Samantha T. Coles

Enclosure

This letter is a straightforward presentation of the candidate's qualifications for the job. In the third paragraph, some notable and highly relevant achievements are highlighted.

Writer: Janet Beckstrom; Flint, MI

14

Jonathan P. Franklin

1854 Broadway Street
Vassar, MI 48555

517-555-0935
or 517-555-8736

Dear Hiring Manager:

I have worked in a manufacturing environment for over 15 years, in positions ranging from die setter to production supervisor. Because I have had experience from both the hourly and supervisory viewpoints, I believe I can be an effective supervisor for your company. I hope you will consider my interest for an appropriate position on your supervisory team.

The enclosed resume describes my employment background. One area that I am particularly knowledgeable about is ISO9002/QS9000. I have worked in several companies that have undergone inspections and eventual certification. In fact, I was placed in my current position at GM Flint Assembly because of this experience. At Flint, I was significantly involved
in preparing several internal departments of the Paint Department for inspection. I developed manuals, trained employees, and generally coordinated the preparations. We expect to be certified by the end of this year.

I don't think you will find a supervisor who is more hard working or dependable. I know what needs to be done, and I work to that end. What I don't know how to do, I teach myself with help from someone who does know. Constantly I am looking for new challenges and ways to improve myself. I'm a hands-on leader who creates a friendly environment for my employees, which invariably translates into a more loyal crew.

After reading this letter, I hope you agree that I have what it takes to be the kind of supervisor you are looking for. Please give me a call to arrange a convenient meeting time. Thank you for your consideration.

Sincerely,

Jonathan P. Franklin

Enclosure

This cold-call letter is intended for use as-is, without personalization. This approach is extremely practical for job seekers who don't have access to a PC to address and modify each letter. In the third paragraph, he communicates important "intangibles" that set him apart from others.

15

Writer: Janet Beckstrom; Flint, MI

Kerry E. Ramsdale

870 Winfield Court
Saginaw, MI 48602

517-555-7649
or 810-555-2581

February 7, 2002

Director of Employment
Saginaw Industries
72 Hooper Mill Road
Saginaw, MI 48600

Dear Director of Employment:

Please accept this letter and my resume as an expression of interest in joining your company in a position that I am qualified for based on my customer service and production background.

I consider myself to be goal oriented with a strong desire to succeed and work toward outstanding results. I take pride in working hard and enjoy challenges and demands.

As my resume describes, I have experience in mail room operations, delivery service, and manufacturing/production. I am certain I can make a valuable contribution to your organization.

I welcome the opportunity to meet and discuss this with you. If you need additional information, or if you would like to arrange an interview, please contact me. Thank you for your time and courtesy in reviewing this material. I will look forward to hearing from you.

Sincerely,

Kerry E. Ramsdale

Enclosure

Without specifying a particular position, this cold-call letter sets forth experience and personal attributes that will be valuable to the company. By describing a hard-working, energetic, and experienced individual, the writer does a good job of appealing to the reader's interests.

Writer: Nancy Karvonen, CPRW, JCTC, CCM; Galt, CA

16

Donald W. Karr

III Adare Way Galt, California 95632 **(209) 555-4075**

January 4, 2001

Kristi Goldby
Director of Guest Services
Sacramento River Cats Baseball, LLC
1001 Second Street
Old Sacramento, CA 95814

Dear Ms. Goldby:

It was thrilling when Andrea Smith called recently and asked me to send in my resume for a *Seating Attendant* position. This gave me the opportunity to support Sacramento's very own professional baseball team, the *River Cats*. For the past five years I have dreamed of being a seating attendant for a baseball team and considered working at the Coliseum or Pac Bell park upon retirement this year from the Department of Corrections.

When the Founding Corporate Partners decided to build a Triple-A stadium in West Sacramento, I was ecstatic! A Minor League ball park right in my own backyard—how lucky could a guy get? As a passionate fan of the Athletics since the club first moved to Oakland, I have remained loyal to the team whether they've been up on top or down in the cellar.

The ability to be tactful, but firm, is important when dealing with people in the wrong seats, fans trying to go onto the field or drinking too much. I would make the fans feel comfortable while maintaining order within my area and adhering to seating rules, policies, and procedures. With my extensive law enforcement background and experience with people from all walks of life, this position seems to be a natural match.

I feel I would be a fantastic seating attendant and have fun at the same time. It is a personal challenge to help bring pleasure to the fans at Raley Field while maintaining order. I look forward to meeting with you soon to discuss how my peace officer background coupled with an enthusiasm for baseball meets the needs of the Sacramento River Cats Baseball team. Thank you for your time and consideration.

Sincerely,

Donald W. Karr

In this letter, the candidate uses his intense interest in baseball as a key selling point. Since enthusiasm for and knowledge of the game are key attributes for a seating attendant, this approach is very effective.

17

Writer: Susan Britton Whitcomb, Fresno, CA

Roger Shamblin

55555 Plains Drive
Denton, TX 75555
(555) 555-5555

March 4, 2002

Manson Manufacturing Company
P. O. Box 12345
Denton, TX 75555

Attn: Welding Department Supervisor

Please consider my resume for the position of welder advertised in *The Denton Times*. I have recently completed a Certificated Welding Program at Denton Community College that included more than 1,000 hours of hands-on training in the following areas:

- **Basic Welding:** Oxy-acetylene fusion welding on plate, pipe, and tubing of mild steel, stainless steel, and cast iron; soft and hard soldering on ferrous and nonferrous materials; use of hand torch, straight-line cutter, and dupli-cutter; electric arc welding on mild steel plate and pipe.

- **Mig-Tig Welding:** Basic mig and tig welding on mild steel, stainless steel, and aluminum; basic plasma cutting systems; welding in flat, horizontal, vertical, and overhead positions with emphasis on working toward A.W.S. plate certification.

- **Welding Fabrication:** Advanced shop welding practices on mild steel plate and pipe; advanced mig welding on mild steel; advanced tig welding on mild steel, stainless steel, and aluminum plate; inner shield, flux core; test and inspection of welds; project design, including flowcharting and project construction.

- **Metals:** Metal process applications, including working with bench metals, forming wrought iron, laying out and forming sheet metals, casting, and forging.

- **Related Courses:** Electricity, blueprint reading, machine shop (turning), CNC milling, and CADD.

Welding instructors at Denton Community College gave me some of the highest grades in the program for my quality workmanship and study habits. In addition, my internship supervisor, Joe Brown at Upright Harvester, was very happy with my performance and asked that potential employers call him directly for a reference (Mr. Brown's number is 555-5555).

Thank you for your time. I look forward to hearing from you.

Sincerely,

Roger Shamblin

Enclosure (Resume)

In addition to addressing, in detail, all the specific skills and qualifications needed for this job, the job seeker uses the second-to-last paragraph to communicate a few intangibles (excellent academic record and strong personal recommendation) to further sell himself as a strong candidate for the position.

Chapter 9

Winning Cover Letters for Young Professionals/ New Graduates

The Top Five Cover Letter–Writing Tips for Young Professionals/New Graduates

1. Highlight "professional" skills that you have developed through both professional and nonprofessional experiences. For example, if you have worked on important team projects while at school, communicate that you know how to get results in a team environment.

2. If technology skills are important in your chosen field, be sure to emphasize your skills in this area.

3. Mine your academic experiences for evidence of leadership skills. These are important in a work environment and are evidence of your potential.

4. Highlight your academic achievements. They indicate your intelligence and competitiveness.

5. Relate your skills, experience, and interests to the needs of the employer. Show that you understand business priorities and are ready to make a contribution; don't simply state, "I've graduated! Now I need a job!"

18

Writer: Laura DeCarlo, CPRW, JCTC; Melbourne, FL

YVONNE P. SMITH
15 Caribbean Isle Lane, #8
Orlando, FL 32808
(407) 555-8790

July 6, 2002

Attn: Ms. Denise Seatl
District Manager
Eckerd Drugs
22 Lake Buena Vista Road
Orlando, FL 32808

Dear Ms. Seatl:

Think of all the things that make a Manager with Eckerd Drugs GREAT....

Drive, dedication, and a willingness to learn and achieve. Exposure to different
levels of the sales process. Current knowledge of Eckerd Drugs store policies and
procedures as an Assistant Manager. A competitive, professional personality. Skills
and talents to exceed goals and set records. Excellent results. *I believe I have what you
are looking for!*

Realizing that this summary, as well as my resume, cannot adequately
communicate my qualifications in-depth, I would appreciate having the
opportunity to discuss with you how I can continue to be an asset to your firm.
I look forward to speaking with you.

Thank you for your time and consideration.

Sincerely,

Yvonne P. Smith

enclosure: resume

This letter starts off with an irresistible "hook," followed by a paragraph that details the qualities that
will be of most interest to the reader. For new graduates, experience is not usually the strongest selling
point. Potential and personal attributes are usually of most interest to employers.

19

Writer: Kathryn Bourne, CPRW, JCTC; Tucson, AZ

SAMANTHA CROSS

117 Greenbriar Way, # 214 ◇ Denver, CO 48210 ◇ 312-555-6794

December 4, 2001

Mr. Kent Laverly, Principal
LW Design
505 West Broadway Avenue
Denver, CO 48232

Dear Mr. Laverly:

Isn't it important to LW Design that:

> Clients feel their project is important to the firm?
> All projects are handled with the utmost professionalism?
> Employee creativity is in a constant state of development?

Of course it is. Superior corporate goals and objectives will ensure that LW Design will remain a premier Denver firm into the new century.

These values are also core to my developing career. As you will see in the enclosed résumé, I recently graduated from the Art Institute of Seattle with a 9-month internship at Newton Architecture. Under their mentoring I gained hands-on experience in space planning, material and finish selections, color board assembly, writing specifications, and compiling architectural finish books.

Another strength I bring to LW Design is the ability to build confidence with existing customers as well as establish rapport and trust with prospective clients. In addition, holding a degree in Business Administration and Marketing, I fully understand the importance of adhering to budgets, maintaining positive vendor relationships, managing day-to-day marketing activities, and applying innovative ideas to capture new projects.

I would appreciate the opportunity to further explore the needs of LW Design and how my strengths could have a positive impact on the company's bottom line. I will be contacting you next week to arrange for a meeting time convenient for you.

Sincerely,

Samantha Cross

Enclosure

This letter appeals to its audience in two ways: First, with an interesting design and font selection, it demonstrates strong graphic skills—communicating an important attribute by showing rather than telling. Second, it leads off with questions that demonstrate knowledge of the company's values.

20

Writer: Vivian Van Lier, CPRW, JCTC; Valley Glen, CA

NOREEN BERGMAN

5555 Magnolia Court • Valley Glen, CA 91405 • (818) 555-6565 • noreen555@ucla.edu

March 27, 2001

Sarah Hartford
Director of Human Resources
Pacific Enterprises, Inc.
2745 Topanga Boulevard
Los Angeles, CA 94005

Dear Ms. Hartford:

In June I will graduate from UCLA with a degree in Business Economics. My willingness to work hard is evident from the fact that I hold part-time professional positions concurrent with my studies. These experiences have enabled me to gain a realistic view of the demands and challenges of the business world.

I would welcome the chance to discuss opportunities with your firm. I believe that my energy, analytic skills, organizational abilities, and creativity in tackling problems can make a positive contribution to your company. I am equally comfortable working independently to meet company goals as well as collaboratively as part of a team. I have always been able to establish and maintain excellent relationships with clients and coworkers at all levels. My professional skills include

- Client relations, research, and account management strengths gained as a Finance Assistant at a brokerage firm

- Experience in managing client records, preparing financial statements, and completing tax returns for a CPA firm

- Assisting low-income clients and students with income tax preparation as a volunteer

- Serving as a group leader—planning and implementing activities as a camp counselor for four summers

Please consider me a serious candidate for a position with your firm. I look forward to a personal meeting so that I can provide you with additional information to supplement what appears on my enclosed resume.

Sincerely,

Noreen Bergman

enclosure: resume

Using a combination of paragraphs and bullets, this candidate conveys important qualifications—academic history, experience, and personal qualities that communicate her potential to become a valuable asset to the firm.

Writer: Don Orlando, MBA, CPRW, JCTC; Montgomery, AL

21

Mark Morstad
1440 Norton Avenue
Montgomery, Alabama 36100
[334] 555-5555 — morstad1@aol.com

February 23, 2001

Ms. Nora W. Morgan
Comptroller
Topline, Inc.
1200 Ventura Avenue
Suite 1000
Montgomery, Alabama 36100

Dear Ms. Morgan:

Where do you look in your organization for the person who does the "nitty-gritty" work to build Topline's future success? Where is the person who frees senior decision-makers for the work only they can do? If you need those profit-enhancing capabilities, I would like to join your team as your newest entry-level project analyst.

Even before I earned my degree, I got great satisfaction from helping businesses succeed. Naturally, when I attended school I majored in the field that seemed just right for me: commerce and business administration.

However, I wanted more practical, hands-on, knowledge than I saw in my college courses. And so I took the jobs others might have shunned to get practical, hands-on, experience. None of the job titles were impressive. But helping pay my way through school as a bartender, doorman (you may read that as "bouncer"), laborer, and assembly worker taught me a lot about how to work with people to get the job done and serve the customers—sometimes very tough customers.

Now I want to put all that I've learned to work. Perhaps a good next step is to hear about your specific needs. May I call in a few days to arrange a meeting?

Sincerely,

Mark Morstad

Enclosure: Resume

This letter demonstrates how a new grad can relate seemingly irrelevant experience to a company's needs. The letter contains terms that clearly show an understanding of what's important to businesses—such as "profit-enhancing," working with people "to get the job done," and "building future success."

22

Writer: Lisa LeVerrier, CPRW, JCTC, M.A., M.S.; Boca Raton, FL

Carol Hobesound

2460 Country Club Boulevard, Deerfield Beach, FL 33442 • (954) 444-8617

September 27, 2001

Shanna Detwiler   RE: Marketing Assistant
VP Human Resources
General Media Corporation
75 High Ridge Road
Stamford, CT 09602

Dear Ms. Detwiler:

"If you wish to reach the highest, begin at the lowest." — Pubilius Syrus

I know my quoting Pubilius Syrus is a sign of youthful idealism. However, I know it takes hard work and proven dedication to move up within an industry. I'd like to reach the highest by starting at the beginning within the PR/Marketing industry.

I recently graduated with a BA in Communications from Wake Forest University in North Carolina. I am seeking an entry-level position with a dynamic PR/Marketing firm in Connecticut, offering opportunity for upward mobility based on performance. I realize it takes hard work and proven dedication to move up within a firm—I'm willing to start at the beginning and prove my skills and dedication along the way.

As my resume indicates, I have excellent customer service skills. This is demonstrated by my proven ability to quickly establish rapport with a diverse range of customers and suppliers. My strong written communication skills are demonstrated by several writing samples prepared during college, which I can furnish upon request. I am also proficient with both PC and Macintosh software including Windows applications, Microsoft Word, WordPerfect, electronic mail, and Internet browsers. Finally, my excellent work ethic and positive attitude are contagious.

I am residing in Florida temporarily to care for an elderly family member. However, I am seeking to relocate to Connecticut by November 2001 and am seeking employment to begin at that time.

I look forward to discussing possibilities to grow within your firm and am very excited about the opportunity to capitalize on my communications background and assist your company in the PR/Marketing arena. Thank you for your time and consideration — I can assure you that I will make a positive contribution to your organization.

Sincerely,

Carol Hobesound

Enclosure: resume

The technique of beginning with a quote is a sure-fire attention-getter, and this candidate continues by relating the quote to her career goals and interest in joining the firm. As in the previous sample, the letter contains ample evidence that she knows what is important to businesses.

Writer: Kirsten Dixson, CPRW; Bronxville, NY

23

Heather Jones

(212) 555-1111
100 East 75th Street #2A, New York, NY 10020
hjones@hotmail.com

April 23, 2002

Ms. Julie McCafrey
DesignPros International
123 Avenue of the Americas, Suite 999
New York, NY 10035

Dear Ms. McCafrey:

Ms. Jane Smith suggested that I contact you to discuss the contribution that I could make to DesignPros in a Contract Design Internship this summer. I am currently a student at The Interior Design Institute and am anxious to begin my professional design career. Unlike many of my peers whose only experience is academic, I offer not only strong educational credentials, but also practical, "hands-on" business experience.

My strength is being able to work with people to generate ideas that work. My career has been focused in the areas of advertising project coordination, customer relations management and events planning. Former managers would describe me as capable, motivated and detail-oriented.

The most rewarding work for me has always centered on creativity and design. As a child, I made barrettes, boxes, and dolls and sold them to local stores. In high school, I took every art and photography course that I could and even won a tri-state photography contest. Then I earned a degree in business administration and began working in marketing. Once I made the decision to make a career change, I began to create again. I made and sold pillows, blankets, painted furniture, pictures with beads, mosaics on tables and mirrors, water-colored lampshades, etc. Friends suggested that I should do it for a living. I agreed and quickly commenced my formal design training. I have excelled in my coursework and am looking forward to bringing my creativity and business acumen to this profession.

I have enclosed my resume to provide more information on my strengths and career achievements. I'm also prepared to show you a preliminary portfolio of my work. I look forward to speaking with you to further pursue this opportunity. Thank you for your consideration.

Sincerely,

Heather Jones

Enclosure

This candidate provides evidence that sets her apart from her peers who may also be applying to this company. The story of her lifelong interest in design is interesting and highly relevant.

24

Writer: Maria Hebda, CPRW; Trenton, MI

Thomas N. Jones

424 Columbia Avenue • Trenton, Michigan 48183
(734) 555-8205

January 15, 2002

Recruitment Center
P.O. Box 2945
Arlington, Virginia 22209

RE: Central Intelligence Agency Employment

I am interested in exploring employment opportunities with the Central Intelligence Agency (CIA). The enclosed resume is in accordance with the instructions stated in the CIA's *Job Kit and Resume Preparation Guide*. I would like to be considered for all possible positions. An acceptable salary would be in the mid-$20K range.

Qualifications I bring to your agency include

- Proven performance in fast-paced and high-stress working environments
- Strong analytical skills with exceptional attention to detail
- Highly motivated and aggressively take on great responsibility
- Planned and implemented over 100 strategic missions with a 100 percent success rate
- Hands-on experience with classified documentation
- Experienced in intelligence report writing, including in-depth reports on high-interest areas of operation

My record is one of great responsibility, dedication, and solid accomplishments. I am confident that my experience and abilities can make a valuable contribution to the CIA. I am available for immediate employment and willing to relocate.

Should any questions arise regarding the information on my resume, please do not hesitate to contact me. I look forward to hearing from you in the near future.

Sincerely,

Thomas N. Jones

Enclosure

With six highly relevant bullet-point qualifications, this letter clearly communicates that the candidate has what the CIA is looking for. Reinforcing this message is the first paragraph, which shows compliance with the standerd operating procedures expected by the CIA.

25

Writer: Rhoda Kopy, CPRW; Toms River, NJ

Heather T. Alberts, R.N., B.S.N.
18 Porter Avenue • Lakehurst, NJ 08733 • 732-555-3378

— Willing to Relocate —

January 8, 2002

Daniel R. Farrantino
Northeast Regional Sales Manager
Omni Pharmaceutical Products
Jackson Lane
Princeton, NJ 08540

Dear Mr. Farrantino:

I am a well-spoken, assertive nursing professional with the motivation, medical knowledge, and ability to promote pharmaceuticals to health care professionals. My resume is enclosed for your review.

Throughout my career, I have interacted extensively with pharmaceutical representatives; I know how important it is for them to be knowledgeable about the efficacy, benefits, contra-indications, and potential side effects of drugs. As health care professionals, we expect them to know the answers; if they don't, they lose credibility.

Having administered and monitored the effects of a wide range of pharmaceuticals, I am confident of my ability to promote these products to medical professionals. My associates refer to me as "Ms. PDR" because of my extensive knowledge of and interest in medications. On a daily basis, I had to clearly present medical information to patients, and frequently had to use skills of persuasion with patients, nurses, and physicians.

With over 15 years of experience in emergency nursing, I have a talent for being focused and decisive in the most challenging of situations. Strong organizational and time management skills are imperative in handling medical crises; I firmly believe I can handle any situation as a result of my background.

If you are searching for an energetic health care professional with the knowledge and determination to succeed as a Pharmaceutical Representative, please contact me to arrange an interview. Thank you for your consideration.

Sincerely,

Heather T. Alberts, R.N., B.S.N.

Enclosure

This letter makes a strong case for the candidate's transition from nursing to pharmaceutical sales. In any kind of career transition, it's important to relate past experience and demonstrated skills to the needs of the new profession.

26

Writer: Jean West, CPRW, JCTC; Indian Rocks Beach, FL

CONNIE BELSTROM
2242 Highland Avenue
Fairfax, Virginia 22302
703-555-2534 • E-mail: cebel@email.com

January 4, 2002

Southwest Airlines Company
People Department
P.O. Box 36644 HDQ 4HR
Dallas, TX 75235-1644

RE: Flight Attendant Position

If Southwest Airlines needs flight attendants who thrive on challenge and change and look forward to new opportunities to build positive customer relationships every day, please consider me a prime candidate.

As a frequent flyer with over 250,000 miles on Southwest Airlines, I have chosen Southwest based on your reputation for customer service, because that is where I excel. I am considered a diplomatic problem-solver who is able to handle all personalities with finesse. Based on both my nursing and business background, I have demonstrated experience in handling crisis situations calmly and efficiently to achieve optimum outcomes. Other strengths include the ability to organize, prioritize, and carry out multiple duties at once in order to meet deadlines. You will find me to be a flexible and willing team member.

Flight attendants are usually the last Southwest employees to deal with your customers. They should convey a certain image to those customers, and I believe I am the type of person you want to leave that lasting impression.

I have enclosed my resume for your review and thank you for this opportunity to interview with you.

Sincerely,

Connie Belstrom

Enclosure: Resume

The second-to-last paragraph of this letter is a strong and effective sales pitch and is complemented by the quantifiable qualifications detailed in the previous paragraphs.

27

Writer: Lorie Lebert, CPRW, JCTC; Novi, MI

ALLISON S. THORNWEBER

1061 HOLLYBERRY ROAD — ROYAL OAK, MICHIGAN 48067
248.555.1061
e-mail: athornweb@hotmail.com

July 17, 2001

Thomas Kent, Ph.D.
Director, Library Services
University of Michigan
Ann Arbor, MI 49109

Dear Dr. Kent:

I am writing in anticipation of a position in Library/Information Sciences, Archival Administration, or related fields/divisions. Highlights of my employment and academic experience include

➤ **Strong Project Management Skills.** With extensive experience working in libraries, museums, and non-profit corporations, I have been involved in planning, research, exhibits, and public service that resulted in significant accomplishments.

➤ **Excellent Academic Record.** Since entering universities at the Master's and Bachelor's levels, I have consistently maintained above-average grades while holding outside employment and volunteering.

➤ **Communications and Public Relations Skills.** In each of my positions I have dealt cooperatively with the general public, co-workers, and superiors. My skills at interpersonal relations and cross-cultural communications are excellent.

➤ **Analytical and Organizational Skills.** Practical employment in areas of my concentration allowed me to demonstrate my strength in data research and analysis, project organization, and computer proficiency.

I am anxious to launch my career in a full-time, permanent position and would welcome the opportunity to meet with you to discuss your specific requirements. I would make myself available at your earliest convenience for a meeting/interview.

Thank you for your time reviewing my credentials. I look forward to speaking with you.

Sincerely,

Allison S. Thornweber

Enclosure: Resume

The attractive formatting and easily skimmed bullet points do a good job of communicating this entry-level candidate's professionalism and potential.

28

Writer: Cheryl Ann Harland, CPRW; The Woodlands, TX

Susan Russell

20 Victory Road ◆ Dallas, Texas 75007 ◆ (972) 555-9870 ◆ E-mail: srussell@gateway.net

February 21, 2001

Human Resources Director
Dell Computers
31 Pasadena Avenue
Phoenix, Arizona 99841

Dear Human Resources Director:

Building cooperative relationships between multi-disciplinary groups is my expertise. As a project manager for Texas Instruments, I have been responsible for coordinating, organizing, and facilitating multimillion–dollar IT projects impacting the entire organization (45,000 employees worldwide). It is my project management experience, coupled with my supervisory, training and development background, that I wish to integrate into an HR/Organizational Development role.

Over the years, I have been successful in building trust and cooperation between employees and management, creating environments that support and reward individual accomplishment and contribution.

Having just completed my BBA in Organizational Behavior, I am ready to combine my 20-year technical/supervisory career into a training and development and/or instructional design position, where I can be instrumental in creating training programs responsive to your company's ever-changing organizational needs.

Thank you for reviewing the enclosed qualifications. I look forward to a personal interview at your convenience.

Sincerely,

Susan Russell

Enclosure

Having recently completed a degree, this candidate presents both education and 20 years' experience as key selling points. Note the effective use of the "building cooperative relationships is my expertise" opening strategy (described in chapter 3).

29

Writer: Lynn Andenoro, CPRW; Salt Lake City, UT

Jeffrey A. Anderson
3605 South 2800 West
West Valley City, Utah 84119
(801) 555-4678

October 17, 2000

KUTV Channel 2 News
2185 South 3600 West
Salt Lake City, Utah 84119

Attention: News Operations Manager

It is with great interest that I respond to your job posting for the News Editor/Engineering Controller position with Channel 2 News in Salt Lake City. I believe I have the qualifications and enthusiasm you are looking for. My resume is enclosed for your review.

During my senior year of high school I worked as a video editor for a local cable TV station in Garden Grove, California. I gained considerable hands-on experience, a wealth of practical knowledge, and a determination to pursue TV and film production as a career. Concurrent to my work at Channel 3A, I also studied TV Production in an occupational studies program in my community.

I quickly learned the technical skills of the trade, injected creativity and energy, and was soon filming breaking news stories in the community, covering local meetings and sporting events, editing news footage for weekly broadcasts, and assisting with studio productions and community access programming.

I would like the opportunity to meet with you and discuss how I might become a beneficial part of your team at Channel 2 News. I will call to follow up with you next week. Before then I may be reached at 955-1640. Thank you for your consideration.

Sincerely,

Jeffrey A. Anderson

Enclosures: resume and tape

The appealing (and relevant) graphic at the top of this letter is an effective enhancement to its traditional formatting.

30

Writer: Donna Farrise; Hauppauge, NY

DIANE M. WILSON
555 Meadow Brook Street
Westbury, New York 12345
(631) 555-5555
e-mail: diane@ooo.com

April 17, 2001

McGraw-Hill
1221 Avenue of the Americas
New York, NY 10020

Dear Sir/Madam:

With innate reading/proofreading ability and demonstrated skills in editing grammatical, typographical, and composition errors, I am actively seeking a challenging **freelance reader/proofreader/editor** position. My work has been recognized for theoretical sophistication and rhetorical clarity. Highlighted qualifications and contributions I would bring to your organization include the following:

- Aptitude to read/proofread complex novels and diverse subject matter/disciplines; i.e., instruction manuals, college textbooks, education manuals, math textbooks, journals, etc.

- Ability to edit into abstract frame, produce plausible and innovative interpretation, and provide written and oral commentary. Mastered skills through reading scholarly texts and diverse disciplines, editing press releases, and teaching experience.

- Conspicuously well-reasoned, possessing solid research ingenuity, progressive text development, and comprehensive results meeting deadlines.

- Experience working with a cross-section of individuals, developed through performance as an educator/counselor.

I have been characterized as a top-quality reader, proofreader, and editor with a remarkable sense of humor. I would welcome the opportunity to meet with you and discuss the possible merging of my talent, experience, and enthusiasm with your **freelance reading/proofreading** needs.

Very truly yours,

DIANE M. WILSON

Enclosure

A simple yet striking page border, combined with a clean format and easily skimmed bullet points, make this a very attractive letter.

31

Writer: Salome Randall Tripi; Mt. Morris, NY

MARYBETH LONG

48 Lake Avenue ✦ Buffalo NY 14202
716/555-0909 ✦ *E-mail:* marybeth@myemail.com

February 8, 2001

Mr. Edward P. Murphy
Deputy Superintendent
Mayfield Central School District
19 Main Street
Mayfield NY 14623

Dear Mr. Murphy:

I am interested in being considered for a position within your Guidance Department and have enclosed a completed application and my resume for your review.

During my three years with Brunswick Junior/Senior High School, I have had the opportunity to work with a diverse student population at the middle and high school grade levels. Currently, I manage a caseload of 200 students in the middle school, where individual and group counseling as well as crisis intervention and peer mediation comprise a large portion of my time. In addition to academic and future planning, I assist teens with self-esteem, anger management, social skills training, drug abuse, and sexual abuse issues. I view primary prevention as a critical aspect in assisting young people through the stages of their lives, balanced with a focus on student development and academic excellence.

I have benefited professionally from the experiences and knowledge gained at Brunswick and am confident I can share that effectively with your school district. Additionally, I believe that my excellent work ethic; strong interpersonal, organizational, and communication skills; and ability to establish a solid rapport with students, families, and peers alike would make me an effective member of your Guidance team. I have taken the liberty to enclose letters of reference that reflect the quality of work for which I strive.

I would appreciate the opportunity to interview for a Guidance Department position at Mayfield. Please feel free to contact me at the above telephone number or e-mail address.

Thank you for your time and consideration.

Sincerely,

Marybeth Long

Enclosures

Primarily a straightforward presentation of qualifications, this letter is enhanced by the last sentence in paragraph 2, where the candidate communicates her educational philosophy.

32

Writer: Shanna Kemp, M.Ed., JCTC; Carrollton, TX

DANIELLE ALBRIGHT

922 LAKEVIEW LANE, #4122
LEWISVILLE, TEXAS 75067

972-455-8383 HOME
972-678-3484 MOBILE
danielle_albright@yahoo.com

Dear Personnel Manager:

Are you searching for a dynamic, goal-oriented individual with a strong desire to succeed and lead others to success? Are you searching for an enthusiastic, proactive team member with strong interpersonal skills and a desire to work with people? Look no further.

I am a driven and focused individual who knows how to set goals and work to achieve them. This is clearly exemplified by my time in college. When I started my degree program, I set my sights on finishing early and doing well in all my courses. Since I also needed to earn the money to pay for my schooling, I knew I had set a demanding goal for myself. I persevered, however, and expect to graduate in December from the University of North Texas in just 3 $\frac{1}{2}$ years with a 3.0 GPA while working 20+ hours per week and taking course loads of 18 hours per semester.

Is this the type of person you want working for you?

My degree is in psychology. I have always enjoyed working with and helping people. It has become my desire to work with people in a business atmosphere—to assist others with the professional side of their needs and work in a company where I can set long-term goals for success.

I have enclosed my resume for your consideration. I would appreciate the opportunity to meet with you in person to discuss how I may further the goals of your company. I look forward to your call.

Sincerely,

Danielle Albright

Enclosure

Capturing the reader's attention with interest-generating questions makes for a strong opening paragraph. The information the candidate shares about her personal qualities and school experience is interesting, relevant, and powerful. The attractive letterhead design enhances the total presentation.

33

Writer: Michele Haffner, CPRW; Glendale, WI

MARIE GILMAN
2110 East Kane Avenue
Shorewood, Wisconsin 53211
Cellular: (414) 555-6025 — Home: (414) 555-0619
E-mail: mgilman@aol.com

January 14, 2001

Dr. Robert Deahl, Dean, College of Professional Studies
Marquette University
P.O. Box 1881
Milwaukee, WI 53201-1881

Dear Dr. Deahl:

As a single working mother who recently completed undergraduate and graduate degrees,
I can certainly empathize with the students who are enrolled in your Professional Studies
program. At times while working on my own degree, I recall feeling overwhelmed.
Fortunately, community resources such as yours help adult working students thrive in their
environments. I emerged from the experience motivated and ready to assist others in the
spirit of your mission statement: "…providing service that expresses the highest degree of
understanding, respect, honesty, compassion, and guidance."

Therefore, I would like to be considered for the position of Adult Student Advisor. You
will see from the enclosed resume that my background and education closely match your
requirements for the job. As a community counselor, my work has included assisting single
mothers and their children as the family adjusts to major life changes such as returning to
school or work. In addition, my recent graduate training has included course work in career
counseling and career development within four-year colleges. The needs of special groups
(delayed entrants, mid-life changers, displaced home workers, etc.) were covered thoroughly.

I can arrange to be available for an interview at your earliest convenience and look forward to
meeting with you.

Sincerely,

Marie Gilman

Enclosure: Resume

This candidate effectively relates her personal situation to the needs of the job for which she is applying. This is entirely appropriate since these personal experiences give her an appreciation for the
needs of students and the demands of college life.

34

Writer: Deborah Wile Dib, CCM, NCRW, CPRW, JCTC; Medford, NY

Anjelique Tarakas

Freedom Quad, P.O. Box 0021
University at Albany, Albany, NY 12222
518-555-0101 ● anta@cnsvax.albany.edu

Permanent Residence
45 Sloane Drive, Great Neck, NY 11702
516-555-0303 ● anjel@mindspring.com

April 21, 2002

Mr. William Cousins
Director of Human Resources
Chase
25 Park Avenue
New York, NY 10101

Dear Mr. Cousins:

You have advertised for an entry-level Financial Analyst in Sunday's *New York Times*. As a soon-to-graduate university senior majoring in Business Administration with a concentration in Information Systems Management, my qualifications should meet your requirements.

Taking initiative has always been my academic and career focus. I certainly understand responsibility, hold an intense work ethic, and strive to do my best in any situation. During four years of work and internship experiences, I have enthusiastically sought challenging projects and have made strong contributions not normally expected of an intern. Highlights include

- The development of an Access-to-Excel migration spreadsheet that organized a company-wide PC inventory system for MedFlo instruments.
- The creation of an Excel spreadsheet that permitted MedFlo to implement more rapid vendor payment.
- The successful learning and selling of high-profit liability coverage while an intern at Budget Rent-a-Car (normally done only by experienced sales force).
- The planning and implementation of a large warehouse document relocation project for Symbol Technologies.
- The fulfillment of positions as Vice President of Finance and as Community Service Coordinator for Pi Sigma Epsilon, Professional Sales and Marketing Fraternity.
- The attainment and successful performance of Teacher Assistant positions for two educators.

A demanding course load, multiple campus leadership positions, challenging internships, and a variety of work experiences have prepared me for the rigors of an entry-level Financial Analyst's position at Chase. My technical and business background is balanced by courses in art and the humanities, creating the ability to grasp business and technology needs as well as the skills to think past the obvious aspects of a situation. I have an intense interest in pursuing and overcoming difficult challenges, I work hard, and I have the drive to make a difference.

I'd like to meet and discuss the ways in which I can contribute my experience and energy to Chase. I can be reached at my academic address via phone or e-mail and look forward to speaking with you.

Sincerely,

Anjelique Tarakas

Enclosure: resume in traditional and computer-scannable versions

This candidate presents both quantifiable qualifications (in a bulleted list) and intangible qualities that show she is very well suited for the job for which she is applying. Note that she is enclosing both traditional and computer-scannable resumes.

35

Writer: Christine Magnus, CPRW; Bronx, NY

Christina Thomas

120 Fifth Avenue
New York, NY 10250
(212) 555-1023

February 3, 2002

Yvonne Harris
Metropolitan Children's Therapies
123 Maple Way
New York, NY 10002

Dear Ms. Harris:

Over the last three years I have become familiar with all aspects of service delivery for speech-impaired clients. Since 1996, I have been instrumental in overseeing/coordinating service delivery for a speech-impaired child—my son.

Since his birth, I have participated in every facet of his care, from recruiting qualified service providers to administering therapy. This experience has inspired me to embark on a career as a Speech Therapist or Special Education Teacher. My hard work and tireless efforts to facilitate his progress have resulted in marked improvements.

The areas in which I have made considerable contributions are Diagnostic Planning, Case Management, and Speech Therapy. My resume provides an overview of my role and achievements in each of these areas. Additionally, I am pursuing a degree in Speech Therapy / Special Education at Westchester Community College. I am confident that the knowledge and experience I have acquired to date will help your clients achieve their goals.

I would like to schedule a personal interview where we can discuss my strong enthusiasm and qualifications for a position in your organization. I can be reached at the address and phone number listed above. Thanks in advance for your time and consideration. I look forward to your response.

Sincerely,

Christina Thomas

This letter is another example of relating personal experiences to the needs and demands of a specific job. The graphic under her name is a striking and attractive enhancement.

36

Writer: Nancy Karvonen, CPRW, JCTC, CCM; Galt, CA

Ernest White

5068 Beacon Street • Hackensack, New Jersey 07601 • (201) 555-4032

February 10, 2001

Gregory Mahaffey
President
International Trading Corporation
7047 West Market Street
Hackensack, NJ 07640

Dear Mr. Mahaffey:

International Trading Corporation is known for valuing solid professional skills, creativity, a strong work ethic, and the desire to excel. Since these qualities are mine in abundance, my search for an entry-level *International Marketing* position begins with your firm.

The past four years have provided exposure to a wide variety of advertising, public relations and financial-related activities through positions with top agencies in New Jersey while pursuing my BA in Marketing Management/International Business and Trade. These experiences have confirmed my desire for a career on the creative side of international marketing; however, at this point I am seeking an entry-level public relations or marketing position to increase my skills while contributing to the organization's growth and profitability.

As my enclosed resume attests, my diverse career background demonstrates progressive administrative, marketing, account development, and public relations experience. With key project-planning and profit-building expertise, I have extensive background working with a wide range of customer needs. My professional growth reflects my commitment to achievement of corporate objectives, delivering an outstanding level of customer satisfaction, and effectively cultivating and successfully managing account relationships.

With an enthusiastic desire to meet with you and explore opportunities within International Trading Corporation, may we schedule an appointment to discuss current or anticipated needs at your firm and how I can become a key contributor to your operations? I would greatly like to contribute my energy and experience to your future bottom-line successes.

Thank you for your consideration. I will follow up with a phone call next week

Sincerely,

Ernest White

Enclosure: Resume

Starting off by identifying the company's values and priorities, this candidate subtly flatters the company by indicating that it is his "first choice" for professional employment.

37

Writer: Ross Macpherson, MA, JCTC; Pickering, Ontario

DANIELLE GREEN ———

1999 Port Smith Road   (905) 555-6789
Pinehurst, Alberta N5L 5M5   dgreen@mail.com

——— *Goal: Pharmaceutical Sales* ———

January 23, 2002

Mr. Bryan Hodgins
PharmLab Canada
44 Industry Way
Pinehurst, Alberta
N5N 7M7

Dear Mr. Hodgins:

I understand that PharmLab Canada is introducing a new cardiovascular medication, Milocaid, and that you are looking for salespeople within the Pinehurst area.

Throughout my professional and academic careers, I have consistently driven myself to meet challenges and achieve goals, and it is within this type of challenging and results-oriented environment in which I particularly thrive. Likewise, it is exactly these qualities that attract me to a highly competitive and exciting career in pharmaceutical sales, and in particular to PharmLab Canada as an industry leader that can provide both the challenge and opportunity I am seeking.

With both professional experience in a technical lab environment and an honours degree in Biomedical Science, I have an excellent background in health and biomedical settings and am both comfortable and proficient with highly technical terminology and communication. This advantage, combined with my demonstrated sales and marketing accomplishments, makes me confident that I would be a valuable contributor to the PharmLab Canada sales team.

Success in sales is measured in **results**, and I can bring the following results-oriented qualities to PharmLab Canada:

> **Demonstrated proficiency in selling to customer needs, fostering client relationships, and managing key accounts to maximize revenue and retention**
> **Outstanding teamwork and leadership skills, where I have demonstrated my ability to both contribute and motivate**
> **A goal-driven work ethic and dedicated approach to all tasks and undertakings**

I would appreciate the opportunity to meet and further share with you my qualifications and enthusiasm for joining the sales team at PharmLab Canada. I invite you to review my attached resume and thank you for your consideration.

Sincerely,

Danielle Green

Enclosure

The attention-getting bullet points in this letter relate potential (what the candidate can do) rather than specific qualifications—these are covered in the earlier paragraphs.

Writer: Janet Beckstrom; Flint, MI

Jeremy S. Yale

2384 Sparrow Road • Kingston, MI 48534 • 810-555-3449

Dear Employment Director:

You are the master of your own destiny.

That's what I tell other sales representatives when I am trying to help them understand how a successful career in sales is within their reach. Within a short three-year period, I have developed strong sales skills that have enabled me to build a record of sustained sales increases. I enjoy helping others improve their sales skills by using some of the methods that have been successful for me. The enclosed resume highlights some of my specific accomplishments. It supports my interest in a position with your organization.

My experience demonstrates that I have the ability to transition into selling diverse products and services. After all, sales is sales. My strongest sales tool, I believe, is that I am willing to truly listen to my customers. Since I hear what they are saying, I am prepared to identify and offer the product or service they need at a price they cannot turn down. It's a win-win situation.

After reviewing my material, I hope you will agree that I am the kind of highly motivated, successful sales professional that you are looking for. Please contact me at the above number to arrange a convenient meeting time so that I can elaborate on how my track record in sales can benefit your organization. Thank you for your time and consideration.

Sincerely,

Jeremy S. Yale

Enclosure

The compelling philosophy stated in the first sentence of this letter should grab the attention of every reader. The letter becomes even more effective when the candidate goes on to relate the importance of that philosophy to his career success to date.

A Magic Example

Writer: Susan Britton Whitcomb, NCRW, CPRW; Fresno, CA

CHARLES MARTIN EDWARDS III

555 South Fairfield
San Francisco, CA 95555
(415) 555-5555
cme3@compuserve.com

June 23, 2001

Hudson Parker, Hiring Partner
Jones, Marriott & Parker, Attorneys at Law
555 West Kennowith
San Francisco, CA 95555

Dear Mr. Parker:

Having graduated with honors from Hastings School of Law and recently passed the Bar, I am seeking interviews with civil litigation firms that devote a portion of their practice to international law. The enclosed resume details my education, experience, skills, and legal interests. Among my qualifications are the following:

- Scholarship developed as an extern for California Supreme Court Justice Louis Madigian and as a staff writer for *The Hastings Law Review*;

- Courtroom skills learned while conducting preliminary hearings as an intern with the Alameda County District Attorney's Office;

- Leadership gained as a college quarterback and volunteer team leader with Habitat for Humanity; and

- International experience acquired while studying law in London, England, and traveling extensively throughout Europe, Mexico, and Central America.

Given the combination of these experiences, I am confident I have developed a professional resourcefulness and personal diversity that will enable me to become a capable member of your firm. Your consideration of my qualifications for associate attorney positions will be appreciated.

Sincerely,

Charles Martin Edwards III

Enclosure

The four bullet points in this letter convey the job seeker's key qualifications—so a quick skim of the letter would quickly convey the most important information.

Chapter 10

Winning Cover Letters for Mid-Career Professionals

The Top Five Cover Letter–Writing Tips for Mid-Career Professionals

1. Focus on your career accomplishments. By describing what you have done for other employers, you will demonstrate your potential to make similar contributions for this employer.

2. If you have managed staff, be sure to communicate team and managerial accomplishments as well as individual achievements.

3. Relate your accomplishments to the overall goals of the organization as well as your unique sphere of influence.

4. Emphasize career progression. Your advancement indicates reward for past achievement and shows your readiness to continue to move upward.

5. Don't take up valuable space by including college or early career information; in most instances, your most recent experience will be most relevant.

40
Writer: Debra O'Reilly, CPRW, JCTC; Bristol, CT

Jayne Smyth
101 Main Street
Friendship, CT 06000
203-555-1010

February 10, 2001

Hallmark Cards, Inc.
ATTN: Human Resources Director
P.O. Box 10001
Kansas City, MO 64141

Re: Positions for **Sales Professionals**

Dear Human Resources Director:

When you care enough to send the very best...send me!

The opportunity to represent Hallmark Cards, the perennial industry leader, would be a dream come true. Because I share your philosophy that only my best is good enough to offer, I have consistently been a top-producing sales representative for my current employer, constantly exceeding sales quotas and earning recognition from clients, peers, and supervisors. Accomplishments include the following:

- Among 50 sales representatives, rank in the top 3 for the past 2 years, supporting the achievement of departmental sales goals averaging $500,000 per month.
- Regularly produce 30 percent or more over daily sales goals.
- Selected to manage key national accounts.
- Commended by peers for providing sales assistance/support with accounts in a competitive environment.
- Chosen to mentor new hires.

I offer you solid sales experience, a strong customer focus and effective leadership skills, in combination with an "only the best will do" work ethic. I eagerly anticipate the opportunity to discuss your goals for your new territory and the ways in which I might help Hallmark achieve and exceed them. Thank you for considering my qualifications.

Sincerely,

Jayne Smyth

Enclosure

The opening line of this cover letter is perfectly tailored for its recipient. After capturing the reader's attention, the letter follows up with strong accomplishments that support this candidate's claim to be "the best."

41

Writer: Michele Haffner, CPRW; Glendale, WI

George E. Brown

3265 North Bartelt Street   E-mail: geb3@earthlink.net
Milwaukee, Wisconsin 53211   Telephone/Message: (414) 555-3081

November 30, 2000

Mr. Daniel Tilman
Roadway Express, Inc.
6880 South Howard Avenue
Oak Creek, Wisconsin 53154

Dear Mr. Tilman:

Having visited your company's website, my impressions were of an organization that is forward thinking and always looking for new ways to improve. An open-door type of relationship appears to be prevalent between you and your customers. Therefore, it would seem necessary for your sales representatives and management personnel to possess strong communication abilities in order to effectively carry out your mission.

As you can see from the enclosed resume, my educational concentration in communications has been balanced by actual work experience. I have been required to conduct financial analysis, solve technical difficulties (sometimes remotely), and give the highest possible levels of customer service. I am certainly willing to learn all about the industry and your organization so that
I can be a productive team member.

My promise is that a meeting will not be a waste of time, yours or mine. In addition, I can make myself available at your convenience to discuss your needs in detail. Thank you for your consideration of my qualifications, and
I look forward to hearing from you.

Sincerely,

George E. Brown

Enclosure: Resume

In this letter, the job seeker creates rapport by identifying with the target company's mission. Mentioning that he has researched the company by visiting its Web site is another way to communicate that he knows the company he's approaching and can indeed be a "productive team member."

42

Writer: G. William Amme, JCTC; Deerfield Beach, FL

John H. Libby, Ph.D., N.C.C., L.M.H.C.
2400 Germantown Avenue
Philadelphia, Pennsylvania 19004
(215) 798-2018
jlib007@aol.com

Job Posting L-1711
Mental Health Magazine
P.O. Box 10007
Philadelphia, PA 19001

Dear Sir or Madam:

I am very interested in the position of Clinical Supervisor as advertised in the July issue of *Mental Health* magazine.

The enclosed resume reflects both my 15 years of counseling and psychotherapy experience and my outstanding educational credentials. I am now seeking additional challenges and opportunities in the mental health counseling field. If you can use a well-trained and highly competent professional with exceptional real-world experience, *I am your ideal candidate*. The following highlights how my background meets your stated position requirements.

You require:	*My qualifications:*
Master's degree.	*A Doctorate in Psychology and a Master's in Health Services as well as a post-Master's degree as Specialist in Mental Health Counseling.*
24 graduate semester hours in Psychology.	*More than 115 graduate semester hours in Psychology and Neuro-Linguistic Programming.*
Experience teaching at the college level.	*Experience teaching at both the junior college and university graduate levels.*
Background as Licensed Therapist or Mental Health Counselor.	*More than 15 years of successful practice as a Licensed Therapist and Mental Health Counselor.*
The ability to teach both day and evening classes.	*The ability to teach day and evening classes as demonstrated by my current employment schedules.*

You may note that along with my educational and college-level teaching credentials, I have had substantial success in working with Mood Disorders including Major Depression and Anxiety Disorders in both individual and group therapy. In addition, my experience in rehabilitation and career counseling may provide collateral benefits to your institution.

Letters and resumes help you sort out the probable from the possible, but they are no way to judge the caliber of an individual. I would like to meet with you and demonstrate that along with my credentials, I have the personality and skills that make for a successful counselor, instructor, and supporting team member. Recognizing the demands of your schedule, I will call you soon after you receive this letter. I would appreciate my application being treated as confidential as I am currently employed.

Sincerely,

John H. Libby, Ph.D., N.C.C., L.M.H.C.

encl: Resume

In addition to a close match between specific requirements and his qualifications—as demonstrated in a well-organized table—this candidate sells himself by providing additional highly relevant qualifications and describing himself as the "ideal candidate."

Writer: Georgia Adamson, JCTC, CPRW; Campbell, CA

ROGER ARNOLD

466 Geneva Street
San Rafael, CA 90000

(555) 555-5555
rarnold@isp.com

February 28, 2002

Ms. Deborah Jacobsen
Vice President, Corporate Security
Megacorp Enterprises
1111 Allen Road
San Francisco, CA 94000

Dear Ms. Jacobsen:

Could you use a law enforcement management professional with a successful track record in security program planning, implementation and operation, as well as a reputation for effective leadership and exceptional team-building? If so, I believe you will find the enclosed resume worth a close look.

Throughout my law enforcement / security career, I have focused on empowering my subordinates to succeed by encouraging them to develop their strengths and grow professionally. In many cases where individuals were dissatisfied, I resolved the underlying problems and turned their attitude around. This approach consistently produces highly effective, supportive teams under my command.

Prior to my current work in the executive protection field, I managed up to 250 police officers and 50–100 civilians as a Watch Commander, Division Commander, and SWAT Team leader with the Haslett County Sheriff's Department. I also managed custodial facilities that housed over 3,000 inmates and dealt frequently with operational issues that included budgets, staffing, and scheduling. As president of the Deputy Sheriffs' Association, I successfully negotiated several union contracts and resolved a variety of personnel problems.

In addition to becoming a Certified Executive Protection Specialist, I ensure my continuing ability to handle demanding responsibilities by maintaining excellent physical condition. For example, I compete as an amateur boxer and recently won a World Title in this sport.

Based on my experience and strong commitment, I am confident that I can add significant value to your security function. If appropriate, I would like to schedule a meeting to discuss your needs and the contribution I can make to the success of your organization. I look forward to speaking with you soon.

Sincerely,

Roger Arnold

Encl.

The opening question in this cold-call letter should capture the reader's attention, and it is followed up by well-written and well-organized paragraphs that communicate strong qualifications.

44

Writer: Deborah Wile Dib, CCM, NCRW, CPRW, JCTC; Medford, NY

Martina Marchesi

42 Laurel Road
Aquebogue, NY 11732
631-555-1010

Specialty Foods Consultant ♦ **Fresh Produce Authority** ♦ **Organics Specialist**

June 14, 2001

Mr. Tim Mathesion
Vice President of Operations
The Greenery
2523 Links Road
Chicago, IL 12543

RE: The Greenery Regional Produce Coordinator—Southwest Region

Dear Mr. Mathesion:

You are looking for a dynamic marketer and manager with broad industry experience and the skills needed to bring in the margins necessary for profitable operations and long-term growth. My accomplishments with The Greenery and other well-known industry leaders clearly demonstrate my ability to creatively react to today's rapidly changing natural foods marketplace while retaining a keen focus on the bottom line.

Mr. Mathesion, although you are probably aware of my work as manager of The Greenery's Southampton location, I'd like to review the highlights of my tenure with The Greenery:

♦ Converted a negative 6-point contribution margin to a positive 3-point contribution in the Southampton produce department.

♦ Created better price image by walking the competition weekly to select "meet or beat price" items, resulting in a stabilized market share from a downtrending market share.

♦ Improved bottom line by increasing quality standards, establishing proper receiving and stocking methods, and improving team members' morale and pride in their stores.

♦ Mentored a team member, Thomas DeMatia, into a successful Southampton produce team leader.

♦ Selected by Alesia Reynolds to write the new Southwest regional produce training manual.

In over 10 years in the natural foods business, I have held positions in all areas of the industry—Produce Manager and Buyer, Store and Display Designer, Store Opening Manager, Specialty and Organics Food Consultant, and Wholesale Produce Distributor. I am accustomed to maximizing productivity and increasing corporate profits through expert cost and inventory control, forecasting, planning, trend spotting, spoilage reduction, display creation, vendor relations, and employee development. In addition, I have a strong understanding of what it takes to get the product from the field to the table.

In an unusual and attractive two-page format, this candidate presents her qualifications for a significant promotion with her current employer. When applying for internal promotions, it's important not

Martina Marchesi   page two

The following accomplishments demonstrate previous experience that I will bring to the position of Regional Produce Coordinator:

♦ Opened five stores in the past nine years, from a 1,000-square-foot organic produce store to a 20,000-square-foot full-service natural foods store.

♦ Learned to recognize, create, and uphold the highest standards through work in the Bay Area, New York City, and the Hamptons, all among the most competitive and discriminating regions in the United States.

♦ Worked with some of the best distributors in the world through two years' employment in the Seattle Produce Terminal.

♦ Developed an appreciation of the freshest food and the art of selling into the customers' hands through several summers running farmers' markets and farm stands in San Francisco and Southampton.

♦ Continually trained staff in leading-edge and classic whole-foods marketing, display, and operations styles and techniques.

♦ Consistently built loyal customer base by hands-on sales techniques, impeccable standards and quality, enticing displays, fair pricing, educational events, and personal service.

Mr. Mathesion, as an industry veteran, I have long respected The Greenery for its market leadership, sound operations, value orientation, and presentation standards. Now that I work with The Greenery, I'm continually excited by the company and its goals. I very much enjoy my current position but feel strongly that I am ready to make a more substantial contribution by bringing my industry expertise and my commitment to excellence to the Southwest Regional Produce Coordinator's position. If you feel that my experience and drive can benefit The Greenery in this or other positions, let's talk!

Sincerely,

Martina Marchesi

to assume that senior managers will know everything you've done for the company; spell it out just as you would in a letter to a stranger.

45

Writer: Shanna Kemp, M.Ed., JCTC; Carrollton, TX

BRETT KINCAID

421 East Washington
Carrollton, TX 75006
Home: (972) 555-3099
Fax: (972) 555-2561

"First, you've got to get the best possible people to
work with you." Norman Brinker

April 27, 2001

Charles Durham
Vice President, Human Resources
Brinker International
725 Ranch Parkway
Dallas, TX 75001

Dear Mr. Durham:

While it would be an exaggeration to say that I can leap tall buildings in a single bound, or restore the safety of humanity with a mighty "heigh-ho Silver," it would be perfectly accurate to say that I am the best possible person to add to Brinker's research and development team.

Mr. Brinker's philosophies on hiring the best people and creating strong teams of employees have resulted in repeated success. He has discovered that it is imperative that the people you work with are inwardly motivated, have a "can-do" attitude, and are enthusiastic and energetic. Using those words to describe me would not be an exaggeration.

As you can see from my enclosed resume, I have a strong history of successfully building new business and developing new products. My success stems from my love for the work and my ability to create strong teams of employees and develop personal relationships with my business allies.

Like Mr. Brinker, I believe a job should be challenging and fun. I am ready for a new challenge and would like to find it at Brinker International. As you read my enclosed resume, you will not find a superhero, but you will find an outstanding employee and leader, ready to take the next step, work hard, have fun, and make superhuman efforts toward success.

It will be a pleasure to meet with you at your convenience to discuss my credentials in detail. I can be reached at the above numbers when you are ready to set up a time to meet. I look forward to your call.

Sincerely,

Brett Kincaid

Enclosure

The quote that starts this letter is particularly effective since the person being quoted is the founder of the company to which the job seeker is applying. The "superhero" theme mentioned in the first paragraph is used effectively in the closing.

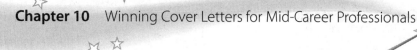

46

Writer: Kirsten Dixson, CPRW; Certificate in Career Planning and Development; Bronxville, NY

Julie H. May

411 Meadow Lane
Yonkers, NY 10709
914-555-6666 res./msg.
914-555-7777 fax
bestteacher@aol.com

June 28, 2001

Dr. William Lewis
Principal
P.S. 42
Tuckahoe, NY 10707

Dear Dr. Lewis:

I noted with interest your June 13, 1999, advertisement in *The New York Times* for a **Grade 2 Teacher** for a leave replacement (9/01–12/01). As a certified teacher with experience teaching this grade level and first-hand knowledge of P.S. 42 through extensive volunteer activities, I believe that I am an excellent candidate for this position.

I understand that you need someone who is self-directed and who possesses the necessary qualities for managing another teacher's class—flexibility, good humor, rapport with parents, familiarity with the school culture, and the ability to go beyond the lesson plans in accordance with meeting the current needs. At this point, I welcome the challenge of making a positive impact on the minds of elementary school–aged children. I am committed to achieving this goal through ongoing professional development to learn the latest effective teaching methods.

I have enclosed my resume to provide more information on my strengths and career achievements. I am also open to other opportunities in the school. If, after reviewing my material, you believe that there is a match, please call me. Thank you for your consideration.

Sincerely,

Julie H. May

Enclosure

In an attractive format, this letter does an excellent job of responding to the specific qualifications listed in a job advertisement.

47

Writer: Christine Magnus, CPRW; Bronx, NY

SHARON A. ROBINSON

10 Hone Street
Bronx, NY 10452

Telephone/Fax
(718) 555-8382

April 17, 2001

Michael Thomas
Human Resource Director
Cablevision
18 Madison Avenue
New York, NY 10022

Dear Mr. Thomas:

As a longstanding member of 49th District Community Committee, I have had the distinct pleasure of communicating with you in the course of conducting business with Cablevision.

I am writing to you because, after many years serving the community, I have decided to use some of my capabilities in a corporate setting. Following is an overview of my skills and background:

- **Administration.** Over 12 years of experience as CEO of the Community Affairs Organization—reduced operational costs, raised funds, administered daily activities.
- **Sales/Marketing.** Successfully procured donations for scholarships; sold advertising space; generated ticket sales for numerous events. Developed ministry's mailing list from nil to virtually 900 names.
- **Staff Training and Supervision.** Supervised corporate and volunteer staff.
- **Program Development.** Crafted well-received events, workshops, and financial, social, and recreational programs.

I have watched Cablevision become a leader in the telecommunications industry and would be honored to contribute to its growth and success. I am confident my skills and background can help achieve this. I genuinely appreciate your time and help and look forward to hearing from you.

Sincerely,

Sharon A. Robinson

To make a connection with the person to whom she's writing, this job seeker uses a "self-referral" technique. She mentions a prior association and then relates that experience to the job she is seeking. Her qualifications, well highlighted in bold, lead off a concise list of bullet points.

Writer: Jean West, CPRW, JCTC; Indian Rocks Beach, FL

Anna Smith
17 Pomeroy Road
North Reading, MA 01867
978-555-9393 • Fax: 978-555-3834 • E-Mail: asmith@email.com

July 17, 2001

Conversent Communications
Attn: Human Resources
90 Maple Street
Stoneham, MA 02180

Re: Sales Careers with Conversent Communications

Would a person with 15 years of sales, marketing, training and management experience for three Fortune 500 companies interest you? What if that person could couple her experience with the ability to build productive business relationships and effectively interface with all levels of management, staff and customers? If this describes the professional you want to represent your company, please give me your valued consideration.

I am a consistent, "hands-on" manager who contributes to and supports corporate merchandising programs. I have built strong, effective, and loyal teams who take pride in being the best in the company. A sense of urgency characterizes my management style. I take great pride in getting things done right the first time around.

My résumé provides more details, but some highlights of my experience include:

- Launching new products and programs to increase market share, consistently exceeding sales quotas.
- Start-up operations and management of retail sales and service centers.
- Strong management, team building, motivation and training experience.

My objective is to obtain a position where I can apply my talents, energy and problem-solving expertise to positively impact a company's growth. I am willing to travel and am fluent in Spanish.

I feel confident that my 15 years' experience in the telecommunications field will be an important asset for your company. I look forward to talking with you soon.

Sincerely,

Anna Smith

Enclosure: Résumé

This cold-call letter leads off with some thought-provoking questions and then summarizes qualifications in both paragraph and bullet format.

49

Writer: Bernice Antifonario; Tewksbury, MA

DANIEL J. STEWART
14 Rock Ledge Drive
Nashua, NH 03063
603 / 555-2676

May 10, 2002

Mr. Glenn Roberts
Blackstone Corporation
122 Center Street
Malden, MA 02148

Dear Mr. Roberts:

As an experienced production supervisor with a record of success in process improvement, I am interested in the Production Supervisor position you advertised recently. A review of your requirements suggests a good fit with my experience and skills.

Your requirements	My experience
Improve quality, capacity	In an ISO 9001, FDA, CGMP environment with critical quality standards, work with R&D and Engineering to maintain standards and schedules.
	Recommended improved manufacturing standards that resulted in $687K in annual savings.
	Reduced floor space by 25 percent and eliminated second shift without impacting output volume.
Leadership	Key player in implementing continuous improvement processes and training and motivating team members.
Safety standards, personnel	Maintain OSHA standards for all aspects of operation. Hire, train, review, evaluate, and supervise staff.
Analytical, organizational skill	Continually analyze multiple production-related factors to ensure efficiency and productivity.

Personal abilities I offer include strong interpersonal and communication skills, a flexible attitude, and attention to detail. I am a highly motivated, high-energy individual, with the leadership ability to motivate a staff to achieve team success.

A copy of my resume is enclosed for your review. I would appreciate the opportunity to discuss your needs and my background in person. I will call you next week to see when we can arrange a meeting. Thank you very much for your consideration.

Sincerely,

Daniel J. Stewart

Enclosure

Making the most of the comparison-list style, this candidate mentions some key accomplishments relating to the required qualifications. In the next paragraph, intangible qualities are mentioned as additional selling points.

Matthew Kincaid
110 North Knisel Street
Riverside, Iowa 52327
319.354.7822
mkincaid@earthlink.net

February 18, 2002

Xena Marketing Corp.
Attn: Susan Quinn, Director
179 Executive Park Drive
Iowa City, Iowa 52240

Dear Ms. Quinn:

It is not the strongest of the species that survive, nor the most intelligent, but the one most responsive to change. — Charles Darwin

Fast, fluid, and flexible — isn't that what Darwin <u>really</u> meant?

Marketing certainly can be viewed as a survival of the fittest, and I:

Thrive on managing the myriad details necessary to propel the ordinary to excellence;

Relish the opportunity, and responsibility, to motivate and coach my staff to achieve their potential; and,

Embrace the challenges key to demonstrating pride of mastery in marketing quality products to dominance.

My salary requirements are realistic and, given the strengths and attributes I possess, make me an excellent value for your company's compensation dollar. I also realize flexibility is essential and am therefore open to discussing your company's salary range for a professional with my background and business acumen.

Would your organization benefit from these attributes? Please call me at your earliest convenience to discuss my focus on bringing a fresh perspective to the marketing arena.

Very truly yours,

Matthew Kincaid

Enclosure

With short, punchy sentences and paragraphs, an interesting quote, and bold type highlighting key attributes, this letter would be as effective as an online cover letter as it is in a traditional paper document.

51

Writer: Laurie Smith, CPRW; Alexandria, VA

Patricia Bates

4983 CLEAR BROOK COURT
FALLS CHURCH, VA 22043
(703) 534-8945
BATES3498@EARTHLINK.NET

June 17, 2001

Mr. James Ryan
Cooper & Associates
1400 Peach Tree Lane
Atlanta, GA 30330

Dear Mr. Ryan:

Is your organization looking for a customer service manager who is:

υ   An effective communicator, able to talk to and write effectively for audiences at all levels;

υ   Determined and persistent ... does not back off when the situation gets tough;

υ   A team player, not easily rattled, confident without self-importance;

υ   Ever-vigilant for wasted time, effort, resources, or money; and

υ   Able to develop/implement processes and procedures to keep your company profitable?

If so, I believe my qualifications will interest you. Throughout my 15 years in the direct mail order/telemarketing business, I have consistently created environments, processes, and procedures that spurred my teams to increased productivity, sales, and camaraderie. Serving in diverse roles spanning Credit, Distribution, Customer Service/Telemarketing, and Operations, I played an important part in the growth of a family of companies over 10 years from $1 million to $35+ million in revenues.

I look forward to the opportunity to discuss how I might contribute to your company's growth and increased profitability through excellence in customer service. You may reach me during business hours at (301) 845-2308, or evenings at (703) 534-8945. Thank you for your consideration.

Sincerely,

Patricia Bates

Starting off with a bulleted list of key attributes, this letter captures immediate attention and then goes on to summarize experience and accomplishments.

Writer: Cynthia Kraft, CPRW, JCTC, CCM; Valrico, FL

52

SALLY SUE SMITH
813-555-8765
sallysmith@aol.com

1384 Stone Hill Way, Brandon, FL 33511

February 18, 2001

Mr. Robert Jones
Kline Pharmaceuticals
1803 Lois Avenue
Tampa, FL 33619

Dear Mr. Jones:

    A successful consultative sales person has the ability to develop and nurture long-term relationships. My success in this area is well documented. My customers will tell you I am... efficient and organized... a helpful people person with superior follow-through... and excellent at building rapport and fostering mutually beneficial relationships. My supervisors look at the bottom line and acknowledge my overall contributions to the company.

    Although my resume is practical in nature, it cannot convey the full level of my eagerness to undertake new challenges. I would like to continue my successful growth in the field of pharmaceutical sales. You will find that I am a rapid learner with a great deal of excitement and enthusiasm in all my endeavors.

    I believe that I can make a positive contribution to Kline Pharmaceuticals and look forward to discussing my capabilities in more detail. I am available for a personal interview at your earliest convenience, and will call you next week to arrange a convenient time when we might meet to discuss in detail your objectives and challenges.

                  Very truly yours,

                  Sally Sue Smith

Enclosure

Rather than discuss specific accomplishments, this job seeker focuses on core attributes and uses others' opinions to reinforce her statements about herself. Note the aggressive closing—very suitable for someone seeking a sales position.

53

Writer: Don Orlando, MBA, CPRW, JCTC; Montgomery, AL

WILLIAM CROSS, COLONEL, USAF
554 Kinchloe Drive
Burleson Air Force Base, Wisconsin 53000
✆ [414] 555-5555 (Office) – [414] 555-6666 (Home)
cross024@aol.com

February 29, 2001

General Marshall Morgan, USA (ret.)
Chancellor
Gallatin Military Institute
1400 Gallatin Road
Gallatin, Tennessee 37500

Dear General Morgan:

When you look at your organizational chart, where do you find the person responsible for meeting the expectations of your cadets and their families, your instructors and your staff, and admissions officers at leading colleges? Of course, everyone at Gallatin Military Institute contributes to that vital mission. However, I would like to serve as your "expectations multiplier." You call that position Commandant of Cadets. The difference is more than semantic.

For most of my military career, I have been fortunate to pursue my real vocation: molding groups of strangers into capable, confident, educated young people. I love that process because it can only be done by reaching out to individuals. Even today, in my senior position, those people include faculty, staff, students, and even—sometimes—parents.

Today it's fashionable to speak of nearly everyone as a "mentor." And it's politically incorrect to talk about "tough" academic programs. But I have never believed the two were anything but complementary. Instructors at military schools are the best mentors because they hold students to demanding standards—and then provide every means to reach them. It is hugely rewarding to see "unpolished" cadets demonstrate to themselves, and everyone else, that they can guide their education and therefore their lives.

If I could continue molding young minds and bodies into new leaders, I would never leave the Air Force. However, although they have consistently promoted me over some tough competitors, the Air Force must soon send me to positions too far removed from my life's work. That is why I am seeking eagerly to contribute to a private military school. Experience tells me that a good first step might be to explore Gallatin Military Institute's specific needs. May I call in a few days to arrange a time to do that?

Sincerely,

William Cross, Colonel, USAF

Enclosure: Resume

Transitioning from military to civilian life presents unique challenges. This letter expertly relates the candidate's Air Force experience to the needs of the organization and the position for which he is applying.

54

Writer: Christine Magnus, CPRW; Bronx, NY

JEREMY N. BROSNAN

1225 August Road　　　　　　　　　　　　　　　　　Phone: (718) 555-1244
New York, NY 10100　　　　　　　　　　　　　　　　　Prevent00@aol.com

Proficient Loss Prevention Expert
Committed to Helping You
Achieve a Healthier Bottom Line!

Dear Employment Manager:

　　Each year, retailers lose an estimated $26 billion in merchandise to shrinkage, primarily through theft and employee error. This means 1 to 2 percent of total sales are lost, and for larger companies, this loss totals in the millions. Some companies find themselves in this predicament because of an ineffective loss prevention program, or lack of one.

Here's how I can help...

❖ Draw on practical experience to identify and solve loss-related problems.

❖ Develop and implement sound strategies to arrive at effective solutions.

❖ Use effective management techniques to train loss prevention staff.

❖ Collaborate with team members to address current problems and anticipate future challenges.

　　My background includes four years in loss prevention management and a career in law enforcement that spans six years. If you feel your company can benefit from someone with my background and expertise, please feel free to contact me through the telephone number or e-mail address listed above.

　　Thank you for taking the time to review my material. I look forward to hearing from you soon.

Sincerely,

Jeremy N. Brosnan

Don't be fooled by the brevity of this letter! It is hard-hitting and highly effective. The attention-getting headline and strong first paragraph appeal to the employer's most pressing concern (minimizing financial losses), and the bullet points zero in on key qualifications.

55

Writer: Cheryl Ann Harland, CPRW; The Woodlands, TX

Beth Lyons

205 West Shadlowlake Circle ✧ The Woodlands, Texas 77381 ✧ (281) 555-7555

February 21, 2000

Ms. Lucy Fields
Dean of Admissions
Montgomery College
527 University Road
Conroe, Texas 77418

Dear Ms. Fields:

With 20+ years of administrative management experience at the collegiate and university level, I bring to your facility a wealth of knowledge and experience in student admissions, financial aid administration, alumni relations, fund-raising, bookstore operations, and departmental leadership. Over the years, I have consistently delivered strong operating, productivity, cost, and quality gains through workforce reengineering, streamlining operations, and quality/performance-improvement initiatives.

Currently, I am employed by Follett Higher Education Group as their District Manager for Textbook Operations. In less than one year, I have significantly improved the quality and overall performance of each of their six operating facilities.

Although proud of my achievements, I wish to return to an administrative management role within a college or university environment where I can provide hands-on leadership. Thank you for reviewing my qualifications. I look forward to a personal interview at your earliest convenience.

Sincerely,

Beth Lyons

Enclosure

Communicating strong results in administrative/operations positions both in academia and in the private sector, this letter also provides a rationale for the job search.

Writer: Beverly Harvey, CPRW, JCTC, CCM; Pierson, FL

56

JASMINE L. FORESTER

E-mail: jaslforester@gate.net   Home: (561) 596-7458   1518 Rambling Rose Court
Fax: (561) 843-2585   Cellular: (561) 362-7519   Boca Raton, Florida 33486

October 27, 2002

Frederick Longini
Miami Industries, Inc.
27-A Bayside Avenue
Miami, FL 33160

Dear Mr. Longini:

Dr. Albert Thalheimer recommended that I forward my resume to you in the interest of a sales management position with your company.

Building market share and driving revenues is my main area of expertise. Whether challenged to build presence in new markets, lead sales organizations in highly competitive markets, or create strategic marketing programs to deliver rapid growth, I have consistently delivered strong, innovative results. Most notably, my contributions include the following:

- As Pharmaceutical Sales Representative for Pharmacia & Upjohn, I became the top sales performer within 18 months and was promoted to District Manager responsible for eight representatives throughout Southeast Florida.

- As District Manager for Merck & Company, I identified market needs and won support of increased allocations of resources and funding from internal product marketing teams to improve market share in the South Florida area.

- As the top-producing sales representative for Pfizer, I grew the diabetes product line from 33 to 104 percent of quota and increased three cardiovascular lines 150 percent.

- As Sales Representative for the *Orlando Sentinel,* I improved revenues and was promoted to Contract Sales Manager within two months, managing their largest national account.

These achievements reflect the core of my career — create strategic market plans, build new markets, negotiate partnerships and strategic alliances, and drive long-term revenue and profit growth. Just as notable are my strengths in organizational development, team building, and leadership.

Although secure in my current position, I am interested in a more challenging opportunity. I would welcome the opportunity to discuss the contributions I can make to your organization.

Thank you for your consideration.

Sincerely,

Jasmine L. Forester

Enclosure

Note how this letter follows the "first rule of referral letter writing"—the name of the referring party is mentioned in the very first sentence. Additionally, the candidate reinforces the referral with strong results that are relevant to the sales position she's seeking.

57

Writer: Meg Montford, CCM; Kansas City, MO

Ellen E. Palmer

10620 E. 98th Terrace, Apartment 12, Kansas City, MO 64134 (816) 555-9999

March 16, 2001

Mr. U. Zeke
Principal
Alternative Education Center
1000 Harrison
Kansas City, MO 64108

Dear Mr. Zeke:

Although successful in my current position at Franklin High School, the opportunity to contribute to the education of students at an alternative school excites me. My rewards of teaching occur when the light comes on in a student's eyes as he grasps the math concepts I am presenting. Since small groups and individual tutoring situations provide me the most effective teaching arenas, the mathematics instructor position at your institution would offer the perfect medium for my teaching talents.

Traveling and living in other parts of the world has been my good fortune, allowing me to study and interact with other cultures. I would like to share these life experiences with your students. Art history has always been a passion of mine. I have toured the National Archaeological Museum in Athens, Greece, as well as the Rijksmuseum and Van Gogh Museum in Amsterdam, The Netherlands. Additionally, I have traveled throughout the United States, visiting museums from coast to coast. With my life experiences, plus the knowledge derived from elective coursework in college, I can develop for your students a cultural course of study. Included in the course would be art history and trips to Kansas City–area museums, plus access to other art-related resources within our community. This could satisfy the culture credit the alternative students need for graduation.

Will you be available next Monday for me to call to discuss my qualifications further? If you wish to contact me sooner, please call me at home any evening at 816-555-9999.

Thank you for your consideration.

Sincerely,

Ellen E. Palmer

Some professions are more "quantifiable" than others; for some, less-tangible qualities are extremely important. Teaching is a good example. In this letter, the job seeker communicates what she would bring to the position—not in terms of results, but in terms of life experiences and teaching philosophy.

58

Writer: Kristie Cook, CPRW, JCTC; Olathe, KS

SHANE J. BAKER
6741 E. Summit
Pittstown, NJ 08867
908-555-0098

GROWTH-DRIVEN DIRECTOR WILL TAKE YOUR DEALERSHIP TO THE NEXT LEVEL

Your search for a top-flight director is over if you seek someone who can ignite sales, increase OSI/CSI objectives and commit to your dealership's success. I present to you my resume for your consideration for a position on your management team.

I bring to you and your team:

- Over 15 years of award-winning experience in automotive management
- Dynamic career of consistently increasing sales and improving customer service and quality
- Energy, enthusiasm, perseverance, and motivation
- Proven record in sales, leadership, and management that shines with superior achievements

My key strength is initiating and implementing changes to turn departments into profit machines. This process starts with building rapport with my employees and colleagues at the onset, motivating others to exceed expectations and delivering the extra effort necessary to achieve the goals of the department and dealership. I have been commended many times for outstanding performance as both a team player and individual contributor. The awards mentioned on my resume provide evidence of my dedication to success.

I am confident that I can make similar contributions to your dealership. My goals are to help you meet your overall objectives in any way I can. I am determined, motivated, and excited to make a difference at your store.

I am willing to relocate for the right opportunity—one that provides a challenge, a way for me to make an ongoing, positive impact and the potential to grow with the dealership. I would appreciate the chance to talk with you to further discuss your needs and goals. Please call me at (908) 555-8533 to schedule a meeting at your convenience.

I look forward to meeting with you in the near future. Thank you for your time and consideration.

Respectfully,

Shane J. Baker

The headline is used very effectively in this cold-call letter written for a specific niche industry. Numerous relevant accomplishments in the body of the letter support the "brag" in the headline.

59

Writer: Mark Berkowitz, NCCC, CPRW, JCTC; Yorktown Heights, NY

Nicole Savarino

P.O. Box 626

Katonah, NY 10536

(914) 767-5555

To teach is to touch a life forever!

June 17, 2002

Ms. Helene Kane, Principal
Furnace Woods Elementary School
25 Schoolhouse Road
Chappaqua, NY 10514

Dear Ms. Kane:

I am contacting you at the suggestion of Tony Savastano, a guidance counselor at Blue Mountain Middle School, who felt that my background and experience would be an excellent match for the Kindergarten teaching vacancy at your school. I am well aware that in today's job market you will find teachers with more years of experience than I have had, though **you won't find anyone willing to work harder.** My record is one of solid accomplishments in my teaching assignments.

Review of the accompanying resume will show how well my qualifications match those of the position. Among my qualifications are

- ➾ *Enthusiastic, high-energy educator* with proven tack record in fostering academic learning and enhancing student creativity. I believe in making learning as much fun as possible.
- ➾ *Recognized* by both *parents* and *administrators alike* for *classroom effectiveness.*
- ➾ *Proven expertise* in taking academic subject matter and *"making it come alive"* for the student through well-planned, hands-on activities that foster development of creative and critical-thinking skills.
- ➾ *Acknowledged for raising the bar* in elevating students' standards and *igniting* their *curiosity.*
- ➾ *Demonstrated ability* to *consistently individualize instruction,* based on students' interests and needs, at the most appropriate level.

I am confident that this background provides the skills you require for this position. I look forward to the opportunity to discuss in greater detail how my experience would benefit Furnace Woods Elementary School. In the interim, thank you for your consideration, attention, and forthcoming response.

Very truly yours,

Nicole Savarino

Enclosure: Resume

Clever graphic elements are attractive and appropriate for this teacher's cover letter. Note how the referring person's name is "dropped" right away to make sure this letter is not passed over.

60

Writer: Arthur I. Frank; Palm Harbor, FL

ROY H. HAMILTON
1513 Lakes Trail, Indianapolis, IN 51234   (931) 555-2254   (515) 221-8907   E-mail: hamil@aol.com

August 15, 2001

Gloria Baker
VP Sales and Marketing
Regal Worldwide Traders
2575 Carmel Boulevard
Indianapolis, IN 46240

Dear Ms. Baker:

After contributing to the rapid growth and success of several fast-track organizations for 14 years, I am seeking new challenges with an enterprising group in need of someone with exceptional planning, leadership, and Sales and Marketing Management qualities. **Taking command of a sales force... then training, motivating, and driving it to become an industry leader, is my greatest strength.**

As evidenced in the enclosed resume, my experience encompasses all aspects of corporate business development including strategic planning, systems integration, internal management consulting, resource utilization, and human resource management. My ability to analyze needs and develop unique programs designed to yield a profitable outcome has proven to be one of my greatest assets.

Credited with significantly impacting bottom-line profitability wherever I have worked, I excel at streamlining less-than-efficient or stagnant sales operations. My record of achievements is exemplary, as I have successfully directed and managed a wide variety of assignments while meeting or exceeding projections. **Proactive management enabled me to boost revenues from $2 million in annual sales to $54 million within five years,** while serving as the top sales and marketing executive at Crown Marketing Group.

Characterized by others as visionary and decisive, I possess keen instincts and intelligence, am results-driven and have an aptitude for solving business problems. The essence of what I have done for others and what I can do for you as well is best summed up by a thread running through all of my performance evaluations, namely that *"Roy's attitude and aggressive style motivates his fellow workers. He has the desire and drive to be the best at whatever he does."*

Weighing the combination of these factors, I am certain I can be a high-impact player in most any area of sales management, marketing, and administration.

I know that resumes help you sort out the probables from the possibles; however, I would like to meet with you and demonstrate that along with my credentials, I have the personality and horsepower suitable for your organization. Be assured your investment of time will be amply repaid.

Sincerely,

Roy H. Hamilton

Enclosure

P.S.: I would be delighted to share with you a few of the techniques I've applied to boost sales and improve closing ratios irrespective of economic conditions, if you feel your current selling staff needs a shot in the arm.

For sales professionals, measurable results are the most important thing to communicate in both the resume and cover letter. In this letter, boldfacing and underlining make the results stand out. The "P.S." is a highly effective attention-getter; the P.S. is the first *and* last thing perused by most readers.

61

Writers: Jane Roqueplot and Chris Palmer; Sharon, PA

Steven A. Daniels
254 State Line Road
Martin's Corners, MD 16133

(724) 555-7223
msg. (724) 555-1441

May 15, 2001

District Church of Zion
District Office
Attn: Reverend Howard S. Templeton, *District Superintendent*
884 Northern Pike
Zelienople, PA 16001-8326

Dear Reverend Templeton:

The prospect of working as the Director of the **District Church of Zion Camp** would be the fulfillment of a major goal and vision since my rebirth in Christ. I am submitting my resume as a statement of my intense interest in achieving this objective.

My past relationship with the camp has been positive and rewarding, and I trust that my energy and enthusiasm for the camp's operation can contribute to the continued success and expansion of the facility. Since a need has been expressed for a proactive director, I am confident I can answer that call and apply my considerable skill and spirit to the future success of the operation, ensuring that this valuable resource will be available for the benefit of future generations. I envision groups of all ages using the camp as a setting for meetings and events founded in and perpetuating Christian doctrine.

My professional experience and skill as a business owner and contractor will allow me to address every physical need of the camp. My administrative experience will allow me to plan and oversee its smooth daily, weekly, monthly, and yearly budgeting and operation. My unfaltering faith will allow me to recognize, protect, and further the most important interest involved—the spiritual.

A personal meeting is an excellent opportunity for us to have a detailed discussion about the benefits I can bring to the camp as Director. I will be happy to provide you further documentation of my background at that time. Please contact me at your earliest convenience to schedule a time and place to meet.

Respectfully,

Steven A. Daniels

Enclosure

Personal qualities can be strong selling points. In this letter to a Christian camp, the writer's faith is relevant and important to highlight…but note that he goes further by including important accomplishments and experience that qualify him for the position.

62

Writer: Loretta Heck; Prospect Heights, IL

ROBERT P. BIRNARD
402 East Maude Avenue
Arlington Heights, Illinois 60004
(847) 555-7035

June 23, 2002

Schneider Lock Company
Human Resources Department
1915 Jamie Drive, Suite 165
Colorado Springs, CO 80920

Dear Sir or Madam:

Creating successful sales programs is more of a challenge than ever before. With the advent of multiple electronic technologies, in tandem with the already existing marketing channels, a Sales Manager is faced with unlimited options for business development. My success lies in my ability to evaluate each of these channels, determine the most appropriate mix of sales and marketing tools, and create the campaigns that deliver results.

Throughout my professional career, I have facilitated the strategic planning, development, and implementation of marketing programs designed to accelerate base business while launching the introduction of numerous new products, services, and technologies. My ability to build and lead cross-functional teams of creative design, marketing, and management personnel has been critical to my performance.

I am knowledgeable and comfortable selling and managing in various industries. It is with pride that I possess a selling management style that has given me a unique viewpoint for developing innovative selling presentations for tough, demanding customers. This along with excellent listening and communication skills has earned me the reputation for creating a profitable bottom-line situation for both parties.

At this point in my career, I am seeking new professional challenges where I can continue to provide strategic, tactical, and creative sales leadership. As such, my interest is meeting with you to explore opportunities with Schneider Lock Company.

Thank you for your consideration.

Sincerely yours,

Robert P. Birnard

enclosure: resume

The first paragraph of this letter establishes rapport by identifying common concerns and then describing solutions.

63

Writer: Karen Wrigley, CPRW, JCTC; Round Rock, TX

JENNIFER P. KNIGHT

6119 West 91st Street, #60 • Overland Park, Kansas 66210
Home: (913) 555-6126 • Mobile: (816) 555-8432

September 30, 2001

HR – SEM
KC Star
9172 Grand Blvd.
Kansas City, MO 64108

Dear HR Authority:

In response to your ad for a **Special Events Manager** in the January 27th edition of the *Kansas City Star*, I have enclosed my confidential resume for your review and consideration. The position described sounds like just the kind of new challenge and opportunity I am seeking. As my resume will indicate, my experience uniquely qualifies me for this position!

You require:	*My experience:*
Revenue and expense goal accountability	**Presently leading organization to be first in company history to hit forecasted sales of $50 million while operating within budgeted expenses!**
Vendor, sponsorship, exhibitor sales relations	**Successfully manage contract negotiations and independent contractor relations, including monitoring service performance.**
Track record of revenue-producing special events	**Conceptualized, planned, and implemented revenue-producing and PR promotions, including a basketball game event that resulted in a daily sales increase of 20 percent.**
Three years sales and staff management/leadership	**Over 12 years managing sales staffs. Appointed Resource Manager to lead very diverse groups of individuals into productive team members and environments.**
Detail-oriented	**Selected to oversee all aspects of detail-oriented assignment — Physical Inventory for all Kansas stores.**
Able to meet deadlines with limited resources	**Decreased payroll deficit by $7,000 during busiest retail season while maintaining excellent customer servicing.**
Able to work weekend hours throughout the year	**Twelve years working weekend and "retail hours"!**

As my resume is only a brief overview of my qualifications, I would appreciate the opportunity to meet with you personally so that we may further discuss how I can meet the particular needs of *KC Star*. I will contact you this week to verify your receipt of this information and to arrange for an interview.

Your consideration is greatly appreciated!

Sincerely,

Jennifer P. Knight

Enclosure: resume

The attractive formatting of this comparison list makes it easy to skim yet provides substantive information to "sell" the candidate.

Writer: Jean West, CPRW, JCTC; Indian Rocks Beach, FL

64

SUSAN JONES
819 Beach Boulevard
Daytona Beach, Florida 32153
727-555-2534

October 4, 2001

Victor Prince
President
Prince Media Works
73 Seminole Drive
Daytona Beach, FL 32150

Dear Mr. Prince:

As an experienced manager in several facets of the communications industry, I have the reputation for tackling and completing any project with enthusiasm to achieve corporate goals.

As a highly motivated person with tremendous energy, my goal is to find a position with broader responsibilities where I can put my experience and knowledge to work to benefit a company's bottom line. Please note that I am willing and able to travel outside of the U.S. and am fluent in Spanish.

Having the background, experience, and ability to make a strong contribution in a management position with your company, I would welcome the opportunity to talk with you.

Sincerely,

Susan Jones

Enclosure: Résumé

What People Say . . .

◎ *"Today (we) are **growing beyond expectations based on suggestions by Susan**. She has brought a wealth of knowledge in marketing these services.*
*"She handled **high-level executives with professionalism and integrity** and **received many compliments** from other Directors and Vice Presidents associated within the organization **on her suggestions and marketing strategies**."*

James Weston
New Frontiers Technology

◎ *"**Her creativity** in introducing new techniques **and her ability to coach her team to peak performance has been a motivation to her fellow managers** . . .*
*"Susan has the potential and background to handle a number of management jobs within the organization. **She should especially be considered for openings requiring organization and motivational skills**."*

Frederick Smith, Director
Cellular Communication

◎ *"**Her hard work, dedication, and leadership skills were invaluable. She is one of the key reasons that the office was so successful**."*

Roger West
Manager, Bell Telephone

Notice how effectively these quotes sell this candidate! This letter is well designed, making it easy to read both the letter and the testimonials.

A Magic Example

65

Writer: *Susan Britton Whitcomb, NCRW, CPRW; Fresno, CA*

TERRI HOLLINGSWORTH

555 North Peach
Dallas, TX 75555

terrih@earthlink.net

Business: (555) 555-5555
Cellular: (555) 544-4444

December 12, 2001

Ms. Jennifer Carter, CEO
Dami, Vasquez & Lindstrom
555 Sunnyside
Dallas, TX 75555

Re: Your Need of a Financial Manager

Dear Ms. Carter:

Numbers drive business decisions — without solid data, planning is ineffective and progress is immeasurable.

Throughout my career in finance, I have implemented systems that captured meaningful data and enhanced decision-making processes. I am equally skilled at general management functions and offer a solid understanding of the business cycle, from marketing and sales through production and distribution. Minimal employee turnover and high productivity evidence my ability to communicate, motivate, and build teams.

Currently, I serve as the senior financial officer for a Dallas-based manufacturing and distribution firm. At the time I joined the company, it was experiencing a number of financial and internal challenges. One of my first initiatives was to create financial performance-monitoring models for virtually every area of the company. This included the development of formalized budgeting and planning processes, credit and collections policies, and monthly variance reports. I also negotiated favorable loan agreements and monitored loan activity against budgeted projections. The combination of these efforts supported significant financial improvements:

> ➤ a threefold increase in operating funds
> ➤ a 60 percent increase in annual revenues
> ➤ a 36 percent increase in collection of outstanding receivables (from 62 to 98 percent)
> ➤ a 30–40 percent increase in individual customer revenues with the introduction of
>   new customer financing programs

I look forward to delivering similar results for your organization. May we talk at your earliest convenience?

Sincerely,

Terri Hollingsworth

Enclosure

This letter is an effective combination of a strong opening paragraph, "meaty" paragraphs describing relevant experience, and brief, hard-hitting bullet points.

Winning Cover Letters for Senior Managers and Executives

The Top Five Cover Letter–Writing Tips for Senior Managers and Executives

1. Be sure your letters are sophisticated in their language and presentation.

2. Highlight your major achievements that impacted the entire company or organization.

3. Use dollars, numbers, and percentages to drive home the value of your contributions.

4. Since your ability to achieve organizational goals depends greatly on other people within the organization, be sure to communicate strong leadership skills.

5. Mention any experience you have that relates to key issues and challenges the company is currently facing—such as rapid growth, recovery from Chapter 11, acquisition integration, e-commerce launch, and other significant organizational challenges.

66

Writer: Laurie Smith, CPRW; Alexandria, VA

Benjamin R. David

230 OAKWOOD CIRCLE
SAVANNAH, GA 45452
(912) 323-4940

February 21, 2001

Mr. James Baker
President
International Telesales, Inc.
460 Concord Parkway
Philadelphia, PA 11663

Dear Mr. Baker:

In today's intensely competitive consumer marketplace, the ultimate success of any telemarketing operation requires management that can

- organize a call center or fleet of call centers to draw maximum quality and production from available staff, resources, and databases;

- instill self-confidence and motivation in managers, supervisors, and sales and customer service staff, and train them for maximum achievement in sales and customer satisfaction;

- clarify and strengthen the organization's core values and principles to facilitate dynamic business growth and profitability enhancement, while keeping the people side of the business strong; and

- take advantage of the latest call center and Internet technologies to make customer communication quick, low-cost, rewarding for all parties, and seamless.

I believe my track record as outlined in the enclosed resume demonstrates that I can ensure all of the above for your organization. In my current position as Vice President of Operations for an industry-leading telecommunications firm, I have led my team to deliver a 40-fold increase in a key business segment, and more than tripled operating margins through a variety of quality, performance, employee incentive, and process reengineering efforts.

During my tenure as Call Center Director for a showcase telemarketing operation, my team produced over $25 million in profits on $55 million in revenues over 10 years (nearly a 50 percent profit margin), smoothly transitioned operations from manual to fully automated with no decrease in production, and launched a "package savings" program that increased profit per order by 300 percent. Immensely successful programs in the areas of employee training, dispute resolution, strategic marketing, and organizational transition/ restructuring were adopted as models company-wide. I have been called upon on numerous occasions to consult internally as well as with telemarketing organizations of major telecommunications and financial industry corporations.

I attribute my consistent success in large part to the ability to build and maintain a principle-centered environment that preserves the company's core values while stimulating growth and progress. Equally important is a strong focus on ensuring positive customer contacts at all levels, both internally and externally. You will find that I am very skilled at developing sound action plans, as well as in oversight of and follow-through on those plans.

I will welcome the opportunity to explore my potential contributions to your telemarketing operation's quality, revenues, and bottom line. Thank you for your consideration of my qualifications; I look forward to discussing the possibilities.

Sincerely,

Benjamin R. David

After starting with a list of bullet points that capture the reader's attention, this letter goes on to summarize career achievements that are directly related to those points—and to the bottom line of the organization.

67

Writer: Cynthia Kraft, CPRW, JCTC, CCM; Valrico, FL

EDGAR ALFONSO
813-555-7245
entrepreneur@usa.net

3455 Oceanside Drive, Palm Harbor, FL 34685

February 12, 2001

Stacy Smith, Human Resources Manager
Barney's Gourmet Coffee
3184 Coffee Lane
Denver, CO 80001

Dear Ms. Smith:

The wise Will Rogers said, "Even if you're on the right track, you'll get run over if you just sit there." Barney's has done an outstanding job of implementing change, innovation and creativity to become a leader in the 21st century.

My career experience has been as a "change agent," implementing forward-thinking ideas, concepts, and programs that motivate highly successful teams, generate strong and sustainable profitability, and ensure customer loyalty. My past experience includes ...

♦ Providing proactive leadership, with the understanding that when my team is successful we are all successful, allowing me to be effective in spearheading innovative projects and programs which established long-term profitability. Eckerd's first-time entry into the Denver market **generated 110 percent more profitability** than new stores in existing markets.

♦ Implementing quality customer service programs that foster long-term customer loyalty. By conducting research and analyzing market data, **we gathered extensive information on the nature of our shopper and what she expected and responded to in the market place, and then created an environment to enhance her shopping experience.**

♦ Analyzing market trends and identifying opportunities that provide long-term profitability. I was able to **position the North Florida region as the ONLY region in the company to exceed its bottom-line profit projections.**

Barney's is well positioned for growth. Managing growth requires expertise in driving change, building highly motivated teams, improving performance, and directing operational efficiency. May I offer my expertise?

Sincerely,

Edgar Alfonso

Enclosure

This letter gets off to a strong start with an effective quote and a tie-in to the company. The bullet points, with bold print highlighting strong numbers, support this candidate's ability to deliver results in several important areas.

68

Writer: JoAnn Nix, CPRW; Beaumont, TX

CAROLYN BROWN

62 Rosewood Lane
Houston, TX 77702

Residence: (713) 555-3891
E-Mail: cbrown2@hotmail.com

Dear Selection Committee:

As a **Senior Portfolio Manager** with 11 years of experience in the financial service industry, one of my primary goals has been to follow the advice of Henry Kissinger: *"The task of a leader is to get his people from where they are to where they have not been."* As you will soon learn, one of my greatest strengths is mentoring and guiding my colleagues so they may reach great professional heights. I truly believe in empowering my peers...competent professionals deliver results and enhance a corporation's image.

I joined American Capital Corporation in 1990, advanced to Senior Portfolio Manager in 1992, and have been a valuable resource and critical link between clients, management, and interdepartmental team members. Currently I spearhead an $18 million portfolio comprising 16 complex accounts and manage a staff of seven professionals. My 10-year career has afforded me an opportunity to gain a wealth of finance/accounting knowledge.

In short, I am a leader both by example and through effective management of individuals, and provide financial leadership and guidance to my clients. It is essential that I develop very close relationships with each client to know the intimate details of their financial status to help steer the companies toward financial independence.

I have reached a juncture in my career where I am highly interested in moving up the management ladder and feel it is time to examine other career opportunities. I am most interested in a position that offers additional opportunities for advancement, a chance to continue to mentor and guide my peers, and the ability to use my rich mix of skills. I am an extremely strong manager who is vision-driven, intelligent, aggressive, intuitive, and extremely tenacious! I am considered "as sharp as a tack" by those who know me, and I know as a manager I can add tremendous value to an organization.

If you believe that my qualifications and experience would greatly contribute to your organizational goals, I would welcome the opportunity to introduce myself and my credentials to you in a personal interview. I will take the liberty of contacting your office next week to arrange a meeting. I look forward to meeting or speaking with you soon.

Sincerely,

Carolyn Brown

Enclosure: Resume

Starting with a personal philosophy of management, this letter gives compelling evidence of leadership skills. The language is "executive level" from start to finish.

69

Writer: Linsey Levine, MS, JCTC; Chappaqua, NY

Robert Brown
111 Riverside Drive #12B
New York, NY 10025
Home: 212-555-8943   E-mail: robbro@msn.net

April 5, 2001

Ms. Alice O'Riley
President, The Riverside Foundation
2573 Central Park West, Suite 8-B
New York, NY 10021

Dear Alice:

I enjoyed speaking with you on the phone, and pursuant to that conversation, I have enclosed my resume.

I'm looking for a unique executive opportunity where I can provide critical management functions—vision, leadership, strategic planning, finance, marketing, administration, legal insight, operations control—to enable an organization to accomplish its goals.

My career in the corporate and not-for-profit arenas has been accelerated based on my ability to deliver results despite financial, market, and organizational challenges. The blend of my business, legal and financial skills, and the ability to translate vision into meaningful action, has proved successful in the following areas:

- managing businesses and organizations to turn around performance and achieve full potential
- developing and implementing long-range plans, including marketing, product, operations, financial, and acquisition/divestiture strategies
- analyzing and controlling all aspects of operations to reduce costs and improve profits
- organizing, reorganizing, training, and motivating to improve individual and group effectiveness
- negotiating favorable partnerships, strategic alliances, and joint ventures

At this time, I am interested in exploring new executive challenges and opportunities where I can continue to provide decisive and effective operating leadership. I would appreciate the chance to meet and discuss your ideas and thoughts at your earliest convenience.

I certainly appreciate your time and consideration and will phone next week to speak with you further.

Best regards,

Robert Brown

This is an excellent example of an effective networking letter. To give the reader a sense of how she might be helpful in his search, the candidate provides an overview of his capabilities and current goals. Note how he keeps control of the follow-up.

70

Writer: Nina Ebert, CPRW; Toms River, NJ

VICTOR JOSEPHS

| 70 Ellen Drive | Marlboro, New Jersey 07746 | (555) 758-0448 |

January 12, 2001

Box VJ234, Wall Street Journal
545 E. John Carpenter Freeway #400
Irving, TX 75062

Dear Prospective Employer:

Either I am a talented salesperson and smart sales manager, or I have been very lucky throughout my 23+ year career. Personally, I doubt that luck has much to do with anyone's success.

Inherent management and communications skills are my strengths. I have extensive experience in the areas of profit and loss responsibilities, staff hiring, training and development, marketing and account development, and sound decision making. Smart business planning and straightforward management practices have propelled my career.

I hire the right people for the right job, implement a strong business plan, make my expectations very clear, provide excellent training, and track the numbers. I do not micro manage. I build strong teams. (I terminated only two employees throughout my career and remain in touch with all of the others.) I travel to meet my customers in person and am recognized by them for initiating innovative solutions to challenging problems.

Since my resume provides an overview of my background, I look forward to the opportunity to meet with you in person to provide you with further insight into my professional value. Until we meet, thank you for your consideration.

Yours truly,

Victor Josephs

Enclosure

This is a rather unusual letter for a sales management professional in that it sells with words, not with numbers. The strong opening will be helpful in catching the attention of readers who will probably be inundated with resumes in response to their *Wall Street Journal* advertisement.

71

Writer: Kathryn Bourne, CPRW, JCTC; Tucson, AZ

JOSÉ L. GONZALES

4412 East Springfield Road, Havasu, AZ 84132
Res: (520) 555-7323   Fax: (520) 555-7324
E-mail: lane45@sprynet.com

January 31, 2001

Mr. James P. Purdy, Vice President
Lifton, Inc.
310 Center Parkway Drive
San Diego, CA 95612

Dear Mr. Purdy:

We have read the articles, we have seen the news items on television—the growing Hispanic business and consumer markets are the new frontiers. Is your company poised to enter this dynamic environment? Are you eager to move ahead but not quite sure where to begin? Then we should to talk. I can get you where you need and want to be!

Developing and increasing international and national market value is my expertise. Whether the challenge originated with a start-up business venture or with an established company, my successful career in marketing management has led companies to profitability and growth. With an established presence in Mexican markets and the knowledge of the Latin American area as a whole, I can be the catalyst for your next major expansion.

As you will see in the enclosed resume, I have consistently designed and implemented strategies, plans, and actions that have delivered strong and sustainable revenues and profit growth. My strengths include

- Proven leadership skills—evidenced by smooth internal reorganizations and transitions.
- Proficiency and success in multi-cultural business environments—I am bicultural/bilingual in Spanish and English and highly adept in cross-cultural communications.
- Astute analysis and understanding of market surveys—to assure growth of both revenue and profit.

My goal is to secure a senior management position with an organization in need of strong and decisive leadership to open new markets. I would welcome the opportunity to discuss the needs of Lifton, Inc., and explore how I can significantly benefit the organization. I will contact you next week to arrange a meeting at a mutually convenient time.

Sincerely,

José L. Gonzales

Enclosure

Appealing to a specific market niche (Latin America), this letter opens strongly and then goes on to sell this candidate based on his capabilities and results.

72

Writer: Lorie Lebert, CPRW, JCTC; Novi, MI

BRIAN C. COOPERSMITH, CPM

Senior Real Estate Marketing & Management Executive

1061 QUAILS RIDGE DRIVE
WEST BLOOMFIELD, MICHIGAN 48322
E-Mail: bccoopersmith@aol.com
Residence: 248.555.6101
Fax: 248.555.1601

September 25, 2001

David Winston
President
Wolverine Properties Ltd.
252 Creek Road
Bloomfield, MI 48320

Dear Mr. Winston:

In the 1970s, a group of like-minded visionaries and I had an idea for a new business venture. That idea transformed into a multimillion-dollar conglomerate with operations in five states and more than 120 properties in a variety of interests. With more than two decades of strong and profitable property management expertise, I bring experience and wisdom that come from extensive general administration.

Implementing hands-on strategies and providing personal contact, I believe, are key to building successful business relationships. I am effective at establishing and maintaining business alliances, as well as developing strategic programs that increase revenue and add value.

Throughout my career, I have experienced full responsibility and leadership of entire corporate real estate, property management, and financial functions. The scope of responsibilities has been diverse and included financial and strategic planning, property analysis, corporate management, and internal administration. Concurrent executive management responsibility involved corporate expansion and sales management.

Currently, I am exploring opportunities that would benefit a company's success and serve as a source of new possibilities. I believe my expertise would be of value to a company looking for effective leadership and direction. The enclosed resume summarizes my achievements, experience, and other information you will find helpful in understanding my background.

If you are seeking leadership from someone with my qualifications, experience, and track record, I would welcome a personal interview. I appreciate you taking time to review my credentials.

Sincerely,

Brian C. Coopersmith, CPM

Enclosure

Telling the story of his early success is an original and effective opening for this letter. Leadership skills are emphasized throughout.

Writer: Susan Guarneri, NCCC, CPRW, CCM, JCTC; Lawrenceville, NJ

73

Thomas A. Kensington
17 Sarah Court, Pennington, NJ 08534
609-555-1834 • Tomaken@home.com

January 28, 2001

Dear Hiring Manager:

Your recent job posting for a **Regional Director of Sales** caught my eye. With 20 years of experience in sales and sales management (technical products), as well as MBA-equivalent coursework with AT&T and a Bachelor's degree, I feel I am uniquely qualified for this position.

My resume is enclosed for your review. I would like to call attention to the similarities between your requirements and my qualifications.

YOUR REQUIREMENTS	MY QUALIFICATIONS
☑ *Experience in managing sales force and technical sales*	☑ 20 years experience in sales and sales management, 8 as a Regional Sales Manager for Fortune 200 accounts in the highly competitive telecommunications industry.
☑ *College degree*	☑ Master of Business Administration (equivalent coursework), AT&T; Bachelor of Science, Rider College.
☑ *Track record of achieving goals*	☑ Proven record of meeting and/or exceeding sales and new business development goals (see resume).
☑ *Excellent communications skills*	☑ Demonstrated versatility communicating with a wide range of individuals, such as senior-level manager, business clients, professional staff, and vendors.

I am confident that I can make an immediate impact on your bottom line. I would appreciate an opportunity to describe my potential contributions in more detail and look forward to a personal interview. Thank you for your consideration.

Sincerely,

Thomas A. Kensington

Enclosure: Resume

Using a straightforward comparison-list style, this letter clearly demonstrates that the candidate has everything the company is looking for.

74

Writer: Beverly Harvey, CPRW, JCTC, CCM; Pierson, FL

RAYMOND PHRAMPUS

560 Mourning Dove Circle
Lake Mary, Florida 32746
Cell: (407) 620-9533
E-mail: tronv@aol.com

Home: (407) 322-9543
Office: (407) 322-9587

July 17, 2001

Gordon Smith
CEO
Consolidated Corporation
75 Biscayne Bay Boulevard
Miami, FL 33162

Dear Mr. Smith:

I am a successful entrepreneur who has developed, marketed, and built four new ventures, plus numerous joint ventures, strategic alliances and partnerships within the consumer products industry. Combined revenues have exceeded $525 million annually, with my most recent project forecasted to generate $275K in its first-year sales. I have met the challenges of startup, turnarounds, and high-growth expansions while delivering strong revenue and profit growth.

The wealth of experience I bring to a venture is vast, with particular emphasis on the identification and development of new business opportunities, strategic and tactical planning, new product development and launch, marketing, sales force development, distribution channel development, and the maximization of sales potential domestically and internationally. Just as significant are my strengths in general, operations, manufacturing, and administrative management. My leadership style is decisive, yet flexible in responding to the constantly changing market, economic and business demands.

Based on my achievements, I have been featured in industry-leading publications as well as the local newspaper. Articles cited my innovativeness; industry leadership; and expertise in market growth and penetration, business management, and profitability.

At this juncture in my career, I am seeking the opportunity to transition my qualifications into a high-growth corporation in need of strong executive leadership. Therefore, I have enclosed a brief summary of my career. I would welcome the opportunity to meet with you to determine the contributions I could make to one of your portfolio companies. Thank you.

Sincerely,

Raymond Phrampus

Enclosure

Businesslike and to the point, this letter respects the time constraints of the CEO and immediately gives him information he can use. The candidate's career accomplishments are notable, so he uses them as primary attention-getters and selling points.

75

Writer: Arthur I. Frank; Palm Harbor, FL

Marshall B. Ingram

1742 Warwick Drive   (321) 555-2202
Bar Harbor, Maine   ingra@aol.com

May 17, 2001

Elizabeth Troutman
Northeast Executive Recruiters
215 State Street
Boston, MA 02120

Dear Ms. Troutman:

Throughout my 20 years of professional employment, I have always been recognized as someone who could get the job done. As a Marine Officer, law firm associate, and junior partner, I was often given responsibilities ahead of my peers and those senior to me. I was recognized as a trustworthy, loyal, and energetic team leader.

Over the past 12 years I have achieved exceptional success as **CEO, MANAGING PARTNER,** and **COO** of several transactional and management consulting practices. I played an integral role in the acquisition, overhaul, and substantial growth of numerous organizations including near-failed banks and other ineffectual business entities. I can be characterized as a focused and disciplined business builder, with powerful negotiating skills and strong listening abilities. Contracts that I have written and proprietary deals that I have negotiated have demonstrated insight and vision, and have been replicated by others. In each consecutive assignment my rapport and credibility throughout an organization have been instrumental in breaking impasses that were inhibiting growth.

As a change catalyst or business builder, I initiated transformations requiring comprehensive re-structuring that included top-to-bottom operations redesign and the repositioning of an entire workforce. The success achieved was in large part due to my ability to persuade others to see the value of change. I have demonstrated that even a large and cumbersome organization can be transformed if the changes are correctly presented to employees.

Other abilities I can bring to any job:
- ❑ Improved administrative function linked to expense control.
- ❑ Advanced skills in relationship-building.
- ❑ Improved communications with boards and constituencies of both a "hard" nature (financial data/strategic planning), and a "soft" nature (access, accountability, and public relations).
- ❑ Using my law and mediation background on a daily basis to solve the competing demands that are inherent in this field. This includes deft "ego-management" skills.
- ❑ An innate talent to be effective without alienating the affected constituencies.
- ❑ A contemporary management style enabling me to work with a wide cross-section of people and cultural diversity.
- ❑ Numerous key contacts with lobbyists, politicians, bankers, and attorneys.
- ❑ Character qualities that engender loyalty and integrity in the workplace.

If you know anyone seeking a market-driven operating executive with a proven track record who can make an immediate and enduring contribution, your timely introduction could be beneficial to all concerned. Please take a moment to review the enclosed resume.

I thank you for your consideration and look forward to speaking with you soon.

Sincerely,

Marshall B. Ingram

Enclosure

In this letter to a recruiter, the candidate provides much detail about his background and career. The bullet-point list of potential contributions will strike a chord with many of the recruiter's clients.

76

Writer: Ross Macpherson, MA, JCTC; Pickering, Ontario

Robert A. Bertram

100 Pebble Drive
Banff, Alberta A5B 6D7
Home: (403) 555-7600
Cell: (403) 555-2222

February 7, 2001

Brian Talbot
Executive Vice-President
eGrocers.com Ltd.
2200 Brock Street, Suite 2000
Toronto, Ontario
M1N 2N1

Brian,

After all of our voicemail exchanges, it was a pleasure to have finally spoken with you in regards to joining your team as CFO. As promised, I am providing a "scribbled account" of my experience and qualifications in the accompanying resume; I think you will agree they are an excellent match to your specific current and future needs.

As you may have gathered, I am a results-driven financial and operational executive with a strong entrepreneurial spirit. My particular strengths lie in my ability to create solid and cost-effective foundations, focus on both macro and micro issues, apply innovative thinking, and remain adaptive not only to spot opportunities but also to capitalize on them.

I had an opportunity to sample your grocery service this weekend, and also to review Ted's message on the Internet, and I feel we have a strong connection of values, specifically with regard to your focus on family and customer service. Additionally, the type of innovative and fast-paced Internet/Service company you describe is precisely the environment in which I will excel.

I will be in touch within the next 24 hours to follow up and discuss matters further. I am looking forward to receiving my groceries "between 7 and 10 pm—<u>guaranteed.</u>"

Sincerely,

Robert A. Bertram

Enclosure

Having already networked with an Internet start-up about its CFO position, this candidate specifically did not want to seem to be "applying for the job"—he saw this as a business transaction, not an application process. The casual and personal tone of the letter lets his personality come across.

Writer: Vivian Van Lier, CPRW, JCTC; Valley Glen, CA

77

KEVIN JONES

1234 Pacific Shores Place
Malibu, CA 95555

Home (310) 555-6655
Mobile (310) 555-6620

October 27, 2000

Sabine Muller
CEO
Pacific Traders, Inc.
2723 Ocean Parkway
Malibu, CA 95553

Dear Ms. Muller:

In today's global economy, balancing the technical intricacies of international trade with the complex subtleties of working with diverse cultures and international business protocols is essential to achieving profitable results. *This is the expertise that I bring to the table.*

I have developed the key strategic alliances required to facilitate the most complex projects—whether it is sourcing artisans in remote locations, managing private-label production processes, or negotiating international credit and shipping terms. My background includes

- More than 10 years of successful import/export experience in diverse areas of consumer products
- In-depth knowledge of import regulations, tariffs, duties, and international trade agreements
- Project and product management strengths
- Expertise in vendor sourcing, manufacturing, distribution, and shipping
- Cross-cultural communication skills
- Well-respected international reputation for integrity and reliability

If your organization is seeking expansion in international markets, I would welcome the opportunity for a personal meeting. I appreciate your time in reviewing my qualifications.

Sincerely,

Kevin Jones

enclosure

A great deal of information is conveyed in this relatively brief letter. First, the candidate conveys his expertise and how this can help a company in today's competitive business environment. Second, he provides "quick-read" bullet points that drive home his capabilities.

78

Writer: Kristie Cook, JCTC, CPRW; Olathe, KS

ROBERT MILLER
4950 Pierce St.
Olathe, KS 66061
(913) 555-0496

March 4, 2000

Kay Curtis
ERI, Inc.
1345 151st St.
Olathe, KS 66061

Dear Ms. Curtis:

Are you looking for an executive-level candidate with strong skills in turning around revenues and profits, and expertise in the agricultural industry? If so, we have good reason to meet, as I can make a significant contribution to one of your clients. Please find my resume enclosed to review and forward to your clients in need of a professional with my qualifications.

My resume demonstrates my fast-track progress to Vice President, the position I have held for over five years. When I took over this position temporarily, the Kansas division was making little money and no profits, and had a 100 percent annual turnover rate. Immediately I turned around the division, proving to the President of the company that I was the right person for the permanent Vice President position.

In the past five years, I have increased revenues to over $5 million, and they are steadily rising. The annual turnover rate has dropped to 10 percent. I have made remarkable improvements to the six-state division in every aspect, including marketing, customer service, employee relations, and operations. I am the only division manager with written revenue goals and an action plan to meet those objectives. Unfortunately, there is nowhere to progress in my career with my current employer.

I seek an opportunity where I can make a valuable contribution to the bottom line of an agricultural company and grow professionally with the organization. If you would like to work with a candidate with my qualifications, please call me at (913) 555-0496. I believe I can help you create a win-win-win situation for your clients, you, and myself. Thank you for your time and consideration. I look forward to meeting you in the near future.

Sincerely,

Robert Miller

enclosure

In this letter to a recruiter, the candidate provides a rationale for his job search and does a good job of appealing to the interests of both the recruiter and his client, the hiring company.

79

Writer: Carole Barns; Woodinville, WA

EMILY K. LANGSETH
345 Lincoln River Road ◆ Dallas, TX 75275 ◆ 469 / 455-9101 *(Home)* ◆ 469 / 709-3005 *(Fax)*

February 29, 2000

Leonard Brown, CEO
Children First
25 Sleepy Hollow Lane
Baltimore, MD 21202

Dear Mr. Brown:

- ◆ **Leading** sales and marketing organizations to multimillion–dollar status is my experience.
- ◆ **Creating** a network of international sourcing channels is my expertise.
- ◆ **Inspiring** multidisciplined teams to deliver their best performance is my talent.
- ◆ **Understanding** technology and manufacturing processes and how to leverage them for improved growth, service, and quality is my strength.
- ◆ **Providing** unparalleled service to customers is my passion.

This experience, expertise, talent, strength, and passion is what I can bring to Children First as its Vice President of Sales and Marketing.

Currently I am an executive with Crescent Clothes, a leading wholesaler of family apparel with international sales of over $175 million. In recognition of the significant contributions I've made to the company's growth and bottom line during my 15-year sales and marketing career with it, I was promoted two years ago to Executive Vice President of Sales.

While secure in my position, I am confidentially seeking an opportunity to expand my range of leadership and become part of a company that mirrors my commitment to family. My goal is to work in an environment that is grounded in hard work but acknowledges the value of creativity and humor in boosting productivity and profitability. Children First—with its emphasis on quality and service—is an organization where my ability to manage people, projects, and resources to their highest potential can help guide the transition to your next level of success.

Let me highlight some of the achievements that reflect the quality and caliber of my professional career, as well as bottom-line contributions I have made:

- ◆ **As Executive Vice President of Sales,** increased overall sales volume by 24 percent through product diversification, new account development, exclusive manufacturing sourcing, and hiring top-notch personnel.
- ◆ **As Sales Executive,** won a 38 percent market share of core accounts and increased sales in the Children's Division by 27 percent.
- ◆ **As Product Engineer, Children's Division,** led from my Taiwan base the effort to increase sales 19 pecent in one year.
- ◆ **As Production Control Manager,** reduced manufacturing costs 14 percent.

My strengths lie in my ability to recognize new opportunities, conceive and implement the action plans to capture those opportunities, and negotiate strategic partnerships to drive global market expansion and revenue/profit growth. Equally strong are my qualifications in general management, P&L management, and staff selection and training.

I believe I am the candidate who can take the past and present sales/marketing successes of Children First, grow and expand them, and provide a rich future for the organization, its customers, and employees. I look forward to discussing in greater detail with you the ways in which my experience and expertise can drive that future. I will call you within the next week to schedule a conversation.

Sincerely,

Emily K. Langseth

Enclosure: Resume

The matching lists of bullet points—one describing general areas of expertise and the other detailing specific accomplishments—begin and end this letter on a strong note.

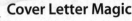

Writer: Don Orlando, MBA, CPRW, JCTC; Montgomery, AL

CONFIDENTIAL

Shinwell Johnson
4114 Burberry Mews
Malton, Alabama 36000
johnn346@aol.com
☎ [334] 555-5555

Tuesday, 07 December, 2002

Mr. Charles W. Morgan
President and CEO
Topline, Inc.
1200 Ventura Avenue
Suite 1000
Montgomery, Alabama 36100

Dear Mr. Morgan:

On the next pages you will find nine documented capabilities that can add to Topline's success. Each one is complete with quantified results that went right to the bottom line. I would like to put every one of them at your disposal by joining your management team.

My company values what I do. Overall, I've led us to a 63 percent increase in sales since 1986. And, although I love what I do, and we are growing in our limited field, I miss the challenges under which I thrive. That is why I am looking, confidentially, for new opportunities of mutual benefit.

May I call in a few days to explore how well I might match Topline's specific needs?

Sincerely,

Shinwell Johnson

Enclosure: Resume

CONFIDENTIAL

The brevity of this letter is one of its strengths. It is focused, hard-hitting, and appeals to the reader's interests. By writing in terms of benefit to the reader ("nine documented capabilities that can add to Topline's success"), the candidate piques the reader's interest and draws him to read further.

Writer: Deborah Wile Dib, CCM, NCRW, CPRW, JCTC; Medford, NY

81

Declan McBride
35 East 58th Street, New York, NY 10010
phone: 212-555-1010   cell: 212-555-0303   fax: 212-555-4404   e-mail: declanmcb@aol.com

---

September 17, 2001

Mr. Thomas H. Clemens
Vice Chairman
Citibank
200 Fifth Avenue
New York, NY 10017

Dear Mr. Clemens:

Roger Davidson spoke with you on Wednesday, September 15th, and suggested that you and I meet. Roger feels that my expertise in domestic and international real estate, corporate finance, and business building might benefit Citibank. I'd like to meet with you and find out.

First, some background—

As a true generalist in my field, I have successfully tackled numerous projects that cannot be pigeonholed into a niche-hiring model. I think and act "outside the box," and a company that values profitable problem-solving will value me, for that is what I do best. What I can bring to Citibank is a vast knowledge of real-estate and corporate finance that spans fifteen countries, four continents, and multi-billions of dollars in acquisitions, disposals, developments, financing, and joint ventures for major corporations, governments, and privately held firms.

Everything that I have accomplished in my twenty years in business has demonstrated adding value and problem-solving along the length of the real estate value chain. It would be impossible in a brief letter to discuss all the features of my experience that may engage you. I think you will be interested to know that my credentials include achievements in:

- Technology—improving efficiency by process and knowledge management
- Operations—adding value at the physical property level
- Finance—creating value through innovative financing
- Strategy—positioning companies optimally in relation to key constituents

In addition, I've seen, survived, and thrived in the up-and-downswings of two full market cycles, even developing a $150 million project (521 Park Avenue) that sold out at record prices at the bottom of the market. My career itself has been outside the box—a cross-cultural, cross-border journey that took me from work in my native Ireland, to management of a state-owned real estate fund in Saudi Arabia, to an internationally renowned investment bank in New York City, to running my own firm, to acting as international advisor to ABC News and other entities.

Mr. Clemens, the enclosed information illustrates many of my successes—profitable projects that demonstrate the types of abilities I can bring to Citibank. I would very much enjoy an informal meeting to talk over Citibank's needs and how I might make a difference to the company. I'll be in touch with you this week.

Best regards,

Declan McBride

Enclosures

This candidate successfully positioned his "generalist" background into a selling point rather than the detriment it was when he looked at lower-level positions requiring "niche" expertise. He got many interviews for high-level international financial and consulting positions.

82

Writer: Vivian Van Lier, CPRW, JCTC; Valley Glen, CA

CHRISTINE STONE

5555 Valley View Drive
Woodland Hills, CA 91555

(818) 555-6655
Fax (818) 555-6620

August 20, 2001

Matthew Taylor
Executive Vice President
The Commerce Companies
2755 Brentwood Boulevard
Los Angeles, CA 90024

Dear Mr. Taylor:

Strong human resources leadership can have a tremendous impact on operating results.
By building and managing an effective HR infrastructure, developing successful
productivity, efficiency, quality, and performance management, I have consistently made a
direct contribution to corporate goals. Highlights of my professional career include

- Fifteen years of senior-level experience as an HR Generalist providing HR
  planning and leadership in union and non-union environments across diverse
  industries

- Implementation of HRIS technology and applications to improve information
  flow and use in strategic planning initiatives

- Strong qualifications in employee relations with ability to build confidence and
  trust between employees and management

- Introduction of loss control, safety, and worker's compensation fraud programs

- Authoring employee manuals to provide employee guidelines in compliance
  with changing regulatory environments

Most significantly, I have positioned myself and the HR function as a partner to senior
management to work together toward producing top-performing workforces able to meet
operating challenges. I am currently seeking a new opportunity as a senior-level HR
professional with an organization seeking talent, drive, enthusiasm, and leadership
expertise. As such, I would welcome a personal interview to explore such positions with
your organization. Thank you.

Sincerely,

Christine Stone

enclosure

With concise bullet points that capture her most salient qualifications, this candidate is able to convey
her expertise and relevant experience in a fairly brief letter.

Writer: Lorie Lebert, CPRW, JCTC; Novi, MI

83

Thomas R. Leonard, Jr.

1061 Chesapeake Drive • Holly, Michigan 48442
Residence: 248.555.4844 • Pager: 810.555.1601

E-mail: jrtomleon@aol.com

Executive Level Sales, Marketing, & Management Professional

October 4, 2001

Meredith Andrews
President / COO
Forward Strategies, Inc.
257 Michigan Parkway
Lansing, MI 48906

Dear Ms. Andrews:

If you got a personally written thank-you note from the owner of the company, wouldn't you appreciate it? My customers do. I know that it takes a lot of time, but when people place their trust in me, I appreciate it and show my gratitude by a personal note. This is an example of the way I do business.

Throughout my career, I have experienced full responsibility and leadership. My scope of responsibilities has been diverse and included corporate administration, strategic planning, program management, and financial analysis. I have been successful at implementing strategies and executing tactics that cut costs and saved dollars. These initiatives accomplished multiple deliverables that gained market share in a highly competitive industry.

I established long-term relationships and developed solid business practices that have increased sales, strengthened market positioning, and gained a secure foothold on long-term return on investment. I am extremely knowledgeable at utilizing personal and professional experience to benefit sales and support.

Currently, I am exploring new career challenges and opportunities where I can continue providing excellent leadership and motivation. The ideal situation would require combined strategic and operating leadership in an organization poised to go forward in the new millennium with intelligence and discernment.

Anticipating your need for leadership with my background, I am enclosing my resume, which summarizes my achievements, experience, and other information you will find helpful. I am confident that the strength of my experience, combined with my dedication, energy, and commitment, will add measurable value to your organization. Thank you.

Sincerely,

Thomas R. Leonard, Jr.

Resume enclosed

The "headline" in this letter immediately identifies the candidate's level and career goals. The first paragraph is interesting and attention-getting, and conveys his leadership philosophy.

84

Writer: Lisa LeVerrier, CPRW, JCTC, MA, MS; Boca Raton, FL

John Glogau

5000 S. 92nd Street
Boca Raton, FL 33496

Phone (561) 982-1109
Available for Relocation

February 15, 1999

John Brown, CEO
International Telecommunications, Inc.
12900 Riverside Avenue
San Bernardino, CA 98770

Dear Mr. Brown:

As Director of International Development for ABC Freight Systems, I led a start-up international transportation services division through critical start-up, growth, and operations cycles. For the past seven years, I built international market presence, accelerated revenue growth, and outperformed the competition. Notable achievements include

- Expansion into 47 countries within the first year and 160 countries within four years

- Gross margins in excess of 30 percent after first year of operation

- Consistent annual growth in sales volume resulting in revenue increases of 25 percent per year

As Director, I also established an International Customer Service Center and Telemarketing Center. I recruited and trained all staff and played a significant role in developing an automated billing, tracing, and accounting system that significantly improved customer response time.

Complementing my ability to produce sales dollars and lead start-up sales organizations are equally strong qualifications in training and leading professional sales teams. While at ABC, I conducted front-end analysis, researched training needs, and implemented a powerful sales and negotiation training program that helped reduce sales force turnover from 18 percent to 8.5 percent in five years.

I lead by example and provide strong decision-making, problem-solving, and project-management skills. In fact, I have never missed a project deadline. If decisive and action-driven leadership are your goals, we should meet. I welcome the opportunity for a personal interview and can assure you that my expertise will be of value in your sales and global expansion efforts. Thank you.

Sincerely,

John Glogau

Enclosure: Resume

This letter is extremely well written, with an executive-level tone, concise language, and strong focus on bottom-line results. Numbers included are impressive.

Writer: Don Orlando, MBA, CPRW, JCTC; Montgomery, AL

CONFIDENTIAL

JOSIAH AMBERLY

444 Ponder Drive Midlane City, Alabama 35000 ☎ [256] 555-5555 (Home)

November 16, 2001

Ms. Nora W. Morgan
President and CEO
Topline, Inc.
1200 Ventura Avenue
Suite 1000
Montgomery, Alabama 36100

Dear Ms. Morgan:

For more than ten years, I've had full profit and loss responsibility for a manufacturing company. My company's business is making wood products; *my* business is making sales. And I like that part of the business so well, I want to devote all my energies and talents to serving as a senior sales professional.

As a first step, I have attached a "research document" designed to illustrate sales-related performance. In it, you will find more than a half dozen sales contributions to my company's bottom line. Behind the numbers is this personal, professional code that guides all I do:

- ✧ A positive attitude is a major sales tool. It makes my company come alive for customers, colleagues, and management.

- ✧ A good sales record rests on *tomorrow's* numbers. My goal is to have our customers think of us as the sole source they can't do without.

- ✧ A corporate reputation for honesty is the best "cold-calling" sales tool.

If my approach to business and my track record appeal to Topline, I would like to explore how I can serve your specific needs. May I call in a few days to set up an appointment?

Sincerely,

Josiah Amberly

Enclosure: Resume

CONFIDENTIAL

Starting off with a compelling rationale for seeking a sales rather than general management position, this job seeker goes on to highlight sales philosophy and strong results that should capture his reader's attention.

86

Writer: Martin Buckland, CPRW; Oakville, Ontario

PHILLIP TROTTER
2020 - 444 Water Street, Toronto, Ontario, M7R 1K1
(416) 333-3333

18TH February 2000

Mr Paul Smith
Director of Human Resources
City of Toronto
666 Bay Street
P.O. Box 213
Toronto
Ontario, M5R 2V2

Dear Mr Smith:

"Success is a journey, not a destination" is my company philosophy, and it applies to this vibrant city also. The City of Toronto is becoming an increasingly popular place to visit. I am proud to live and serve my home community in a number of ways: through the medium of television by producing and hosting the "Neighbour to Neighbour" show, as a volunteer with a variety of organizations and being selected to officiate as the Master of Ceremonies with your municipality at the "Sound of Music Festival" and the "Lakeside a la Carte."

The advertised position, Executive Director of Tourism Toronto, sounds exciting and fits exactly into my realm of community involvement and spirit. My resume is enclosed. One of my greatest strengths is the ability to motivate and cultivate support for events, which is a quality this position requires. I am also regarded as an effective communicator, another requisite that enhances my feeling that I should be considered for the Executive Director position.

I would welcome a personal interview to discuss how I can continue to promote the City of Toronto. I appreciate your time in reviewing my resume.

Sincerely,

Phillip Trotter

Enc.

Obviously, this letter was written just for this opportunity as Executive Director of Tourism for Toronto. It conveys passion for the city as well as strong qualifications for the position.

87

Writer: Rhoda Kopy, CPRW; Toms River, NJ

CARLA B. ALEXANDER
537 Tiptop Terrace ➤ Hazlet, NJ 07730 ➤ 732-555-1610

February 16, 2002

Ms. Marianne Maxwell
Commission Auditor
Celeste County Governmental Center
Seventh Avenue
Crystal Lake, FL 30941

Dear Ms. Maxwell:

As a Senior Finance and Operating Executive who has propelled the growth of a multimillion-dollar, 25-site organization, I can offer the leadership, drive, and integrity required for the Celeste County Administrator position.

My background includes ten years of senior executive experience, during which time I have demonstrated strengths in strategic planning, business development, financial management, operations management, negotiation, marketing, MIS, and employee relations.

Celeste County is a growing community, and the County Administrator must have the foresight, planning skills, and flexibility to successfully manage its growth. In my present position, I have

- Drastically improved earnings and profits and led the company out of severe financial crisis.
- Spearheaded the development of financial control, budget, and forecasting systems able to handle the rapid growth and expansion of the company.
- Instituted a wide range of successful cost-control measures.
- Maximized investment earnings and increased benefits and financial incentives for employees.
- Created a positive, team-oriented atmosphere and gained the loyalty and trust of employees.

If you are searching for an innovative, proactive leader who will have a positive impact on the county organization and the community, please contact me to arrange an interview. I am eager to learn more about the challenges facing Celeste County and clarify how I can make a difference.

Thank you for your interest and consideration.

Sincerely,

Carla B. Alexander

Enclosure

The powerful first paragraph of this letter is an excellent introduction and "sales pitch" for the candidate, and it is followed by facts and figures that support her candidacy for the job.

88

Writer: Diane Burns, CPRW, CCM, JCTC; Columbia, MD

John P. Michaels   **4678 Littleton Way • Chicago, IL 60646**
                              Tel: (555) 555-5555 • JPM@yahoo.com

November 26, 2002

Mr. Andrew Seth
Services Corporation
275 Steffens Drive
Chicago, IL 60612

Dear Mr. Seth:

Distinguished executive experience in Logistics and Transportation Management, an exceptional record of complex issue resolution, and numerous deployments throughout Europe and the Middle East with senior oversight for logistics operations and planning qualify me for consideration with your organization. I have enclosed my resume with brief highlights of experience for your consideration.

Over the years I consistently improved and coordinated various logistical operations:

- Managed, programmed, and estimated all logistical accounts, negotiated contracts, processed earnings, and reconciled automated findings reports
- Held complete oversight for petroleum, oils, and lubricants accountability for bulk and coupon issue
- Maintained warehouses in state-of-the-art posture

My expertise is recognized through superior performance ratings, numerous letters of commendation, and prestigious awards. My skills and experience would be a genuine benefit to your operations; I can provide aggressive and attainable results, streamlined and efficient operations, training, and executive management. These attributes have been highly sought by logistics managers throughout my military career:

> *"Magnificent performance from a truly quality officer."*

> *"His technical expertise knows no bounds and has resulted in dramatic improvements in the repair parts supply policy."*

> *"His outstanding accomplishments…reflected his unquestionable commitment to precision planning, exacting management, and quality staff work."*

> *"I would fight to have him assigned to any of my future units."*

You may contact me at the above address or phone number to further discuss my qualifications and how I can best serve your requirements, enhance your operations, and increase your posture in logistics and transportation. I will be happy to provide you with additional information or references. Thank you for taking the time to review my qualifications.

Sincerely,

John P. Michaels

Enclosure

There is little to indicate that this letter is from a transitioning military officer; it does a good job of communicating military experiences in "civilian" terms. The quotes definitely help to sell this candidate.

Writer: John O'Connor, MFA, CPRW; Raleigh, NC

89

JANE J. JOHNSON

112 American Way
Anywhere, North Carolina 27615
janejohnson@internet.com
(919) 555-5555

December 13, 2001

Rudnick & Wolfe
203 North LaSalle Street
Suite 1800
Chicago, IL 60601-1293

To Whom It May Concern:

Please review and consider my credentials for an Attorney position with Rudnick & Wolfe.

After much personal and professional career analysis, I am very excited about forwarding my credentials for relocation back to the Chicago area. Currently, I serve with the law firm of Manning, Fulton & Skinner in Raleigh, North Carolina, where I have utilized skills in real property and real estate law and mortgage law to develop a large, highly respected practice.

I feel that my background in business analysis and business consultation with insurance and banking industry companies provides your firm with the opportunity to develop and grow business in these industries. Without reservation, I offer you the highest level of professional and personal commitment.

Some of the key areas where my experience is strongest are:

- Property Sales and Acquisitions
- Corporate Analyst/Process Liaison
- Business and Holding Entity
- Leasing of New Properties and Renewals
- Real and Personal Property Loans
- Environmental Problems and Problem Resolution
- Strong Representative Client Base/Professional Industry Leadership

My career history emphasizes significant achievements and transferable leadership performance that will allow me to develop new clients and keep current professional relationships. My salary requirements are $120,000+ depending upon compensation package.

Thank you for your time and consideration. I look forward to speaking to you soon.

Sincerely,

Jane J. Johnson

Enclosure

Focusing on areas of expertise within the legal field, this letter is a straightforward business communication. Its lack of "sales pitch" is very appropriate for its conservative law firm audience.

CAROLE SCHULTZ

555 Shell Drake Circle
The Woodlands, Texas 75555   cschultz@earthlink.net

Residence: (555) 555-5555
Voice Mail: (555) 544-4444

September 27, 2001

C. J. Olson
Executive Recruiters, Inc.
555 Southside
Houston, Texas 75555

Dear Mr. Olson:

"Treat employees like partners and they act like partners."
Fred Allen, CEO, Pitney Bowes

As a business leader, I believe strongly in giving employees ownership of their work. This empowerment model has been key in my success as an engineering manager, global manufacturing manager, and, most recently, vice president of international business development for a multimillion-dollar tech organization. The enclosed resume outlines my 12 years of senior management experience, highlights of which include the following:

➢ **Strategic Planning:** Authored strategies for growth management, turnaround, and market contraction for Data-Tech, Inc. Identified profitable acquisition and diversification opportunities and facilitated negotiations for sale of software division to Fortune 500 company.

➢ **Growth Performance:** Increased unit sales 25 percent and captured $25+ million in revenue growth per year, despite shrinking price points. Member of sales closing team for contracts with the top five manufacturers of computer equipment.

➢ **Profit Enhancement:** Cut costs in major expense category by $10 million through design integration and innovative alliance programs with vendor partners such as Lucent and NEC.

➢ **Human Resources:** Managed diverse, geographically dispersed workforce of 300+ in R&D, manufacturing, and business development. Unified marketing, sales, and engineering on a global scale. Noted for exceptional team-building, motivational, and leadership skills.

➢ **Manufacturing:** Oversaw technology manufacturing operations in Asia, Europe, and the United States. Persuaded overseas contract manufacturers to invest $50+ million in capital improvements. Brought 20 new products to market with significant commercialization value.

I'd like to put these strengths to work in another strategic/directional role. Should one of your client companies have need of an executive with my track record, I would appreciate an opportunity to talk.

Sincerely,

Carole Schultz

Enclosure

Writing to a recruiter, this executive relates three areas of expertise that are supported by brief summaries of her achievements in these areas. Leadership philosophy is communicated in the first paragraph and enhanced by the quote that leads off this letter.

Winning Cover Letters for Technical and Scientific Professions

The Top Five Cover Letter–Writing Tips for Technical and Scientific Professions

1. Be sure to spotlight your most significant and most "saleable" technical qualifications as they relate to the specific company to which you are writing.

2. Demonstrate how your technical skills have positively impacted the operations, productivity, and financial performance of the company.

3. It is beneficial for technical professionals to cite evidence of "people" skills. Tell how you've worked with teams, communicated with non-technical people, improved morale, or made contributions other than just technical feats.

4. Relate your technical skills to overall business needs; don't try to sell "technology for technology's sake."

5. It's important to use technology in your job search. For instance, communicate as much as possible by e-mail; whenever it's an option, use an online application; and post your resume at a private URL.

91

Writer: Martin Buckland, CPRW; Oakville, Ontario

MARK ROBERTS, B.Sc. Mech Eng

650 Lakeshore Road East, Oakville, Ontario, L6J 3X9
Phone: (905) 344-0000 Fax: (905) 344-0001 E-mail: mroberts@tew.ca

14th December 2000

Mr. Jack Aldwin
Human Resources Manager
Tarnoch Engineering Inc.
222 Lea Way
Oakville, ON, L6M 6P4

Dear Mr. Aldwin:

As we enter the new millennium, the NASA International Space Station program will be taking mankind on an exciting leap forward in space research. The enclosed resume highlights my successful career in project management and engineering, in particular my previous work with NASA.

The Senior Program Engineer opportunity with Tarnoch Engineering, Inc., matches exactly the attributes and experience I have developed within the aerospace industry. With full responsibility for the entire cycle, I have directed teams of professionals selected to research, design, produce and deliver outstanding products. Two highlights of my career are the International Space Station arm, which is the larger and more complex version of the "Canadarm," and the ABC-450 engine design for the Beechcraft King Air C-43, Otter and Beaver aircraft. I am familiar with Canadian Space Agency and NASA requirements. Specialties include the following:

< Knowledge of Mil and NASA specifications
< Government procurement
< Chairing internal and customer design reviews
< Advanced knowledge of CATIA and Pro-E software
< FAR and JAR, International Aviation requirements
< Government and private-sector negotiation
< ISO 9000, 9001, 9002
< Building and leading mechanical and technical teams

I am actively seeking a new challenge and opportunity. The Senior Program Engineer position with Tarnoch Engineering will be my second project for the prestigious International Space Station. I would welcome a personal interview, scheduled at your convenience, to enable me to explain further how my expertise can assist you.

Thank you for your consideration.

Yours Truly,

Mark Roberts, B.Sc. Mech Eng

Enc.

In addition to communicating a close match with the advertised position, this letter conveys career highlights and specific technical qualifications.

92

Writer: Lorie Lebert, CPRW, JCTC; Novi, MI

SEAN GLADDER

1061 HEATHER CREEK
BLISSTON, MICHIGAN 48058

734.555.1601

e-mail: sgladder@provide.net

August 20, 2001

QRP Consulting
333 Bridge Street SW
Grand Rapids, MI 49504

Dear Hiring Authority:

If you are interested in candidates who are not only computer jocks, but work well with people and know how to handle large-scale projects...the enclosed resume will be of interest to you.

I have a degree in electronics, a degree in robotics, and have almost finished a B.S.T. degree with a minor in Computer Science. Also, my Novell C.N.A. certification is in process. With this education and hands-on computer/electronics experience for almost ten years, I believe I would be a valuable addition to your team.

Currently, I am a Database Administrator and perform all the duties of a Lead Instrument/Electrical Designer. Project involvement encompasses initial database development, bid information, and standards preparation, along with continued updating and maintenance until the project is completed.

Along with my technical expertise, I know how to deal with customers, colleagues, and management to ensure project accuracy and customer satisfaction.

I would appreciate a personal interview, where I can expand on my qualifications to meet your current staffing needs. If you have any questions in the meantime, however, please call me.

Thank you for your time in reviewing my credentials and considering me for permanent employment. I look forward to speaking with you in the near future.

Sincerely,

Sean Gladder

Enclosure: Resume

The first sentence communicates a sense of humor and also conveys interpersonal skills that are not always a strength of technical professionals.

Writer: Cynthia Kraft, CPRW, JCTC, CCM; Valrico, FL

ROBERT M. LEE
941-555-8753
1386 Pony Lane, Lakeland, FL 33384

February 18, 2000

BankAmerica
1811 BankAmerica Drive
Any City, USA

Dear Hiring Manager:

A project manager with aggressive turnaround leadership and team-building capabilities, and a thorough understanding of operations, can dramatically impact a company's bottom line.

My success in each of these areas is well-documented and includes…

➢ Spearheading the continuing education conversion from outside to in-house, reducing costs by more than $40,000 in the first year.

➢ Initiating leadership programs that motivated employees with low morale, poor attendance, and unacceptable productivity levels to work together as a top-producing team.

➢ Negotiating with vendors to ensure department peaks were adequately staffed and products were timely delivered.

➢ Designing applications that dramatically reduced operator error and increased productivity as much as 50 percent.

I am confident that I can make a positive contribution to BankAmerica and look forward to discussing my capabilities in more detail. I am available for a personal interview at your earliest convenience.

Very truly yours,

Robert M. Lee

Enclosure

This letter is made up almost entirely of well-chosen, highly relevant bullet points. The letter is concise, to the point, and easy to read.

94

Writer: Myriam-Rose Kohn, CPRW, JCTC, CCM; Valencia, CA

DELIA CAPO

21785 Trident Lane   Saugus, California 91350   661 555-0807

February 9, 2001

Taft University
Human Resources
333 Bluff Road
Los Angeles, California 91520

Requisition Number: H-14022

I was highly excited to come across your advertisement for a **Staff Research Associate II** in the Neuroenteric Disease Program laboratory at the Taft University School of Medicine. Laboratory research has always been most intriguing to me—so much so that I studied to obtain a Bachelor of Science degree in Biology and plan to continue my studies even further. When I started my Bachelor's, I was working as a Registered and Licensed Vocational Nurse in hospitals and physicians' offices, as well as a back-office Veterinary Assistant where I participated in activities such as post-operative animal care and the administration of intravenous and intraperitoneal medications. I have worked with human and animal patients, so I bring hands-on experience to the job.

The enclosed resume details my background and knowledge in pharmacology as well as my clinical laboratory skills, which encompass the placement of intravenous catheters and electromyographic electrodes. In addition to live animals in vet hospitals and in the field, I have also worked with laboratory animals and have dissected quite a few. I am quite familiar with the operation of a variety of lab equipment. In all of my positions, I have demonstrated the ability to prioritize and complete numerous concurrent assignments while meeting time and organizational goals. I am results oriented with strong interpersonal skills and can work either independently or with a team.

I hold a Bachelor of Science in Biology with a minor in Chemistry. Because of my passion and love for the field, I feel I could contribute considerably to the Taft University School of Medicine and am eager to become part of such a team.

A perfect fit seems to exist between your requirements and my qualifications. I would greatly appreciate an interview, during which we could further explore the possibilities of a mutually beneficial relationship.

Sincerely,

Delia Capo

Enclosure

The job seeker conveys passion and enthusiasm for her chosen field, and the information she provides about her educational background is both interesting and relevant.

95

Writer: Laura DeCarlo, CPRW, JCTC; Melbourne, FL

CHARLOTTE S. WALLINGTON, RDCS
33 Park Swing Lane
Cocoa Beach, FL 32955
(321) 555-6869

February 3, 2001

Mr. Stuart Kolter
Human Resource Manager
Harlton Corporation
121 Plymouth Place
Orlando, FL 32912

Dear Mr. Kolter:

I am sure you can easily find a number of individuals who are qualified Registered Diagnostic Cardiac Sonographers. However, I believe I can offer you a higher caliber of professionalism and qualifications than the average applicant. Please consider some of my skills and credentials:

- **Experience:** Registered Diagnostic Cardiac Sonographer with 12+ years of experience in the medical / cardiovascular field.

- **Initiative:** Consistently pursue additional training to meet company goals and needs. Recently added skills including arterial and venous vascular duplex/color flow imaging.

- **Research / Problem Solving:** Recognized for seeking opportunities to make improvements, achieve cost savings, and increase patient satisfaction. Recently negotiated for new ultrasound equipment and researched and collected information for accreditation of cardiac and vascular labs.

- **Excellence in Patient Relations:** Developed an excellent reputation for putting patients at ease, resolving problems, and providing gentle and qualified care.

Most important is my professionalism. I am exceedingly dedicated and willing to accept new challenges and opportunities. In short, I believe in giving my all in every situation to ensure positive results.

If I sound like the type of individual you would like on your team, please contact me. I have enclosed my resume for your review. Thank you for your consideration.

Sincerely,

Charlotte S. Wallington, RDCS

enclosure

In the first paragraph, the candidate very directly sets herself apart from her competition, and the bullet points and bold type highlight her key qualifications.

Writer: Nina Ebert, CPRW; Toms River, NJ

96

LAWRENCE SAUNDERS, JR.

190 Bridle Lane   Toms River, New Jersey 08753   (555) 244-2211

March 4, 2000

Tim Flannery, Director of Human Resources
SpeedWay Vehicles, Inc.
25-A Race Way
Toms River, NJ 08753

Dear Mr. Flannery:

Patrick Head has noted that a prerequisite for innovative design is the engineer's ability to "get close to the hardware." My hands-on expertise is, perhaps, my greatest attribute.

Skilled in the areas of design engineering, manufacturing, and fabrication and machining, I am knowledgeable of the materials and processes that turn designs into hardware. I am eager to turn hardware into winning race cars.

"The real satisfaction comes from new solutions to old problems," according to John Barnard. Although something new is exciting, I savor troubleshooting. I approach problems holistically, pushing design concepts to the boundaries, remaining focused on pre-determined goals.

Whatever task or project I undertake, I perform it to the best of my ability. My focus, drive and determination, coupled with my acute attention to detail, have progressed my career to date. I intend to continue to apply this same level of expertise as a member of your team.

Since my resume is an overview of my background and accomplishments, I look forward to providing you with further insight into my professional value during a personal interview. Until we meet, thank you for your consideration.

Yours truly,

Lawrence Saunders, Jr.

Enclosure

This well-written letter, incorporating two quotes, is both interesting and persuasive. Intangible qualities and approach to engineering challenges are emphasized.

97

Writer: Richard Porter; Portage, MI

Mary A. Potter
330 Galileo Drive
Aurora, IL 60504

630.555.6008   **potter1957@aol.com**

December 8, 2000

James A. Jackson, Ph.D.
President
Advantage Laboratories, Inc.
1061 Precision Drive
Kalamazoo, MI 49024

Dear Dr. Jackson:

Thank you for taking the time to speak with me on the telephone yesterday. From our discussion, it appears that you are in need of an experienced environmental laboratory quality professional who will assume a leadership role in managing Advantage Labs' new quality assurance department. As an 18-year "veteran" in overseeing laboratory quality control for a Fortune 500 environmental contract laboratory in the Chicago area, I believe I have the qualifications and experience necessary to assume the role of director of quality assurance for your laboratory.

As you will note on my attached resume, my particular expertise lies in coordinating quality control activities and managing laboratory analytical data, while at the same time serving as a technical resource to laboratory personnel, client services personnel, and customers. In addition to these qualifications, I will bring to Advantage Labs a strong background in general management and administration, most notably effective technical staff supervision. Highlights of my career that may be of particular interest to Advantage Labs include the following:

> ➢ Validation of GC/MS, GC, ICP, HPLC, and classic chemistry data to assess compliance with USEPA guidelines
> ➢ Development and implementation of a TQM system for laboratory processes from sample reports to final data reports, ensuring 100 percent accuracy and reliable laboratory results
> ➢ Validation of laboratory compliance with current state and USEPA SW-846 methodologies to achieve common goals and performance objectives
> ➢ Implementation of an analytical results database developed in conjunction with site well demographic data to ensure proper compliance of water-monitoring wells
> ➢ Strong qualities in leadership, particularly as they pertain to instilling and motivating a spirit of teambuilding among coworkers to achieve corporate goals
> ➢ Complete familiarity with federal, state, and local regulations pertaining to CERCLA, CERCLIS, CAA, CLP, EPCRA, and RCRA

Although I am secure in my present position, I am interested in pursuing new challenges and opportunities in a more senior-level administrative position such as that offered by your lab. As we discussed on the telephone, I am open to relocation, and I would welcome an interview with you. I will contact you within the next few days to schedule a convenient time. Thank you.

Sincerely,

Mary A. Potter

Enclosure

As a follow-up to an initial phone conversation, this letter does a good job of communicating specific technical qualifications.

98

Writer: Elizabeth Axnix, CPRW, JCTC; Iowa City, IA

IAN DURRINGTON · (319) 555-4819

110 North Knisel Street · Riverside, Iowa 55555

February 11, 2000

Bert Adams, Executive Officer
Waste Management Assistance Division
Iowa DNR
3 Retread Drive
Des Moines, Iowa 55555

Dear Mr. Adams:

RE: Environmental Specialist Opportunity — Market Assistance / Market Development Area

Many aspects of my professional background are relevant to your Environmental Specialist
staffing needs, and I have enclosed my resume in application. I interact frequently with the Iowa
DNR, federal regulatory representatives, and members of the general public, and I enjoy sharing
my knowledge base locally and throughout the federal waste management / recycling arena.

The Veterans Affairs Medical Center in Iowa City features an integrated waste management
program that has earned system-wide recognition for its innovative initiatives and, most
importantly, results. We've been able to effect an average 30 percent diversion rate in the waste
stream annually and are continually searching for other opportunities to positively impact our
environment.

In addition to being a trained facilitator who regularly leads panel discussions, focus groups and
patient informational meetings, my functions include recycling task force leadership, project
management and public speaking experience. I oversee the implementation of federal or state
regulatory controls and am currently contributing to market development activities involved in
maximizing the effectiveness of a multi-site laundry operation serving VA facilities in two states.

My current position is challenging, rewarding, and very close to my loyalties because I am a
veteran. However, as a native Iowan, I am deeply committed to our state, and I would like to
transition my skills to an opportunity that would draw more heavily upon my environmental
knowledge base and affinity for a clean natural environment. As this letter cannot convey my
enthusiasm to discuss this opportunity, I will take the liberty to call your office next week and
briefly follow up on this letter. I hope we can arrange a personal meeting soon to discuss your
staffing needs and my expertise as it relates to recycling and the environment.

Sincerely,

Ian Durrington

Enclosures

By making a clear connection between position requirements and his qualifications, this candidate
enhances his chance for an interview. Note the assertive closing.

99

Writer: Laurie Smith, CPRW; Alexandria, VA

Kevin R. Foster

239 MAPLE DRIVE
BALTIMORE, MD 22412
410-949-2309

April 4, 2001

Claude R. Hampton
President/CEO
Technology Pathfinders, Inc.
1644 Edmonds Street
Atlanta, GA 45723

Dear Mr. Hampton:

As a seasoned IT executive who fully understands the importance of strategic positioning of technology to achieve and maintain competitive advantage in global markets, I believe we should meet. With more than 20 years of experience providing strategic direction and leading design, creation, and deployment of technology solutions to address enterprise-wide business issues, I am confident I can help your company meet the information management challenges outlined in your recent *Wall Street Journal* advertisement.

I bring to the table a "big picture" perspective of organizational and marketplace dynamics derived from a diverse career spanning Finance, General Management, and IT Management. This perspective has enabled me to create successful responses to new challenges, including the emerging electronic commerce marketing and sales channels that are key to marketplace competitiveness for virtually every business today. It has also provided an unusually keen understanding of the issues and priorities facing various organizational units that facilitates the kind of cooperation, effective interaction, and buy-in at all levels that are key to success of any IT initiative.

Representative successes detailed in the enclosed resume include:

- Implementation of an enterprise-wide five-year IT strategy, worldwide communications infrastructure upgrade, and Y2K compliance program for a high-technology manufacturer
- Replacement of a multibillion-dollar company's 100+ legacy systems with state-of-the-art, Y2K-compliant systems on a two-year fast track
- Dramatic expansion of potential markets for an international communications company delivered through entry into the e-commerce arena with projected first-year new revenues of $15 million

I will welcome the chance to pursue the CIO position with you, and will follow up with you next week. Please note that I am currently employed and appreciate your confidentiality in this matter.

Sincerely,

Kevin R. Foster

enclosure

For this executive-level (CIO) candidate, leadership skills and strategic planning abilities are as important as technical competence. All of these key qualities are communicated in this letter.

100

Writer: Lisa LeVerrier, CPRW, JCTC, MA, MS; Boca Raton, FL

Craig Simmons

299 SW Yamato Road   Phone (561) 555-0581
Boca Raton, FL 33432   csimmons123@mindspring.com

November 17, 2000

Edward Barry
National Account Manager
Southeast Management Recruitment, Inc.
27 Bayshore Boulevard
Boca Raton, FL 33432

Dear Mr. Barry:

Telecommunications, customer service, and coaching/supervising teams are my areas of expertise. For the last nine years, I have worked in both the telecommunications and hospitality industries to streamline business processes, improve customer service delivery, and build strong and motivated teams. Here are a few of my noteworthy achievements and results:

Achievements	Results
• Contributed to project team to obtain new government contract at Siemens	• Net revenue of over $100 million
• Designed and implemented new inventory control system to track EWSD voice switching test equipment	• Reduced staff time trying to locate necessary test equipment and improved tracking procedures
• Streamlined check-in process for frequent customers at Biltmore Hotel	• Personalized express customer service delivery for VIP customers
• Designed, developed, and implemented training and operating procedures for staff	• Standardized performance expectations and improved consistency and quality of staff performance
• Streamlined reporting of sales and occupancy by implementing automated procedures	• Decreased labor costs involved in performing reporting function manually

I am currently exploring avenues to take my skills and expertise in telecommunications, customer service, and management through a new door. If my experience and abilities are a match for one of your current searches, I would welcome the opportunity for a personal interview. I can assure you that my expertise will be of value to your client's organization. Thank you.

Sincerely,

Craig Simmons

Enclosure: resume

This letter shows a new take on the traditional comparison-list style of letter. Rather than matching qualifications to job requirements, this candidate matches activities with results in a highly readable format.

101

Writer: John O'Connor, MFA, CPRW; Raleigh, NC

JANE J. JOHNSON

112 American Way Drive
Round Rock, TX 78683
janejohnson@internet.com
(512) 555-5555

December 1, 2001

CISCO
CFP-Manufacturing Division
Attn: Brett Scott
25 Technology Drive
Round Rock, TX 78680

REQUISITION: 305566

Dear Mr. Scott:

Thank you for considering my credentials for the **project management** position with your company. I would like to meet with you and your team to discuss my qualifications and how I could be of benefit to your organization's curriculum and training goals.

I can offer you strong senior-level project management and problem-solving skills developed in consulting, enterprise information systems engineering, and related roles. In these positions, I have dealt with and solved multiple IT issues, developed technology strategies, and managed new IT and related operational/technical management projects. These qualifications include serving as Risk Assessment Project Manager, Y2K Test Team Coordinator, and in various technical project and industrial engineering roles.

This position and other positions have allowed me to develop extensive skills in a variety of areas. Some of my management skills include team leadership, team visioning, technical software skills, industrial engineering expertise, and project management. My foundational skills include systems programming as well as extensive senior-level work in developing and implementing business-critical IT projects and processes. All of my achievements focus on building and keeping the organization working efficiently and providing keen direction to internal entities.

If you need a proven visionary leader and team player, I will be able to meet and exceed your requirements. My record shows consistent ability to innovate and provide senior-level management.

Throughout my career, I have effectively developed business solutions to problems while working closely with personnel and projects, building a reputation of quality with overall results.

Thank you for your time and consideration. I look forward to speaking to you soon.

Sincerely,

Jane J. Johnson

Enclosure

Here is another example of combining technical qualifications with intangible qualities ("visionary leader and team player") that will be important to the organization.

Writer: *Deborah Wile Dib, CCM, NCRW, CPRW, JCTC; Medford, NY*

102

Antony M. Tisane

June 14, 2000

Mr. George Lyons
CIO
Symbol Technologies
2 Expressway Drive
Islandia, NY 11743

Dear Mr. Lyons:

Do you have a need for an experienced and certified technology specialist with a cross-functional background in hands-on software development, team management, and operational problem solving? If so, I would welcome learning about your needs and how I may contribute to your technical team.

Relevant credentials include over 15 years' technical and managerial experience with American Airlines, Cisco and Microsoft certifications (CCNA and MCSE) from Technology Career Center's 1080-hour WAN/LAN certification program, and an MBA focusing on Total Quality Management (Fall 2000 completion).

As Manager of American's Flight Operations Crew Allocations Department and as Supervisor of American's Data Systems Department, I analyzed and documented software problems, tested software changes, and assisted programmers in the development of new software solutions. In these positions I...

- Revitalized a malfunctioning, multimillion–dollar SABRE-produced software project.
- Recommended software enhancements instrumental in saving millions of dollars.
- Crisis-tested and proved effectiveness of new automated Crew Management System.
- Managed ground-zero to full-operation logistics of cross-country department relocation.
- Directed massive flight crew rescheduling during irregularities and wildcat strikes.

As a Cisco Certified Network Associate and Microsoft Certified Systems Engineer, I have hands-on experience configuring and troubleshooting a TCP/IP environment with Cisco routers and switches; and Microsoft NT 4.0 Workstation, Server, and Enterprise environments.

Mr. Lyons, I'm a high achiever with a thirst for growth and new challenges. Each of my business accomplishments has involved learning quickly, using technology to solve operational problems, working under pressure, and meeting tight deadlines. I'd like to discuss how these skills and experiences can benefit Symbol Technologies, and I look forward to hearing from you.

Sincerely,

Antony M. Tisane

132-43 35th Avenue, Flushing, NY 11358 • 718-555-1010 • toptech@aol.com

This job seeker's challenge was to show knowledge of current technology (through his recent education) combined with proven street smarts gained from years of meeting real-world technical challenges.

103

Writer: Jewel Bracy DeMaio, CPRW; Elkins Park, PA

MARK R. MERRILL

10 Tomasine Way   Day: (856) 555-5510
Tanning, NJ 08651   Eve: (609) 555-0904
                            mmerrill@erols.com

September 27, 2000

Engineering Outlooks, Inc.
444 Newman Road
New York, NY 21435

Dear Hiring Manager:

My electrical engineering background, specifically my successes working on many defense, combat, and Navy projects, is the chief asset I would bring to the position of **Systems Engineer** in San Diego, CA.

I understand that the primary function is to provide guidance for Navy SATCOM systems in electro-magnetic environmental effects, shock and vibration, antenna blockage, and radar cross section. I am thoroughly familiar with Navy acquisition programs in general, and I have also dealt almost exclusively with Navy civilian and uniformed personnel throughout my career, so I am well-versed in Navy project specifications, requirements, and protocol.

In my current position as Senior Systems Engineer for Electric Solutions, Inc., a firm dealing primarily in Navy contracts, I supervise the software systems and testing associated with the AEGIS Weapon System. And as the Chief Consulting Engineer with Merit Systems Associates, I deal with not only Navy security classification issues, but also those involving the Department of Defense.

Previously, as the manager of Development & Special Projects Test Engineering for Lockman Testing, I participated in the development of the Navy's DDG-51 Test and Evaluation Master Plan for the DDG-51 Acquisition Program. While working with the DDG-51 AEGIS Combat System Integration and Test Team, we produced the first operating DDG-51 class AEGIS Combat System within extremely short time constraints, an accomplishment that led to the successful completion of the DT/OT milestone event.

My strengths are not only in development, but also in testing and analysis. Again at Lockman Testing, when faced with the loss of data during an initial shock trial of the AEGIS cruiser, I developed the following solution: We located video cameras at key equipment indicator panels and display consoles. The equipment recorded the data processes, which I analyzed, then suggested corrective action. A similar video-recording technique was used to solve a problem on the SATCOM antenna.

Please consider that I am also enthusiastic about consultant or part-time opportunities. And another asset is that since I am retired from the Navy and from Lockman Testing, I will not be taking advantage of your company's health and dental benefits.

I believe my Navy and electrical engineering background is a quality match for the requirements stated for this position. Kindly review my résumé, then please contact me at your earliest convenience to schedule a professional interview.

Sincerely yours,

Mark R. Merrill

Right off the bat, this letter makes a strong connection between the candidate's background and the company's needs. In the second-to-last paragraph, he offers the company a financial incentive for hiring him and opens the door for other opportunities.

104

Writer: Carole Barns; Woodinville, WA

MARK RENSHAW

1004 – 47th ▣ Seattle, WA 98105 ▣ 206 / 555-9876 ▣ FAX: 206 / 555-8761

February 9, 2001

Benson Engineering
10 – 6th Avenue, Room 1200
Seattle, WA 98103

RE: Structural AutoCAD Drafting position advertised in <u>The Seattle Times</u>

As an individual with excellent skills in drafting and AutoCAD plus experience in the engineering and construction industries, I am particularly qualified for the Structural AutoCAD Drafting position currently open at Benson Engineering. My career as a draftsman has its basis in hand-generated structural drawings using illustrative and mathematical skills that have enabled me to more accurately envision the final products that I now create on computers.

I am particularly proud of my ability to adapt to changing technologies and environments. The bulk of my professional life has been spent working for organizations that transitioned from one company to another through a series of mergers and acquisitions. While secure in my current position with The Truss Company, I am confidentially exploring opportunities that will allow me to use my analytical and structural design capabilities beyond truss design. Let me highlight a few ways in which I've achieved success as a design draftsman:

▣ Selected as one of two design draftsmen to move from residential truss design to the more complex, and costly, commercial arena. Commercial clients are in King, Snohomish, and Pierce counties and have included federal buildings, restaurants, and large residential complexes.

▣ Work closely with architects and sales representatives on the interpretation of designs, ensuring the final products meet the intended plan. I am particularly skilled in translating the technical to nontechnical individuals.

▣ Successfully introduced computerized design into organizations and taught on a one-on-one basis the use of both AutoCAD and PrimeCAD.

I look forward to discussing in greater detail with you the ways in which I can make a significant contribution to Benson Engineering. I will call you next week to schedule a conversation.

Sincerely,

Mark Renshaw

Attachment: Resume

The bullets are an attractive graphic element that is repeated in the header of this well-written letter.

105

Writer: Shanna Kemp, M.Ed., JCTC; Carrollton, TX

VICTORIA ADAMS
3535 S. Prairieview Road
Irving, TX 75033
(972) 555-1276

February 8, 2001

Jane Robbins
Technical Advantage, Inc.
1424 Broadview Lane
Dallas, Texas 75057

Dear Ms. Robbins:

I am exploring employment opportunities as a technical support specialist where I can merge my customer service skills and interest in technical fields. Technical Advantage, Inc., seems to offer such an opportunity.

I have enclosed my resume, which outlines my dedication, qualifications, and credentials in this field. I appreciate your taking the time to review it.

You will notice that I have an outstanding background in customer service and am especially skilled in my ability to build relationships, solve problems, and implement organizational methods. It is my goal to transfer these skills to a technical market. Toward that end, I am pursuing educational training in telecommunications to increase my technical skills and knowledge.

My success in the past and my future successes stem from my strong commitment and sense of professionalism. I maintain high work standards for myself and have always served as a positive role model and motivator to other employees.

I look forward to speaking with you personally so that we may discuss the specific needs of Technical Advantage, Inc., and how I can fulfill them. I will be calling you next week to set up an appointment. In the meantime, if you have any questions or would like to contact me in advance, I can be reached at the number above.

Sincerely,

Victoria Adams

Enclosure

In this cold-call letter, the job seeker concisely presents her qualifications and is upfront about what she's seeking.

Writer: Lynn Andenoro, CPRW; Salt Lake City, UT

CARTER ALAN CAMPBELL
4479 S. Blue Moon Drive Apt. 321 ▪ Taylorsville, Utah 84123
(801) 555-3676 ▪ ccampbell@uswest.net

January 5, 2001

Marvin Zimmerman
Innovative Engineering
3480 Research Drive
Salt Lake City, Utah 84108

Dear Mr. Zimmerman:

If you are looking for an innovative, performance-driven mechanical/design engineer who consistently delivers solid results as an individual or team leader, then you will be interested in the experience and accomplishments highlighted in the enclosed resume.

During my four years with I-Sim, I have made significant contributions to the development and quality of the product line and to bottom-line performance:

- Designed and implemented motion base systems for high-end truck and automobile simulators.

- Co-developed real-time simulator dynamics, including software models for road-tire interaction, drive train, and vehicle dynamic response.

- Led C++ software development for motion control and I/O processing for embedded digital signal processors in automobile simulators.

- Captured $15,000 per unit cost savings by advocating outside purchase of motion base rather than developing the part in-house.

- Successfully installed new prototype through extraordinary effort that ensured sale of 16 police car simulators in the first week.

In order to advance my career, I am seeking new challenges with a mechanical engineering/design firm like Innovative Engineering. May we meet to explore your needs and how my skills, strengths, and experience can deliver similar results for your organization?

Thank you for your consideration.

Sincerely,

Carter Alan Campbell

The relevant bullet-point accomplishments are the heart of this letter. Specific technical abilities are highlighted.

107

Writer: Maria Hebda, CPRW; Trenton, MI

Kenneth Richards

16364 St. Joseph • Grand Ledge, Michigan 48837 • (517) 555-2968
E-mail: krichards@mysite.com

January 15, 2001

Mr. William Stark, Personnel Director
Star Commodities, Inc.
2698 Logan
Lansing, Michigan 48910

Dear Mr. Stark:

As a highly proficient and experienced project manager with a passion for technology, I am routinely faced with challenges and the need to evaluate diversified programs and their ability to meet operating requirements.

As you will note, my resume may not look like others you receive. My resume is beyond reciting job titles and duties — it reveals results. Having a complete picture of my expertise and experience is very important. For several years, I have spearheaded and developed various programs to meet organizational needs.

I possess solid experience in systems integration, hardware and software analysis, and systems life cycle management. In addition to my managerial and technical experience, I will offer your company decisive leadership, dedication, and commitment to excellence.

The enclosed resume is submitted in confidence. I prefer that my present employer not be contacted until a position is officially offered. Your time and consideration are appreciated. I will contact your office next week to follow up and answer any questions you may have. Please feel free to contact me if you would like to speak sooner.

Sincerely,

Kenneth Richards

Enclosure

This candidate discusses project successes and his approach to project management. Note this letter's assertive close.

108

Writer: Salome Randall Tripi; Mt. Morris, NY

OLIVER T. KEITH   8002 Lakeside Road • Buffalo NY 14202 • 716/555-0099

February 8, 2000   **VIA FAX to: 518/555-0101; 3 pages total**

Mr. Peter Robinson
Vice President, Engineering
Eastern NY Telecommunications
10 Fourth Street
Albany, NY 12888

Dear Mr. Robinson:

My resume follows for employment consideration with your organization.

I possess 15 years of experience as a Communications Engineer with specific background in fiber optics, microwave, and voice and data transmissions. I have honed my technical skills through independent and team work primarily in the areas of maintenance, repair, troubleshooting, and testing. Additionally, I have managed assigned projects and directed staff in day-to-day duties.

I am confident in my ability to make a significant contribution to Eastern NY Telecommunications and would appreciate the opportunity to discuss my background in light of potential employment with you. Feel free to contact me at 716/555-0099 at your convenience.

Thank you for your time and consideration.

Sincerely,

Oliver T. Keith

Attachment

This concise letter would be as appropriate for online transmission as it is for fax or standard mail. It focuses on "just the facts."

109

Writer: Loretta Heck; Prospect Heights, IL

Dan Van Essen
462 Bridle Path
Wheeling, IL 60090
(847) 555-1749

April 4, 2001

Patrice Sullivan
Dynamic Technologies, Inc.
45 Wheeling Parkway
Wheeling, IL 60093

Dear Ms. Sullivan:

I am writing to express my interest in senior-level project management opportunities. Highlights of my professional career include

- Over 15 years of experience leading complex design projects, engineering and troubleshooting difficult and intermittent problems (electrical, mechanical, or programming)

- Outstanding technical, engineering, design, and analytical qualifications

- Leadership of cross-functional project teams working cooperatively to achieve common goals and job objectives

- Consistent success in delivering projects on time and within budget

- Ability to optimize programs and operations, thereby improving manufacturing output

The core of my experience is in automated machinery, electrical design, and programming. My goal is to continue as head of large projects, solve difficult problems, and be in a leadership role where I believe my experience and competencies are of most value.

I would welcome the opportunity to speak with you regarding your current management requirements and appreciate both your time and your consideration of my qualifications.

Sincerely,

Dan Van Essen

This well-written letter is readable, concise, and focused. The candidate's skills and achievements are clearly communicated, and the tone throughout is very professional.

Writer: Kristie Cook, JCTC, CPRW; Olathe, KS

KATHERINE M. CLAUSSEN
561 N. Frederick St.
Arlington, VA 22203
703-555-7776

September 29, 2001

Jonathan Spears
Garrison Communications
8742 Germantown Road
Gaithersburg, MD 20882

Dear Mr. Spears:

As new technology continually emerges, progressive companies recognize the pressing need for someone to train employees on new hardware and software. I understand your company is seeking someone to meet that need. Please find my resume enclosed for your review and consideration as a Computer Trainer.

With over six years of experience training new and converted software users, I possess a variety of teaching techniques that transform even the most reluctant students into knowledgeable computer users. I am proficient in most mainstream software and have a knack for learning new and proprietary software quickly and efficiently. My experience includes training one-on-one, and with small and large groups, in both classroom and on-the-job settings. I understand the need to teach users from their perspective—I quickly learn what each student needs to know for real-world use and design classes around those needs. My goal is to help people learn their software and systems in a practical way that is useful to them.

If this goal contributes to your objective for a Computer Trainer, we have good reason to meet. I would appreciate the opportunity to speak with you about how I can help your company live its mission by improving customer service, productivity, and efficiency through information technology. I will call in a few days to arrange a meeting that is convenient for you. In the meantime, if you need more information, please feel free to call me at 703-555-7776. Thank you for your time and consideration. I look forward to meeting you in the near future.

Respectfully,

Katherine M. Claussen

enclosure

With an interesting opening, assertive close, and persuasive middle paragraph, this letter captures and keeps the reader's attention.

JOSÉ ROMERO

555 Skyline Drive
Mountain View, CA 95555 E-resume: www.CareerFolios.com/JRomero.html

Cell: (555) 555-5555
jromero@aol.com

December 30, 2000

Mr. Victor Petrocelli
Procurement Manager
MajorTech Company
555 Granite Bay Road
Granite Bay, CA 95555

Re: Software VAR Procurement Specialist

Dear Mr. Petrocelli:

Gene Mortillano spoke to me recently about your need for a Software VAR Procurement Specialist at the Granite Bay site. Although not actively pursuing a career change, I am very interested in the position for a number of reasons. First, MajorTech's name is synonymous with "best-of-breed" product engineering and technology solutions. Further, the company's reputation for attracting and retaining quality individuals isn't happenstance. In part, it is attributable to MT's commitment to diversity, employee development, mentoring, and performance-based advancement opportunities.

What would I bring to the table? A record that represents a good mix of creativity, drive, intellect, and leadership, along with solid knowledge of OS and Web applications. Highlights of my recent contributions for ABC Services (a software subscription/upgrade outsource company) are these:

✓ Supported a 23 percent increase in revenue and a 32 percent increase in profit (recent quarter), primarily through development and management of VAR channel programs for software companies and partnership support to UNIX install-base.

✓ Doubled company's sales with launch of new Web products division as a result of relationship selling and a partnering commitment with industry leaders such as 3Com and Intel.

✓ Earned Netscape's Preferred Reseller award, reserved for top-performing groups among 400 reseller partners.

Given my technical knowledge, management skills, and partnership-management strengths, I believe I have much to offer MajorTech as it approaches an exciting turning point. I will be in touch and look forward to learning more about your needs for this position.

Sincerely,

José Romero

Having been referred for this position, the candidate mentions this fact right up front and then follows with specific reasons that the reader should be interested in his background and capabilities.

Part

III

The Total Job Search: Thank-You Letters, Recruiters, and Resumes

Winning
Thank-You Letters

Ask yourself this question: "When should you send a thank-you letter after an interview?"

If you answered "always," you're right! Regardless of the circumstance, the position, or your level of interest in the opportunity, you should *always* send a thank-you letter. It's proper job search etiquette; and, frankly, it's expected in an intensely competitive job search market.

Remember back when you were a child, when your mother forced you to sit down and write thank-you notes after each holiday season? You thought it was a laborious task, and you didn't understand why you couldn't just go play with your new toys. Well, believe it or not, and whether your mother knew it or not, she was teaching you an extremely valuable business skill.

 Tip Simply put, sending a thank-you letter after an interview is good manners!

People remember other people who go the "extra mile" and put forth extra effort. When you send a thank-you note after an interview, you are communicating the following:

- I appreciate your time and consideration in interviewing me.
- I am interested in the opportunity. (Even if you're not, you certainly do not want to "burn any bridges." In fact, you want to leave every door open for future opportunities.)
- I am well versed in business etiquette and protocol.
- I know how to deal with people and win their trust.
- I am a good communicator with excellent interpersonal skills.
- I follow through on tasks I have initiated.
- I will put forth extra effort for you and for the company.
- I am determined to get what I want.

Remember the discussion from the Introduction about the history of cover letters and how they have transitioned from transmittal letters to cover letters to marketing communications over the past several decades? Well, the same can be said about thank-you letters. Fifteen years ago, you sent a thank-you letter that communicated two key concepts:

1. Thank you for your time.

2. I'm quite interested in the position.

Here's an example:

```
Dear Mr. Marsh:

Thank you for taking the time to meet with me last Thursday.
I enjoyed learning about Triple X and meeting the other mem-
bers of the Engineering department. As I mentioned, I am
quite interested in your position for an Engineering Manager
and look forward to returning for a second round of inter-
views. I'll wait to hear from Sally about scheduling.
```

That's it. The letter was brief and to the point. It was simply a formality.

Today, thank-you letters have evolved into what we refer to as "second-tier" marketing communications—letters that highlight your qualifications and "sell" you for a specific position. Consider that your resume and cover letter were your "first-tier" marketing tools. They got you in the door for the interview and, thus, served their purpose. Now, you're ready to go on the attack again, marketing your skills and qualifications, communicating your expertise, and demonstrating your value to that specific organization with your "second-tier" tool—your thank-you letter.

How Thank-You Letters Can Help You

Well-written thank-you letters can be powerful marketing communications that can advance your candidacy in a number of important ways.

Reinforce Points from the Interview

Thank-you letters give you the opportunity to reiterate the skills, qualifications, and experiences you bring to the company that are directly related to their current and long-range needs.

Your interviewer could not possibly remember each and every detail that was discussed during your interview. Therefore, it is your responsibility to highlight the information about yourself and your career that is most relevant to the position and to the company. Don't ever leave your interviewer wondering whether you can or cannot do something. Spell it out so that your qualifications are clear and readily identifiable.

> As you will recall, I bring to your company six years of progressively responsible experience in insurance claims processing, along with award-winning performance in customer service/customer satisfaction. In addition, I spearheaded the implementation of new client/server technology to support our growing infrastructure, much like the project that you are currently undertaking.

With these two sentences, not only did we highlight years of experience and success, we focused on the individual's technical expertise as it relates directly to that company's current needs.

Communicate New Information

Thank-you letters allow you to share new information that was not addressed during the interview.

Although you go into each interview with your own agenda of information that you want to share, there may be instances where you have not been able to communicate everything you had intended. It may be that the allotted interview time was too brief or the interviewer's agenda did not lend itself to a discussion of a particular topic. Or it may be that you simply forgot to mention something that, in hindsight, you consider essential to communicate. Use your thank-you letter to share that information and bring it to your interviewer's attention.

> One key facet of my career that we did not discuss on Friday is my experience in vendor sourcing. With Chevron, I am responsible for researching and identifying new vendors worldwide to supply both our administrative and field operations. To date, I have contracted with more than 200 vendors for over $100 million in annual purchases. In addition, I am currently in the final stages of implementing a vendor quality program that is projected to cut 8 percent from our costs.

This paragraph highlights what the candidate forgot to mention during the interview, using concrete numbers to demonstrate the scope of his responsibility. He then follows up with an achievement that communicates two critical concepts: performance improvement (vendor quality) and cost savings.

Respond to Objections from the Interview

Thank-you letters allow you the opportunity to respond to any objections that were discussed, or inferred, during the interview.

Often during an interview, your interviewer will identify one or two concerns she has about your qualifications, experience, skills, and candidacy for the position. This is where your thank-you letter can have a tremendous impact. It provides you with a vehicle to respond to those objections and, hopefully, overcome them.

Suppose you are applying for a position in real estate in a city in which you have never worked. To really excel in that position, you must have local contacts that you can leverage to your advantage. This is what the hiring company is most concerned about in relation to your ability to handle the job. Here's an example of how to deal with that in your thank-you letter:

> You're right. I have never worked in the San Diego market. However, I have worked in other new markets nationwide where I have quickly ingratiated myself within the local business community and driven significant revenue growth. Furthermore, I have extensive business contacts in San Diego who are more than willing to open new doors and introduce me to the people in town who I need to know.

In this paragraph, the candidate responded to the fact that he has successfully met the challenge of building new markets in his earlier positions. What's more, all of a sudden he's not an outsider; already he has contacts in San Diego.

Share Relevant Personal Information

Thank-you letters are an excellent vehicle for sharing personal information when, and only when, you believe it to be relevant to the position, the company, or the people you will be working with.

Although job seekers are generally told to refrain from sharing personal information, there are situations in which this type of information can be valuable in facilitating a positive hiring situation. Consider the following example:

```
In reference to our discussions regarding relocation, let me
share with you that my wife is a Nursing Administrator and,
therefore, it should be relatively easy for her find a posi-
tion in Detroit. If you have any specific contacts or recom-
mendations, I'd appreciate it. In addition, I noticed several
photographs of you on the golf course. I am also an avid
golfer and would like to know where the best course in town
is. Maybe on my next trip, we can fit in nine holes.
```

What have we communicated here? Simply put, that the candidate and his wife are quite interested in the position, are willing to relocate, and can quickly assimilate into the community. What's more, the candidate and the interviewer share a common interest. This type of information is obviously most appropriate for more senior-level candidates for whom relocation and spousal employment are primary considerations.

Keep Your Qualifications on the Manager's Mind

Thank-you letters keep you and your qualifications in the forefront and on the mind of the hiring manager.

Consider this. You're applying for a pharmaceutical sales position and you know that the competition is stiff. There may be perhaps 200 or more candidates for one opening. The interviewer has reviewed all of the resumes and talked with more than 50 people. At that point, everyone blurs together and the interviewer really can't remember who's who.

Just then your thank-you letter appears on her desk. All of a sudden, not only does she remember who you are, she also remembers your past track record of sales performance, your outgoing personality, and your knowledge of pharmaceutical products. You've just positioned yourself in the forefront of her mind! When you call the next day to follow up, she knows who you are and immediately invites you back for a second round of interviews.

Distinguish Yourself from Other Candidates

Thank-you letters competitively distinguish you from other candidates, particularly those who do not put forth the extra effort to send a thank-you letter.

We'll use the same scenario as above. By sending a thank-you letter, you have not only put yourself in the forefront of the hiring manager's mind, but you've also put yourself ahead of the other candidates for the position. Those who have not gone to the effort of sending a thank-you letter are simply lost in the shuffle and will most likely never hear back from her.

Build a Relationship

Thank-you letters help you build a relationship with influential hiring authorities.

A typical job search involves many interviews, and, obviously, not all of these will result in a job offer. But it is always in your best interests to create a positive image of yourself and your professional capabilities. Who knows where this might lead! It's not inconceivable that you could build a referral network with people who interview you but don't select you for a specific position! Your thank-you letters help you build a relationship and convey a consistently positive and professional impression.

> *Tip* Thank-you letters really do make a difference. Our professional colleagues who are recruiters or hiring managers tell us they're "astounded" at how few candidates take the time to send a thank-you letter. There are no negatives to sending a thank-you letter—provided that it is well-written and relevant to your interview situation. Send your thank-you letters today, and give yourself a competitive edge!

Frequently Asked Questions

A question often asked about thank-you letters is how many pages they should be. Again, as with most other activities in your job search campaign, there are no definite answers and no specific rules. Generally speaking, we recommend that thank-you letters be one to two pages long, depending entirely on the amount of information you want and need to communicate to your interviewer.

The question also arises as to whether thank-you notes should be hand-written or word-processed. Unless you are writing a brief "bread-and-butter" thank-you note similar to the first example in this chapter, it is our strong recommendation that these letters be typed for a professional appearance that's consistent with your resume and cover letter. Handwriting is difficult to read and does not convey a businesslike image. Although a brief hand-written note can be a charming and personal touch, do not attempt to convey more than a few sentences by hand.

Thank-You Letter Checklist

Once you've written a thank-you letter, take a moment to review the list below. Does your thank-you letter communicate the following?

- Performance
- Success
- Energy
- Enthusiasm
- Personality
- Commitment
- Results
- Interest in the position
- Interest in the company
- Your value to the company
- Your potential contributions to the company

If your letter does communicate most of this, great. Proofread it one more time and get it out ASAP. If it doesn't, you might want to go back and re-write or edit it. Remember that you are writing a marketing letter, so be sure to *sell yourself!*

> *Tip* No two thank-you letters you write will be the same, because no two situations are ever the same. To have impact, thank-you letters must be individually written to highlight what is most significant to that person and that company.

> *Tip* When you've interviewed with more than one person, either individually or in a group, take the time to write a separate thank-you letter to each person. And be sure that the content of each letter is unique, because there's a good chance your letters will be shared or added to your interview file. Focus on an area of rapport you developed with each interviewer, and try to connect your letter to what you feel are each person's strongest interests and concerns.

One Final Recommendation

When you are sitting in an interview and you think of something that would be important to include in your thank-you letter, jot down a quick note—a word or two—to remind yourself. It communicates a positive message if your interviewer sees that you're so interested in the position that you have to take notes! If the situation does not lend itself to notetaking, the moment you leave that interview, find a quiet place and write a few notes to yourself about the company's core issues, needs, and challenges. You'll then know what to focus on when writing your thank-you letter that same day or the next.

Sample Thank-You Letters

Following are five thank-you letters. Each is quite different from the others in style, tone, format, and message. Each was written for a particular person in a particular situation. Some are traditional; some are more creative. Some are short and to the point; others are much more detailed. We share these with you just to give you a sampling of what thank-you letters are all about.

Writer: Carole S. Barns; Woodinville, WA

CALISTA MARIE KINGSTON
12 North Terrace View Drive ◆ Fresno, CA 93714 ◆ (559) 325-3232
lakeview@seanet.com

February 16, 2000

Ms. Wilhelmina Jackson
Director of Training
SunSystem.com
123 Highline Circle
San Jose, CA 95150

Dear Ms. Jackson:

Gracias! Merci! Danke schoen! Thank you!

In any language, my appreciation is genuine for the time you, Linda, and Darrell gave me Tuesday. It's such a joy when a job interview is not only informative, but also filled with interesting conversation. I was particularly impressed with the depth of your commitment to quality training. Obviously you "walk the talk" that knowledgeable employees are critical to an organization's success *and* necessary to continue SunSystem.com's phenomenal growth. I left your offices totally psyched—energized, enthusiastic, and eager to put into play for SunSystem.com a variety of personnel-training and staff-development projects as a member of your team.

Based on my broad credentials in training, coaching, project management, vision-based strategic planning—as well as knowledge of UNIX, Web-based design systems, and HTML—I am uniquely qualified to fill the role of Learning Content Manager. We discussed in detail most of my qualifications on Tuesday. Let me itemize some additional reasons to hire me:

◆ *Responsibility for anticipating, designing, and implementing changing training needs.* In both current and former positions, I created programs to meet changes in procedures, cultures, and economic situations that provided each individual with strong support and overall direction in keeping with company core values, mission, and key deliverables.

◆ *Management of personnel.* Not only do I have experience and skill in managing people of diverse responsibilities, levels, ages, and cultures, I am aware of the special considerations that are needed to guide co-workers in a matrix/project management setting with other managers.

◆ *Development and administration of budgets.* Key to the success of my Education for Success clients has been the attention I've given to developing strong business plans, short- and long-term budgets, and solid P&L statements.

My vision for the Learning Centers is to work with you to develop a team of individuals who are customer-focused, have performance standards aimed at meeting the needs of their constituency, and possess the tools to support that direction and the company's mission and goals. Throughout my career I have been characterized as a decisive business leader who is able to envision and deliver results and who has earned the respect of all personnel in each organization, from those in entry-level positions to members of the senior executive team. It is this strength in leadership and dedication that I bring to SunSystem.com.

Thank you, again, for such an interesting and informative meeting. I look forward to moving to the next step in the selection process.

Sincerely,

Calista Marie Kingston

Energy and enthusiasm are communicated immediately in the first words of this letter, and the job seeker gives compelling reasons to further her candidacy.

Writer: Mark Berkowitz, NCCC, CPRW, JCTC; Yorktown Heights, NY

Graham T. Johnson

235 Shady Hill Lane
Thornwood, NY
10504
(914) 747-5555

November 2, 2000

Rev. Monsignor Trent P. James, Pastor
St. Bernadette Roman Catholic Church
1127 Main Street
Danbury, CT 06810

Dear Pastor James:

It was a pleasure meeting you and the Director-of-Music Search Committee on Sunday, October 25th. I wanted to take the opportunity to thank you and the committee for taking the time to both interview and audition me.

I found St. Bernadette Church to be an exciting and liturgically rich and active parish and am totally confident that my qualifications are head-on with your position requirements. I am certain that with my education and experience, I would quickly become a valuable asset to the life and ministry of St. Bernadette.

In conversations with committee members, I learned that they believe my expertise would be a welcome addition to the music ministry and staff of St. Bernadette, as they were impressed with the following:

- My knowledge of Catholic liturgy/ritual
- Proficiency in organ
- Proven ability to recruit and direct youth/children, contemporary and adult choirs/cantors

I look forward to meeting with you again so that we may take matters to the next level, as I am convinced that my background and expertise make an excellent match for the needs of your parish. In the interim, thank you for your consideration, attention, and time.

Sincerely,

Graham T. Johnson

In this letter, the candidate effectively uses the impressions of others to sell him for the position.

Writer: Carole S. Barns; Woodinville, WA

SALLY GLORIA CARBONNE
18730 Occident Avenue ◆ Silverado, CA 92676 ◆ (805) 555-3269
gloryglory@email.net

January 24, 2001

Mr. Eric Holesen
Vice President, Marketing
I-Net Co.
500 Union Street, Suite 745
Seattle, WA 98101

Dear Eric:

"Enthusiastic" was how I characterized my feelings toward I-Net Co. following our telephone conversation last week. After meeting with you and Susie on Tuesday, I decided **"ENTHUSIASTIC!"** was a more accurate description of my eagerness to join your team and bring to the I-Net family my vision, marketing expertise, and skill in creating a demand for product.

Thank you for the great session and for sharing so openly your plans and goals for the I-Net product. It was refreshing to talk with someone whose opinions and views on the concept of brand so closely match mine. Yes, brand is *not* logo; it truly is that intangible feeling a consumer has toward a product that, when managed successfully, results in sales, loyalty, and more sales.

I believe my level of corporate marketing and brand management experience (national, international, large, small, high-profile, start-up, ad agency, packaging, and distribution)—coupled with my ability to take the corporate message and create an appropriately targeted marketing plan—are exactly what a "product first" company such as I-Net needs. I can hit the ground running and deliver results quickly.

My previous correspondence, my resume, and my conversations with you these past two weeks detailed the many successes I've had—growing K-2 revenues 706 percent and its market share to 40 percent, management of multimillion–dollar budgets, and supervision of several dozen employees. I am convinced I am the right person to build similar successes for the first of the next generation of online companies.

I look forward to the next step in your selection process and, ultimately, to strategizing with you on ways to ensure all Internet users can add security, privacy, and speed to the flexibility and convenience of "surfing the Web."

Sincerely,

Sally Gloria Carbonne

This job seeker builds on the rapport she obviously established during her initial interview, then goes on to share a strong rationale for her candidacy.

Writer: Elizabeth Axnix, CPRW, JCTC; Iowa City, IA

HEATHER CARTER
555.472.7360

103 South Burlington, #1   Fairfield, Iowa 55555

March 22, 2001

Mr. Richard Torres
General Manager
Royal Flush Corporation
555 Golden Street
Deadwood, SD 55555

Dear Mr. Torres:

Thank you for your time and hospitality in meeting with me this past weekend. I appreciated very much the opportunity to interview for the general manager position and learn more about your company. Enclosed is a list of my professional references.

The astute business manager bases decisions on in-depth research, empirical evidence, and documented numbers. When I'm faced with making a critical business decision, I certainly use all three tools. However, in making personal decisions, I add one more criteria—intuition. My business sense indicates that my management skills and knowledge of the hospitality industry would easily transition to a general management role with your company, while my sense of intuition tells me that I would be very happy making my home in the Deadwood area.

My decision to relocate to the Deadwood area is equally divided between business and personal. The term "culture shock" was mentioned frequently in the interview. I currently live in a town of 350 people in one of our nation's most rural states, Iowa. My husband and I have researched the suitability of the Deadwood area very carefully through frequent and lengthy visits and, frankly, it is the isolation that attracts us primarily. The economic opportunities are also attractive. The growth in the area's gaming industry has spurred corresponding growth in the hospitality sector, and that's where my expertise lies.

Although my gaming experience is limited, I have successfully addressed a number of situations from which parallels could be drawn. I've had guests expire in the parking lot, I've assisted law enforcement authorities in apprehending armed drug smugglers (in front of a full lobby, of course!), and I've dealt with hundreds of rabid, unruly, and inebriated sports fans. To my way of thinking, guests intent on playing games of chance do not compare with athletes suffering from high levels of steroids! In any event, I am a very quick learner and am eager to expand my knowledge of the hospitality industry.

I fully understand the economic, cultural, and demographic realities of Deadwood. I've experienced its hospitality, and I have calculated the risks and rewards of relocating to the area. You will not make a poor business decision if you hire me, because my business sense tells me that I can strengthen guest and employee loyalty, control variable expenses, and deliver consistent, profitable results for Royal Flush Corporation.

Sincerely,

Heather Carter

Enclosure

P.S.: Doesn't your gut feeling have you wanting me to work for you rather than your competitor?

In this letter, the candidate effectively overcomes some potential objections she noted during her interview. And doesn't the P.S. grab your attention?

Writer: Christine Magnus, CPRW; Bronx, NY

Katherine Morgan
1022 West Bend Avenue
Mount Vernon, NY 10560
Phone: (718) 555-5052

November 16, 2000

Cheryl Washington
Hiring Manager
Tri-State Healthcare Service
357 Fifth Avenue
New York, NY 10022

Dear Ms. Washington:

Thank you for taking time out of your busy schedule to meet with me on November 15th to discuss career opportunities with THS. I would also like to thank you for your flexibility and patience in scheduling our meeting.

From our conversation, I am confident in my ability to meet and exceed your expectations. Your clients will benefit from a dedicated professional who has expertise collaborating with nurses and social workers to deliver quality care and services. In addition, I am capable of achieving the following:

- Assessing a patient's psychological, emotional, and financial needs
- Providing counseling to patients and family
- Linking patients and family to other community services
- Resolving abuse/neglect problems
- Advocating for patients' rights and helping patients negotiate the social service delivery system

Since being founded in 1925, THS continues to be a leading provider of home health care and community-based health services. I look forward to becoming part of an organization that has such an impressive history.

Again, thank you for your time and interest.

With strong interest,

Katherine Morgan

This is a fairly normal, traditional approach to a follow-up letter. The bullet points highlight key qualifications, and in the following paragraph the candidate compliments and identifies with the organization.

Chapter

14

Cover Letter Insights from Recruiters

At this point, you've probably devoted several hours, if not more, to writing your cover letter. You've read this book, flipped back and forth between sections, rewritten, edited, and proofread. Now, you've finally got a letter ready to go. Great! You've got the right marketing materials (your resume and cover letter) and are moving forward with your search full steam ahead!

Now, we're going to change direction 180 degrees and focus our attention on recruiters and cover letters. This is a two-pronged conversation in which we will discuss

- Cover letters that recruiters write to their clients (companies) to introduce a candidate (hopefully, you!).

- Cover letters written by candidates to recruiters (the type of letter that you write).

Cover Letters Recruiters Write to Their Client Companies

To understand the first set of letters, you must understand the recruiter-company relationship. If you hire a professional resume writer, career coach, employment agency, or outplacement consultant, *you* are the client. You have hired them and you are paying the fee (or perhaps your employer is paying it on your behalf). With recruiters, the relationship is entirely different. Their clients are the companies that pay their fee, not you, the individual job seeker. In fact, they don't even refer to you as clients. You are their "candidates."

This is a critical concept to grasp. All too many job seekers believe that recruiters will go out and find them a job. That is simply not true. In fact, the opposite is true. Recruiters are paid by companies to go out and find *precisely* the candidate they are seeking. Unfortunately, unless you meet the job specifications almost verbatim, you are, in essence, a worthless commodity to that recruiter. We don't mean to sound so tough, but a quick reality check is vital in proactively managing your relationships with recruiters.

Do you want to work with recruiters in your job search? Most likely, the answer is "yes." But you must realize that they will not be working for you! You are considered a commodity in a competitive and volatile job search market. If you don't meet the specs for a particular position, you will most likely never even hear from that recruiter. In fact, it will most likely be impossible for you to call and get him on the phone. The recruiter sees no immediate value in spending any time with you or exerting any effort on your behalf, because it will not yield him a placement fee.

The only time this will not be the case is when you *are* the perfect candidate. In this situation, the recruiter has the potential to make tens of thousands of dollars if the company (her client) hires you. You'd better believe she'll be your best friend, go out of her way to accommodate you, and work to make the entire hiring process as easy and quick as possible. Wouldn't you do the same if someone were going to pay you $10,000, $20,000, or more?

Don't misinterpret what we are communicating here. There are thousands and thousands of recruiters nationwide. They are committed to their profession and to their clients. The only issue that you must remember is that you are not the client. Understand how the recruiter–job seeker relationship works and you'll be better able to manage your campaign "within the established process."

Let's look more closely at the recruiter-company relationship and workflow process. The company gives the recruiter detailed information about the candidate they are seeking. This generally includes professional qualifications, technical skills, educational credentials, management and leadership qualifications, industry experience, years of experience, technical skills, U.S. citizenship status, and other information directly relevant to the position at

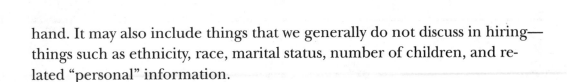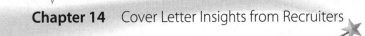

hand. It may also include things that we generally do not discuss in hiring—things such as ethnicity, race, marital status, number of children, and related "personal" information.

You can look at the recruiter-company relationship as a partnership. The company has defined who they want. It is now the recruiter's task to find that person. Once the right candidate has been identified, the recruiter will generally conduct a preliminary phone interview or in-person screening to verify the candidate's credentials, qualifications, and experience. Then, if the candidate matches the qualifications to a "T" and also has a strong component of the "intangibles" being sought, the recruiter will most likely forward the candidate's resume to the hiring manager at his client company, along with a brief cover letter addressing very specific issues, many of them personal.

Tim Dermady: Contingent Recruiter in Telecommunications, Software, and Engineering

Tim Dermady, President of ExecutiveFIT (526 Old Liverpool Road, Syracuse, New York 13088; 315-451-5457; tim@executivefit.com), states, "I use cover letters as a booster to present candidates. The cover letter comes directly from me, so I know that the company reads it. My letters are short and concise, and do not reiterate the resume, other than to quickly identify 'who' the candidate is. That's it. I then go into things that the client wants to know, such as dual-career-couple status, diversity, compensation, reason for leaving, citizenship, ability to travel, geographic preferences, kids, and the like. This content then serves as a useful ice-breaker for hiring managers. I make a point of staying away from smarmy wordsmithing, and I really like lots of white space."

Let's take a look at some of Tim's letters. You'll get a much better idea of how he approaches his cover letters, what type of information he includes, and the style in which they are written. Note that we are *not* recommending that your cover letters be written in this manner. These are letters that Tim has written to his client companies. They are included in this book just to demonstrate the difference in style and presentation from the more "traditional" cover letters you will be writing, and to give you an idea of the kinds of information a recruiter will be sending employers about you.

Executivefit.

P.O. Box 8
202 Strathmore by the Park
Syracuse, NY 13207.0008
315.425.9025
315.424.9473 fax

URL: www.executivefit.com
email: tim@executivefit.com
Tim Dermady
Ellen McCauley

December 22, 2001

John Miller
President & CEO
Miller Technologies, Inc.

Re. **Walter C. Roven,** Vice President Sales; Candidate

John:

We are presenting Walter Roven for your VP position. I discussed your company with him, and he subsequently visited your Web site. In response, he indicated you share the same clients he had with Unisys and USoft. Walter stated that half of his sales-management experience in IT at Unisys was in the public sector. Most of his experience was with state governments that included NY, CT, MA, PA, and VA. Many of his connections within these agencies as well as account managers that reported to him remain informally today.

The reason he is in the market is due to a recent merger. Walter received an attractive package recently and is considering the best firm to pursue going forward, having a nice runway.

He fits the profile you have been pursuing: 160mm in revenue goal(s), achievement in the public-sector IT market, 10 direct reports & 100+ sales reps, ME to VA. Walter is earning a base of 150K + bonus that led him into a 250K range. This excludes earned options.

Although he has been away from Unisys for four years, the relationships among subordinates and clients usually don't fade, given his tenure. The longer, the better, when they reconvene. Our experience is that the hot, "flash in the pan" persona hasn't worked out well in the government market. Tradition and familiarity seem to prevail in their risk-aversive culture.

Look forward to your feedback.

Tim

Executivefit.

P.O. Box 8
202 Strathmore by the Park
Syracuse, NY 13207.0008
315.425.9025
315.424.9473 fax

URL: www.executivefit.com
email: tim@executivefit.com
Tim Dermady
Ellen McCauley

December 9, 2001

John Miller
President & CEO
Miller Technologies, Inc.

Re. **Henry R. Charles, CFO candidate**

John:

Here is your heavy hitter, with all the right connections on Wall Street.

Charles is a great financial persona for your company. He is the finest we have seen so far for your IPO objectives. Open for relocation to Albany.

Tim

Executivefit.

P.O. Box 8
202 Strathmore by the Park
Syracuse, NY 13207.0008
315.425.9025
315.424.9473 fax

URL: www.executivefit.com
email: tim@executivefit.com
Tim Dermady
Ellen McCauley

Percy Preston
President & CEO
Preston Technologies, Inc.
105 Johnson Circle
Albany, NY 12145

Re. CFO Candidate **Lewis L. Lester**

Percy:

I am pleased to present Lewis L. Lester. I have attached his resume to this e-mail for your assessment. Lewis has reviewed your Web site already to get a perspective on Preston. He has a strong background in finance, IPO experience, M&A, investment banking, SEC, and E-Commerce.

He is familiar with Scient, Viant, iXL, and Razorfish.

Lewis has Wall Street connections from the early 80s from LBO activity with Chase Manhattan. He also knows many high-profile VC groups. I asked him for specifics in this area. The following is a list of firms that would be of interest to you:

Goldman Sachs, NYC
Oppenheimer, NYC
Morgan Stanley Dean Witter, NYC
Prudential Securities, NYC
Bear Stearns, NYC
BankBoston, Boston

There are about six other notable firms as well.

He is seeking 150K in base with an ability to increase his compensation through an IPO with stock options. Lewis owns property in North Chatham, NY, a close suburb near Albany. He is open for relocation to the area.

Lewis already has two written offers now. He was intrigued by your Web site, though. I would recommend a phone meeting, shortly, if you have interest. There is a timing issue with our sourcing of this candidate for you now.

Tim Dermady

Executive**fit.**

P.O. Box 8
202 Strathmore by the Park
Syracuse, NY 13207.0008
315.425.9025
315.424.9473 fax

URL: www.executivefit.com
email: tim@executivefit.com
Tim Dermady
Ellen McCauley

November 28, 2002

Chris Robinson
CRS Corporation

Enterprise Architect Candidate – **Randy Steinhock**

I have submitted Randy Steinhock for your review. He reviewed the job description prior to our weekend call. We agreed it looked like a good fit. I used Johnson and Patterson as benchmarks, and compared his credentials to them before and during our sourcing process. He has been a team leader from a low of 4 to a high of 35+ employees. Randy had reviewed your Web site thoroughly before he called me yesterday. We discussed his management style. It was clear to me (through our conversation) that he has a strong team orientation. He was not grandstanding, which is what I listen for. He has range in his personality to perform well in a matrix organization. Randy thought Computerworld gave the company excellent insights on the culture of the company.

He is a U.S. citizen, open for relocation to CRS, and has visited Homefair.com to strike a comparison for cost of living differences between Huntsville, AL, and Upstate NY. He would be seeking a package of 100K, with a base of 85K. His wife is a draftsperson for an architectural firm. They have a teenage son. The family is open together toward moving.

Tim Dermady

Rolande LaPointe: Contingent Recruiter
for a Wide Range of Local Industries

Rolande LaPointe of RO-LAN Associates, Inc. (725 Sabattus Street, Lewiston, Maine; 207-784-1010; rlapointe@aol.com), approaches recruitment from a somewhat different perspective than most. In addition to her recruiting practice, she is also a Certified Professional Resume Writer, working "both sides of the fence"—the preparatory process (resume and cover letter development) and the career marketing and job search process (placement).

Rolande shares two of her favorite cover letter examples with us. Remember, these are letters that she is writing to her client companies to encourage that they interview one of her candidates. It could be you!

The first example is the style she prefers because it is much more personalized and not so standardized.

RO-LAN ASSOCIATES, INC.

725 Sabattus Street
Lewiston, ME 04240

Office	Fax	Email
(207) 784-1010	(207) 782-3446	RLapointe@aol.com

2 February, 2000

Bernard Stevenson
Goldman Brown & Steep
1 Auto Drive
Freeport, RI 06754

Dear Bernard:

We're happy to forward the resume of Leslie Wilson for your consideration for your General Manager's position. You will see from her credentials that she has all of the qualifications and skills you require. What we are sending you (today) is the resume we have developed for Leslie after an extensive interview process. She has not yet seen this finished product. Her visit to the office for "proofing" will coincide with an interview with you.

As I told you, she is not rushing to change her present employment. She is looking to continue growing professionally – but, in a smaller environment. She is currently employed by Service King in Freeport. It is very difficult to capture on paper all that Leslie is and can offer an employer. I feel confident that when you meet her, you will understand my enthusiasm in presenting her as an "ideal" candidate for your organization and this new position.

In the interim, I look forward to receiving from you the days and times you may be available to meet with Leslie (at our location) possibly next week.

Have a wonderful day and remainder of the week.

Very truly yours,
RO-LAN ASSOCIATES, INC.

Rolande L. LaPointe, CPC, CIPC, CPRW, IJCTC
President

Enclosure

RO-LAN ASSOCIATES, INC.

725 Sabattus Street
Lewiston, ME 04240

Office	Fax	Email
(207) 784-1010	(207) 782-3446	RLapointe@aol.com

February 9, 2000

Delores Foster
Vice President, Campbell Manufacturing Co.
777 East Elm Road
Watertown, NY 15601

Dear Delores:

We are faxing you the resume of an excellent candidate for your Operations Manager position. His name is Martin Richardson. Martin is an experienced troubleshooter and is highly computer literate. We feel very comfortable in presenting Martin to you based on his qualifications and also the fact that he is personally known to staff members of RO-LAN Associates, Inc.

The following is a summarized list of Martin's skills and qualifications, including (but not limited to):

Pertinent Skills & Qualifications:
- Expertise in management at both Paper Direct and EMG Manufacturing.
- Successful in presenting a plan for installing a PC network for all departments of EMG Manufacturing.
- Extensive experience in identifying problems and providing workable solutions – a job he is now doing with Paper Direct.
- Managed shipping, order processing, and scheduling at both Paper Direct and EMG.

Pertinent Education & Training:
- Completed numerous business administration and computer courses.

Personal Data:
- Returned to Paper Direct in February 1998 as a Troubleshooting Manager.
- Very organized and a team player.
- Enjoys a manufacturing environment with responsibilities involving quality control, expediting, production, and overall management.
- Seeking employment with a growing company like Campbell Manufacturing.
- Lives in Watertown and is able to interview and begin work with notice.

We are looking forward to your comments on our candidate. Please feel free to call with any questions.

Sincerely,
RO-LAN ASSOCIATES, INC.

Rolande L. LaPointe, CPC, CIPC, CPRW, IJCTC
President

Enclosure

Sample #2 that Rolande shares with us is a style that most of the other recruiters at RO-LAN Associates use. It is much more structured and standardized, therefore making the writing process a bit easier. Obviously, the information about the candidate that is highlighted in this letter is directly in line with the company's hiring criteria.

Recruiters' Tips for Effective Cover Letters

We've explored how different the style and tone of letters that recruiters write to their client companies are from letters you would write. Now let's return our discussion to you, the job seeker, and what recruiters like to see when you write letters to them.

Barrie Hubbard: Retained Recruiter and HR Consultant

Barrie Hubbard, a recruiter and Vice President for Centennial, Inc. (1014 Vine Street, Cincinnati, Ohio 45202; 513-381-4411; barrie@centennnial-inc .com), sees hundreds of cover letters a week. "What catches my attention are letters that have been written to address the specific requirements for a position. These letters instantly communicate what the job seeker can do for my client. This is particularly important when the candidate is applying for a position that is different from his past experiences. For example, if I run an advertisement for a Marketing Manager and receive a resume from a Sales Executive, I am much more inclined to read that resume if the cover letter has highlighted that person's experience in marketing."

As you can see, Barrie's comments support everything that we have said in this book—specifically, that cover letters must be written to address the specifications of a particular job, and they must highlight the experiences, qualifications, and achievements the candidate brings to the table that are directly relevant to that position.

Barrie goes on to say that she sometimes receives cover letters with errors, misspellings, poor word usage, and other unacceptable mistakes. "What a shame. Many of these candidates are well qualified but have not taken the time to carefully review their cover letters. Often, it's just carelessness that results in a huge price to pay. I rarely, if ever, will present a candidate who cannot even send me error-free correspondence. Remember, the cover letter is my introduction to that person. It must be perfect and create a positive impression."

When we asked Barrie if she wrote and sent her own cover letters to her client companies when forwarding a candidate's resume, she said that was not common practice for her. Generally, she completes the pre-screening, speaks with the company about the candidate, gives them particular information as to why that individual is so well qualified, and then passes along a copy of the resume. The only exception is when the company is doing the pre-screening process themselves. In this instance, she will forward the job seeker's letter that she received.

Gary D'Alessio: Legal Industry Recruiter with Nationwide Placements

For a different perspective on cover letters, we contacted Gary A. D'Alessio of Chicago Legal Search (33 N. Dearborn Street #2302, Chicago, Illinois 60602; 312-251-2580; chgoleg@interaccess.com). As the company name indicates, Gary specializes in the placement of attorneys and other legal practitioners with law firms and corporations nationwide. After 14 years in the recruitment industry, Gary thinks that all too many attorneys falsely believe that cover letters are either not read or serve only as an introduction to their resume.

Gary comments, "Well-written cover letters incorporate several key concepts and information. First of all, they address why you're writing to that specific employer and what you know about the company. Second, well-written cover letters highlight specific information and relevant experience that will intrigue and entice the reader. Third, well-written cover letters are engaging, riveting, and revealing. They do not simply regurgitate what is already on the resume."

Gary shares a few more cover letter–writing rules with us. "It is bad form to submit a resume without a cover letter, no matter how casual the contact. It is an unprofessional presentation. What's more, cover letters should always be one page. If longer than one page, they are often considered cumbersome, too elaborate, and distracting.

"Remember, you've only got a recruiter's attention for 30 to 40 seconds to review both your cover letter and your resume. Attorneys should analogize a cover letter to an appellate brief or motion where, based on your written words, you want the opportunity to present your case orally. Cover letter writing is the same process, where your case is now the interview. You need to be persuasive to get what you want."

In discussing the particular components of a well-written letter, Gary also commented that each letter should have three distinct sections—the introduction (why you are writing to that specific employer or recruiter), the marketing pitch (why you are so well qualified), and the closing (where you ask for an interview or an informational meeting). He also describes the three most typical types of cover letters—the transmittal letter (most appropriately used when you've just been in contact with someone and they've asked for a copy of your resume), the network or contact letter (where you are writing at someone else's recommendation and you're sure to mention that person's name as the very first thing in the letter to capture your reader's attention), and the unsolicited letter (the most difficult of all to write).

A few other tips that Gary shares with us include the following comments. "Never use a form letter, for it is immediately recognizable. Definitely use numbers and percentages whenever possible to appropriately 'weight' your experience. Be conservative in your presentation. Use white or ivory paper— nothing outrageous or outlandish. In your closing paragraph, always indicate when you will follow up with that individual if you do not hear back from them. For example, 'I will phone the week of March 12th to schedule an interview.' This demonstrates that you're following through and taking the initiative, both of which are admirable qualities in any candidate— attorney or otherwise. And, most significantly, remember that the letter is really the first writing sample that you are submitting to that company or law firm. Nothing short of perfect is ever acceptable."

Rolande LaPointe

Earlier in this chapter, we highlighted two cover letters written by Rolande LaPointe of RO-LAN Associates, Inc. These were examples of cover letters written by recruiters to hiring companies. Now Rolande shares her insights on what she likes and dislikes in cover letters written by job seekers:

Likes

- Clearly states the candidate's objective or the type of position being sought.

- Makes communication easy by including all contact information (address, home phone, work phone, fax, and e-mail). Also includes a statement about the best times to reach the candidate.

- Includes salary requirements, availability for interviews, and availability for relocation.

- Includes information about why the candidate is relocating (if pertinent).

- Includes personal data about the spouse and the spouse's employment situation, children, and any special needs they may have.

- Includes references so that if there is an immediate interest, her firm can begin the reference-checking process.

As a recruiter, Rolande is interested in the whole person, not just the credentials. Because there are so very many personal factors that can halt a successful placement, the more she knows about the person and his personal situation, the better equipped she is to positively manage the placement.

Dislikes

- Standardized or form letters in which it is obvious that the candidate has sent the same letter to hundreds of recruiters.

- Unclear goals and objectives ("I don't know what to do with the candidate.").

- Poor spelling, grammar, punctuation, or visual presentation says a great deal about a candidate, none of it positive.

- Multiple resumes from the same candidate to support different objectives clearly communicates that this candidate is uncertain about career direction.

- No fancy presentations, binders, or folders. ("They don't fit into my files. Send paper, not frills.")

- Letters that are too pushy. ("I don't need to be impressed. I want to work with that individual and get them an interview. They don't need to sell me when my objective already is to screen them in, not out.")

Tip Rolande shares four other critical points you should consider when forwarding your job search materials to a recruiter. Remember these, because they are vital!

⚹ The quality and presentation of your resume and cover letter are extremely important. Never let any recruiter tell you otherwise.

⚹ Use a bullet-style format when writing cover letters to recruiters. It makes it much easier to quickly identify the candidate's core qualifications and allows the recruiter to know what that individual's top selling points are. That way, a recruiter is better prepared to present the candidate to client companies.

⚹ Recruiters are not necessarily experts in each and every profession. Again, the bullet-style format makes it easier for a recruiter to understand "who" the candidate is.

⚹ After you've forwarded a resume to a recruiter, you can call to check in once or twice. Find out what the recruiter's standard procedures are and stick to them. Don't call constantly.

Candy Mirrer: Executive Recruiter for Start-Up Technology Ventures

Candy Mirrer, President of MirrerSearch.com (868 33rd Avenue, San Francisco, California 94121; 415-387-7997; candy@mirrersearch.com), specializes in executive searches for start-up technology ventures in Silicon Valley. Because of the specific market she works in, her perspective is somewhat different from other recruiters.

Candy works entirely in today's new economy and prefers that all candidates submit their resumes and cover letters to her via e-mail. "If they forward their information via fax or mail, it clearly communicates the message that they 'just don't get it.'" Candy points out that if she receives a resume and cover letter for a position or industry in which she does not specialize, it takes only a moment to pass the e-mail along to another executive search consultant in her network.

Candy also prefers the following:

- All resumes and cover letters should be submitted as a Word attachment. The resume can also be put in text within the e-mail, but it should not substitute for the attachment.

- Include both the resume and cover letter in the same file so there is only one attachment to open and one file to keep track of in her database. *Do not* send Zip (compressed) files. "It's another step in the process, another demand on my time."

- Do not send an e-mail that has just an attachment and no note about the position for which the candidate is applying.

- Be sure to use a virus-checking program. "If I receive an e-mail message and a virus is identified, I simply return the message to the sender and alert him of the virus."

- Save all of your Word documents to display at 100% size (by selecting Zoom under the View menu). At 75%, your reader has to strain. At 150%, it's overkill. "I'm not blind!"

In relation to the content of the cover letter, Candy comments, "Tell me the position for which you are applying and your relevant background. Use bulleted sentences that are quick and easy to review. My general practice is a quick review of the letter, with much more attention paid to the content of the resume, the specific work experience, and exact technical qualifications. What's more, if relocation would be necessary, you've got to really stress the qualifications you bring to the table. Most start-up ventures will not go to the expense to relocate an individual unless they are extremely well qualified for the position—more qualified, perhaps, than local candidates."

"Key words are also an important consideration," continues Candy. "I run every resume I receive through a key word search."

When Candy submits a candidate to a hiring company, she forwards a standardized resume (the candidate's words reformatted into her company's standardized resume format) along with a brief summary of the candidate's qualifications, including both benefits and concerns. The hiring executive can then quickly review the summary page and take it into account during the interview.

Nadine Rubin: Retained Recruiter Specializing in Telecom and Infrastructure-Development Industries

Nadine Rubin, President of Adams-Bryce, Inc. (77 Maple Avenue, New City, New York 10956; 914-634-1772; nadine@adambryce.com), specializes in retained placement in the telecommunications and infrastructure development industries. With 22 years of experience, Nadine knows what she likes and dislikes in a cover letter. "Don't just send me a letter that says 'See my attached resume.' I want a letter that: (1) provides a synopsis of what I'm going to read in the resume; (2) highlights the parameters of the candidate's search (who they are and what type of position they're looking for); and (3) provides full contact information with a note as to when is the best time to contact them."

According to Nadine, an excellent example is this cover letter introduction:

```
I am writing to you because I am seeking a position as VP
of Marketing in the Tri-State area. My experience includes
10 years with IBM, where I have progressed from field sales
to sales management to my current position as Key Account
Marketing Manager with revenue responsibility for $22+
million annually.
```

Note that this introduction is a brief synopsis of the candidate's entire career, just as Nadine prefers.

When asked if anything in a cover letter excites her, Nadine commented that creativity is important, particularly for individuals interested in positions in sales, marketing, or executive management. Here's an example for a marketing candidate:

```
If your clients are looking for a strong marketing strate-
gist, I've launched more than 15 campaigns for Digital that
have not only received tremendous market visibility, but have
been a key contributor to double-digit revenue growth.
```

Nadine further comments, "It really impresses me when candidates have done their homework and provide insightful information about a particular company or industry. When they do this, they make my job easier, providing me with just the right information to demonstrate to the hiring company why this candidate can help them, solve their problems, and deliver measurable results."

When we asked Nadine about her use of cover letters when forwarding resumes to her client companies, she commented that she transmits all candidate resumes electronically and includes only a brief note to the hiring manager, with copies to other decision makers within the organization. In her subject line, she writes "Resume of *Candidate's Name*" and includes a short note with pertinent information such as type of position the candidate is seeking, geographic preferences, and, as appropriate, salary requirements. "I don't like to use the written word to replace what I can say in person or on the phone. When I'm communicating directly with the hiring manager, I can verbally overcome obstacles that may have totally negated the placement if provided via e-mail."

Each of these recruiters has taken the time and effort to share their cover letter insights with you. Take their advice to heart and use it wisely. Remember, although recruiters don't work for you—the candidate—they can be an invaluable resource in your campaign and can get you right in front of top decision-makers. Operate within their system and structure, and it will work to your advantage.

Chapter 15

Winning Resume Strategies

This chapter was the greatest challenge of all for us. How could we write just one chapter on resumes when, between the two of us, we've written three whole books? Yet we felt that it was important to include some basic information on resume strategy, development, writing, and presentation. After all, we assume the reason that you're reading this book is because you

★ Are just starting or are in the midst of a job search.

★ Have either a completed resume or one under development.

★ Need to know how to write powerful cover letters to accompany that resume.

Frankly, we can't think of any other reason why you'd be reading this book!

First, we address three critical components of resume preparation: strategy, writing, and presentation. Then, to illustrate these concepts, we've included a detailed section with recommended resume formats and samples. Each of these formats has been designed for specific job search situations and types of job seekers.

Wouldn't it be great if you could select one of those samples and just plug your career information right in? Ten minutes and you'd be done! No problem! However, the chances of that happening are quite slim. Each job seeker has different skills, qualifications, and experiences, and each resume must be custom-designed. No two situations are ever exactly the same. These samples are offered simply to give you ideas for content, format, presentation, and impact. Use them wisely and to your advantage.

The final section in this chapter is "Magical Tips on Resume Writing," which contains ideas, techniques, and insights that we have learned during our more than 25 years of resume writing and career marketing. If you're interested in a more comprehensive discussion of resume writing, we refer you to our companion book, *Résumé Magic*, by Susan Britton Whitcomb, CPRW, NCRW, JCTC.

Resume Strategy

We've spent a great deal of time in this book discussing the fact that cover letters and thank-you letters are really marketing communications. They should be designed to "sell" your qualifications and position you for a new career opportunity. This concept is even more critical when you're writing your resume! Consider your resume as your own personal advertisement that highlights the features, benefits, and value of the product you are selling—*you!*

There are several vital strategic issues that you will want to address before you write one word of your resume, because they will provide the foundation for virtually everything that you include in your resume *and* everything you omit.

Focus and Perception: Who You Are

Who are you and how do you want people to perceive you? A resume does not work if your reader cannot immediately understand who you are, your primary skill sets, and the value you bring to his or her organization.

How do you accomplish that in your resume? To quickly give a snapshot overview of who you are, use either of these two strategies to begin your resume:

★ Strategy 1: Write a clear and well-defined Objective that states the type of position you are most interested in. For example: "Seeking a challenging management position leading customer service operations for a high-growth consumer products company."

★ Strategy 2: Omit an Objective and start your resume with a Summary or Career Profile that succinctly describes who you are and quickly grabs your reader's attention. For example:

SENIOR SALES & MARKETING EXECUTIVE

Building Revenues and Market Share Throughout National Markets

Dynamic 15-year career leading sales, marketing, and service
organizations. Delivered strong and sustainable revenue gains
in both emerging and mature business markets. Excellent sales
training and team leadership skills. PC proficient and
Internet savvy.

Whether you decide to use an Objective or a Summary, your reader will be
able to quickly and accurately define who you are and where you fit into his
or her organization.

> *Tip* Without a doubt, current resume styles favor the use of the Summary or Profile rather than an Objective. From a marketing standpoint, it's more beneficial to use a Summary, which tells the reader "Here's what I have to offer," than an Objective, which states, "Here's what I want." If you do use an Objective, try to include language that implies benefit to the organization and not just what is important to you.

For guidance on writing Objectives and Career Summaries, refer to pages
335–337 of this chapter.

Career Goals and Objectives: Who You Want to Be

Always remember the following: *Your resume needs to focus on the type of position
you are currently seeking, which may or may not be in line with what you have done
in the past.* Your current objectives will determine what information you
include in your resume and how you present it. Your challenge is to write a
document that positions you for the type of job you are currently seeking,
not a document that simply reiterates what you have done in the past.

In theory, you want to take everything that you have ever done in your
career and lay it on the table. Then choose those items that are most closely
related to where you are currently headed in your career. Those are the
items that you will want to highlight in your resume. Does this strategy
sound familiar? It should! It's precisely the same approach we recommended for preparing your cover letters. Bring to the forefront the items
you want someone to "see" about you and your career.

> *Tip* Just as with cover letters, your resume should include only *relevant* information. It is not a "biography" and does not have to include everything you've ever done. Always keep your career goals in mind when choosing information to include on your resume.

How do you define "how" you want to be perceived in a resume? Consider this. For the past 12 years, you've worked as a Laboratory Specialist for the American Red Cross. If you were interested in remaining in this line of work, your Summary might read something like this:

```
Twelve years of progressively responsible experience in high-
volume blood bank operations for the American Red Cross.
Excellent technical, scientific, and laboratory-management
skills. Extensive experience in the use of sophisticated
laboratory equipment and instrumentation.
```

Now suppose that you're ready to shift your career focus to a position in Health Care Administration that has nothing to do with laboratory operations. Your Summary might read something like this:

```
Twelve years of progressively responsible experience with a
major health-care organization. Excellent qualifications in
project planning and management, budgeting, materials acqui-
sition, technology procurement, and team building/leadership.
Introduced processes that increased productivity, improved
quality of operations, and contributed to double-digit cost
savings.
```

These two summaries sound like they're about two different people. Yet we were 100 percent honest and accurate, simply shifting our focus from one set of skills to another to support the job seeker's current objective. In the resume trade, this is referred to as "painting the picture you want someone to see while remaining in the realm of reality."

Sales and Merchandising: What You Have Accomplished

Your resume should be more than a list of past jobs. It is the first opportunity you have to distinguish yourself from the competitive crowd of other candidates, and it should be written as a personal sales and marketing tool that attracts and impresses employers. Your qualifications, words, format, and presentation must all be favorably presented to attract your reader's interest. Take credit for your experience and accomplishments, know what makes you marketable, and sell it!

How do you accomplish this in a resume? You can most positively position your qualifications by defining the scope of your responsibilities and then highlighting your achievements and successes. That means not saying just what you did, but also how well you did it.

Poor Example:

- Managed accounting and finance operations for a $22 million company.

Good Example:

- Independently planned and directed a team of 27, responsible for accounting and financial affairs for a $22 million NASDAQ company with three operating locations and 500 employees.

Poor Example:

- Supervised IT operations in Dow Chemical's headquarters facility.

Good Example:

- Chief Information Officer with full responsibility for the strategic planning, development, and leadership of the entire information technology organization for Dow Chemical's $800 million headquarters facility. Introduced PC-based client/server architecture, SAP and SPC technologies, and an internal software-development team to optimize performance and productivity.

Poor Example:

- Coordinated office affairs for the President and Executive Committee.

Good Example:

- Independently and sensitively managed all administrative affairs on behalf of the President and Executive Committee of a $42 million industrial manufacturing company.

To create a hard-hitting resume, ask yourself what you have accomplished in your career, what quantifiable achievements you have delivered, what special projects you have managed, what honors and awards you have won, what unique skills and qualifications you have developed, and what distinguishes you from other candidates applying for the same position. Then use that information as the ammunition for your resume. This will allow you to write a document that is powerful, positive, and competitive.

For more information on writing job descriptions, refer to pages 338–340 of this chapter.

Resume Writing

Now that you've given some thought to the strategy behind your resume, let's look at how to compose each of the distinct sections that make up most resumes. We'll address both content—what to include—and writing—how to communicate this information for maximum impact.

The most difficult part of resume writing is getting started. Where do you begin? You've got lots of information, but you aren't sure what to do with it all. Here's a step-by-step action plan that will make the process easier and faster. Follow it closely, and you will see that it is not nearly as difficult a task as you had imagined.

Content

Begin by compiling the raw information about yourself and your career, some of which will be included in your final resume and some of which will not. Then, proceed through the following steps:

1. Type your name, address, home phone number, and e-mail address. Include your work phone, cell phone, fax, and pager numbers if appropriate.

2. Write your objective(s) and a list of *all* the skills you possess that support that objective.

3. List your job titles, employers, locations, and dates for each position you've held, along with basic information about that job, your responsibilities, the company, and your achievements. Jot down this information in note form and don't waste time on specific wording and sentence structure. We'll worry about that later.

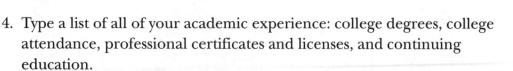
4. Type a list of all of your academic experience: college degrees, college attendance, professional certificates and licenses, and continuing education.

5. List any of the following information that is applicable to you and your career:

>   Professional memberships

>   Civic memberships

>   Computer and technology skills

>   Honors and awards

>   Volunteer experience

>   Publications

>   Public-speaking experience

>   Media recognition

>   Foreign-language skills

>   International experience

Objectives and Career Summaries

Now that you have compiled the raw data for your resume, it's time to begin actually writing the text. The most important thing to consider in this process is what your current career objectives are, because this will dictate what information you include, where you include it, and how you include it. Remember, you're "painting a picture."

Begin by deciding whether you want to include an Objective on your resume. Including an Objective is optional and depends entirely on you and your goals. If you know that you are looking for a position as a Field Service Dispatcher and nothing else, you may want to include an Objective. However, if you're looking at several different opportunities, we recommend that you leave off the Objective. In this situation, your Objective would either be limiting or so broad that it said nothing.

Here's an example of a well-written Objective:

> Seeking a Customer Service Management position in the Tele-
> communications industry.

Why is this Objective so good? Because it clearly states what type of position this individual is seeking and in what industry. There are no unanswered questions about what this person wants to do. In fact, if she had wanted to take it a step further, she could have written this:

> Seeking a Customer Service Management position where I can
> apply my six years' experience in the Telecommunications
> industry.

This Objective is even better because not only does it communicate the type of position and industry in which the candidate is interested, it also communicates that she has experience that is directly relevant.

If you do not use an Objective, consider using a Career Summary, Professional Profile, or Qualifications Statement at the beginning of your resume. When you write an Objective, you are telling your reader what you want. When you write a Summary, you are communicating what you have to offer—your value. It is a much more powerful introduction that immediately entices someone to read on. Consider these examples:

SENIOR FINANCE EXECUTIVE

Corporate Finance Executive with 18 years' experience leading
the financial-management functions of a multinational corporation. Combines strong analytical skills and creative thinking with outstanding financial and investment expertise.
Delivered consistent gains in revenues and profitability
while reducing annual operating costs and optimizing organizational productivity. MBA in Finance.

- Strategic Business & Financial Planning

- Acquisitions / Joint Ventures / LBOs

- Treasury, Banking, & Cash Management

- Equity & Debt Financing

- U.S. & Foreign Tax Regulations

- ESOP & 401K Plans

- International Trade Finance & Credit

- Information Systems & Technologies

Or

```
QUALIFICATIONS PROFILE:

Special Events — Meeting & Conference Planning — Trade Shows
— Fund-raising

Creative professional successful in planning, coordinating,
and managing programs and special events for up to 5000
guests. Sourced vendors, negotiated contracts, managed
budgets, coordinated schedules, recruited volunteers, and
facilitated press coverage. Outstanding organizational,
communication, decision-making, problem-solving, and
project-management skills. Enthusiastic and energetic.
```

Now, wouldn't you agree that these sample Summaries are dramatically more powerful than a traditional Objective? We certainly believe so. Each individual's career goals are clearly communicated, not with a passive Objective statement, but with a powerful presentation of their skills and qualifications.

> *Tip* The next decision you have to make is whether to follow with Education or Experience. The answer is simple. Look at your Objective or Summary, and then decide if your Education or Experience is most supportive of that. If you are a recent college graduate seeking an entry-level professional position, chances are that your Education will follow. If, on the other hand, you're an experienced Chemical Engineer who graduated 10 years ago and has been working professionally ever since, Experience should be your next section.

Education

The Education section of your resume should include college degrees (or attendance if you do not have a degree), certificates, licenses, seminars, workshops, and other continuing education. Be sure to include all relevant information (for example, major courses of study, names of colleges and universities, academic honors, demonstration of leadership capabilities). If your education ended with high school, list the name of the school, its location, and your graduation date. If you are a college graduate, there is no need to include high school unless you graduated from a prestigious private institution.

Here are a few examples to get you started:

EDUCATION:

M.B.A.—Harvard University—1992

B.A.—Management & Economics—Princeton University—1990

Graduate, 200+ hours of continuing professional education

Or

EDUCATION & PROFESSIONAL CERTIFICATIONS:

| CENTRAL MICHIGAN UNIVERSITY | Bachelor of Arts — 1987 |
| Grand Rapids, Michigan | **Business Administration** |

  Internship: Langley & Stewart
  Investors, London, England, 1986
  Foreign Exchange: Paris, France,
  Summer 1985

NASD Registered Investment Representative, 1994

Certified Insurance Counselor (CIC), 1992

Life & Health Insurance License, 1992

Real Estate Sales License, 1989

Or

CENTRAL VIRGINIA COMMUNITY COLLEGE, Lynchburg, Virginia

Currently pursuing **A.A. Degree in General Studies** (to be conferred in June 2001)

High School Graduate, Virginia Episcopal School, Lynchburg, Virginia, 1998

Employment Experience

The Experience section of your resume will most likely be the longest and the most detailed. It will also take you the longest to write. In this section you want to highlight, as briefly as possible, the key responsibilities and accomplishments of each of your positions using powerful words to create a powerful presentation.

By now you should realize that resumes are not job descriptions. They may certainly include some information that is in your job description, but a resume is a sales document, not just a listing of duties and responsibilities. It must be well worded and carefully merchandised to capture your reader's attention. You must include precise information about your job functions

and achievements, not just generalized statements of overall responsibilities. Include specific figures, percentages, and results when describing your accomplishments to clearly communicate your skills and expertise.

Here's an excellent example of an impactful experience description. It effectively communicates overall scope of responsibility in the first paragraph and then presents measurable accomplishments in an easy-to-skim bullet format.

> Directed the planning, staffing, budgeting, and operations of a six-site logistics operation for $800 million plastics distributor. Scope of responsibility was diverse and included purchasing, vendor management, materials handling, inventory control, distribution planning, and field delivery operations. Managed a staff of 55 through six supervisors. Controlled a $45 million annual operating budget.
>
> - Introduced continuous improvement and quality management programs throughout the logistics organization. Results included a 25% increase in productivity and a 64% increase in customer satisfaction.
>
> - Spearheaded cost-reduction initiatives that reduced labor costs by 18%, overtime by 34%, and material waste by 42%.
>
> - Renegotiated key vendor contracts for a 28% reduction over previous year's costs.
>
> - Facilitated the integration of logistics and supply chain management operations following the $2.8 million acquisition of Ellerson Plastics Components.

Prospective employers who read this description can quickly sense the scope of this candidate's responsibilities (size of company, number of people, budgets) and clearly identify his achievements (cost savings, productivity improvements, waste reductions, acquisition integration, customer satisfaction). Remember, recruiters and employers won't read between the lines for relevant information. You must spell it out.

As you're writing your job descriptions, remember that they should generally get shorter and shorter as you go back further in time. Obviously, you are not going to include as much information about a job from 10 years ago as you are about your current position. Use your previous positions to highlight notable achievements, major responsibilities, special projects, and performance improvements.

"Older" Experience

If you've been working for 15, 20, or more years, you will have to decide how much of your older experience you want to include. This will depend entirely on how relevant that information is to your current career objectives. If you can optimize that experience and demonstrate value, include it, but be brief and leave off the dates (particularly if they're prior to 1970) if you're concerned that they may immediately exclude you from consideration. Here's an excellent example:

```
Previous professional experience includes several responsible
operations-management positions with Ryder Dedicated Logis-
tics, Federal Express, and Airborne.
```

Note that the value you get from this sentence is the impressive name recognition of your past employers.

OR

```
Promoted rapidly throughout early career in sales and cus-
tomer service. Personally negotiated and closed a $17 million
sale to Chrysler, the largest sale in the history of IBM.
```

Here the value is the financial result you delivered.

Spelling, Punctuation, Grammar, and Syntax

Your resume must be perfect, with absolutely no errors. A typographical error, poor word choice, inconsistencies in syntax, or incorrect punctuation can be the kiss of death. Ask yourself whether you'd hire someone who sent a resume that was filled with errors. Your answer is mostly likely no. So, why would anyone else? Remember, your resume demonstrates the quality of work you will produce on that company's behalf. If it's not perfect, it's not acceptable.

Proofread your resume not just once or twice, but repeatedly to identify and correct any typographical or wording errors. Then ask three to five of your friends or colleagues to review it as well, just to double-check that you have not missed anything.

Also, be sure to choose language that is appropriate to the position you are seeking. If you're an entry-level professional, don't use "Ph.D." language. On the other end of the spectrum, if you're in line for a CEO slot, use appropriate management and leadership terminology to create a resume that has the right tone and impact for a candidate at that level.

Writing in the First Person

Write your document in the active first-person voice, never the third-person. There are no exceptions to this rule.

One quirk in resume writing that sometimes causes confusion about which voice is being used is the fact that, almost invariably, pronouns in resumes are omitted. For instance, you would not say "I direct a six-person sales administration team that supports all 47 of our field sales engineers." Instead, you would word this statement in the following idiosyncratic "resume language": first person, pronouns omitted.

```
Direct six-person sales administration team that supports all
47 of the company's field sales engineers.
```

Another question that frequently arises is whether to write in the present or past tense. As a rule, the activities and responsibilities of your current position should be written in the present tense, while all past positions and all completed accomplishments should be written in the past tense.

Length

The same one-page versus two-page dilemma that we explored about cover letters is also a major point of discussion in relation to resume writing. Twenty years ago, it was "standard practice" to have a one-page resume. Today, the rules have changed, the market has changed, and the competition has increased phenomenally. Most individuals would now agree that a resume does not necessarily have to be just one page.

What it does have to be is a document that sells you. We recommend that you begin by writing the text and then determining whether it will fit most comfortably on one page or two. However, if you're going to use a second page, be sure that you do indeed need it. If you have only two or three lines on the second page, go back and edit your text, delete a line here and there, and get your resume onto one page.

 Tip You will find that the response to your resume will be directly proportionate to how well you've marketed your qualifications and achievements, and not the number of pages in your resume.

Resume Presentation

There are countless ways to arrange the contents of your resume, and dozens of different fonts and formatting styles you can choose. The underlying foundation for all of your design decisions should be to communicate the most important information about your qualifications quickly, easily, and logically. Your resume should be inviting and easy to read, yet provide enough detail to convey the depth of your experience. The key points should be easily grasped in a 10-second skim-through, and all formatting enhancements (such as headers, bold type, bullet points, underlines, and so forth) should help readers notice and remember your strongest "selling points."

Format

Format should *not* be your primary consideration when writing your resume. Often job seekers will see a format that they like and then try to make their information fit into it. It simply doesn't work! You can review other resumes for ideas, but you must craft your document to sell only you.

A much better strategy is to decide on a resume format after you have written the text and seen what information you have to work with. At this point, the most effective format should easily present itself just from the type of information you have written. Then all you'll need to do is

- Set your headings and margins.
- Adjust spacing for readability and impact.
- Insert horizontal rules or other graphic elements to improve appearance and organization.
- Select which type enhancements (**bold,** *italics,* or <u>underlining</u>) you wish to use and where.
- Then edit the text to comfortably fit on each page.

If possible, adhere to these formatting guidelines:

- Don't expect readers to struggle through paragraphs that are 10 to 15 lines long. Substitute two or three shorter paragraphs, or use bullets to offset new sentences and sections.
- Don't overdo your use of bold, italics, or underlining. Excessive use defeats the purpose of these enhancements. If half of the type on the page is bold, nothing will stand out.

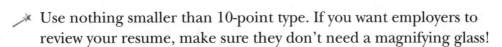

⚡ Use nothing smaller than 10-point type. If you want employers to review your resume, make sure they don't need a magnifying glass!

⚡ Don't clutter your resume. Everything you've heard about "white space" is true. Let your document "breathe" so that readers don't have to struggle through it. Ease of readability is a key factor in the effectiveness of your resume.

⚡ Use an excellent printer, preferably a laser printer. Smudged, faint, heavy, or otherwise poor-quality print will discourage red-eyed readers.

Visual Presentation

Since your resume is actually a marketing document, its appearance is critical. To survive in the job search market and outperform other well-qualified candidates, your resume must be sharp and powerful in its presentation. Do not type it on an outdated word processor using an antiquated resume style and then print it on onion-skin paper with a nice blob of white-out covering the mistakes! Those days are long gone.

Instead, give your document an up-to-date style that attracts attention. This doesn't mean using an italic typeface, cute logos, or an outrageous paper color. Instead, be conservatively distinctive. Choose a sharp-looking typeface such as **Bookman**, Soutane, **Tahoma**, or Fritz. If your font selection is limited, choose the more familiar Times New Roman or Arial typefaces. Unless you're seeking a position in graphic arts or some other creative career track, don't put logos or artwork on your resume.

Your choice of paper color is entirely based on your personal preference, although we do recommend something conservative—such as white, ivory, or light gray—because you never know who may be looking at your resume, and you can't go wrong with these selections. However, a bit of creativity can give you a real boost and help your resume stand out from the crowd. Review the discussion on cover letter paper in chapter 5, and choose matching or complementary paper for all your job search materials.

Recommended Resume Formats

Following are ten resume formats (with full sample resumes) that have been designed with specific types of job seekers in mind.

Blue-Collar Job Seeker

Peter Swann
75 Beech Street
North Branford, CT 06471
(203) 555-7854   peterswann@aol.com

SUMMARY

Skilled **Vacuum Furnace Operator** recognized for quality, productivity, and work ethic. In every position, earned track record of contributing to improved operations and positive results through dedication, leadership, and effective problem-solving.

EMPLOYMENT

Vacuum Furnace Operator   **1997–Present**
ACME MACHINE COMPANY, BRANFORD, CONNECTICUT

Perform extremely close-tolerance metal fabrication work for the aerospace industry as an outsourced service provider to customers including Pratt & Whitney, Boeing, General Motors, the U.S. Navy, and the Department of Defense. As sole Vacuum Furnace Operator on shift, operate three furnaces simultaneously to keep fabricators supplied and maintain productivity in cell-based, ISO 9000 manufacturing environment.

Troubleshoot furnace problems to sustain high quality within the vacuum environment. Maintain outstanding quality record, consistently complying with stringent close-tolerance standards.

- Successfully completed training in **Basic Vacuum Practices** (Varian, Chicago, Illinois) and **Vacuum Furnace Operation** (Vacuum Furnace Systems, Pittsburgh, Pennsylvania).

- Increased productivity of the vacuum furnace operation by eliminating redundant paperwork and shortening several required forms.

- Took initiative to plan and orchestrate furnace move during recent plant consolidation. Successfully completed move with no unscheduled downtime.

Building Manager   **1994–1997**
EAST END APARTMENTS, NEW HAVEN, CONNECTICUT

Served as on-site manager for 14-unit apartment building. Scheduled all repair and remodeling work.

- Raised occupancy from 30% to 100%.

- Organized and led neighborhood pride events that were featured on local television (WNHT-TV).

Corporal   **1990–1994**
UNITED STATES MARINE CORPS, SAN DIEGO, CALIFORNIA

Participated in Operation Desert Shield/Storm. As Equipment NCO, responsible for approximately $350,000 of equipment.

- Recognized for exemplary performance and outstanding dedication by Commanding Officer.

Commercial Painter   **1989–1990**
ELM CITY PAINTING, NEW HAVEN, CONNECTICUT

EDUCATION

Southern Connecticut Technical College   **1997–Present**
Major: MECHANICAL ENGINEERING TECHNOLOGY (DESIGN) PROGRAM

INTERESTS

Church choir, golf, biking, and reading.

This format is recommended because it highlights skills, training, and experience, and the job seeker's profession is clearly evident.

Graduating Student with Minimal Work Experience

LAURA S. LEWIS

4998 Irene Avenue, Apt. #202
Baltimore, Maryland 21211
(555) 783-2372 / fft@aol.com

CAREER OBJECTIVE: **Entry-Level Professional Position in Corporate Law & Litigation.**

QUALIFICATIONS PROFILE:

- Legal Research & Writing
- Case Strategy & Management
- Client Negotiations
- Legal Briefs & Memoranda
- Pleadings & Motions
- Depositions & Interrogatories

PC proficient. Strong organizational and project-management skills. Analytical and decisive.

EDUCATION:

UNIVERSITY OF MARYLAND SCHOOL OF LAW, Baltimore, Maryland
J.D. Degree, December 1999
<u>Honors & Activities</u>:   Top 35% of Class; Member, Moot Court Board

UNIVERSITY OF SAN DIEGO, San Diego, California
B.A. Degree in History; Minor in English; Cum Laude, May 1996
<u>Honors & Activities</u>:   Top 10% of Class; Dean's List; Golden Key National Honor Society
Phi Alpha Theta (National History Honor Society)
Sigma Kappa Sorority (Scholarship Chair)

EMPLOYMENT EXPERIENCE:

Server / Customer Service Associate   1998 to Present
KIVA GRILL, Baltimore, Maryland
CRATER'S, Baltimore, Maryland
Fast-paced customer-service positions with two upscale restaurants. Emphasis on quality service, up-selling, cross-selling, public relations, and customer loyalty/retention.

Law Clerk   Summer 1998
OFFICE OF ATTORNEY GENERAL, Baltimore, Maryland
Selected from a competitive group of more than 50 candidates for a 4-month intensive clerkship. Assisted staff attorneys with client interviews and investigations. Researched and wrote memoranda, documented findings, and prepared legal materials for courtroom litigation.

Law Clerk   Summer 1997
LAW OFFICE OF JACK GREENE, ESQ., Baltimore, Maryland
Three-month clerkship with private law firm specializing in contracts, torts, and real estate transactions.

Server   1995 to 1997
PUSSER'S, San Diego, California
GREEN STREET INN, San Diego, California
HYATT REGENCY, San Diego, California
Worked in several exclusive hotel and privately owned restaurants. Recognized for outstanding customer service and selected to train newly hired wait staff.

This format is recommended because it brings the job seeker's relevant skills to the forefront (based on her objective) and highlights her strong academic career.

Young Professional Uncertain About Career Objectives

Kelly Townsend
27-A High Street
Danbury, CT 06811
(203) 555-8910   kellytownsend@juno.com

QUALIFICATIONS SUMMARY

- **COMPUTER TRAINING ABILITIES:** experience training novice and experienced users in standard and custom software applications, technology tools, and business operational procedures.
- **IN-DEPTH KNOWLEDGE** of Windows operating system and the entire MS Office suite of products.
- **STRONG COMMUNICATION SKILLS:** track record of delivering effective presentations and excelling in sales and training positions.
- **BACKGROUND IN EDUCATION** including curriculum development and multiple teaching strategies… skilled at adapting training methods to match group and individual learning styles.
- **PROJECT AND PEOPLE MANAGEMENT SKILLS:** proven ability to oversee complex projects and effectively manage people to high levels of performance.

PROFESSIONAL EXPERIENCE

1997-Present   SOLUTION SYSTEMS, INC., Danbury, CT
HIGH-TECH BUSINESS SYSTEMS, INC. (acquired by Solution Systems in April 2000)
Hardware & software resellers

District Manager, May 2000-Present

Chosen to lead service/implementation team in support of the company's #2 account manager, a top producer with $15 million in monthly revenue including the company's #1 account.

- Following corporate merger, maintained focus on team goals and customer service commitment during corporate transition; maintained 100% staff retention.
- Currently managing project roll-out for a key client, CVS Pharmacies, requiring complex coordination of technical installations nationwide.

Project (Training) Specialist, March 1999-May 2000

Selected for newly created 100% training position, serving as primary operations and applications trainer for all new hires. Additionally, became the region's primary presenter to clients and prospects on the company's implementation and customer-service procedures.

- Developed standardized training activities and worksheets to ensure consistent new-hire training.
- Maintained 100% "pass" rate for newly trained employees on the company's Oracle system.
- Developed online applications and tools to establish "best practices" for the department. Ensured consistency, streamlined procedures, and eliminated redundancies.

District Manager, December 1997-March 1999

Led a team of technical marketing representatives in providing high levels of customer service and communication to support hardware and software system deployment.

- Recruited, trained, and supervised staff toward the goal of long-range skills assessment, development, and professional growth. Designed and implemented training programs, motivational tools, and recognition programs that developed district staff skills and built teamwork.
- Provided intensive, hands-on application training for new hires.
- Delivered presentations on company services to internal customers and prospective clients.

This format is recommended because it highlights a cross-section of skills and qualifications that are relevant to a number of different types of positions, companies, and industries. This format is flexible

Kelly Townsend
— PAGE 2 —

PROFESSIONAL EXPERIENCE

continued   HIGH-TECH BUSINESS SYSTEMS
Technical Marketing Representative, February–December 1997

Managed IT rollouts, special projects, and daily account maintenance for Fortune 1000 clients. Researched and designed technical solutions for clients' corporate computer standards. Managed procurement and deployment schedules.

- Consistently shipped $1.5 million in monthly revenue — outperforming goal of $650K through high levels of energy, persistence, customer follow-up, and solution selling.
- Maintained ongoing communication with customers and field sales representatives.
- Co-chaired Northeast Area Team Building Committee in design of programs to improve team morale and cooperation.

1993-1997   TECH SOLUTIONS, INC., Hartford, CT
Hardware & software resellers
Inside Sales Representative

Coordinated delivery of services to local, national, and international customers, serving as centralized point of contact for customers, outside sales force, inside systems experts, and vendors.

- Documented and developed processes for smooth and successful deployment of complex, integrated systems.
- Promoted to train and supervise the inside sales team.
- As appointed member of Tech Solutions' Quality Council, worked with team members to document, develop, evaluate, and revise internal processes.
- Named the region's "Outstanding Performer" for 1996.

EDUCATION

UNIVERSITY OF CONNECTICUT, Storrs, CT
M.Ed.: Currently enrolled; anticipate completion in 2001.

SOUTHERN CONNECTICUT STATE UNIVERSITY, New Haven, CT
B.S. in Communication Disorders: 1992

- Developed and delivered educational programs for students with communication difficulties — English as a second language, speech and language disabilities — through internships, part-time and volunteer positions, and teacher training.

TRAINING-RELATED COMMUNITY ACTIVITIES

- Trained Literacy Volunteer: Literacy Volunteers of New England.
- University of Connecticut English as a Second Language Program: Tutor graduate students and their spouses from numerous countries around the world.

and appropriate in countless different situations—it allows the job seeker to explore a variety of career opportunities while still giving readers a sense of her skills and strengths.

Career Changer

JOHN CEO
789 Craigmont Avenue
Duluth, Minnesota 33383
(555) 333-3726

SENIOR EXECUTIVE PROFILE
Strategic Human Resources Leadership / Organizational Development / Change Management
Performance Optimization / Leadership Training & Development / P&L Management / Harvard MBA Degree

Dynamic management career leading organizations through start-up, change, revitalization, turnaround and accelerated growth. Cross-functional expertise with proven success in optimizing organizational growth, productivity and efficiency. HR Generalist experience in benefits, compensation, recruitment, training and HRIS technology. Expert team building, team leadership, communication and interpersonal relations skills. Strategic and analytical with outstanding problem-solving and negotiating performance.

PROFESSIONAL EXPERIENCE:

Chief Executive Officer   1997 to Present
MED HEALTH SOLUTIONS, Duluth, Minnesota

CHALLENGE: *To lead the organization through a comprehensive organizational development and change management program to support growth, diversification and expansion.*

Senior Executive recruited to plan and orchestrate a complete redesign of strategic planning, HR/OD, administrative, information technology, marketing and operating functions to increase revenues and bottom-line profitability. Manage within a tightly regulated and competitive industry.

- One of two senior executives credited with transitioning Med Health Solutions from 1997 revenues of $7000 per month to current revenues of $1.5 million per month (57% increase within two years). Drove profit growth by better than 45%.
- Spearheaded an aggressive internal change initiative. Partnered core operations to support organizational redesign and performance reengineering initiatives.
- Built a best-in-class HR organization, implemented advanced HRIS technology, designed benefit and compensation programs, established a formal salary structure, and introduced employee training, counseling and coaching programs.
- Revitalized all core financial functions, implemented client/server architecture to optimize technology performance, and created a team-based/customer-based corporate culture.
- Negotiated $2.8 million acquisition of competitive company and facilitated seamless integration of personnel, technology and product lines.

President / General Manager   1990 to 1997
DYNAMIC SOLUTIONS, INC., Tampa, Florida

CHALLENGE: *To launch and build an entrepreneurial venture within an intensely competitive consumer market and create a strong organizational infrastructure to support continued growth and market penetration.*

Senior Executive with full responsibility for strategic planning, business development, staffing, HR administration, operations, marketing and P&L performance of an independent venture. Built the entire organizational infrastructure, created accounting and financial reporting processes, and implemented computer technology to support operations.

This format is recommended because it transitions every position to focus on the candidate's new HR career path and not on what he has really devoted the vast majority of his time to (CEO responsibilities). By using this strategy, we can change how someone perceives this individual. He is no longer

JOHN CEO – Page Two

- Built new venture from concept to over $1 million in annual sales with a 23% profit margin.
- Created performance-based training programs for all hourly and management personnel.
- Achieved and maintained a stable workforce with less than 5% turnover in an industry with average turnover of better than 20%.
- Launched a series of innovative community outreach programs as part of the corporation's strategic marketing and business development efforts.

Chief Executive Officer   1983 to 1990
LSI SOCIEDAD, S.A., Santa Domingo, Dominican Republic

CHALLENGE: *To orchestrate the growth of new international venture within the financial services industry, and transition through organizational change and market repositioning.*

Senior Management Executive and HR Director building a new professional services organization. Created organizational infrastructure, recruited/trained personnel, designed marketing and business development programs, and created all administrative and internal reporting systems.

- Built new company from concept into a $12 million annual revenue producer with EBTA of $1 million annually. Achieved/surpassed all corporate revenue and profit objectives.
- Led the organization through a successful internal transition and recreated core business processes to support massive change and recreate corporate image.
- Recruited and trained a team of more than 60. Introduced incentives linked to performance and focused on customer development, retention and growth.
- Negotiated health and insurance benefit contracts for the corporation. Designed salary structures, incentive programs and executive compensation plans.

Personal Assistant to CEO   1981 to 1983
BANCO DEL COMBRERO, Santa Domingo, Dominican Republic

CHALLENGE: *To facilitate market and revenue growth for a specialty import/export company.*

Recruited by CEO to assist with building a profitable international business venture. Scope of responsibility spanned all core executive functions with particular emphasis on organizational design, policy/procedure development, recruitment and training, sales and marketing.

- Instrumental in driving growth from $2.5 million to $5.5 million in annual revenues.
- Recruited former Procter & Gamble executive to the organization to provide critical industry and market leadership. Recruited sales producers from leading Latin American companies.
- Created organizational infrastructure and HR support to facilitate diversification and expansion into both emerging and established consumer markets.
- Designed HR policies, compensation plans, performance review schedules, and a series of employee training and development programs.

EDUCATION:
Executive MBA – Harvard University – 1989 (*Distinguished Alumnus Award*)
BS – Business Administration – Lillymount University – 1981

PROFESSIONAL AFFILIATIONS:
Society for Human Resource Management (SHRM)
American Society for Training & Development (ASTD)

"John the CEO," but rather "John the HR executive." In addition, note that his Summary highlights skills and qualifications directly related to his current objectives and not his past experience, immediately "painting a picture" of an accomplished HR executive.

Industry Changer

EDWARD EXECUTIVE
executive@inmind.com

1 Mission Circle
Miami, Florida 33389

Phone: 555.315.3334
Fax: 555.315.3332

SENIOR MANUFACTURING INDUSTRY EXECUTIVE
President / Vice President / Chief Operating Officer / General Manager
Incorporating Advanced Information & Manufacturing Technologies to Optimize Productivity

- Multisite Operations Management
- Global Sales & Marketing Leadership
- Key Account Relationship Management
- Process Redesign & Performance Optimization
- Opportunity Development & Profitability

- Multi-Site P&L Management
- Budgeting, Finance & Cost Reduction
- Joint Ventures & Acquisitions
- Product R&D & Commercialization
- Robotics & Automated Processes

Entrepreneurial spirit and drive with outstanding strategic planning, problem solving, decision making and negotiating skills. Creative with strong communication, team building, leadership and interpersonal performance. Bottom-line driven.

PROFESSIONAL EXPERIENCE:

Vice President & General Manager   1998 to Present
PREMIER PLASTICS CORPORATION, Reading, PA
($40 million manufacturer with state-of-the-art technology center)

Recruited as #2 executive in a small, growth-driven, global manufacturer. Given full responsibility for re-creating the business infrastructure, redesigning domestic and international sales and market development programs, realigning engineering and manufacturing operations, eliminating excessive costs, and introducing advanced information and manufacturing technologies. Joint P&L responsibility with company president.

- **Revenue & Profit Growth**. Reduced breakeven by $1.5 million within first nine months. Currently projecting 30% revenue growth and 400% income growth in 2000.

- **E-Commerce**. Established the corporation's first Web site to launch massive E-commerce initiative currently on track to generate $2.5 million in first-year sales.

- **Technology Advances**. Directed technology team responsible for software development, customization and implementation of advanced EDI system. Spearheaded acquisition of $200,000 in automated manufacturing technologies, systems and processes.

- **Sales & Marketing Leadership**. Created a best-in-class global sales organization that captured three multi-million dollar, exclusive customer accounts with Flint Ink, PPG Industries and Sherwin Williams. Currently negotiating final agreement with DuPont. Total value of $5-10 million in revenue.

- **International Business Development**. Built and led a completely new European sales organization projected to deliver $8 million in sales in 1999 and $15 million in 2000.

- **Product Engineering & Development**. Revitalized Engineering, introduced automated productivity improvement tools, implemented accurate tracking and reporting systems, and launched major initiative to develop and market new products. Currently completing applications for four new product patents.

- **Manufacturing Operations**. Spearheaded cost reduction, quality improvement and productivity improvement programs projected to reduce annual expenses by 12% while enhancing product quality and customer satisfaction/retention. Currently finalizing ISO 9001 for certification in 2000.

This format is recommended when a candidate is seeking to transition his skills from one industry to another. This presentation focuses on the candidate's transferable qualifications with virtually no mention of his previous and long-time experience in the plastics industry. Also note that his

EDWARD EXECUTIVE – Page Two

Vice President & Chief Operating Officer   1996 to 1998
NEUMANN, INC., Gladstone, PA
($20 million US division of $300 million world class manufacturer)

Recruited to US division of German-based manufacturer supplying major corporations worldwide (e.g., BASF, DuPont, Hershey, Sun Chemical) to revitalize lackluster operations and reposition for long-term growth and profitability. Full operating, engineering, manufacturing, R&D, sales, marketing, HR and P&L responsibility for US operations supplying customers throughout North America.

- **Revenue & Profit Growth**. Delivered first-year revenue growth of 50.3% and profit growth of 544.6%, achieving 10% EBIT in a traditionally low-margin market. Sustained performance results through year two and positioned for continued accelerated growth.
- **Information Technology**. Led transition from UNIX-based to PC-based technology infrastructure.
- **Sales & Marketing Leadership**. Transitioned sales into a value-added partner to the manufacturing organization. Recruited direct sales force, introduced incentive program, developed Web site and product catalog, expanded product line offerings and create a targeted sales/market penetration program.

General Manager & Chief Operating Officer   1987 to 1996
TECHFORM CORPORATION, Valley Forge, NJ
($35 million international division of $350 million manufacturer)

Recruited to plan and orchestrate an aggressive reengineering and turnaround of this specialty manufacturer faced with tremendous competition, cost overruns, poor market penetration and faltering sales performance. Held full planning, operating, marketing, HR, technology and P&L responsibility for the entire international division, including 14 manufacturing locations, two company presidents and a 200-person staff. Challenged to drive earnings growth and ROA while repositioning and stabilizing the organization.

- **Revenue & Profit Growth**. Drove revenues from $18 million to $35 million over seven years with a better than 18% increase in bottom-line profitability. Credited with creating the business and marketing plans that successfully revitalized and repositioned the organization.
- **Technology Development**. Led project team in the design, development, prototyping and full-scale manufacturing of several new product technologies to advance market positioning.
- **Cost Reduction & Performance Improvement**. Launched a massive cost reduction initiative, introduced automated production techniques, lowered headcount and reduced production costs by 30-70% over two years. Added $500,000+ to profits.
- **Operating Turnaround**. Reversed $250,000/month negative cash flow in Latin American division and restored to positive cash position.
- **High-Growth Performance**. Increased revenues and net income year-over-year in Mexico and Brazil during periods of hyperinflation (2000%) resulting from economic and political turmoil.

Previous Professional Experience with Automatic Lighting Company ($250 million industrial manufacturer) in Griswold, NJ. Promoted from Sales Engineer to Engineering Manager to Manager of International Operations with full operating responsibility for $30 million international division.

- **International Business Development**. Five-year senior management career developing international distribution channels throughout Europe, South Africa, Latin America, Canada and Australia. Led buy-out of Japanese joint venture. Heavy focus on international technology transfers.
- **Product R&D**. Five-year management career in product R&D included one patent, three major new product lines and numerous line extensions to meet expanding customer demand. Led 30-person team.

EDUCATION: **BS – Industrial Engineering** – Newark College of Engineering – Newark, NJ – 1972

technology experience is brought to the forefront in each of his positions and that his e-mail address is immediately below his name to draw attention to his technical proficiency (which is crucial in the industry in which he is currently pursuing opportunities).

Mid-Level Management Candidate

Susan C. Boone

2525 Dogwood Trail
Raleigh, NC 27612
Home (919) 555-2929 • Office (513) 555-3030 • E-mail susanboone@aol.com

Expertise Providing effective leadership to customer service and sales support teams and departments within a manufacturing environment. Experience / track record includes

- Seamless coordination and delivery of support activities across global boundaries and internal departments, through corporate mergers, in a high-pressure, 24-hours-a-day, 7-days-a-week environment.
- Profit, cost-center, and budget management.
- Staff training, mentoring, and development.
- ISO 9001 procedure writing and internal auditing.
- Sales and proposal presentations to internal and external customers.
- Measurable improvements in service delivery time, customer satisfaction, results tracking, and other performance criteria.

Professional Experience

EMPIRE PAPER TECHNOLOGY, Raleigh, NC, 1978–Present
$50 million division of British-owned machinery manufacturer for the paper-making industry

Manager, Customer Service, 1996–Present

Selected to lead newly formed department, consolidating Technical Services and Spare Parts operations following corporate merger. Managed growth of department from 8 people in 1996 to 16 currently. Interact with corporate HQ in London, parts facilities in Ireland and Mexico, and customers throughout US, Latin America, and Canada; travel to corporate and customer facilities as needed. Audit and maintain departmental procedures in compliance with ISO 9001 requirements. Responsible for Product Safety.

Oversee the activities of Field Technical Service Engineers, Commissioning Engineers, and Spare Parts team; manage $5.5 million sales budget. Additionally, provide direct service to key accounts, resolving issues and problems in a high-pressure service environment for customers whose productivity depends on machine reliability.

- Increased sale of services 25% while maintaining budgeted percentage of direct hours and profit margins.
- Managed the department as a revenue generator while maintaining consistently positive customer relations.
- Created a tracking system to identify key customer concerns and monitor average response times. Used data as an analytical tool for department decision-making. Successfully and continually reduced average response times.
- Developed departmental procedures and guidelines for customer response; trained staff in service delivery to ensure consistent and customer-focused service.
- Focused on swiftly addressing customer issues; succeeded in slashing active customer concerns by 50%.
- Directed proactive response to a rash of injury claims by devising a plan, then forming and leading a team that succeeded in maintaining insurance premiums at existing levels.
- Supported growth and development of individual staff members through ongoing training, incentive programs, and opportunities for decision-making and autonomy.
- Participated on company-wide task force that developed a new national sales program.

This format is recommended because it clearly presents both broad management skills and strong, quantifiable accomplishments.

Manager, Sales Administration, 1989–1996

Assumed management of Spare Parts department while retaining all prior Sales Supervisor responsibilities. Directed 8-member staff and managed $3 million spare parts budget.

- Increased profit margins 25% while growing spare parts business 20%.
- Reduced order-entry time and customer-confirmation time by 50%.
- Created spare-parts database that provided immediate access to pricing and usage information for all key accounts and was easily updated to reflect current activity.
- Wrote and revised departmental procedures that contributed to successful achievement of ISO 9001 certification.

Sales Supervisor, 1986–1989

Led 4-person team in the development of sales/service proposals for projects ranging from $500K to $50 million. Interacted extensively with customers and field sales team on project specifications.

- Spearheaded development of a database for proposal components; successfully reduced preparation time and promoted uniformity in proposals that encompassed hundreds of pages and numerous technical specifications.
- Acquired degree in Business Administration.
- Instrumental in the development of a Sales Department PC computer system.

Senior Sales Correspondent, 1983–1986
Sales Correspondent, 1982–1983

Provided inside sales support to field sales team. Gathered specifications and wrote proposals. Accompanied sales team on customer visits to provide proposal and sales support expertise.

Estimator, 1980–1982
Junior Estimator, 1978–1980

Generated detailed cost estimates for parts, machine components, and entire machine purchase and installation.

Education and Professional Development

NORTH CAROLINA STATE UNIVERSITY, Raleigh, North Carolina
- Bachelor of Science in Business Administration

EMORY UNIVERSITY, Atlanta, Georgia
- The Role of Hazard Analysis
- Establishing and Implementing the Product Safety Program
- The Role of Warnings and Instructions

IN-HOUSE COURSES
- Team Building — completed training and participated on corporate team-building task force
- Conducting Business Overseas
- ISO 9001 Training

DALE CARNEGIE
- 12-week Communications program

Computer Skills

Proficient in Microsoft Word, Excel, and PowerPoint — FileMaker Pro database — BPCS operating system — AS400 and PC computer systems

Technologist or Scientist

Rose Anne Larkin

7525 Dante Drive, Cincinnati, OH 45213 ◆ 513-555-8787 ◆ roselarkin@worldnet.att.net

TECHNOLOGY TEAM / PROJECT LEADER
Client / Server Projects — Object-Oriented Design Methodologies

Experienced technical professional with a track record of delivering sound technical solutions, effective project and team leadership, and innovative problem-solving. Proven ability to deliver projects on time, within budget, and with results that exceed client expectations. Talent for mentoring and leading teams of highly experienced technical professionals; key strength is communicating project goals and maintaining focus on results throughout project life cycle. Record of rapidly learning new programming languages, development tools, applications, and other technical skills as needed for project implementation.

TECHNICAL COMPETENCIES

Languages	Java, PowerBuilder, Rexx, Insight/Trident, C, Modula 2, CORBA
	Additional familiarity with Visual Basic, Pascal, Fortran, Ada, C++
Operating Systems	Microsoft Windows 98, Microsoft Windows 95, Microsoft NT 4.x, DOS
Applications	Microsoft Word, Excel, Publisher, Project

PROFESSIONAL EXPERIENCE

NATIONWIDE AIRLINES, Cincinnati, Ohio, 1996–Present

Progressively challenging consulting / project leadership positions in support of INFLIGHT, Nationwide Airlines' proprietary scheduling and flight-management system.

— **Principal Consultant,** August 2000–Present

Currently leading a team of six consultants in converting the airline's reservation system to a Java-based bridge system that will enable deployment of a new, high-productivity hardware infrastructure. Oversee code production; provide technical and project coaching to team members; make final design decisions.

  ◆ Bridge solution increases processing speed and provides significant cost savings by enabling 18-month delay of investment in new hardware.
  ◆ Requires virtually no staff retraining, thereby maintaining productivity and eliminating training costs.
  ◆ All project phases on target for January delivery — on schedule and within budget parameters.

— **Senior Consultant I and II,** 1997–2000

Projects included:

RESERVATIONS SYSTEM: Led a team of four consultants in a high-profile project to design a converter for the existing reservation system's client platform from a proprietary language to Java. Designed, documented, and constructed the runtime classes to be used to support the converted code.

  ◆ Promoted to Principal Consultant to lead implementation of this project.

TICKET DELIVERY SERVICE (TDS): Wrote white paper proposing software changes to migrate the INFLIGHT fulfillment applications into the Travel Distribution Framework (TDF), providing a facility by which application objects and services can be shared company-wide via CORBA.

  ◆ Proposal currently being used to create a business case for presentation to senior executives.

TDS PRINTER EMULATOR: Called in to troubleshoot a critical problem with the printer emulator that was unresolved five months into the project.

  ◆ Within four days, identified solution that reduced error rate from 1% to less than 0.1%, exceeding client expectations and enabling forward progress on the project. Solution reduced manpower requirements by one full-time staff member who had been assigned to monitor and resolve ticket-printing errors.
  ◆ Led a team of three consultants in developing and implementing solution using PowerBuilder 5.0.

This format is recommended because it highlights specific technical qualifications (languages, operating systems, and applications) while also detailing the specific business benefits that have resulted from this candidate's technology projects and leadership performance.

Nationwide Airlines, continued

TDS EDITOR/CONTROLLER: Led two teams in the design, coding, and testing of Editor and Controller processing engines for the INFLIGHT system, using PowerBuilder 5.0 and IBM DB/2.

- ◆ Nine-month project successfully completed on schedule.
- ◆ After implementation, spearheaded project to upgrade the system to PowerBuilder 6.5.

TDS MASK PROCESSING: Designed and implemented a mask processing engine within the Editor application for INFLIGHT.

- ◆ Engine enables TDS to create custom processes for all ticketing masks, automating several processes formerly handled by agents.

TRAVEL-AIR AIRLINES, Erlanger, Kentucky, 1991–1997

— **Senior Programmer-Analyst / Programmer-Analyst / Programmer Trainee**

Consistently promoted to higher-level leadership responsibilities. Projects included:

RESERVATIONS SYSTEM: Led a large team of programmers, reservation agents, and analysts in major redesign of the reservation agent platform, using a proprietary language built to communicate with the INFLIGHT and AATMS hosts. Directed process reengineering activities using object-oriented design methodologies.

- ◆ Maintained cohesion within large team by establishing documentation, design, and construction standards and conducting design reviews and code walkthroughs.
- ◆ Coached and counseled team members on technical issues.

AIRPORT TICKETING: Designed and developed a user interface for ticket agents, using a proprietary language.

- ◆ Improved agent productivity by simplifying ticketing transactions.
- ◆ Conducted on-site alpha and beta tests; implemented new interface at five airports in US and Europe.

PROGRAMMING TOOL DEVELOPMENT AND DOCUMENTATION: Authored the reference manual for a proprietary language used by Travel-Air Airlines. Designed, developed, and implemented tools to increase programmers' efficiency, including a code generator that translated screens into source code.

MICROSOFT CORPORATION, Redmond, Washington, 1990–1991

— **Product Support Technician**

Delivered technical support for Microsoft Windows and Windows applications, including Microsoft Excel. Researched and tested complex system configurations; conducted training for support personnel; wrote technical articles for Microsoft's Online KnowledgeBase.

EDUCATION

UNIVERSITY OF WASHINGTON, Seattle, Washington: Bachelor of Science, Computer Science, 1991

TECHNICAL TRAINING / PROFESSIONAL ACTIVITIES

Weeklong courses in Java, PowerBuilder, and C

Attended JavaOne conference, 1999

INTERESTS

Personal Web page development using FrontPage 98

Digital photography

Candidate Leaving the Military or Government for a Corporate Position

COMMANDER CRAIG
432 Colonel Marshall Way
Lovingston AFB, Colorado 38837

Phone: (555) 352-4726
Fax: (555) 354-3827

Voice Mail: (555) 352-3827
E-mail: commander@aol.com

CAREER PROFILE:

High-caliber Management Executive with over 15 years' experience building and leading top-performing, efficient, and cost-effective operations for a global organization. Strong general management qualifications in strategic planning, reengineering, process redesign, quality, and productivity improvement. Excellent experience in personnel training, development, and leadership. Skilled public speaker and executive liaison.

PROFESSIONAL EXPERIENCE:

MANAGEMENT EXECUTIVE   1972 to Present
UNITED STATES NAVY – U.S. & WORLDWIDE ASSIGNMENTS

Fast-track promotion through a series of increasingly responsible management positions directing large-scale operating, resource management, finance, and human resource organizations. Acted in the capacity of Chief Operating Officer, General Manager, and Management Executive, developing and leading high-profile business units supporting global operations. Expertise includes:

General Management / Operations Management

- Planned, staffed, and directed business affairs for organizations with up to 4,200 personnel assigned to over 15 different sites worldwide. Held full decision-making responsibility for developing annual business plans and long-range strategic plans, evaluating human resource and training requirements, and implementing advanced information technologies.

- Consulted with senior executive management team to evaluate long-term organizational goals and design supporting business and financial systems to control operations.

- Managed over $300 million in annual budget funds allocated for operations, research and development, and general expenses. Slashed 22% from the budget through reallocation of resources, personnel, and technologies.

- Conducted ongoing analyses to evaluate the efficiency, quality, and productivity of diverse operations (e.g., administrative, equipment, maintenance, transportation, human resources, inventory control). Streamlined operations and reduced staffing requirements by 18%.

- Negotiated and administered multimillion–dollar vendor contracts supporting over $80 million in field construction and renovation projects. Delivered all projects on time and within budget.

- Appointed to several headquarters committees working to professionalize the U.S. Navy, introduce proven business-management strategies, and enhance internal accountabilities.

This style is recommended because it uses a format that highlights the candidate's general business skills and qualifications. By using "corporate" language, not military or government lingo, it appears as though the candidate already belongs in "corporate America."

COMMANDER CRAIG – *Page Two*

Human Resource Leadership

- Directed staffs of up to 100+ technical, professional, and support personnel. Fully accountable for personnel scheduling, job assignments, performance reviews, merit promotions, and daily supervision. Coordinated manpower planning to meet operational requirements and realigned workflow to optimize productivity.

- Designed and led hundreds of personnel training and professional skills development programs throughout career. Topics included budgeting/finance, leadership, team building, information technology, communications, reporting, and diversity.

- Introduced innovative training technologies (e.g., remote, video, telecommunications).

Information & Telecommunications Technology

- Spearheaded the selection, acquisition, and implementation of over $45 million in technologies over the past 10 years (e.g., Internet and Intranet, data mining, data warehousing, CADCAM, Microsoft Office, GIS).

Asset Management

- Controlled over $175 million in capital equipment, materials, and supplies. Redesigned logistics support programs and reduced inventory costs by $3 million annually.

Career Path
Commanding Officer (1992 to Present)
Resource Management Director (1987 to 1992)
Executive Officer (1985 to 1987)
Business/Finance Manager (1982 to 1984)
Operations Officer (1976 to 1982)
Administrator / Program Coordinator / Educational Officer (1972 to 1976)

Received several distinguished awards and commendations for outstanding leadership qualifications, management expertise, quality/productivity improvements, and cost reductions.

EDUCATION: **MS – Executive Management** – Naval Postgraduate School – 1978
BS – Management – U.S. Naval Academy – 1972
Graduate – 500+ hours leadership / executive management training

AFFILIATIONS: Who's Who Worldwide (1995)
Sydney Roads Total Quality Management Council
American Society of Military Leaders
American Management Association

Senior Manager or Executive

Theresa Santiago
santiago-t@yahoo.com

2775 Hyde Park Place
Chicago, IL 60616
(312) 555-0001 Home
(312) 555-5556 Office

PROFILE

Corporate attorney and management executive with a background in *finance* and *regulatory compliance.* Creative consensus-builder with a history of driving change and improvement to achieve positive business results.

Strengths

- Negotiation, communication, and relationship-building with both internal and external customers.
- Effective leadership of corporate departments and initiatives; management and development of staff; true team orientation.
- Analytical and organizational skills combined with strong ability to envision both process and results.

EDUCATION

Juris Doctor, 1996—Licensed to practice law in Illinois.
NORTHWESTERN UNIVERSITY COLLEGE OF LAW, Chicago, Illinois

Bachelor of Business Administration, summa cum laude, 1987—Majors: Finance and Marketing
UNIVERSITY OF CHICAGO, Chicago, Illinois

PROFESSIONAL EXPERIENCE

1988–Present   MIDWEST MUTUAL INSURANCE COMPANY, Chicago, Illinois

Regulatory Compliance Department

Vice President, March 2000–Present

Promoted to senior officer and charged with centralizing and overseeing all of the company's legal activities and government affairs, while maintaining majority of responsibilities of prior position. Manage $1 million department budget and $2.5 million legal fees budget.

- Initiated legal affairs centralization with an in-depth assessment of company-wide legal affiliations and activities; primary goal is to identify opportunities to save cost by bringing services in-house. Developing recommendation and plan for presentation to executive management in spring 2001.
- Assumed responsibility for the company's government affairs and PAC activities. Currently developing plan to build relationships with key Illinois legislators.
- Investigated business incentive opportunities with 3 states; concluded successful negotiation that captured $8 million incentive for relocation and consolidation.
- Implemented centralized contract analysis, review, and sign-off procedures and took on responsibility of overseeing all corporate contracts.

Assistant Treasurer, 1997–2000
Department Head, 1994–2000

Provided strategic direction to 18-member department created from start-up to centralize the company's tax, securities, and licensing activities.

- Spearheaded the formation of the department… developed in-depth organizational plan and secured senior management approval to implement. After 2 years of operation, department selected for Midwest Mutual's **President's Award,** reflecting our contributions to corporate profit and continued commitment to corporate values.

Led and managed the department with a strong customer-service focus, inclusive team-building approach, and support for staff development and advancement.

Key responsibility was ensuring compliance with tax and securities laws and directing the licensing process with state departments of insurance. As well, communicated changes in regulations and provided legal and financial advice.

This format is recommended because of its executive-level language, tone, style, and impact. All of these combine to create a powerful, upscale, and executive presentation.

Theresa Santiago Page 2

PROFESSIONAL EXPERIENCE

continued **MIDWEST MUTUAL INSURANCE COMPANY**

Built appropriate professional relationship with the IRS and state insurance departments. Represented the company on audits and appeals of federal, state, and local tax issues.

- Virtually eliminated the assessment of tax penalties since formation of the department—attributable to cohesive tax strategy, centralized activities, highly effective negotiations during audits, and department-level focus on tax-related issues.

Maintained thorough knowledge of Midwest Mutual's strategies, objectives, products, and long-term business plans to ensure effective and appropriate advice on tax and securities consequences of specific activities and transactions as they fit within the larger scheme of the corporation's overall direction and objectives.

As a member of the company's due diligence team, conducted tax, finance, and legal research on potential acquisitions and liquidations.

Reviewed and coordinated filing of SEC registration statements. Developed, implemented, and maintained corporate insider trading policy and procedures. Contributed to development of corporate disclosure policy and procedures.

Corporate Tax Manager, 1992–1994

Oversaw all tax-related activities for the company and held responsibility for compliance with federal, state, and local taxation laws. Supervised staff of 4 in preparation of tax returns and related financial documents.

- Took on assignment with no prior experience in corporate taxation… began law school to increase knowledge of tax and regulatory issues.

Developed positive relationship with IRS through consistent demonstration of professionalism, preparedness, and good business ethics.

- Captured tax savings of more than $3.5 million through successful IRS appeals negotiations.

Director of Private Placements, 1989–1992

Implemented investment strategies for private placements averaging $300 million annually. Analyzed proposed investment vehicles; negotiated terms and conditions directly with borrowing company; monitored existing portfolio and post-closing documentation.

Established operating procedures for the handling of confidential information.

Represented the company at campus recruiting sessions.

Investment Analyst, 1988–1989

PROFESSIONAL AFFILIATIONS

Trustee, Midwest Mutual Foundation

- Directed legal and administrative set-up of the foundation. Contributed to development of charitable giving policy and procedures.

Board Member, Illinois Insurance Institute

Board Member, United Way of Cook County—Member, Budget Allocation Committee

Member, Tax Executives Institute

Member, American Bar Association and local affiliates

Consultant

RAYMOND R. PALANSKI
82 Grisham Road
Seafert, DE 19898
Phone: 555-839-2876   E-mail: rrpalanski@aol.com   Fax: 555-839-9643

EXECUTIVE PROFILE

Corporate Development Executive/Business Development Strategist with 15+ years across broad industries, products, services, and technologies in U.S. and foreign markets. Intuitive, insightful, creative, and intelligent. Confidential advisor to CEOs, CFOs, Chairmen, and other senior executives. Impeccable ethics and integrity. MBA Degree. CPA.

- Growth & Development Strategy, Value Analysis, Vision, & Leadership
- Mergers, Acquisitions, Joint Ventures, Strategic Alliances, & Partnerships
- Capital Formation, Investment Banking, & Venture Capital Funding
- Complex Financial Analysis, Modeling, & Transactions Structuring
- Executive Mediation, Negotiation, Facilitation, & Partner/Liaison Affairs
- Acquisition Integration & Post-Integration Leadership

CAREER PROFILE

CORPORATE DEVELOPMENT CONSULTANT   1994 to Present
THE PALANSKI COMPANY
Strategic & Financial Advisor/Investment Banker to U.S. and foreign corporations committed to acquisition-focused growth strategies. Provide turnkey leadership for major acquisition, strategic alliance, joint venture, and refinancing programs, from initial business planning, candidate/partner selection, due diligence, deal structuring, and negotiations through final execution. Project highlights include:

- **Forum International** – Developed and executed strategy to employ high market capitalization of U.K. medtech company for U.S. expansion. Delivered strategy that achieved profit targets to counter R&D costs; product/service outsourcing; and roll-up consolidation. Point person for two acquisitions, driving client revenues from $2 million to $30+ million. Listed company on London Stock Exchange.

- **Leverson Global** – Authored business plan for strategic alliance to establish a U.S. consulting firm joint venture for $2 billion Dutch corporate division. Executive committee voted full funding for $750,000.

- **Bross & Company** – Conceived competitive strategy for Fortune 1000 Bross client to increase market share and profitability within the changing health-care reimbursement market.

- **Biotech Partners** – Currently leading effort to acquire larger, publicly held competitor to build critical mass, expand product line, and achieve public listing with less costly and more creative "back door" strategy.

VENTURE PROJECTS DIRECTOR   1988 to 1994
LOUISIANA GENERAL HOSPITAL (LGH), Baton Rouge, Louisiana
Recruited by Chairman of the Board as **Venture Projects Director** to orchestrate an aggressive expansion throughout highly competitive health-care industries, technologies, and services. Conceived, developed, and led successful corporate development projects (strategic alliances, joint ventures, start-up ventures). Served as **CFO, Treasurer or Director of Finance** for new projects. Member – Corporate Strategies Committee. **Board Member** – MGH portfolio companies.

- **CRESSTAR, Inc.** – CFO tasked to either restore this medical imaging technology transfer venture to profitability or close. Sought funding to energize company, expand operations, and strengthen financial performance. Achieved all financial objectives.

  — Negotiated $2 million strategic alliance with 3M and $5 million contract with Procter & Gamble.
  — Developed capital strategy and business plan leading to acquisition by French merchant bankers.

- **Fox Runn Partnership** – Partnered with two for-profit companies to develop a $100 million retirement community. Negotiated complex $75 million construction loan and subsequent permanent mortgage financing package. Restructured loan status when FDIC took over bank. Structured and negotiated successful buyout of corporate partner facing bankruptcy to eliminate partnership liability.

  — Returned $7+ million profit on $2.3 million investment (despite poor regional real estate market).

This format is recommended because it places the emphasis on depth and scope of consulting projects, notable results and achievements, and reputation and diversity of clients.

RAYMOND R. PALANSKI – *Page Two*

VENTURE PROJECTS DIRECTOR *(Continued)*

- **Louisiana Biomedical Research Corporation** – Singlehandedly structured a complex financial model for $125 million bond financing for development of 650,000 sq. ft. of biomedical research labs. Met debt covenants, grant restrictions, market lease rates, FASB 13, and debt burden limits.

    — Created financial plan in place for six years. Co-led company's $30 million operations during tenure.

- **Acute Disease Care Center** – Authored strategic, financial, and business plans approved for $22 million in new venture funding by the Board of Trustees.

- Conceived, developed, and/or launched several other successful new ventures/portfolio companies:

    — **XRT** – Partnered with Paris-based venture capital firm to develop international telemedicine partnership.
    — **LGHIC** – Launched diagnostic imaging venture. Increased utilization and reimbursement by $5 million.
    — **American Express** – Partnered hospital with American Express to establish profitable in-house travel agency.

VENTURE PROJECTS CONSULTANT/INTERIM CFO   1985 to 1988

- **LGH** – Developed and implemented strategic business plan to establish innovative marketing initiative. Subsequently recruited as Venture Projects Director with this $1+ billion corporation.

- **Crescent Ventures** – Developed and automated accounting and financial management systems for seven partnerships of this $160 million new-venture firm (now one of the world's largest VC firms). Directed investor relations with corporations and pension funds. Managed $40 million cash fund.

- **Paris Stores, Inc.** – Created and implemented financial and administrative infrastructure to lead Canadian-based retail chain into U.S. market (18 stores in Eastern and Midwestern regions).

- **Seventh Avenue Deli** – Developed strategic business plan for retail food company that attracted majority ownership investment offer from Beatrice Foods.

CHIEF FINANCIAL OFFICER / SENIOR VICE PRESIDENT   1983 to 1985
BUCKMAN & LEWISTON, Boston, Massachusetts (*22-office regional investment brokerage*)
Promoted from Vice President of Finance to CFO with full leadership responsibility for the firm's finance, investment, credit, accounting, MIS, and human resource operations. Teamed with Chairman and CEO in negotiating the profitable sale of the firm in 1985 (*declined offer to remain with new corporation*).

MANAGER – INVESTOR RELATIONS   1980 to 1983
DRG CORPORATION, Westborough, Massachusetts
Communicated financial results and strategic direction to Wall Street, strengthening DRG's market credibility (*despite negative industry press*). Authored corporate press releases and speeches.

ASSISTANT TO THE PRESIDENT   1977 to 1980
MID-EAST ROYALTIES, Chattanooga, Tennessee
Managed SEC affairs through two security offerings for $100 million oil and gas company.

EDUCATION

M.B.A. – Finance	EMORY UNIVERSITY – 1984
B.A. – Economics	UNIVERSITY OF TENNESSEE – 1976
C.P.A.	STATE OF LOUISIANA – 1977

Magical Tips on Resume Writing

With more than 25 years of resume writing experience between the two of us, we've come to know certain things that will help you create resumes that get noticed. Follow these magical tips to ensure that your resume is appropriate, on target, and a powerful sales document.

No Rules—Just Write

If anyone ever tells you that there are "rules" to resume writing, walk away. The fact that there are no rules is what makes the resume writing process so challenging. What works for one individual does not work for another, and each document must be custom-designed to that individual's specific experiences, qualifications, credentials, and track record of performance.

Sell It to Me; Don't Tell It to Me

The "sell it to me; don't tell it to me" strategy is one of the most effective in resume writing. Read the following sentence carefully:

```
Responsible for recruitment, training, benefits, compensa-
tion, and employee relations.
```

That sentence very succinctly "tells" the reader what you did.

A much better strategy is to "sell" your accomplishments by using a sentence such as this:

```
Directed recruitment, training, benefits, compensation, and
employee relations for a 400-employee corporation with 25%
annual growth and worldwide market presence.
```

Can you see the difference? The first is passive; it simply states overall responsibilities. The second is assertive; not only does it highlight responsibilities, but it clearly communicates the large and dynamic environment in which the job seeker worked. Sell your success. No one else is going to!

Be Honest, But Not Modest

If you are ever going to "toot your own horn," now is the time, and the vehicle is your resume. You *never* want to lie or misrepresent yourself. However, you do want to sell what you have accomplished and capture your reader's interest. It is time to remember all the great things you've done throughout your career and let the world know about them.

Include Employment and Education

Your resume must include your employment history and academic credentials. Although we have said that there are no rules for resume writing, it is expected that you will include your employment history and education qualifications. A prospective employer or recruiter must be able to quickly review your employment (companies and positions) and your academic credentials (college degrees, certificates, and continuing education). If you do not include this information, you have left the reader with virtually nothing to evaluate your skills, competencies, and potential value to that company.

It's OK to Leave Out Some Things

Your resume *does not* have to include each and every position you've ever held. Understand that we are not recommending that you misrepresent anything about yourself or your career. However, at some point in time, your older work experience becomes less important to your current career objectives, particularly if you've been working for 20 or more years.

If this is your situation, you may elect not to include your earlier experience at all, or you may summarize it if it is relevant to your current goals or offers you some competitive distinction from other candidates. This might include names of prominent companies you worked for, prominent client accounts you managed, significant and quantifiable achievements, or interesting and unusual experiences.

The other situation in which you might not include each and every position you've ever held is when you had a job that was particularly short in tenure. Suppose you worked in real estate sales for six months in 1994 between your two industrial sales management positions. Unless that experience is directly related to the type of position you are currently applying for, you may elect to delete it from your resume. It was short in duration, six years ago, and unrelated to your professional career. It was simply a "filler."

Be advised that we recommend you share any information you have left out of your resume at the time of an interview. We do not want you to create a veil of misconception. When you're face to face in an interview, tell the interviewer about those other positions so that you are disclosing all information. Just explain that the experience was irrelevant to your current career goals and, therefore, not worth including on your resume. You never want there to be any question as to your personal integrity, ethics, and values.

Never Include Salary Information on Your Resume

If a prospective employer or recruiter has asked for that information and you choose to comply, include it in your cover letter. That is the appropriate place—not your resume.

Wordings to Avoid

Do not start job descriptions with the words "Responsible for" or "Duties included." These phrases are dated and make for boring resume reading. You will significantly improve the tone and impact of your resume if you write using action verbs such as *managed, directed, trained, supervised, designed, developed, improved, increased, saved, reduced, facilitated, spearheaded…* the list goes on. If you're interested in reviewing a comprehensive list of action verbs, refer to appendix B.

Compare these two sample resume sentences to see the difference action verbs can make:

```
Responsible for planning and managing new product
introductions.
```
```
Spearheaded the introduction of six new products that
generated over $2 million in first-year revenues.
```

See the difference in impact and tone? The first is passive. The second is energizing and immediately communicates success and achievement.

Presentation Counts

The visual presentation of your resume must be powerful, attractive, and easy to read. When your resume first passes in front of someone, you've got only a few seconds to catch her attention. You can best accomplish this by preparing a document that is visually pleasing, has lots of white space, and can be quickly perused. If you don't catch her attention visually, she may never read your resume, and you may never have the opportunity for an interview.

Include Your E-Mail Address

If you have an e-mail address, include it on your resume (and your cover letter). Virtually the entire business world now communicates via e-mail. Let people know that you're "in the loop," and provide your e-mail contact information. Not only does this demonstrate that you're with the times, it also provides a prospective employer or recruiter with an easy and fast channel to communicate with you.

Don't use your current employer's e-mail address on your resume! Not only is this "bad form," implying that you use business tools for personal use, but there is the very real chance that you could jeopardize your current position if someone at your company intercepts or sees your job search–related e-mail messages. With numerous sources of free e-mail access widely available, it's a simple task to sign up for an e-mail address when you start your job search.

Take Everyone's Advice with a "Grain of Salt"

No matter who you speak with or who reviews your resume, you will get different opinions. Remember, that's part of what makes the entire job search process such a challenge. It is not an exact science, but rather is open to extensive personal interpretation. Listen carefully to what everyone says about your resume, and then integrate only the information you believe is appropriate to your career, your current objectives, and your personal situation.

Is Your Resume Working for You?

☐ Are you proud when you look at your resume?

☐ Does your resume leave a memorable visual impression?

☐ Is your resume easy to peruse and easy to read?

☐ Have you left adequate white space?

☐ Are your career objectives and strongest qualifications crystal-clear upon quickly scanning the resume?

☐ Have you included all relevant work experience?

☐ Have you included relevant degrees, training, and educational credentials?

☐ Does your resume highlight your most significant career accomplishments?

☐ Have you included measurable results that demonstrate your contributions?

☐ Does your resume include your e-mail address?

☐ Have you triple-checked for grammar, punctuation, and spelling errors?

☐ Does your resume highlight your technical qualifications (if appropriate)?

☐ Does your resume clearly communicate your value to a prospective employer?

☐ Does your resume *sell* you?

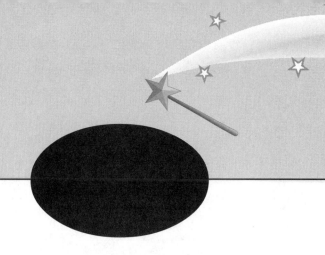

Appendixes

Appendix A

Using Key Words to Win in Your Job Search

Five years ago, no one had ever heard of *key words*. Today, they are everywhere!

- You talk to a resume writer, recruiter, career counselor, corporate human resources professional, or career coach, and each of them mentions the importance of key words.

- You read about the Internet and online job search, and the emphasis is on key words and key-word scanning.

- You listen to a CNN news brief about the latest employment trends, and the reporter highlights the importance of key words in today's competitive job market.

- You attend a job search training and networking seminar, and the focus in on key words.

- You purchase a book on resume writing and job search, and the emphasis is on key words and their importance in the development of resumes, cover letters, broadcast letters, and other job search marketing communications.

Then, you ask yourself:

- ★ What are key words, and where did they come from?
- ★ What is all this talk about key words and scanning?
- ★ How do I use key words in my cover letter?
- ★ Where else can I use key words?
- ★ Which key words are right for me, my profession, and my industry?

The following sections will answer all of these key-word questions.

What Are Key Words, and Where Did They Come From?

Key words are nothing new. They are buzzwords— the "hot" words associated with a specific industry, profession, or job function—that clearly and succinctly communicate a specific message about a job function, qualification, accomplishment, or responsibility. Key words are usually nouns—words such as *benefits plan design* (for human resources), *market share ratings* (for marketing and sales), *logistics management* (for transportation), and *platform architecture* (for information technology).

Trends today, greatly influenced by the tremendous competition in the job market, require that resumes, cover letters, and other job search communications clearly present your skills and qualifications in an action-driven style. Your challenge when preparing these documents is to demonstrate that you can deliver strong performance results. And there is no better manner in which to accomplish this than with the use of powerful key words and phrases that demonstrate your qualifications, capabilities, skills, and value to a hiring organization. Key words get you noticed, not passed over.

 Examples of General Key Words

Here are some "general management" and "professional" key words for use in your resume and cover letter. Use these key words to supplement the key words you've already selected from your designated profession or industry.

- ★ Strategic planning
- ★ Performance and productivity improvement
- ★ P&L responsibility

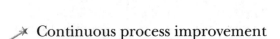

- ✦ Continuous process improvement
- ✦ Organizational design
- ✦ Business process design and reengineering
- ✦ Infrastructure development
- ✦ Business process optimization
- ✦ Team-building and leadership
- ✦ Business turnaround and revitalization
- ✦ Change management
- ✦ Start-up ventures and new enterprises
- ✦ Information technology
- ✦ New media, Internet, and e-commerce
- ✦ Consensus-building
- ✦ Executive presentations and negotiations
- ✦ Project design and management
- ✦ Competitive market and product positioning
- ✦ Investor and board relations
- ✦ New product and new service introduction
- ✦ Oral and written communications
- ✦ Problem-solving and decision-making

The list could go on. You can probably think of many more key words to integrate into your job search materials.

What Is All This Talk About Key Words and Scanning?

Key words are the standard by which thousands of companies and recruiters screen applicants' resumes to identify core qualifications and skills.

First, upon arrival at a company that uses scanning technology, all resumes, and sometimes their accompanying cover letters, are scanned into the company's database. This process makes all the words in the resume accessible via a computerized search. And what are the criteria used for the search? Quite simply, they are the key words that match the specific hiring criteria. As you can imagine, these key words are vastly different from position to position, even within a company, and perhaps for similar positions with different companies. The companies themselves select the key words they will use for the search. Therefore, it is critical that you include an appropriate assortment of key words in your resume, cover letter, and all other job search communications so that your documents will be "found" by the scanning technology used at your target company.

Whether or not this strategy and mechanism for evaluating a candidate's qualifications is appropriate, the fact remains that key-word scanning has become an increasingly dominant tool in today's hiring market. The fact remains, however, that scanning technology is in use only by companies and recruiting firms that receive a vast number of resumes, when the amount of work saved by the scanning technology makes the investment worthwhile.

But since you cannot be certain whether your target companies are using scanning technology, make certain you give yourself every chance for consideration. Do not allow yourself to be passed over because you do not have the "right" words in your resume and cover letter. Integrate the key words in this chapter into your resume as they accurately reflect your experience. Not only will you meet the technological requirements for key-word scanning, you will also create powerful career marketing tools. And, we all know that the winners in job search are those who can "sell" their qualifications, highlight their achievements, and distinguish themselves from the competition.

How Do I Use Key Words in My Cover Letter?

Key words are remarkably effective tools to use in developing your cover letters, broadcast letters, thank-you letters, and other job search correspondence. They strengthen the presentation of your skills, qualifications, and experience, as well as demonstrate your competencies, achievements, and successes. Use key words to highlight information as it directly relates to the position for which you are applying.

As on your resume, you can use key words in various cover letter sections, styles, and formats. The following are brief cover letter excerpts to demonstrate how best to integrate key words into your letters.

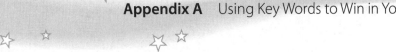

 ## Integrating Key Words into the Text

My career is best summarized as follows: Years of senior management experience with two global corporations—Excelsior Bank and Voice of America—and now my current position as President/CEO of a start-up technology venture. The breadth of my experience is remarkably broad, from managing VOA's entire Latin American operation to the more finite functions of building an operating architecture and business infra-structure for a new and highly specialized enterprise.

Using Key Words in a Separate Skills Section

Highlights of my professional skills that may be of particu-lar interest to you include the following:

- Strategic sales and market planning
- New product introduction
- Competitive sales negotiations
- Sales team training and leadership
- Account development and management
- Client retention and loyalty
- New product design and development
- U.S. and international sales management

Using Key Words in Career Highlights

Highlights of my career that may be of particular interest to you include the following:

- Ten years' experience as Managing Director, Senior VP, Executive VP, COO, and now President/CEO.
- Success in start-ups, acquisitions, turnarounds, high-growth companies, and multinational organizations.
- Innovative performance in business development through internal growth, mergers, acquisitions, joint ventures, and strategic alliances.
- Outstanding P&L performance measured via revenue and profit growth, cost reduction, market penetration, and other key indices.
- Expertise in sales, marketing, and the entire customer development/management/retention process.
- Strong information technology expertise.

Using Key Words in a Double-Column Format

Your Qualifications	My Experience
M.B.A. degree	M.B.A. degree from Harvard Business School
Human Resource Management	10 years' experience in HRM and OD
HRIS technology	Implementation of $2.8 million HRIS technology system
Benefits and compensation	Design of IBM's benefits and compensation systems
Management recruitment	Recruitment and development of IBM's newest executive team

Where Else Can I Use Key Words?

Key words are also powerful tools to incorporate into your other job search materials (such as resumes, leadership profiles, career biographies, Internet postings, and networking letters). In fact, you can also use them in general business correspondence, proposals, reports, capital financing requests, venture capital and Wall Street solicitations, advertisements, marketing communications, publicity, publications, and public speaking presentations. Their usefulness in professional documents is unlimited!

Retain your key-word list for use in future writing and documentation.

Which Key Words Are Right for Me, My Profession, and My Industry?

We've made it easy for you! Below is a comprehensive list of key words for your use as a tool and resource. Review each key word and ask yourself whether it represents one of your important qualifications or job functions. Then make certain that you include the most relevant of these key words in your resume and cover letters.

Not only will you be delighted with the impact of your new job search communications, you can rest assured that your documents will be located by the scanning software whenever a company is searching for a position that matches your skills.

 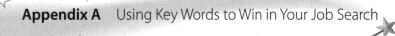

Administration

Administration	Front-Office Operations
Administrative Infrastructure	Government Affairs
Administrative Processes	Liaison Affairs
Administrative Support	Mail and Messenger Services
Back-Office Operations	Meeting Planning
Budget Administration	Office Management
Client Communications	Office Services
Confidential Correspondence	Policy and Procedure
Contract Administration	Product Support
Corporate Recordkeeping	Productivity Improvement
Corporate Secretary	Project Management
Customer Liaison	Records Management
Document Management	Regulatory Reporting
Efficiency Improvement	Resource Management
Executive Liaison Affairs	Technical Support
Executive Officer Support	Time Management
Facilities Management	Workflow Planning/Prioritization

Association and Not-for-Profit Management

Advocacy	Industry Association
Affiliate Members	Industry Relations
Board Relations	Leadership Training
Budget Allocation	Marketing Communications
Budget Oversight	Media Relations
Chapter	Member Communications
Community Outreach	Member Development
Corporate Development	Member-Driven Organization
Corporate Giving	Member Retention
Corporate Sponsorship	Member Services
Education Foundation	Mission Planning
Educational Programming	Not-for-Profit
Endowment Funds	Organization(al) Leadership
Foundation Management	Organization(al) Mission
Fund-Raising	Organization(al) Vision
Grass-Roots Campaign	Policy Development

Political Affairs (Political Action Committee—PAC)

Press Relations

Public Policy Development

Public Relations

Public/Private Partnerships

Regulatory Affairs

Research Foundation

Speakers Bureau

Special Events Management

Volunteer Recruitment

Volunteer Training

Banking

Asset Management

Asset-Based Lending

Audit Examination

Branch Operations

Cash Management

Commercial Banking

Commercial Credit

Consumer Banking

Consumer Credit

Correspondent Banking

Credit Administration

Credit Analysis

de novo Banking

Debt Financing

Deposit Base

Depository Services

Equity Financing

Fee Income

Foreign Exchange (FX)

Global Banking

Investment Management

Investor Relations

Lease Administration

Letters of Credit

Liability Exposure

Loan Administration

Loan Processing

Loan Quality

Loan Recovery

Loan Underwriting

Lockbox Processing

Merchant Banking

Non-Performing Assets

Portfolio Management

Receivership

Regulatory Affairs

Relationship Management

Retail Banking

Retail Lending

Return on Assets (ROA)

Return on Equity (ROE)

Return on Investment (ROI)

Risk Management

Secondary Markets

Secured Lending

Securities Management

Transaction Banking

Trust Services

Unsecured Lending

Wholesale Banking

Workout

Customer Service

Account Relationship Management
Customer Communications
Customer Development
Customer Focus Groups
Customer Loyalty
Customer Management
Customer Needs Assessment
Customer Retention
Customer Satisfaction
Customer Service
Customer Surveys
Field Service Operation
Inbound Service Operation
Key Account Management
Order Fulfillment
Order Processing
Outbound Service Operation
Process Simplification
Records Management
Relationship Management
Sales Administration
Service Benchmarks
Service Delivery
Service Measures
Service Quality
Telemarketing Operations
Telesales Operations

Engineering

Benchmark
Capital Project
Chemical Engineering
Commissioning
Computer-Aided Design (CAD)
Computer-Aided Engineering (CAE)
Computer-Aided Manufacturing (CAM)
Cross-Functional Team
Customer Management
Development Engineering
Efficiency
Electrical Engineering
Electronics Engineering
Engineering Change Order (ECO)
Engineering Documentation
Environmental Engineering
Ergonomic Techniques
Experimental Design
Experimental Methods
Facilities Engineering
Fault Analysis
Field Performance
Final Customer Acceptance
Hardware Engineering
Industrial Engineering
Industrial Hygiene
Maintenance Engineering
Manufacturing Engineering
Manufacturing Integration
Mechanical Engineering
Methods Design
Nuclear Engineering
Occupational Safety and Health Administration (OSHA)
Operating and Maintenance (O&M)
Optics Engineering
Plant Engineering

Process Development

Process Engineering

Process Standardization

Product Design

Product Development Cycle

Product Functionality

Product Innovation

Product Lifecycle Management

Product Manufacturability

Product Reliability

Productivity Improvement

Project Costing

Project Planning

Project Management

Prototype

Quality Assurance

Quality Engineering

Regulatory Compliance

Research and Development (R&D)

Resource Management

Root Cause

Scale-Up

Software Engineering

Specifications

Statistical Analysis

Systems Engineering

Systems Integration

Technical Briefings

Technical Liaison Affairs

Technology Development

Test Engineering

Turnkey

Work Methods Analysis

Finance, Accounting, and Auditing

Accounts Payable

Accounts Receivable

Asset Disposition

Asset Management

Asset Purchase

Audit Controls

Audit Management

Capital Budgets

Cash Management

Commercial Paper

Corporate Development

Corporate Tax

Cost Accounting

Cost Avoidance

Cost Reduction

Cost/Benefit Analysis

Credit and Collections

Debt Financing

Divestiture

Due Diligence

Employee Stock
Ownership Plan (ESOP)

Equity Financing

Feasibility Analysis

Financial Analysis

Financial Audits

Financial Controls

Financial Models

Financial Planning

Financial Reporting

Foreign Exchange (FX)

Initial Public Offering (IPO)

Internal Controls

International Finance

Investment Management

Investor Accounting

Investor Relations

Job Costing

Letters of Credit

Leveraged Buy-Out (LBO)

Liability Management

Make/Buy Analysis

Margin Improvement

Merger

Operating Budgets

Operational Audits

Partnership Accounting

Profit and Loss (P&L) Analysis

Profit Gains

Project Accounting

Project Financing

Regulatory Compliance Auditing

Return on Assets (ROA)

Return on Equity (ROE)

Return on Investment (ROI)

Revenue Gain

Risk Management

Shareholder Relations

Stock Purchase

Strategic Planning

Treasury

Trust Accounting

Workpapers

General Management, Senior Management, and Consulting

Accelerated Growth

Acting Executive

Advanced Technology

Benchmarking

Business Development

Business Reengineering

Capital Projects

Competitive Market Position

Consensus Building

Continuous Process Improvement

Corporate Administration

Corporate Communications

Corporate Culture Change

Corporate Development

Corporate Image

Corporate Legal Affairs

Corporate Mission

Corporate Vision

Cost Avoidance

Cost Reduction

Crisis Communications

Cross-Cultural Communications

Cross-Functional Team Leadership

Customer Loyalty

Customer Retention

Customer-Driven Management

Decision-Making Authority

Efficiency Improvement

Emerging Business Venture

Entrepreneurial Leadership

European Economic Community (EEC)

Executive Management

Executive Presentations

Financial Management

Financial Restructuring

Global Market Expansion

High-Growth Organization

Infrastructure

Interim Executive

Leadership Development

Long-Range Planning

Management Development

Margin Improvement

Market Development

Market-Driven Management

Marketing Management

Matrix Management

Multifunction Experience

Multi-Industry Experience

Multisite Operations Management

New Business Development

Operating Infrastructure

Operating Leadership

Organization(al) Culture

Organization(al) Development

Participative Management

Performance Improvement

Policy Development

Proactive Leadership

Process Ownership

Process Reengineering

Productivity Improvement

Profit and Loss (P&L) Management

Profit Growth

Project Management

Quality Improvement

Reengineering

Relationship Management

Reorganization

Return on Assets (ROA)

Return on Equity (ROE)

Return on Investment (ROI)

Revenue Growth

Sales Management

Service Design/Delivery

Signatory Authority

Start-Up Venture

Strategic Development

Strategic Partnership

Tactical Planning/Leadership

Team-Building

Team Leadership

Total Quality Management (TQM)

Transition Management

Turnaround Management

World Class Organization

Health Care

Acute Care Facility

Ambulatory Care

Assisted Living

Capital Giving Campaign

Case Management

Certificate of Need (CON)

Chronic Care Facility

Clinical Services

Community Hospital

Community Outreach

Continuity of Care

Cost Center

Electronic Claims Processing

Emergency Medical Systems (EMS)

Employee Assistance Program (EAP)

Fee Billing

Full-Time Equivalent (FTE)

Grant Administration

Health-Care Administrator

Health-Care Delivery Systems

Health Maintenance
Organization (HMO)

 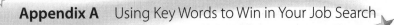

Home Health Care

Hospital Foundation

Industrial Medicine

Inpatient Care

Long-Term Care

Managed Care

Management Service
Organization (MSO)

Multihospital Network

Occupational Health

Outpatient Care

Patient Accounting

Patient Relations

Peer Review

Physician Credentialing

Physician Relations

Practice Management

Preferred Provider
Organization (PPO)

Preventive Medicine

Primary Care

Provider Relations

Public Health Administration

Quality of Care

Regulatory Standards (JCAHO)

Rehabilitation Services

Reimbursement Program

Risk Management

Service Delivery

Skilled Nursing Facility

Third-Party Administrator

Utilization Review

Wellness Programs

Hospitality

Amenities

Back-of-the-House Operations

Banquet Operations

Budget Administration

Catering Operations

Club Management

Conference Management

Contract F&B Operations

Corporate Dining Room

Customer Retention

Customer Service

Food and Beverage Operations (F&B)

Food Cost Controls

Front-of-the-House Operations

Guest Retention

Guest Satisfaction

Hospitality Management

Inventory Planning/Control

Labor Cost Controls

Meeting Planning

Member Development/Retention

Menu Planning

Menu Pricing

Multi-Unit Operations

Occupancy

Portion Control

Property Development

Purchasing

Resort Management

Service Management

Signature Property

Vendor Sourcing

VIP Relations

Human Resources

Americans with Disabilities Act (ADA)
Benefits Administration
Career Pathing
Change Management
Claims Administration
College Recruitment
Compensation
Competency-Based Performance
Corporate Culture Change
Cross-Cultural Communications
Diversity Management
Employee Communications
Employee Empowerment
Employee Involvement Teams
Employee Relations
Employee Retention
Employee Surveys
Equal Employment Opportunity (EEO)
Expatriate Employment
Grievance Proceedings
Human Resources (HR)
Human Resources Generalist Affairs
Human Resources Partnerships
Incentive Planning
International Employment
Job Task Analysis
Labor Arbitration
Labor Contract Negotiations

Labor Relations
Leadership Assessment
Leadership Development
Management Training and Development
Manpower Planning
Merit Promotion
Multimedia Training
Multinational Workforce
Organization(al) Design
Organization(al) Development (OD)
Organization(al) Needs Assessment
Participative Management
Performance Appraisal
Performance Incentives
Performance Reengineering
Position Classification
Professional Recruitment
Regulatory Affairs
Retention
Safety Training
Self-Directed Work Teams
Staffing
Succession Planning
Train-the-Trainer
Training and Development
Union Negotiations
Union Relations
Wage and Salary Administration
Workforce Reengineering

Human Services

Adult Services
Advocacy
Behavior Management
Behavior Modification
Casework

Client Advocacy
Client Placement
Community Outreach
Community-Based Intervention
Counseling

Crisis Intervention

Diagnostic Evaluation

Discharge Planning

Dually Diagnosed

Group Counseling

Human Services

Independent Life Skills Training

Inpatient

Integrated Service Delivery

Mainstreaming

Outpatient

Program Development

Protective Services

Psychoanalysis

Psychological Counseling

Psychotropic Medication

School Counseling

Social Services

Social Welfare

Substance Abuse

Testing

Treatment Planning

Vocational Placement

Vocational Rehabilitation

Vocational Testing

Youth Training Program

Information Systems and Telecommunications Technology

Advanced Technology

Applications Development

Architecture

Artificial Intelligence (AI)

Automated Voice Response (AVR)

Backbone

Benchmarking

Capacity Planning

CASE Tools

CD-ROM Technology

Cellular Communications

Chief Information Officer (CIO)

Chief Knowledge Officer (CKO)

Chief Technology Officer (CTO)

Client/Server Architecture

Computer Science

Cross-Functional Technology Team

Data Center Operations

Data Communications

Data Dictionary

Data Recovery

Database Administration

Database Design

Database Server

Desktop Technology

Disaster Recovery

Document Imaging

E-Business

E-Commerce

E-Trade

Electronic Data Interchange (EDI)

Electronic Mail (e-mail)

Emerging Technologies

End-User Support

Enterprise Systems

Expert Systems

Fault Analysis

Field Support

Fourth-Generation Language

Frame Relay

Functionality

Geographic Information System (GIS)

Global Systems Support

Graphical User Interface (GUI)

Hardware Configuration

Hardware Development/Engineering

Help Desk

Host-Based System

Imaging Technology

Information Technology (IT)

Internet

Intranet

Java Scripting

Joint Application Development (JAD)

Local Area Network (LAN)

Management Information Systems (MIS)

Multimedia Technology

Multi-User Interface

Multivendor Systems Integration

Network Administration

New Media

Object-Oriented Programming

Office Automation (OA)

Online

Operating System

Parallel Systems Operations

PC Technology

Pilot Implementation

Process Modeling

Project Lifecycle

Project Management Methodology

Rapid Application Development (RAD)

Real-Time Data

Relational Database

Remote Systems Access

Research and Development (R&D)

Resource Management

Software Configuration

Software Development/Engineering

Systems Acquisition

Systems Configuration

Systems Development Methodology

Systems Documentation

Systems Engineering

Systems Functionality

Systems Implementation

Systems Integration

Systems Security

Technical Documentation

Technical Training

Technology Commercialization

Technology Integration

Technology Licensing

Technology Needs Assessment

Technology Rightsizing

Technology Solutions

Technology Transfer

Telecommunications Technology

Teleconferencing Technology

User Training and Support

Vendor Partnerships

Voice Communications

Web Sites and Web Pages

Wide Area Network (WAN)

International Business Development

Acquisition

Barter Transactions

Channel Development

Competitive Intelligence

Corporate Development

Cross-Border Transactions

Cross-Cultural Communications

Diplomatic Protocol

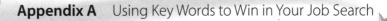

Emerging Markets

Expatriate

Export

Feasibility Analysis

Foreign Government Affairs

Foreign Investment

Global Expansion

Global Market Position

Global Marketing

Global Sales

Import

Intellectual Property

International Business Development

International Business Protocol

International Financing

International Liaison

International Licensee

International Marketing

International Sales

International Subsidiary

International Trade

Joint Venture

Licensing Agreements

Local National

Market Entry

Marketing

Merger

Multichannel Distribution Network

Offshore Operations

Public/Private Partnership

Start-Up Venture

Strategic Alliance

Strategic Planning

Technology Licensing

Technology Transfer

Law and Corporate Legal Affairs

Acquisition

Adjudication

Administrative Law

Antitrust

Briefs

Case Law

Client Management

Competitive Intelligence

Contracts Law

Copyright Law

Corporate Bylaws

Corporate Law

Corporate Recordkeeping

Criminal Law

Cross-Border Transactions

Depositions

Discovery

Due Diligence

Employment Law

Environmental Law

Ethics

Family Law

Fraud

General Partnership

Intellectual Property

Interrogatory

Joint Venture

Judicial Affairs

Juris Doctor (JD)

Labor Law

Landmark Decision

Legal Advocacy

Legal Research

Legislative Review/Analysis

Licensing

Limited Liability Corporation (LLC)

Limited Partnership

Litigation

Mediation

Memoranda

Mergers

Motions

Negotiations

Patent Law

Personal Injury

Probate Law

Real Estate Law

Risk Management

SEC Affairs

Settlement Negotiations

Shareholder Relations

Signatory Authority

Strategic Alliance

Tax Law

Technology Transfer

Trade Secrets

Trademark

Transactions Law

Trial Law

Unfair Competition

Workers' Compensation Litigation

Manufacturing and Production

Asset Management

Automated Manufacturing

Best-in-Class

Capacity Planning

Capital Budget

Capital Project

Cell Manufacturing

Computer Integrated Manufacturing (CIM)

Concurrent Engineering

Continuous Improvement

Cost Avoidance

Cost Reductions

Cross-Functional Teams

Cycle Time Reduction

Distribution Management

Efficiency Improvement

Environmental Health and Safety (EHS)

Equipment Management

Ergonomically Efficient

Facilities Consolidation

Inventory Control

Inventory Planning

Just-in-Time (JIT)

Labor Efficiency

Labor Relations

Logistics Management

Manufacturing Engineering

Manufacturing Integration

Manufacturing Technology

Master Schedule

Materials Planning

Materials Replenishment System (MRP)

Multisite Operations

Occupational Health and Safety (OH&S)

On-Time Delivery

Operating Budget

Operations Management

Operations Reengineering

 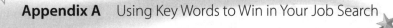

Operations Start-Up
Optimization
Order Fulfillment
Order Processing
Outsourcing
Participative Management
Performance Improvement
Physical Inventory
Pilot Manufacturing
Plant Operations
Process Automation
Process Redesign/Reengineering
Procurement
Product Development and Engineering
Product Rationalization
Production Forecasting
Production Lead Time
Production Management
Production Output
Production Plans/Schedules
Productivity Improvement
Profit and Loss (P&L) Management
Project Budget

Purchasing Management
Quality Assurance/Quality Control
Quality Circles
Regulatory Compliance
Safety Management
Safety Training
Shipping and Receiving Operation
Spares and Repairs Management
Statistical Process Control (SPC)
Technology Integration
Time and Motion Studies
Total Quality Management (TQM)
Traffic Management
Turnaround Management
Union Negotiations
Value-Added Processes
Vendor Management
Warehousing Operations
Work in Progress (WIP)
Workflow Optimization
Workforce Management
World Class Manufacturing (WCM)
Yield Improvement

Public Relations and Corporate Communications

Advertising Communications
Agency Relations
Brand Management
Brand Strategy
Broadcast Media
Campaign Management
Community Affairs
Community Outreach
Competitive Market Lead
Conference Planning
Cooperative Advertising

Corporate Communications
Corporate Identity
Corporate Sponsorship
Corporate Vision
Creative Services
Crisis Communications
Customer Communications
Direct-Mail Campaign
Electronic Advertising
Electronic Media
Employee Communications

Event Management

Fund-Raising

Government Relations

Grass-Roots Campaign

Investor Communications

Issues Management

Legislative Affairs

Logistics

Management Communications

Market Research

Marketing Communications

Media Buys

Media Placement

Media Relations

Media Scheduling

Meeting Planning

Merchandising

Multimedia Advertising

Political Action Committee (PAC)

Premiums

Press Releases

Print Media

Promotions

Public Affairs

Public Relations

Public Speaking

Publications

Publicity

Sales Incentives

Shareholder Communications

Special Events

Strategic Communications Plan

Strategic Planning

Strategic Positioning

Tactical Campaign

Trade Shows

VIP Relations

Purchasing and Logistics

Acquisition Management

Barter Trade

Bid Review

Buy Versus Lease Analysis

Capital Equipment Acquisition

Commodities Purchasing

Competitive Bidding

Contract Administration

Contract Change Order

Contract Negotiations

Contract Terms and Conditions

Cradle-to-Grave Procurement

Distribution Management

Economic Ordering
Quantity Methodology

Fixed-Price Contracts

Indefinite Price/Indefinite Quantity

International Sourcing

International Trade

Inventory Planning/Control

Just-in-Time (JIT) Purchasing

Logistics Management

Materials Management

Materials Replenishment
Ordering (MRO) Purchasing

Multisite Operations

Negotiation

Offshore Purchasing

Outsourced / Outsourcing

Price Negotiations

Procurement

Proposal Review

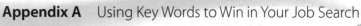

Purchasing

Regulatory Compliance

Request for Proposal (RFP)

Request for Quotation (RFQ)

Sourcing

Specifications Compliance

Subcontractor Negotiations

Supplier Management

Supplier Quality

Vendor Partnerships

Vendor Quality Certification

Warehousing

Real Estate, Construction, and Property Management

Acquisition

Americans with Disabilities Act (ADA)

Asset Management

Asset Valuation

Asset Workout/Recovery

Building Code Compliance

Building Trades

Capital Improvement

Claims Administration

Commercial Development

Community Development

Competitive Bidding

Construction Management

Construction Trades

Contract Administration

Contract Award

Critical Path Method (CPM) Scheduling

Design and Engineering

Divestiture

Engineering Change Orders (ECOs)

Environmental Compliance

Estimating

Facilities Management

Fair Market Value Pricing

Field Construction Management

Grounds Maintenance

Historic Property Renovation

Industrial Development

Infrastructure Development

Leasing Management

Master Community Association

Master Scheduling

Mixed-Use Property

Occupancy

Planned Use Development (PUD)

Portfolio

Preventive Maintenance

Project Development

Project Management

Project Scheduling

Property Management

Property Valuation

Real Estate Appraisal

Real Estate Brokerage

Real Estate Development

Real Estate Investment Trust (REIT)

Real Estate Law

Real Estate Partnership

Regulatory Compliance

Renovation

Return on Assets (ROA)

Return on Equity (ROE)

Return on Investment (ROI)

Site Development

Site Remediation

Specifications
Syndications
Tenant Relations

Tenant Retention
Turnkey Construction

Retail

Buyer Awareness
Credit Operations
Customer Loyalty
Customer Service
Distribution Management
District Sales
Hard Goods
In-Store Promotions
Inventory Control
Inventory Shrinkage
Loss Prevention
Mass Merchants

Merchandising
Multisite Operations
POS Promotions
Preferred Customer Management
Pricing
Product Management
Retail Sales
Security Operations
Soft Goods
Specialty Retailer
Stock Management
Warehousing Operations

Sales and Marketing

Note: Although the two functions are uniquely distinct, sales and marketing are integrated into one section due to the significant overlap in position titles, functions, responsibilities, and achievements.

Account Development
Account Management
Account Retention
Brand Management
Business Development
Campaign Management
Competitive Analysis
Competitive Contract Award
Competitive Market Intelligence
Competitive Product Positioning
Consultative Sales
Customer Loyalty
Customer Needs Assessment
Customer Retention
Customer Satisfaction

Customer Service
Direct Sales
Direct-Mail Marketing
Direct-Response Marketing
Distributor Management
E-Business
E-Commerce
Emerging Markets
Field Sales Management
Fulfillment
Global Markets
Global Sales
Headquarters Account Management
High-Impact Presentations
Incentive Planning

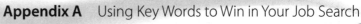

Indirect Sales

International Sales

International Trade

Key Account Management

Line Extension

Margin Improvement

Market Launch

Market Positioning

Market Research

Market Share Ratings

Market Surveys

Marketing Strategy

Mass Merchants

Multichannel Distribution

Multichannel Sales

Multimedia Advertising

Multimedia Marketing Communications

National Account Management

Negotiations

New Market Development

New Product Introduction

Product Development

Product Launch

Product Lifecycle Management

Product Line Rationalization

Product Positioning

Profit and Loss (P&L) Management

Profit Growth

Promotions

Public Relations

Public Speaking

Revenue Growth

Revenue Stream

Sales Closing

Sales Cycle Management

Sales Forecasting

Sales Presentations

Sales Training

Solutions Selling

Strategic Market Planning

Tactical Market Plans

Team Building/Leadership

Trend Analysis

Security and Law Enforcement

Asset Protection

Community Outreach

Corporate Fraud

Corporate Security

Crisis Communications

Crisis Response

Electronic Surveillance

Emergency Planning and Response

Emergency Preparedness

Industrial Espionage

Industrial Security

Interrogation

Investigations Management

Law Enforcement

Media Relations

Personal Protection

Public Relations

Safety Training

Security Operations

Surveillance

Tactical Field Operations

VIP Protection

White-Collar Crime

Teaching and Education Administration

Academic Advisement

Accreditation

Admissions Management

Alumni Relations

Campus Life

Capital Giving Campaign

Career Counseling

Career Development

Classroom Management

Conference Management

Course Design

Curriculum Development

Education Administration

Enrollment

Extension Program

Field Instruction

Grant Administration

Higher Education

Holistic Learning

Instructional Media

Instructional Programming

Intercollegiate Athletics

Leadership Training

Lifelong Learning

Management Development

Peer Counseling

Program Development

Public Speaking

Public/Private Partnerships

Recruitment

Residential Life

Scholastic Standards

Seminar Management

Student Retention

Student Services

Student-Faculty Relations

Tenure

Textbook Review

Training and Development

Transportation and Warehousing

Agency Operations

Asset Management

Cargo Handling

Carrier Management

Common Carrier

Container Transportation

Contract Transportation Services

Customer Delivery Operations

Dedicated Logistics Operations

Dispatch Operations

Distribution Management

Driver Leasing

Equipment Control

Export Operations

Facilities Management

Fleet Management

Freight Consolidation

Freight Forwarding

Import Operations

Inbound Transportation

Intermodal Transportation Network

Load Analysis

Logistics Management

Maritime Operations

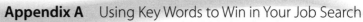

Outbound Transportation
Over-the-Road Transportation
Port Operations
Regulatory Compliance
Route Management
Route Planning/Analysis
Safety Management
Safety Training

Terminal Operations
Traffic Management
Traffic Planning
Transportation Management
Transportation Planning
Warehouse Management
Workflow Optimization

Action Verbs for Cover Letters

When it comes to writing your cover letters, resumes, thank-you letters, and other job search communications, you have two choices:

1. You can write passively, using phrases such as "I was responsible for" and "My duties included."

OR

2. You can write assertively and professionally, using action verbs to communicate what you have done and what you have accomplished.

To help you with this task, we've assembled a list of 250 action verbs. Use the words on this list to transform passive sentences into powerful achievements.

Accelerate	Analyze	Authorize
Accomplish	Apply	Brief
Achieve	Appoint	Budget
Acquire	Arbitrate	Build
Adapt	Architect	Calculate
Address	Ascertain	Capture
Advance	Assemble	Catalog
Advise	Assess	Champion
Advocate	Author	Clarify

Classify	Devise	Experiment
Close	Direct	Export
Coach	Discover	Facilitate
Collect	Dispense	Finalize
Command	Display	Finance
Communicate	Distribute	Forge
Compare	Diversify	Formalize
Compel	Divert	Formulate
Compile	Drive	Generate
Complete	Earn	Govern
Compute	Edit	Graduate
Conclude	Educate	Guide
Conduct	Effect	Hasten
Conserve	Elect	Hire
Consolidate	Eliminate	Hypothesize
Construct	Emphasize	Identify
Contract	Encourage	Illustrate
Coordinate	Energize	Imagine
Counsel	Enforce	Implement
Counteract	Enhance	Import
Craft	Enlist	Improve
Create	Ensure	Improvise
Decrease	Establish	Increase
Delegate	Estimate	Influence
Deliver	Evaluate	Inform
Demonstrate	Examine	Initiate
Deploy	Exceed	Innovate
Design	Execute	Inspire
Detect	Exhibit	Install
Determine	Expand	Institute
Develop	Expedite	Instruct

Integrate	Offer	Realign
Intensify	Officiate	Rebuild
Interpret	Operate	Recapture
Interview	Orchestrate	Receive
Introduce	Organize	Recognize
Invent	Orient	Recommend
Investigate	Originate	Reconcile
Judge	Outsource	Record
Justify	Oversee	Redesign
Launch	Participate	Reduce
Lead	Perceive	Reengineer
Lecture	Perform	Rejuvenate
License	Persuade	Reorganize
Maintain	Pilot	Reposition
Manage	Pinpoint	Represent
Manipulate	Pioneer	Research
Manufacture	Plan	Resolve
Map	Position	Respond
Market	Predict	Restore
Mastermind	Prepare	Restructure
Measure	Prescribe	Retrieve
Mediate	Present	Revamp
Mentor	Preside	Review
Model	Process	Revise
Modify	Procure	Revitalize
Monitor	Promote	Satisfy
Motivate	Propose	Schedule
Navigate	Publicize	Sell
Negotiate	Purchase	Select
Nominate	Quality	Simplify
Observe	Rate	Solidify

Solve	Surpass	Translate
Spearhead	Synthesize	Troubleshoot
Specify	Systematize	Unite
Standardize	Tabulate	Update
Stimulate	Target	Upgrade
Streamline	Teach	Use
Structure	Terminate	Utilize
Succeed	Test	Verbalize
Suggest	Train	Verify
Summarize	Transcribe	Win
Supervise	Transfer	Write
Supply	Transform	
Support	Transition	

C

Job Search Resources on the Internet

With the emergence of the Internet, job search has changed forever. Information that used to take days or even weeks to find can now be accessed in just minutes. It truly is a revolution.

However, the pace of development and the number of new Internet sites that emerge every day make it impossible to provide a comprehensive list of *all* Web sites related to employment, careers, job search, and more. The following list includes some of our favorite sites, some of the largest sites, and some of the best sites.

This list is by no means comprehensive. We strongly suggest that you devote the time necessary to conduct your own independent Web-based research as applicable to your specific job search campaign and career path.

Enjoy the surf!

Career Development Tools

Career Knowledge.net
www.careerknowledge.net

International Career Development Library
icdl.uncg.edu/reference.html

National Occupational Information
www.noicc.gov/

Company Research and Information Sites

AllBusiness.com
www.comfind.com

BigBook Electronic Yellow Pages
www.bigbook.com

Business Directory
www.555-1212.com

Chambers of Commerce
www.uschamber.com/mall/states.htm

Dow Jones
http://www.dowjones.com

EDGAR Online
www.edgar-online.com

Executive Information
people.edgar-online.com/people

Fortune 500 Companies
www.fortune.com/fortune/fortune500

Global B2B Communications
www.vault.com/vstore/lists/companylist.cfm

Hoover's Business Directory
www.hoovers.com

Industry Information
http://home.sprintmail.com/~debflanagan/index.html

Intellifact.com
www.intellifact.com/company_research.htm

New World of Work
www.experiencenetwork.com/newsite/comp_center/index.html

Small Business Information
www.infousa.com

Technology Companies
www.corptech.com/index.cfm

WetFeet.com
http://www.wetfeet.com/asp/companyresource_home.asp

Interviewing Tips and Techniques

Dress for Success
www.dressforsuccess.org

Interview Experts
http://interviewexperts.com/index2.htm

Interviewing Skills
http://jobsearch.about.com/business/jobsearch/msubinterv.htm

Introduction to Job Interviews
www.bradleycvs.demon.co.uk/interview/index.htm

Job Interviews
www.job-interview.net

Northeastern University—Careers
www.dac.neu.edu/coop.careerservices/interview.html

Job Search Sites

6FigureJobs
www.6figurejobs.com

America's Job Bank
www.ajb.dni.us

Career Atlas for the Road
isdn.net/nis

Career Central
www.careercentral.com

Career Magazine
www.careermag.com

Career Mart
www.careershop.com

CareerMosaic
www.careermosaic.com

CareerPath
www.careerpath.com

CareerWeb
www.cweb.com

Careers—All Industries
www.workseek.com

CFO Opportunities
www.cfonet.com

Excite Careers and Education
www.excite.com/careers

FedWorld
www.fedworld.gov

FutureStep
www.futurestep.com

GETAJOB
www.getajob.com

Headhunter.Net
www.headhunter.net/jobs

Health Care Careers
www.healthcareers-online.com

Health Insurance Careers
www.ehealthinsurance.com

Help Wanted
www.helpwanted.com

Insurance Careers
www.insweb.com

Internet Resume Center
www.inpursuit.com/sirc

MBA Careers
www.mbacareers.com

MBA Employment Connection
www.mbanetwork.com/meca

MedHunters.com
www.medhunters.com

Medical Careers
www.medsearch.com

Medical Careers
www.NHRphysician.com

Medzilla (Medical Jobs)
www.medzilla.com

Monster.com
www.monster.com

Pharmaceutical Careers
www.drugstore.com

Professional Careers
www.professionalcareers.com

Professional Careers and Employment Associations

American Bar Association
www.abanet.org

American College of Healthcare Executives
www.ache.org

American Compensation Association
www.acaonline.org

American Counseling Association
www.counseling.org

American National Career Development Association
www.ncda.org

American Psychological Association
www.apa.org

American Society of Association Executives
www.asanet.org

American Staffing Association
www.natss.com

Association for Internet Recruiting
www.recruitersnetwork.com

Association of Career Management Consulting Firms International
www.aocfi.org

British Columbia HR Management Association
www.bchrma.org

Canadian Compensation Association
www.cca-acr.org

Career Masters Institute
www.cminstitute.com

Career Research & Testing
www.careertrainer.com

College of Healthcare Information Management Executives
www.cio-chime.org

Five O'Clock Club
www.fiveoclockclub.com

Home Business Works
www.homebusinessworks.com

Home-Based Working Moms
www.hbwm.com

Human Resource Research Organization
www.humrro.org

Institute of Personnel Development
www.ipd.co.uk

International Association of Administrative Professionals
www.iaap-hq.org

International Association of Career Management Professionals
www.iacmp.org

International Coach Federation
www.coachfederation.org

Jobs for America's Graduates
www.jag.org

National Association of Colleges and Employers
www.jobweb.org

National Board of Certified Counselors
www.nbcc.org

National Résumé
Writers Association
www.nrwa.com

Ontario Municipal HR Association
www.omhra.on.ca

Professional Association
of Résumé Writers
www.parw.com

Recruiters Online Network
www.recruitersonline.com

Society for Human Resource
Management
www.shrm.org

Salary and Compensation Information

Abbott, Langer & Associates
www.abbott-langer.com

Administrative and Office Salaries (Bureau of Labor Statistics)
stats.bls.gov/oco/ocos002.htm

American Compensation Association
www.acaonline.org

America's Career InfoNet
www.acinet.org/acinet/occ_sea1.htm

Broadcast, TV, and Radio Salaries
www.missouri.edu/~jourvs

Bureau of Labor Statistics
stats.bls.gov

Compensation Information
www.claytonwallis.com

CompensationLink.com
www.compensationlink.com

Computer and Internet Salaries (Yahoo!)
yahoo.com/Computers/Employment/Salary_Information

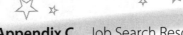

Consultant Salaries

www.cob.ohio-state.edu/~fin/jobs/mco/salary.htm

Engineer Salaries

www.ecn.purdue.edu/ESCAPE/stats/salaries.html

Homefair's Salary Calculator

www.homefair.com/calc/salcalc.html

JobStar Salary Surveys

jobsmart.org/tools/salary/index.htm

Medical Salaries

www.pohly.com/salary.html

MIS Salaries

www.psrinc.com/salary.htm

Monster.com—The Negotiation Coach

http://midcareer.monster.com/experts/negotiation

WageWeb

www.wageweb.com

Working Woman

www.workingwoman.com/salary

Appendix

D

Geographic Index of Cover Letter Authors

The sample cover letters in chapters 7 through 12 were written by professional resume and cover letter writers. If you need help with your job search correspondence, you can use the following list to locate the career professional in your area.

A note about credentials: Nearly all of the contributing writers have earned one or more professional credentials. These credentials are highly regarded in the careers and employment industry and are indicative of the writer's expertise and commitment to professional development. Here is an explanation of each of these credentials:

Credential	Awarded By	Recognizes
CCM: Credentialed Career Master	Career Masters Institute	Specific professional expertise, knowledge of current career trends, commitment to continuing education, and dedication through *pro bono* work
CPRW: Certified Professional Résumé Writer	Professional Association of Résumé Writers	Knowledge of resume strategy development and writing
JCTC: Job and Career Transition Coach	Career Planning and Adult Development Network	Training and expertise in job and career coaching strategies

continues

continued

Credential	Awarded By	Recognizes
MA: Master of Arts MS: Master of Science MBA: Master of Business Administration M.Ed.: Master of Education MFA: Master of Fine Arts	Accredited university	Graduate-level education
NCC: National Certified Counselor NCCC: National Certified Career Counselor	National Board for Certified Counselors (affiliated with the American Counseling Association and the American Psychological Association)	Qualification to provide career counseling
NCRW: Nationally Certified Résumé Writer	National Résumé Writers' Association	Knowledge of resume strategy development and writing

Alabama

Don Orlando, MBA, CPRW, JCTC
The McLean Group; Montgomery, AL
Phone 334-264-2020; Fax 334-264-9227
E-mail: yourcareercoach@aol.com
Web site: www.cminstitute.com

Arizona

Kathryn Bourne, CPRW, JCTC
CareerConnections; Tucson, AZ
Phone 520-323-2964; Fax 520-795-3575
E-mail: CCmentor@aol.com
Web site: www.bestfitresumes.com

California

Georgia Adamson, JCTC, CPRW
Adept Business Services; Campbell, CA
Phone 408-866-6859; Fax 408-866-8915
E-mail: georgiaa@ix.netcom.com
Web site: www.adeptbussvcs.com

Nancy Karvonen, CPRW, JCTC, CCM
A Better Word & Résumé; Galt, CA
Phone 209-744-8203; Fax 209-745-7114
E-mail: Careers@AresumeCoach.com
Web site: www.aresumecoach.com

Myriam-Rose Kohn, CPRW, JCTC, CCM
JEDA Enterprises; Valencia, CA
Phone 800-600-JEDA or 661-253-0801; Fax 661-253-0744
E-mail: myriam-rose@jedaenterprises.com
Web site: www.jedaenterprises.com

Vivian Van Lier, CPRW, JCTC
Advantage Résumé and Career Services; Valley Glen, CA
Phone 818-994-6655; Fax 818-994-6620
E-mail: vivian@CuttingEdgeResumes.com
Web site: www.CuttingEdgeResumes.com

Susan Britton Whitcomb, NCRW, CPRW
Alpha Omega Services; Fresno, CA
Phone 559-222-7474; Fax 559-227-0670
E-mail: TopResume@aol.com
Web site: www.careerwriter.com

Connecticut

Debra O'Reilly, CPRW, JCTC
A First Impression Resume Service; Bristol, CT
Phone 860-583-7500; Fax 860-585-9611
E-mail: debra@resumewriter.com
Web site: www.resumewriter.com

Florida

G. William Amme, JCTC
A CareerPro Inc.; Deerfield Beach, FL
Phone 954-428-4935; Fax 954-428-0965
E-mail: careerpro@mindspring.com
Web site: www.1greatcareer.com

Laura DeCarlo, CPRW, JCTC
A Competitive Edge Career Service; Melbourne, FL
Phone 800-715-3442; Fax 321-752-7513
E-mail: getanedge@aol.com
Web site: www.acompetitiveedge.com

Arthur I. Frank, MBA
Resumes "R" Us; Palm Harbor, FL
Phone 727-787-6885; Fax 727-786-9228
E-mail: AF1134@aol.com

Beverly Harvey, CPRW, JCTC, CCM
Beverly Harvey Resume and Career Services; Pierson, FL
Phone 904-749-3111; Fax 904-749-4881
E-mail: beverly@harveycareers.com
Web site: www.harveycareers.com

Cynthia Kraft, CPRW, JCTC, CCM
Executive Essentials; Valrico, FL
Phone 813-655-0658; Fax 813-685-4287
E-mail: cprwck@gte.net
Web site: www.exec-essentials.com

Lisa LeVerrier, MA, MS, CPRW, JCTC
Competitive Advantage Resumes & Career Coaching; Boca Raton, FL
Phone 954-571-0313 or 954-571-7236; Fax 561-362-5251
E-mail: lisalev@earthlink.net
Web site: www.jobcoaching.com

Jean West, CPRW, JCTC
Impact Résumé and Career Services; Indian Rocks Beach, FL
Phone 727-596-2534; Fax 727-593-7386
E-mail: JobCoach@impactresumes.com
Web site: www.impactresumes.com

Illinois

Loretta Heck
All Word Services; Prospect Heights, IL
Phone 847-215-7517; Fax 847-215-7520
E-mail: siegfried@ameritech.net

Iowa

Elizabeth Axnix, CPRW, JCTC
Quality Word Processing; Iowa City, IA
Phone 800-359-7822; Fax 319-354-2220
E-mail: axnix@earthlink.net

Kansas

Kristie Cook, CPRW, JCTC
Absolutely Write; Olathe, KS
Phone 913-269-3519; Fax 913-397-9273
E-mail: kriscook@absolutely-write.com
Web site: www.absolutely-write.com

Maryland

Diane Burns, CPRW, CCM, JCTC
Career Marketing Techniques; Columbia, MD
Phone 410-884-0213; Fax 410-884-0213
E-mail: dianecprw@aol.com
Web site: www.polishedresumes.com

Massachusetts

Bernice Antifonario
Antion Associates, Inc.; Tewksbury, MA
Phone 978-858-0637; Fax 978-851-4528
E-mail: Antion1@aol.com

Michigan

Janet Beckstrom
Word Crafter; Flint, MI
Phone 800-351-9818; Fax 810-232-9257
E-mail: wordcrafter@voyager.net

Maria Hebda, CPRW
Career Solutions, LLC; Trenton, MI
Phone 734-676-9170; Fax 734-676-9487
E-mail: careers@writingresumes.com
Web site: www.writingresumes.com

Lorie Lebert, CPRW, JCTC
Résumés for Results; Novi, MI
Phone 800-870-9059 or 248-380-6101; Fax 248-380-0169
E-mail: Lorie@DoMyResume.com
Web site: www.DoMyResume.com

Richard Porter
CareerWise Communications, LLC; Portage, MI
Phone 888-565-7108; Fax 888-565-7109
E-mail: rtporter@worldnet.att.net

Missouri

Meg Montford, CCM
Abilities Enhanced; Kansas City, MO
Phone 816-767-1196; Fax 801-650-8529
E-mail: Meg@abilitiesenhanced.com
Web site: www.abilitiesenhanced.com

New Jersey

Nina Ebert, CPRW
A Word's Worth Résumé and Writing Service; Toms River, NJ
Phone 732-349-2225; Fax 732-286-9323
E-mail: wrdswrth@gbsias.com
Web site: www.a-wordsmith.com

Susan Guarneri, NCCC, CPRW, CCM, JCTC
Susan Guarneri Associates; Lawrenceville, NJ
Phone 609-771-1669; Fax 609-637-0449
E-mail: Resumagic@aol.com
Web site: www.Resume-Magic.com

Rhoda Kopy, CPRW
A Hire Image; Toms River, NJ
Phone 732-505-9515; Fax 732-505-3125
E-mail: ahi@injersey.com
Web site: www.jobwinningresumes.com

New York

Mark Berkowitz, NCCC, CPRW, JCTC
Career Development Resources; Yorktown Heights, NY
Phone 888-277-9778 or 914-962-1548; Fax 914-962-0325
E-mail: cardevres@aol.com
Web site: CareerDevResources.com

Deborah Wile Dib, CCM, NCRW, CPRW, JCTC
Advantage Resumes of New York; Medford, NY
Phone 631-475-8513; Fax 631-475-8513
E-mail: gethired@advantageresumes.com
Web site: www.advantageresumes.com

Kirsten Dixson, CPRW,
Certificate in Career Planning and Development
New Leaf Career Solutions; Bronxville, NY
Phone 888-887-7166; Fax 914-206-3611
E-mail: info@newleafcareer.com
Web site: www.newleafcareer.com

Donna Farrise, JCTC
Dynamic Résumés of Long Island, Inc.; Hauppauge, NY
Phone 800-528-6796 or 631-951-4120; Fax 631-952-1817
E-mail: donna@dynamicresumes.com
Web site: www.dynamicresumes.com

Linsey Levine, MS, JCTC;
Career Counsel; Chappaqua, NY
Phone 914-238-1065; Fax 914-238-5822
E-mail: linzlev@aol.com

Christine Magnus, CPRW
Business Services Plus; Bronx, NY
Phone 718-519-0477; Fax 718-405-9894
E-mail: BizServ@aol.com

Salome Randall Tripi
Careers Too; Mt. Morris, NY
Phone and Fax 716-658-2480
E-mail: srttoo@frontiernet.net
Web site: www.frontiernet.net/~srttoo/

North Carolina

Dayna Feist, CPRW, JCTC
Gatehouse Business Services; Asheville, NC
Phone 828-254-7893; Fax 828-254-7894
E-mail: Gatehous@aol.com

John O'Connor, MFA, CPRW
Career Pro Resumes; Raleigh, NC
Phone 919-821-2418; Fax 919-821-2568
E-mail: careerpro2@aol.com
Web site: www.careerproresumes.com

Ontario, Canada

Martin Buckland, CPRW
Elite Resumes; Oakville, Ontario
Phone 905-825-0490; Fax 905-825-2966
E-mail: resumes@fox.nstn.ca

Ross Macpherson, MA, JCTC
Career Quest; Pickering, Ontario
Phone 877-426-8548; Fax 905-426-4274
E-mail: careerquest@primus.ca

Pennsylvania

Jewel Bracy DeMaio, CPRW
Absolutely Perfect Résumés; Elkins Park, PA
Phone 215-782-1460; Fax 215-782-1460
E-mail: mail@boostyourcareer.com
Web site: www.boostyourcareer.com

Jane Roqueplot and Chris Palmer
JaneCo's Sensible Solutions; Sharon, PA
Phone 724-342-0100; Fax 724-346-5263
E-mail: info@janecos.com
Web site: www.janecos.com

Texas

Cheryl Ann Harland, CPRW
Resumes by Design; The Woodlands, TX
Phone 888-213-1650; Fax 888-580-6852
E-mail: cah@resumesbydesign.com
Web site: www.resumesbydesign.com

Shanna Kemp, M.Ed., JCTC
Kemp Career Services; Carrollton, TX
Phone 877-367-5367 or 972-416-9089; Fax 972-478-2890
E-mail: ResPro@aresumepro.com
Web site: www.aresumepro.com

JoAnn Nix, CPRW
Beaumont Resume Service; Beaumont, TX
Phone 409-899-1932; Fax 409-924-0019
E-mail: info@agreatresume.com
Web site: www.agreatresume.com

Karen Wrigley, CPRW, JCTC
AMW Career and Resume Services; Round Rock, TX
Phone 800-880-7088; Fax 512-246-7433
E-mail: coach@amwresumes.com
Web site: www.amwresumes.com

Utah

Lynn Andenoro, CPRW
My Career Resource; Salt Lake City, UT
Phone 801-883-2011; Fax 801-582-8862
E-mail: Lynn@MyCareerResource.com
Web site: www.MyCareerResource.com

Virginia

Laurie Smith, CPRW
Creative Keystrokes Executive Resume Service; Alexandria, VA
Phone 800-817-2779; Fax 800-817-3428
E-mail: ljsmith@creativekeystrokes.com
Web site: www.creativekeystrokes.com

Washington

Carole S. Barns
A Great Career, Inc.; Woodinville, WA
Phone 800-501-4008; Fax 425-489-1995
E-mail: barnsassoc@aol.com
Web site: www.agreatcareer.com

Wisconsin

Michele Haffner, CPRW
Advanced Resume Services; Glendale, WI
Phone 414-247-1677; Fax 414-228-7332
E-mail: mhaffner@resumeservices.com
Web site: www.resumeservices.com

Index

"To manage your career effectively in the twenty-first century, you'll need a solid understanding of the latest job-search techniques. *Résumé Magic* does a great job of explaining those tactics in an easy-to-understand style."

—Tony Lee, Editor-in-Chief and General Manager
careerjournal.com, *The Wall Street Journal's* career Web site

At last—a professional résumé writer reveals her inside trade secrets for creating phenomenal résumés. No other book explains the nuts and bolts of résumé writing so clearly, then illustrates those techniques with Before-and-After résumés. In this book, you'll learn to

* Apply advertising techniques to résumé writing and position yourself above the competition.

* Link your job skills to the 10 "buying motivators" that every employer has.

* Find out what top Human Resource Managers say is the most important résumé feature they're looking for.

* Prepare e-mailable, scannable, and multimedia/electronic résumés.

* Master "résumé-speak," a unique style of writing that combines advertising and business formats to give your résumé energy and interest.

* Use keywords and keep your résumé alive on the Internet.

"To manage your career effectively in the twenty-first century, you'll need a solid understanding of the latest job-search techniques. *Résumé Magic* does a great job of explaining those tactics in an easy-to-understand style."
—Tony Lee, Editor in Chief and General Manager
careers.wsj.com, *Wall Street Journal's* career Web site

Résumé *Magic*
TRADE SECRETS OF A PROFESSIONAL RÉSUMÉ WRITER

Over 50 Before-and-After Résumés

Susan Britton Whitcomb

jist Works

ISBN 1-56370-522-2 ✳ **$18.95** ✳ **Order Code: LP-J5222**